Index to Puerto Rican
Collective Biography

Index to Puerto Rican Collective Biography

Compiled by
Fay Fowlie-Flores

Bibliographies and Indexes in American History, Number 5

Greenwood Press
New York • Westport, Connecticut • London

5811
14.5.88

Library of Congress Cataloging-in-Publication Data

Fowlie-Flores, Fay.
  Index to Puerto Rican collective biography.

  (Bibliographies and indexes in American History,
ISSN 0742-6828 ; no. 5)
  Includes index.
  1. Puerto Rico—Biography—Indexes. 2. Puerto Rico—
History, Local—Indexes. 3. Puerto Ricans—United States
—Biography—Indexes. I. Title. II. Series.
Z5305.P9F68   1987   [CT523]   920'.07295   87-8374
ISBN 0-313-25193-2 (lib. bdg. : alk. paper)

Library of Congress Catalog Card Number: 87-8374
ISBN: 0-313-25193-2
ISSN: 0742-6828

First published in 1987

Greenwood Press, Inc.
88 Post Road West, Westport, Connecticut 06881

Printed in the United States of America

The paper used in this book complies with the
Permanent Paper Standard issued by the National
Information Standards Organization (Z39.48-1984).

10 9 8 7 6 5 4 3 2 1

To Abraham, Camille and Ellen
for their encouragement,
understanding and love

Contents

Preface

The history of any country is directly influenced by the lives of the people who live in it. Since colonial times, Puerto Rico has been fortunate enough to be the home of many illustrious men and women who have had significant roles in the cultural, economic, political, and social development and history of the country. Many of its citizens have truly been "Renaissance men or women," distinguishing themselves in many fields of endeavor.

Until recently, researchers, students, government officials, librarians, and interested readers seeking information on the lives of Puerto Ricans or others closely linked to Puerto Rican history and development were forced to look for that information in scattered sources, and as a result often overlooked useful titles. No indexes to works of Puerto Rican collective biography existed. This book was prepared in an effort to help fill the gap. During the last three years two other indexes have been published.[1] However, because this index covers more titles than the other two, approximately 146 titles which include over 350 volumes, duplication of listed sources has been minimal. Mundo Lo's commendable work, Index to Spanish American Collective Biography, analyzes approximately 100 of the books annotated, while the Indice covers only 25 sources.[2]

In addition, this index includes certain details not found in the other two works. More English-language sources are indexed for more complete coverage and in the hope of serving a wider audience. This is the only index that gives the exact page location of the biographies, which, it is hoped, will prove useful since many of the sources indexed are not in alphabetical order and/or have some errors in the form of entry. Exact volume and page citations facilitate access to the information sought and aid in interlibrary loan requests. Another unique feature of this index is its reference to illustrative material, as will be explained subsequently.

Included in this index are books of collective biography, reference works, collections of essays, histories, and some anthologies, all published before or during 1985. Journals have not been indexed. Books indexed include biographies of people from all walks of life, from colonial times to the present. Puerto Ricans living on the island or on the mainland have been included, as well as Americans and other nationals who have lived on the island and contributed significantly to some aspect of Puerto Rican life, history, government or culture.

Several criteria were considered when selecting books to be analyzed. Only works having a minimum of three biographies were indexed although no maximum number of entries was considered.[3] Other factors taken into account included: authority or importance of the author or compiler, general availability, uniqueness of coverage, and inclusion in basic bibliographies such as those mentioned in BIBLIOGRAPHIES CONSULTED. When more than one edition of a work was available, only the latest was indexed, as is the case with volume fourteen of the Gran enciclopedia de Puerto Rico. The later edition includes far more entries than the first and also gives additional information on many of the biographees who appeared in the first edition. The amount of illustrative material also varies greatly between the two editions.

Most titles chosen for inclusion were indexed completely, that is, all the biographees have been included, unless the information was exclusively subjective or minimal (i.e., birth date or occupation only). Some of the entries in the books by Salvador Arana Soto, Modesto Gotay, Fernando Callejo Ferrer, Manuel Mayoral Barnés and Pepe Quintana, among others, were excluded for these reasons.

Although a special attempt was made to include as many English-language sources as possible, when searching the many standard sources, it was found that coverage of Puerto Ricans was either very limited or uneven. The Dictionary of American Biography and its supplements, for example, include only fourteen biographees related to Puerto Rico. Of these, six were American governors in Puerto Rico, one was the first native Puerto Rican appointed governor, three were resident commissioners in Washington, and one was an American doctor and scientist. The remaining three included a Spanish explorer and governor, a businessman, and a lawyer. It would be interesting to know the criteria used when choosing the fourteen and why other American governors and Puerto Rican resident commissioners were overlooked.

Surprisingly, the first three volumes of Notable American Women do not include any entries on Puerto Ricans at all, while the fourth volume, The Modern Period, includes only three: María Cadilla Martínez, Muna Lee, and Julia de Burgos. However, both Current Biography and Contemporary Authors contain considerably more entries. The former includes approximately twenty-five Puerto Ricans from government, politics, sports, the arts, and literature while the latter lists about forty-three authors who live in Puerto Rico or on the mainland. The Directory of American Scholars has approximately forty relevant entries, though many are not about native-born Puerto Ricans. Obvious omissions include such distinguished scholars as Ricardo Alegría, Ethel Ríos de Betancourt, Arturo Morales Carrión, among others.

The limited and incomplete coverage of Puerto Ricans found in American reference tools seems an interesting subject for further in-depth research. Perhaps with more data at hand, the reasons why relatively few Puerto Ricans appear in such standard works and in specialized reference books could be discovered. A pioneering study has already been completed on the inclusion of mainlanders in a standard Puerto Rican biographical tool.[4]

ABOUT THE INDEX

Each entry in the index includes the following elements: name of biographee, important dates, profession and/or reason for importance, and sources of biographical information. The biographee's last name or names are placed first in capital letters. Birth and/or death dates are given whenever known, though often, the century is indicated if exact dates are not available. An asterisk(*) following a date indicates that different sources give different dates. The date most commonly cited is given. Where there are only two sources, the date cited in the source generally considered to be the most authoritative is used. The sources of biographical information are listed alphabetically by abbreviations for the titles of the works. For each source the exact volume/year and/or page number are indicated, as is the presence of pictures or drawings of the biographee. The latter are signalled by the abbreviation "ill." Sources are separated by semi-colons. Example:

> CASALS, Pablo (1876-1973),
> musician, composer
> BiP 89-90; ConA 93-96:
> 84-87; CuB 1950:82-84,
> ill., 1964:71-74, ill.,
> 1973:452; DiDHM 55, ill.;
> ECPR 6:423; GrEPR 14:65,
> ill., 66-68(ill.); HisD
> 22; L 104-19; PRFAS 55,
> ill.

When the abbreviation "ill." appears within parenthesis, (ill.), following a page number, it indicates that that page has illustrative material only. In the example above, the article in Current Biography (CuB) is illustrated, while pages 66-68 of volume 14 of the Gran enciclopedia de Puerto Rico (GrEPR) have illustrations only. Page 65 in the same source has information and illustrative material. Complete titles for sources identified by abbreviations can be found in the section KEY TO ABBREVIATIONS OF SOURCES INDEXED. Complete bibliographical information for those sources is given in BIBLIOGRAPHY OF SOURCES INDEXED.

Entries are arranged according to the Spanish alphabet. Therefore, "ch", "ll", "ñ", and "rr" are regarded as independent letters so that "Colorado" precedes "Coll", "Cuevas" precedes "Chevremont", "Lugo" precedes "Llorens", etc. Biographees having the same paternal name are alphabetized by the second surname. Simple surnames are placed before compound surnames. Example:

> Ferrer, José
> Ferrer Hernández, Gabriel
> Ferrer Otero, Monserrate
> Ferrer Otero, Pedro

The word "y" in a compound surname is disregarded for alphabetizing.

Cross references have been used but no attempt has been made to include all known pseudonyms. In case of doubt, Lillian

Quiles's <u>Guía de seudónimos puertorriqueños</u> may be consulted.[5]

ACKNOWLEDGMENTS

Grateful acknowledgment is made to the American Library Association for a 1985 Whitney-Carnegie Award that helped make this book possible. Also, the Regional Colleges Administration of the University of Puerto Rico granted me a sabbatical leave, without which the book could not easily have been finished. Special thanks are due to the support and forbearing of my family and to Adelina Coppin-Alvarado for her faith, encouragement, and advice. Maribel Caraballo and Rose Ann Camalo-Hernández generously gave of their time and expertise. I am grateful too for the kind assistance of my colleagues at the Ponce Technological University College of the University of Puerto Rico.

I would gladly recieve suggestions for other titles that could be indexed for a future edition or supplement of this work.

NOTES

[1]<u>Indice biográfico; breves apuntes para un diccionario de puertorriqueños distinguidos</u> (San Juan, P.R.: Colección HIPATIA, 1985), and Sara de Mundo Lo, <u>Index to Spanish American Collective Biography</u>, vol.3, <u>The Central American and Caribbean Countries</u> (Boston: G.K. Hall, 1984), 171-204.

[2]Of these 25, it is unclear whether all entries and volumes are indexed.

[3]Mundo Lo does not index works of more than 300 biographees, thus excluding some basic sources. Her preface states that the index deals mainly with secondary sources.

[4]Charnel Anderson, "An Analysis of Americans in 'Quien es Quien en Puerto Rico', 1933-1949," <u>Homines</u> 8(ene.-jun. 1984): 43-55.

[5]Lillian Quiles de la Luz, <u>Guía de seudónimos puertorriqueños</u> (Barcelona, Spain: Ediciones Rumbos, 1962), 75pp.

General Abbreviations and Symbols

b.	born
ca.	_circa_, about
cent.	century
d.	died
Gov.	Governor
ill., (ill.)	illustrated, illustration
nr	new revision
pt.	part
P.R.	Puerto Rico
suppl.	supplement
U.S.	United States
*	date varies among sources indexed

Key to Abbreviations of Sources Listed

Sources indexed for this book were abbreviated according to their titles. For complete bibliographic information see BIBLIOGRAPHY OF SOURCES INDEXED.

A	Góngora Echenique, Manuel and Amelia Góngora de Parker. Actualidades y semblanzas puertorriqueñas.
AlDJ	Album de Jayuya, 1962-1963.
AlDU	Album de Utuado.
AlHP	Fortuño Janeiro, Luis, comp. Album histórico de Ponce, 1962-1963...
AlHY	Lluch Negroni, Francisco R., ed. Album histórico de Yauco (Puerto Rico).
Algo	Martínez Acosta, C. Algo.
And	Diez de Andino, Juan. Andanzas y perfiles.
Ant	Fernández Juncos, Manuel. Antología de sus obras.
AntHistCag	Lugo Silva, Enrique. Antología histórica de Caguas.
AntPoeCag	Millán Rivera, Pedro. Antología poética de Caguas.
Añas	Carrero Concepción, Jaime A. Añasco y sus hombres, 1475-1893.
Apu	Añeses Morell, Ramón. Apuntes para la historia de Aguadilla.
ArH	Limón de Arce, José. Arecibo histórico.
BeHNPR	Neumann Gandía, Eduardo. Benefactores y hombres notables de Puerto Rico.

BgP   Geigel y Zenón, José and Abelardo Morales Ferrer.
               Bibliografía puertorriqueña.

BiP   Rosa-Nieves, Cesáreo and Esther M. Melón. Biogra-
               fías puertorriqueñas.

BioD   Ohles, John F., ed. Biographical Dictionary of
               American Education.

BoBP   Soto Ramos, Julio. Bocetos biográficos puertorri-
               queños.

BoHP   Méndez Liciaga, Andrés. Boceto histórico del
               Pepino.

BrECP   Rosario, Rubén del, Esther Melón de Díaz and
               Edgar Martínez Masdeu. Breve enciclopedia
               de la cultura puertorriqueña.

CaDeT   Vilar Jiménez, Adolfo. El Caguas de todos los
               tiempos.

CaE   Herdeck, Donald E., ed. Caribbean Writers: A
               Bio-Bibliographical-Critical Encyclopedia.

CaF   Arana Soto, Salvador. Catálogo de farmacéuticos
               de Puerto Rico (desde 1512 a 1925).

CaM   _____. Catálogo de médicos de P.R. de siglos
               pasados (con muchos de éste).

CiBPI   Ribes Tovar, Federico. 100[cien] biografías de
               puertorriqueños ilustres.

CiuP   La ciudad de los poetas...

Co   Puerto Rico. Instituto de Cultura Puertorriqueña.
               Compositores puertorriqueños de siglo XIX.

Com   Compositores de música popular.

ComA   Rivera Santiago, Rafael. Comprensión y análisis:
               entrevistas biográficas, conferencias, ar-
               tículos.

ConA   Contemporary Authors.

Cre   Dalmau y Canet, Sebastián. Crepúsculos literarios.

Crom   Matos Bernier, Félix. Cromos ponceños.

CuB   Current Biography.

DeADeA   Sánchez Morales, Luis. De antes y de ahora...

DeTUP   Guerra, Ramón H. De todo un poco...

DelMu   Cuchí Coll. Isabel. Del mundo de la farándula.

DelRB   Guerra, Ramón H. Del rincón boricua.

Desd	Diez de Andino, Juan. *Desde mi rascacielo.*
Desf	Todd, Roberto H. *Desfile de gobernadores de Puerto Rico 1898 a 1943.*
DiDHM	Reynal, Vicente. *Diccionario de hombres y mujeres ilustres de Puerto Rico y de hechos históricos.*
DiHBC	Hostos, Adolfo de. *Diccionario histórico bibliográfico comentado de Puerto Rico.*
DiM	Arana Soto, Salvador. *Diccionario de médicos puertorriqueños.*
DicAB	*Dictionary of American Biography.*
DicC	Foster, David William, comp. *A Dictionary of Contemporary Latin American Authors.*
DirAS	*Directory of American Scholars.*
Eco	Brau, Salvador. *Ecos de la Batalla.*
ECPR	*Enciclopedia clásicos de Puerto Rico.*
EGMPR	*Enciclopedia grandes mujeres de Puerto Rico.*
EPI	Ribes Tovar, Federico. *Enciclopedia puertorriqueña ilustrada. The Puerto Rican Heritage Encyclopedia.*
EnsB	Figueroa, Sotero. *Ensayo biográfico de los que más han contribuído al progreso de Puerto Rico.*
Esb	Jesús Castro, Tomás de. *Esbozos.*
EsbCrit	_____. *Esbozos críticos.*
Esp	Angelis, Pedro de. *Españoles en Puerto Rico.*
EstCR	Lugo Toro, Sifredo. *Estampas de Cabo Rojo.*
Exp	Infiesta, Alejandro de, ed. *La exposición de Puerto Rico: memoria.*
GenB	Gaudier, Martín. *Genealogías, biografías e historia del Mayagüez de ayer y hoy y antología Puerto Rico.*
GenP	_____. *Genealogías puertorriqueñas...*
GentI	Moretti, Darcia. *Gente importante.*
GrEPR	*La gran enciclopedia de Puerto Rico.*
Guay	Porrata-Doria, Adolfo. *Guayama.*
HePR	Tuck, Jay Nelson and Norma Coolen Vergara. *Heroes of Puerto Rico.*

Hi de CR   Ibern Fleytas, Ramón. Historia de Cabo Rojo.

Hi de Cay   López Martínez, Pío. Historia de Cayey.

Hi de la Ig   Campo Lacasa, Cristina. Historia de la Iglesia en
                  Puerto Rico (1511-1802).

Hi de M   Comité Constituído para la Celebración del Bicen-
                  tenario de la Fundación de Mayagüez. Subco-
                  mité de la Historia de Mayagüez. Historia de
                  Mayagüez, 1760-1960.

Hi de P   López Cantos, Angel. Historia de Puerto Rico.

Hi de Pu   Vila Vilar, Enriqueta. Historia de Puerto Rico
                  (1600-1650).

HisD   Farr, Kenneth R. Historical Dictionary of Puerto
                  Rico and the U.S. Virgin Islands.

HisP   Lidin, Harold. History of the Puerto Rican Inde-
                  pendence Movement. Vol. 1: 19th Century.

HoDMT   Morales Otero, Pablo. Hombres de mi tierra.

HoIPR   Gotay, Modesto. Hombres ilustres de Puerto Rico.

HoPR   Maldonado, Teófilo. Hombres de primera plana.

HoRPR   Hostos, Adolfo de. Hombres representativos de
                  Puerto Rico.

HoYMPR   Carreras, Carlos N. Hombres y mujeres de Puerto
                  Rico.

Hor   Diez de Andino, Juan. Horizontes y verdades.

Imp   LeCompte, Eugenio. Impresiones del momento...

Ind   Coll, Edna. Indice informativo de la novela
                  hispanoamericana. Vol. 1: Las Antillas.

Jes   López de Santa Anna, Antonio. Los Jesuítas en
                  Puerto Rico de 1858 a 1886.

Ka   Atiles García, Guillermo. Kaleidoscopio.

L   Bloch, Peter. La-Le-Lo-Lai...

LM   Delgado Cintrón, Carmelo. Libro de matrícula del
                  ilustre Colegio de Abogados de Puerto Rico,
                  1840-1910.

LPR   Fernández García, E., ed. El libro de Puerto
                  Rico. The Book of Porto Rico.

LiPR   Quiñones Calderón, Antonio, ed. El libro de Puerto
                  Rico 1983.

Lie   Ferrer, Rafael. Lienzos.

LuO	Padró Quiles, José. _Luchas obreras..._
Ma	Rodríguez Troche, Concha. _Maestro._
MeO	Malaret, Augusto. _Medallas de oro._
Med	Balasquide, Lorenzo A. _Médicos notables del antaño ponceño._
Mem	Arrillaga Roque, Juan. _Memorias de antaño..._
Misc	Morales Miranda, José Pablo. _Misceláneas historicas._
MueYV	Matos Bernier, Félix. _Muertos y vivos._
MujDPR	Negrón Muñoz, Angela. _Mujeres de Puerto Rico..._
MujP	Ribes Tovar, Enrique. _La mujer puertorriqueña..._
MujPu	Angelis, María Luisa de. _Mujeres puertorriqueñas..._
Mus en P	Muñoz, María Luisa. _La música en Puerto Rico..._
MusMP	Callejo Ferrer, Fernando. _Música y músicos puertorriqueños._
Not	_Notable American Women._ Vol. 4: _The Modern Period._
Nues	Palacín Mejías, Juan. _Nuestros grandes maestros._
Nuestr	Ruiz García, Zoilo. _Nuestros hombres de antaño._
Orad	Carreras, Carlos N. _Oradores puertorriqueños._
Orig	Pasarell, Emilio J. _Orígenes y desarrollo de la afición teatral en Puerto Rico._
Oro	Cuchí Coll, Isabel. _Del mundo de la farándula._
PaE	Huyke, Juan B. _Páginas escogidas._
PaF	Matos Bernier, Félix. _Páginas sueltas._
PaG	Bloch, Peter. _Painting and Sculpture of the Puerto Ricans._
PaGa	Lefebre, Enrique. _Paisajes mentales..._
PaH	Toro, Emilio del. _Patria..._
PaI	Medina Ramírez, Ramón. _Patriotas ilustres puertorriqueños._
PaP	Todd, Roberto H. _Patriotas puertorriqueños._
Per	Braschi, Wilfredo. _Perfiles puertorriqueños._
Pin	Medina y González, Zenón. _Pinceladas..._

PlE   Rosa-Nieves, Cesáreo. <u>Plumas estelares en las letras de Puerto Rico.</u>

PoA   Limón de Arce, José. <u>Poetas arecibeños, 1832-1904.</u>

PolPr   <u>Political Profiles.</u>

Pon   Vidal Armstrong, Mariano. <u>Ponce: notas para su historia.</u>

PonY   Mayoral Barnés, Manuel. <u>Ponce y su historial...</u>

Por   Van Deusen, Richard James and Elizabeth Kneipple Van Deusen. <u>Porto Rico, a Caribbean Isle.</u>

Port   Maldonado, Adál Alberto. <u>Portraits of the Puerto Rican Experience.</u>

Pq   Amy, Francisco J. <u>Predicar en desierto...</u>

PriC   <u>Primer cincuentenario Senado de Puerto Rico, 1917-1967.</u>

ProA   Quintana, Pepe. <u>Pro-Aguadilla.</u>

Proc   Dalmau y Canet, Sebastián. <u>Próceres.</u>

PQ   Delgado Votaw, Carmen. <u>Puerto Rican Women...</u>

PRFAS   Melón de Díaz, Esther M. <u>Puerto Rico...</u>

PRP   Wagenheim, Kal. <u>Puerto Rico...</u>

PRUSA   <u>Puerto Rico USA...</u>

PuI   Coll y Toste, Cayetano. <u>Puertorriqueños ilustres.</u>

QuR   Sterling, Philip and María Brau. <u>The Quiet Rebels...</u>

QEQ   Asenjo, Conrado, ed. <u>Quien es quien en Puerto Rico...</u>

RepM   <u>The Representative Men of Porto Rico.</u>

S   Vélez Dejardín, José E. <u>San Germán...</u>

San   Vidal, Teodoro. <u>Santeros puertorriqueños.</u>

Sd   Fernández Juncos, Manuel. <u>Semblanzas puertorriqueñas.</u>

Se   Fonfrías, Ernesto Juan. <u>Sementera...</u>

SeDC   Abril, Mariano. <u>Sensaciones de un cronista...</u>

Sil   Chavier, Arístides. <u>Siluetas musicales.</u>

SobM   Diez de Andino, Juan. <u>Sobre la marcha...</u>

Tra	Hanson, Earl Parker. *Transformation: The Story of Modern Puerto Rico.*
Tri	Huyke, Juan B. *Triunfadores.*
Una	Soto Ramos, Julio. *Una pica en Flandes...*
VPR	Geigel Polanco, Vicente. *Valores de Puerto Rico.*
Ver	Neumann Gandía, Eduardo. *Verdadera y auténtica historia de la ciudad de Ponce...*
VerOr	Gaudier, Martín. *El verdadero origen de "La Borinqueña".*
Vida	Grismer, Raymond L. and César Arroyo. *Vida y obra de autores puertorriqueños.*
VisC	Jesús Castro, Tomás de. *Vistos de cerca...*
Vo	Diez de Andino, Juan. *Voces de la farándula...*

INDEX TO PUERTO RICAN COLLECTIVE BIOGRAPHY

A

ABAD, José Ramón (1845?-1912),
journalist
DiHBC 1; DiLP 2, pt.1:1-2;
GrEPR 14:1; HisD 1.

ABADIA, Matías de (d.1743),
governor, soldier
DiDHM 11; DiHBC 1-2; GrEPR
14:1.

ABARCA, Angel, businessman
A 63-64.

ABARCA CORTINA, Angel (19th
cent.), engineer, soldier
DiHBC 2.

ABARCA DE BOLEA, Bernardo,
statesman
DiHBC 2.

ABBAD Y LASIERRA, Iñigo
(1745*-1813), historiographer,
priest
BeHNPR 1:253-60, ill.; BiP
9-10; BrECP 11; CiBPI 48-
50; DiDHM 11-12, ill.; Di-
HBC 3; DiLP 2, pt.1:2-8;
ECPR 6:393; GrEPR 14:1;
HisD 1; PRFAS 11, ill.

ABEILLEZ DE MONTALVO, María
Teresa, educator
EGMPR 4:185-86, ill.

ABELLA BASTON CORTON, Severo
(b.1874), lawyer
LM 127; QEQ (1936-37) 17;
RepM 180, ill.

ABELLA BLANCO, Luis, lawyer,
politician

RepM 221, ill.

ABERCROMBY, Ralph (1734-1801),
British military officer
DiHBC 4; HisD 1.

ABOY BENITEZ, Juan (1876-1901),
poet, novelist
DiLP 2, pt.1:8; Ind 33-34.

ABOY BENITEZ, Ramón, lawyer,
politician
DiHBC 5-6; GrEPR 14:1.

ABOY LONGPRE, Ramón (b.1888),
broker
HoIPR 7, ill; QEQ (1933-34)
177, (1936-37) 17, (1941-42)
13, (1948-49) 7.

ABOY VALLDEJULI, Carmen, author
PQ 22.

ABRIL Y ARROYO, Julio Osvaldo
(b.1846), businessman, political
activist
Apu 51-54; RepM 79, ill.

ABRIL Y OSTALO, Mariano (1861*-
1935), journalist, author
Algo 12-16; BiP 10-11; CaDeT
157-58; CaE 629; CiBPI 210-
12; Cre 31-33; DiDHM 12,
ill.; DiHBC 6-7; DiLP 2, pt.
1:8-10; ECPR 6:393; GrEPR 14:
1; HisD 1; HoIPR 7, ill.; Mem
101-2; Per 1-3; PlE 1:381;
PriC 38, ill.; PRFAS 11-12,
ill.; QEQ (1933-34) 17, (1936-
37) 15; SeDC i-ix; SobM 204-
8; Ver 191.

ACEITUNO, Miguel (16th cent.),
Royal Treasurer
DiHBC 12; GrEPR 14:1.

ACEVEDO, Cándido, music teacher
MusMP 283-84.

ACEVEDO, Francisco "Paco"
(1901-1946), journalist
Per 144-46.

ACEVEDO, Pedro, politician
AlHP 352.

ACEVEDO, Plácido (1906-1974),
musician, composer
Com 1; GrEPR 7:126-27, ill.

ACEVEDO COLON, Salvador (b.
1920), lawyer, politician
GrEPR 14:2; PriC 97-98,
ill.

ACEVEDO CRUZ, Adrián H. (b.
1929), politician
LiPr 123, ill.

ACEVEDO DE SANTIAGO, Ana María
(b.1922), bank official
EGMPR 3:33.

ACEVEDO HERNANDEZ, Francisco
(b.1887), teacher, politician
GrEPR 14:2; QEQ (1948-49)
7.

ACEVEDO LAZARINI, Carlos J.
(b.1958), politician
LiPR 33, ill.

ACEVEDO MARRERO, Ramón Luis
(b.1947), professor, author
PRFAS 12.

ACEVEDO MENDOZA, Juan R. (b.
1898), economist, professor
QEQ (1933-34) 17, (1936-37)
17-18.

ACEVEDO ROSARIO, Manuel (b.
1897), politician
GrEPR 14:2.

ACEVEDO VAZQUEZ, Herminia (b.
1888), teacher
EGMPR 1:229-30, ill.; QEQ
(1933-34) 18, (1936-37) 18,
(1941-42) 13, (1948-49) 7.

ACEVEDO ZENO, Mariano (b.
1899), lawyer

QEQ (1936-37) 18, (1941-42)
14.

ACOSTA, Flavia, opera singer
EGMPR 4:1-2.

ACOSTA, Francisco (19th cent.),
politician
DiHBC 12.

ACOSTA, Mario, broadcaster
A 113, ill.

ACOSTA, Miguel E., factory
owner
A 144.

ACOSTA Y ACOSTA, José Julián (b.
1882), lawyer
ProA 53; QEQ (1933-34) 18,
(1936-37) 18, (1941-42);
RepM 285, ill.

ACOSTA Y CALBO, Eduardo Eugenio
(1823-1868), author, translator,
printer
BeHNPR 2:211-13, ill.; DiLP
2, pt.1:16-17.

ACOSTA Y CALBO, José Julián
(1825-1891), historian, journalist, abolitionist
AlHP 329, ill.; Ant 135-41;
BeHNPR 2:169-90, ill.; BgP
facing p.48, ill.; BiP 11-
13; BrECP 11-12; CiBPI 69
(ill.), 105-8; Desd 139-42;
DiDHM 13; DiHBC 12-13; DiLP
2, pt.1:17-20; ECPR 6:394;
EPI 1:94(ill.), 95, 96; GenP
25; GrEPR 14:2, ill.; Hi de
M 215-16, ill.; HisD 2; Ho-
IPR 7, ill.; HoRPR 27-32;
LPR 970, 971-72, 973, ill.;
PaP 19-29; Por 232-34; PRFAS
13; PuI 106-9; Sd 31-55.

ACOSTA GONZALEZ, Guillermo (b.
1906), doctor
CaF 19; QEQ (1948-49) 7-8.

ACOSTA GRUBB, Carole, government official
EGMPR 3:85-86, ill.

ACOSTA LA SALLE, Mariano R. (b.
1880), lawyer
LM 136; QEQ (1936-37) 18,
(1941-42) 14.

ACOSTA MARQUES, Enrique, politician

GrEPR 14:2.

ACOSTA QUINTERO, Angel (1865-1943), lawyer, judge
    DiHBC 13; GrEPR 14:2, 3 (ill.); HoIPR 8, ill.; LM 122-23; QEQ (1933-34) 177-78, (1936-37) 18-19, (1941-42) 14-15; RepM 238, ill.

ACOSTA QUIÑONES, Antonio V. (b.1894), lawyer
    QEQ (1941-42) 15.

ACOSTA VELARDE, Federico (b. 1896), lawyer, politician
    GrEPR 14:3; QEQ (1941-42) 15.

ACOSTA VELARDE, Mariano (b. 1895), lawyer
    GrEPR 14:3, ill.; QEQ (1936-37) 19, (1941-42) 15, (1948-49) 8.

Acuña, Francisco de Paula see Acuña Paniagua, Francisco de Paula

ACUÑA, Julio (b.1912), painter, teacher
    GrEPR 8:390.

ACUÑA AYBAR, Eduardo (b.1860), politician, lawyer
    GrEPR 14:3, ill.; LM 18-19; RepM 102, ill.

ACUÑA Y PANIAGUA, Francisco de Paula (1839-1929), lawyer, politician
    DiDHM 13-14, ill.; DiHBC 14; Esp 287-88, ill.; GrEPR 14:3; HisD 2; HoIPR 8, ill.; LM 113-14; PRFAS 13-14, ill.

ACHA CAAMAÑO, Ramón, soldier
    DiHBC 14.

ADAMS, Cornele B. (b.1866), engineer, economist
    QEQ (1941-42) 15-16, (1948-49) 8.

ADSUAR, Jorge (1883-1926), journalist, author
    BiP 13-14; CaE 629; DiDHM 14; DiHBC 22; DiLP 2, pt.1: 24-25; GrEPR 4:71; HoIPR 9, ill.; PRFAS 14; SobM 212-20.

ADSUAR BONETA, Amalia (1879-1966), philanthropist
    And 112-16.

AFONSO, Graciliano (1775-1861), poet, translator
    DiLP 2, pt.1:25-27.

AGENJO Y SANTIAGO, Félix F. (b. 1893), pharmacist
    QEQ (1933-34) 18, (1936-37) 19, (1941-42) 16.

AGOSTINI DE DEL RIO, Amelia (b. 1896), author, professor
    DiDHM 14-15; DiHBC 24; DiLP 2, pt.1:27-31; EGMPR 1:231-32, ill.; GrEPR 14:4; MujDPR 251-52, ill.; PQ 22; SobM 134-36, 149-51, 209-11, 227-30.

AGOSTINI ZAPATA, Serafín (1869-1959), teacher, civic leader
    Añas 79-83, ill.

AGOSTO, William, actor
    DelMu 2-7, ill.

AGOSTO ABADIA, Adrián (b.1880), lawyer
    LM 137.

AGRAIT, Gustavo (b.1904), author, professor
    A 61; DiDHM 15; DiLP 2, pt. 1:31-32; GrEPR 14:4, ill.; PRFAS 14-15.

AGRAIT ALDEA, Ricardo (b.1891*), lawyer, politician
    GrEPR 14:4; QEQ (1948-49) 8-9; RepM 159, ill.

AGRAIT CONCEPCION, Tomás S. (b. 1896), educator, musician
    GrEPR 14:4; QEQ (1941-42) 16, (1948-49) 9; S 89.

AGRELOT, José Miguel (b.1927), actor
    GrEPR 14:4, ill.; PRFAS 15-16.

AGUAYO, Joaquín, municipal employee
    Ka 46-47.

AGUAYO Y ALDEA, Nicolás (1808-1878), educator, politician
    DiDHM 15-16; DiHBC 33; EnsB 177-85; GrEPR 14:5; PuI 81-84.

AGUAYO Y SANCHEZ, Alfredo M.
(b.1866), teacher
    GrEPR 14:5; QEQ (1933-34)
    18-19, (1936-37) 19.

AGUERO, Alfonso J., politician
    RepM 325, ill.

AGUEROS, Diego, businessman
    A 121.

AGUEROS, Jack (b.1934), museum
director
    Port 49, 50(ill.)

AGUERREVERE, Angel, doctor
    CaM 20.

AGUERREVERE, Luis, doctor
    CaM 20; Crom 19; DiM 21-23.

AGUEYBANA I, "El Viejo" (d.
1510), Taíno Indian chief
    BiP 14; CiBPI 9-11; DiDHM
    16; ECPR 6:394; GrEPR 14:5.

AGUEYBANA II, "El Bravo" (d.
1511), Taíno Indian chief
    BiP 14; CiBPI 11-14; ECPR
    6:395; GrEPR 14:5.

AGUIAR Y AGUERO, Carlos (1854-
1934), newspaper manager
    DiDHM 16; HoIPR 9, ill.

AGUILAR, Marcos de, Spanish
official
    GrEPR 14:4.

AGUILAR GALARZA, Pablo J. (b.
1892), lawyer, politician
    GrEPR 14:4; QEQ (1936-37)
    19.

AGUILAR MORA, Teodoro (b.1872)
teacher
    GrEPR 14:5; QEQ (1933-34)
    19, (1936-37) 19-20, (1941-
    42) 16-17, (1948-49) 9.

AGUILAR RAMIREZ DE ARELLANO,
Félix A. (b.1888), businessman
    QEQ (1936-37) 20, (1941-42)
    17, (1948-49) 9.

AGUILERA AGUILERA, Tito (1851-
1941), artisan
    San 29-31.

AGUILERA BARCELO, José (19th
cent.), doctor
    CaM 21.

AGUILERA Y GAMBOA, Diego de
(17th cent.), governor
    DiDHM 16; GrEPR 14:5; Hi de
    P 165-70.

AGUILERA PAGAN, Néstor J. (b.
1900), priest
    GenB 413, ill.

AGUILO, José, businessman
    A 172, ill.

AGUIRRE, Francisco (19th cent.),
doctor
    Ka 85.

AGUIRRE, George, businessman,
photographer
    Port 101, 102(ill.)

AGUIRRE DE TORRES, Rufina (b.
1923), nurse
    EGMPR 3:135-36.

AGUSTY RAMIREZ, Joaquín (b.
1894), radio announcer and
engineer
    GrEPR 14:5; QEQ (1936-37)
    177, (1941-42) 17.

ALAEZ, Santiago B. (b.1897),
steamship company manager
    QEQ (1936-37) 20.

ALAFONT Y MARCO, Francisco
(19th cent.), doctor
    CaM 22-23.

ALAMINOS, Antón, Spanish
sailor
    GrEPR 14:5.

ALBENIZ, Clementina (19th cent.),
teacher
    Hi de M 211; VerOr 306.

ALBERTY, Roberto (1930-1985),
painter
    GrEPR 8:390.

ALBIZU, Olga (b.1924), painter
    BrECP 21; EGMPR 4:3-4, ill.;
    GrEPR 8:220, ill.; PaG 203;
    PQ 23; PRFAS 16.

ALBIZU CAMPOS, Pedro (1891-
1965), lawyer, nationalist
leader
    BiP 15-17; BrECP 18-21, ill.;
    CiBPI 231(ill.), 280-85; Di-
    DHM 1718, ill.; DiHBC 35-36;
    ECPR 6:395, 396(ill.); EPI

1:214-23, 3:58-110, ill.;
GrEPR 14:6-9, ill.; Hor
390-412; PaI 149-203, ill.;
PRFAS 16-17, ill.; QEQ
(1936-37) 20; Tra 83-91,
163.

ALCAIDE, Antonio S., businessman
Ka 124.

ALCAIDE, José A. (b.1915),
novelist, government official
DiLP 2, pt.1:39-40; GrEPR
14:10; Ind 34-35; PriC 171,
ill.; PRFAS 17.

Alcides, Gerardo see Domínguez, José de Jesús

Aldaña, Ana María see Negrón
Muñoz, Angela

ALDREY, Antonio de (b.1866),
politician
GrEPR 14:10, ill.; RepM
138, ill.

ALDREY, Jorge de (b.1906),
dentist
QEQ (1933-34) 19, (1936-37)
20, (1941-42) 17.

ALDREY, María Justina de,
musician, teacher
GrEPR 14:10.

ALDREY MONTILLA, Emilio de (b.
1900), lawyer
QEQ (1936-37) 20, (1941-
42) 17-18.

ALDREY MONTOLIO, Pedro de
(1864-1936), lawyer, judge
GrEPR 14:10, ill.; HoIPR
10, ill.; LM 124; QEQ
(1933-34) 19, (1936-37)
20; RepM 51, ill.

ALEGRIA, José S. (1886*-1965)
author, journalist, lawyer
BiP 17-18; CaE 631; CiBPI
227(ill.), 278-80; DiDHM
18, ill.; DiHBC 40; DiLP
2, pt.1:41-43; ECPR 6:395,
397, 399(ill.); GrEPR 14:
11-12, ill.; HisD 6; Per
133-35; PRFAS 17, ill.;
QEQ (1933-34) 19-20,(1936-
37) 20, (1941-42) 18,
(1948-49) 10; RepM 223,
ill.

ALEGRIA, Ricardo E. (b.1921),
anthropologist, historian,
educator
BiP 18-19; BrECP 21, ill.;
ConA 25-28R:18; DiDHM 18-19,
ill.; DiHBC 38-40; DiLP 2,
pt.1:43-45; ECPR 6:397; GrEPR
14:10-11, ill.; HisD 6;
PRFAS 18.

Alegría Santos, José S. see
Alegría, José S.

ALEMAÑY FERNANDEZ, Eugenio (b.
1925), lawyer, politician
GrEPR 14:13.

ALEMAÑY SOSA, Juan (b.1886*),
lawyer
GenB 409-10, ill.; QEQ (1941-
42) 18, (1948-49) 10; VerOr
307-8, ill.

ALEMAR ALEMAR, Carmelo (b.1887),
federal employee
GenB 367-68, ill.

ALERS, Eva, actress
DelMu 10-14, ill.

ALERS, Rafael (b.1903), musician,
composer
GrEPR 14:13.

ALFALLA, Loyda R. (b.1933),
educator
Port 71, 72(ill.)

ALFARO, Luis (16th cent.),
colonist
GrEPR 14:13.

ALFARO DIAZ, Félix (1891-1945),
doctor
CaM 24-25; QEQ (1936-37) 21,
(1941-42) 18-19.

ALFARO Y SANTIAGO, Pablo (1868-
1916), author, lawyer
DiLP 2, pt.1:45-46; RepM
148, ill.

ALFONSO, Félix Simplicio (19th
cent.), pharmacist, politician
CaF 20-21; GrEPR 14:13.

ALFONSO TORRES, Rafael, labor
leader, politician
GrEPR 14:13.

ALGARIN, Miguel (b.1940), author, translator, director,

producer, teacher
    CaE 632; ConA 69-72:19.

ALICEA, José R. (b.1928),
artist
    BrECP 21-22; GrEPR 8:304,
    ill.; PaG 200-201; PRFAS
    18.

ALICEA, Víctor (b.1938), educator, social worker
    Port 21, 22(ill.)

ALICEA CAMPOS, Guillermo,
politician
    GrEPR 14:13.

ALMANSA, Luis de (16th cent.),
soldier
    GrEPR 14:13.

ALMAZAN, Ramón, pharmacy owner
    CaF 21; GrEPR 14:13.

ALMODOVAR, Lillian, painter
    PaG 227.

ALMODOVAR GARCIA, Ismael (b.
1932), chemist, educator
    DiDHM 19.

ALMODOVAR GONZALEZ, Héctor L.
(b.1915), advertising agency
owner
    GenB 428-29, ill.

ALONSO, don (d.1521), Taíno
Indian chief
    GrEPR 14:14.

ALONSO, Alfredo, businessman
    A 134.

Alonso, Campio see Alonso
Pacheco, Campio

ALONSO, Manuel A. (1822*-
1889*), doctor, author
    Ant 125-33; AntHistCag 246;
    BiP 19-22; BrECP 22-24,
    ill.; CaDeT 64, ill.; CaE
    634; CaM 26; CiBPI 72(ill.)
    104-5; DiDHM 20, ill.; Di-
    HBC 42-43; DiLP 2, pt.1:
    49-52; ECPR 6:397; DiM 24-
    29; EPI 1:150-51, ill.;
    GrEPR 14:14; HisD 7; LPR
    968 970, 971; PlE 1:57-70,
    ill.; PRFAS 18-19, ill.;
    PuI 96-100; Sd 9-30.

ALONSO, Sebastián, Spanish
soldier
    GrEPR 14:14.

ALONSO ALONSO, Rafael, lawyer
    PriC 174, ill.

ALONSO CAIÑAS, Fidel (b.1904),
doctor
    QEQ (1948-49) 10.

ALONSO CANCINO, García (15th
cent.), sea captain, colonist
    DiDHM 20; HisD 7.

ALONSO DE MIER, Isabel (1886-
1974), author
    DiDHM 20-21; DiHBC 42; EGMPR
    1:63-66, ill.; MujDPR 206-
    8, ill.

ALONSO DE SOLIS, Juan (d.1641),
bishop
    Hi de la Ig 72-74.

ALONSO FERNANDEZ, Alonso, author,
typographer
    Guay 249.

ALONSO PACHECO, Campio (1826-
1905?), poet, journalist
    CaDeT 181; DiLP 2, pt.1:52-
    53.

Alonso Pacheco, Manuel A. see
Alonso, Manuel A.

ALONSO PINZON, Martín, sailor
    HisD 7.

ALONSO TORRES, Rafael (b.1880),
typographer, politician, labor
leader
    QEQ (1936-37) 177-78.

ALUM PEREZ, José R., doctor,
politician
    DiM 29; GrEPR 14:14.

ALVARADO, Anthony (b.1942),
educator
    Port 67, 68(ill.)

ALVARADO, Arcilio (b.1903), educator, politician
    DiDHM 21; GrEPR 14:15, ill.

ALVARADO, Julio (1886-1970),
musician, composer
    Com 1; GrEPR 7:122.

ALVARADO, Luis (19th cent.),
politician
  Crom 44.

ALVARADO, Margarita, pianist
  MusM 244-45.

Alvarado Alvarado, Arcilio see
Alvarado, Arcilio

ALVAREZ, Ernesto (b.1937),
painter
  GrEPR 8:391.

Alvarez, Francisco see Alvarez
Marrero, Francisco

ALVAREZ, Héctor (b.1926),
painter
  GrEPR 8:430.

ALVAREZ, Hermógenes, musician,
composer
  CaDeT 267-68; MusMP 243.

ALVAREZ, Hernán, pharmacist
  A 103.

ALVAREZ, José Julián (1867-
1934), pharmacist
  CaDeT 257-59, ill.; RepM
  216, ill.

ALVAREZ, Juan M., library aid
  VisC 98.

ALVAREZ, Luis Manuel (b.1939),
composer, professor
  GrEPR 7:324, ill.

Alvarez, Martín see Martínez
Alvarez, Rafael

ALVAREZ, Mauricio (b.1842),
musician, composer
  AntHistCag 348; MusMP 243-
  44.

ALVAREZ, Miguel Angel, actor
  DelMu 16-20, ill.

ALVAREZ, Rafael, Jr., agronomist
  AlDJ 147, ill.

ALVAREZ, Valentín, businessman
  A 136.

ALVAREZ BRUNET, José (b.1913),
politician
  LiPR 118, ill.

ALVAREZ CHANCA, Diego (15th
cent.), doctor
  And 157-60; CaM 123; DiDHM
  21; DiHBC 44; GrEPR 14:95.

ALVAREZ FELDMAN, Carmen,
sculptress
  GrEPR 8:430.

ALVAREZ GARCIA, Francisco (b.
1903), businessman
  QEQ (1936-37) 178, (1941-42)
  19.

ALVAREZ LASANTA, Perfecto (1890-
1950), poet
  AnHistCag 247; AntPoeCag 71-
  73.

ALVAREZ MARTIN, Rafael (b.1903),
singer
  QEQ (1936-37) 178, (1941-42)
  19.

ALVAREZ MARRERO, Francisco
(1847-1881), author
  BiP 22-24; DiHBC 44; DiLP 2,
  pt.1:53-55; Eco 121-25; GrEPR
  14:15; PlE 1:155-68, ill.;
  PRFAS 19; PuI 309-11.

ALVAREZ MIR, Miguel (19th cent.),
government official
  DiHBC 44.

ALVAREZ NAVA, Antonio (1869*-
1922), journalist, orator, lawyer
  DiLP 2, pt.1:55-56; HoIPR 10,
  ill.; LM 123-24; RepM 91, ill.

ALVAREZ NAZARIO, Manuel (b.1924),
philologist, essayist
  And 198-99; BiP 234-35; BrECP
  24; DiHBC 44; DiLP 2, pt.1:
  56-58; GrEPR 14:15; PRFAS 19-
  20.

ALZAMORA, Bartolomé (b.1904),
agronomist
  QEQ (1936-37) 21, (1941-42)
  19, (1948-49) 185.

ALLEN, Charles Herbert (1848-
1934), governor, banker
  Desf 13-18, ill.; DiDHM 21;
  DiHBC 437; GrEPR 14:15, ill.;
  QEQ (1936-37) 178; Rep M
  8, ill.

ALLENDE, Angel E., painter
  PaG 229-30.

AMADEO, Francisco L. (1878-
1948), poet
    DiLP 2, pt.1:59; GrEPR 14:
    15; QEQ (1936-37) 178,
    (1941-42) 19-20.

Amadeo, Jesús María see Amadeo Antomarchi, Jesús María

AMADEO, José A. (b.1899),
doctor
    QEQ (1933-34) 20-21,
    (1936-37) 21.

AMADEO, José H., doctor
    CaM 29; RepM 207, ill.

AMADEO, Santos P. (b.1902),
politician, professor
    Esb 2:31-33; GrEPR 14:16;
    QEQ (1941-42) 233, (1948-
    49) 10-11.

AMADEO ALBERTO, Heraclio L.,
pharmacist
    CaF 23.

AMADEO ANTOMARCHI, Jesús
María (1856-1927), author,
doctor
    CaE 635; DiLP 2, pt.1:59-
    60; DiM 29-31; Ind 35-36;
    PRFAS 20.

AMADEO FERNANDEZ, Heraclio,
pharmacist
    CaF 23.

AMADEO GELY, Teresa (b.1895),
professor
    EGMPR 1:233-34.

AMADEO LOPATEGUI, María de
Lourdes (b.1934), musician
    EGMPR 4:5-6, ill.

AMADEO Y MARTINEZ, Antonio
José, doctor
    CaM 27-28.

AMADEO TORO DE ITURREGUI,
María Teresa, insurance agent
    EGMPR 3:315-16, ill.

AMADOR, Pedro G. (b.1879),
lawyer, politician
    DeTUP 19-20; RepM 126, ill.

AMADOR, Pedro Luis, architect
    GrEPR 9:111.

AMEZQUITA QUIJANO, Juan de
(1598-1650), Spanish soldier
    BeHNPR 1:199-229; BiP 24-
    25; DiDHM 22; DiHBC 44; ECPR
    6:397; GrEPR 14:16; HisD
    7-8; PRFAS 20; PuI 13-15.

AMO Y GONZALEZ, Juan del (19th
cent.), doctor
    CaM 30-31.

AMOROS BELTRAN, Gabriel (1883-
1933), doctor
    CaM 31; QEQ (1933-34) 21,
    (1936-37) 15.

AMY, Enrique (d.1912), politician
    Guay 249-50.

AMY, Francisco J. (1837-1912),
poet, translator, journalist
    BiP 25-26; CaE 635-36; Di-
    HBC 45-46; DiLP 2, pt.1:
    60-62; ECPR 6:397, 399;
    GrEPR 14:16; HisD 8; HoRPR
    192-98; LPR 986-989; Por
    212-13; PRFAS 21.

AMY, Jorge Aurelio (b.1870),
artist
    QEQ (1933-34) 21, (1936-37)
    21, (1941-42) 20, (1948-49)
    11.

AMY, José (b.1953), jockey
    PRUSA 2.

ANDERSON, Axel, actor, director
    DelMu 22-27, ill.

ANDERSON, Joseph, Jr., lawyer
    RepM 100, ill.

ANDERSON, Patricio (19th
cent.), doctor
    CaM 31-32.

ANDINO, Baltasar de (17th
cent.), soldier, userer
    GrEPR 14:16.

ANDINO, Cipriana (1774-1866?),
    EGMPR 4:7; MujPu 15-16.

ANDINO, Eduardo (b.1895),
soldier
    QEQ (1936-37) 178-79, (1941-
    42) 20, (1948-49) 11.

ANDINO, Emigdio (1772-1820),

soldier
   BeHNPR 1:322; PuI 46-47.

ANDINO, Felipa (d.1888), piano
teacher
   MusMP 284.

ANDINO, Hilda, pianist
   A 71, ill.

ANDINO, Julián de (1845-1920),
musician, composer
   BiP 26-27; BrECP 24-25; Di-
   DHM 22-23; HisD 8; ECPR 6:
   399; EPI 3:228; GrEPR 14:
   16; MusMP 215-17; PRFAS 21;
   VerOr 55.

ANDINO, Marcelino (1845?-
1905?), author
   DiLP 2, pt.1:62-63.

ANDINO, Vicente (b.1758),
soldier
   BeHNPR 1:322, ill.

ANDINO Y AMEZQUITA, José de
(1751-1835), soldier, journalist
   BeHNPR 2:11-12; BiP 27-29;
   DiDHM 22; DiLP 2, pt.1:63-
   64; ECPR 6:399; GrEPR 14:
   16; HisD 8; PlE 1:15; PRFAS
   21-22; PuI 25-28.

ANDINO Y CAMPECHE, Silvestre,
painter
   GrEPR 8:18.

ANDRACA DE TIMOTHEE, Rosario
(1873-1946), teacher
   CiBPI 253-55; DiHBC 46;
   ECPR 6:399-400; EGMPR 1:
   235-36, ill.; EPI 3:178,
   183; GrEPR 14:16; HoYMPR
   194-201; MujDPR 147-48,
   ill.; MujP 124; QEQ (1933-
   34) 21-22, 178, (1941-42)
   20.

ANDREU DE AGUILAR, Isabel
(1887-1948), feminist, author
   DiDHM 23; DiHBC 46; EGMPR
   1:67-69, ill.; PQ 1; QEQ
   (1933-34) 21-22, (1936-37)
   22, (1941-42) 20-21, (1948-
   49) 11-12.

ANDREU IGLESIAS, César (1915-
1976), journalist, author
   BiP 29-30; BrECP 25; DiLP

2, pt.1:64-65; DicC 4; ECPR
   6:400; GrEPR 5:53-54, 14:17,
   ill.; Ind 36-39; PRFAS 22.

ANEXI, Jaime (1863-1921), teacher
   HoIPR 10, ill.

ANGELIS, María Luisa de (1891-
1953), author, historian
   DiDHM 73; DiLP 2, pt.1:66-
   69; EGMPR 1:133, ill.

ANGLADE, Enrique J. (b.1901),
pharmacist, politician
   CaF 24.

ANGLADE LUBE, Luis J. (b.1905),
pharmacist
   QEQ (1933-34) 22, (1936-37)
   22.

ANGLERIA, Pedro Martir de
(1457-1526), chronicler
   DiDHM 23; HisD 8.

ANGULO Y LICIAGA, Juan B. (b.
1878), government official
   BoHP 171, 173(ill.)

ANSELMI RODRIGUEZ, Adolfo (b.
1885), pharmacist
   QEQ (1933-34) 22, (1936-37)
   22.

ANSELMI RODRIGUEZ, Francisco L.
(1897-1971), pharmacist, politician
   GrEPR 14:17, ill.; QEQ (1948-
   49) 12.

ANTIQUE, Emigdio (19th cent.),
doctor
   CaM 32-33.

ANTOLINO, Francisco Julián de
(18th cent.), bishop
   Hi de la Ig 123-24.

ANTONELLI, Juan Bautista (16th
cent.), engineer
   DiDHM 23; DiHBC 47; GrEPR 14:
   17.

ANTONETTI ANTONINI, Vicente (b.
1857), sugar mill owner
   DeTUP 25-26.

ANTONETTI MENTRIE, Salvador (b.
1889), accountant
   QEQ (1933-34) 22, (1936-37)
   22, (1941-42) 21.

ANTONGIORGI QUIÑONES, David, agronomist
A 111.

ANTONSANTI, Frank (b.1881), lawyer
QEQ (1933-34) 22, (1936-37) 179, (1941-42) 21; RepM 96, ill.

ANTONSANTI, Orlando J. (b. 1907), lawyer
QEQ (1941-42) 21, (1948-49) 12.

AÑASCO, Luis de (b.1475), soldier, colonist
Añas 10-13; DiDHM 24; GrEPR 14:17.

AÑESES MORELL, Ramón (b.1880), politician
ProA 2-4, ill.; QEQ (1933-34) 22-23, (1936-37) 22, (1941-42) 21.

APELLANIZ STORRER, Luis, politician
GrEPR 14:18.

APONTE, Araceli (19th cent.), singer
MusMP 172.

APONTE, Clotilde, politician
GrEPR 14:18.

APONTE, Edward William (b. 1939), educator, banker
Port 35, 36(ill.)

APONTE, Faustino R. (b.1909), lawyer
QEQ (1941-42) 21.

APONTE, José Agustín (1860-1912), author, orator
DiLP 2, pt.1:100-101; HisD 8.

APONTE, José F., politician
GrEPR 14:18.

APONTE, José J., lawyer, politician
Guay 250.

Aponte, José Rafael see Aponte Ledée, Rafael

APONTE COLON, Eloy (b.1927),

lawyer, politician, professor
GrEPR 14:18.

APONTE CORTES, Felipe (b.1891), poet, customs official
AntHistCag 248; AntPoeCag 89-90; CaDeT 248-49, ill.

APONTE LEDEE, Rafael (b.1938), composer, music teacher
BrECP 31-32; GrEPR 7:321(ill.), 322, 14:18, ill.; Mus en P 160.

APONTE MARTINEZ, Luis (b.1922), Catholic cardinal
DiDHM 24; DiHBC 49; GrEPR 6: 281, 285-87, 14:20(ill.); PRUSA 2.

APONTE MENDEZ, Manuel L. (1897-1955), businessman
HoIPR 11, ill.

APONTE PEREZ, Francisco (b.1928), politician
LiPR 28, ill.

APONTE RIERA, Arturo, lawyer, politician
Crom 55; GrEPR 14:19; QEQ (1941-42) 21-22, (1948-49) 12.

APONTE RIERA, José R. (b.1878), lawyer, politician
GrEPR 14:19, ill.; QEQ (1933-34) 23, (1936-37) 22; RepM 188, ill.

APONTE RODRIGUEZ, Arturo (b. 1906), lawyer, educator, newspaper manager
LM 116.

APONTE RODRIGUEZ, Leandro (b. 1840), lawyer, politician
LM 114.

APONTE SALGUERO, Rafael I. (b. 1892), pharmacist
QEQ (1933-34) 23, (1936-37) 22, (1941-42) 22, (1948-49) 12.

APONTE SANCHEZ, Rafael, politician
GrEPR 14:19.

APONTE TORRES, Gonzalo (b.1895), accountant
QEQ (1936-37) 22-23, (1941-

42) 22, (1948-49) 13.

AQUENZA, Jacinto (1858-1911), author
  DiLP 2, pt.1:101-2.

AQUINO BERMUDEZ, Federico (b. 1925), eductor
  Port 137, 138(ill.)

ARACIBO (16th cent.), Taíno Indian chief
  GrEPR 14:19.

ARAMANA (16th cent.), Taíno Indian chief
  GrEPR 14:19.

ARAN DE GOSNELL, Patria (b. 1906), author, educator
  QEQ (1948-49) 81.

ARAN SOLER, Pedro P. (b.1886), teacher
  GenB 435-37; GrEPR 14:20; QEQ (1933-34) 23, (1936-37) 23, (1941-42) 22, (1948-49) 13.

ARAN ZUZUARREGUI, Luis S. (b. 1885), engineer
  QEQ (1936-37) 179, (1941-42) 23, (1948-49) 13.

ARANA, Alfonso (b.1927), artist
  PaG 209.

ARANA, Felipe N. (1902-1962), author
  DiLP 2, pt.1:102-4.

ARANA RIOS, Cosme (1876-1930), author
  DiLP 2, pt.1: 104.

ARANA SOTO, Salvador (b.1908), doctor, author
  BiP 30-31; DiDHM 24; DiHBC 50; DiLP 2, pt.1:104-6; DiM 31-33; ECPR 6:400; GrEPR 14:20; PRFAS 22.

ARANGO, Sancho de (16th cent.), colonist
  GrEPR 14:20.

ARANZAMENDI, Genaro, composer, musician
  MusMP 217.

ARANZAMENDI, Jenaro de (1829-

1888), author, journalist
  DiLP 2, pt.1:106-8.

ARAUJO, María Dolores (1755-1830), teacher
  EGMPR 1:237; MujPu 8.

ARBAUGH Y BARTHOLOMEW, William George (b.1902), minister
  QEQ (1936-37) 23, (1941-32) 23, (1948-49) 13-14.

ARBONA, Margot, teacher, author
  A1DJ 209, ill.

ARBONA DE ORTIZ, Tití, teacher
  A1DJ 213, ill.

ARBONA IRIZARRY, Guillermo (b. 1910), doctor
  CaM 34.

ARCE, Diego de (16th cent.), Spanish government official
  GrEPR 14:20; HisD 8-9.

ARCE, Ignacio (1858-1928), artisan
  San 23-24, 25.

ARCE, Juan (1862-1932), artisan
  San 23, 25-27.

ARCE, Pedro (1857-1951), artisan
  San 23, 27-28.

ARCE DE VAZQUEZ, Margot (b. 1904), critic, literary historian, educator
  A 59-60; AntHistCag 248-49; BiP 31-33; BrECP 32; CaE 638; CaDeT 179-80; DiDHM 24-25, ill.; DiHBC 51; DiLP 2, pt.1:108-11; DicC 5; ECPR 6:400-401; EGMPR 1:239-40, ill.; HisD 9; MujDPR 254-57, ill.; Oro 52-63, ill.; PlE 2:479-94, ill.; PQ 24; PRFAS 22-23, ill.

ARCE LUGO, Félix (1884-1973), author
  S 87.

ARCE RODRIGUEZ, Julia (b.1915), journalist, politician
  EGMPR 2:9, ill.; GrEPR 14: 20; PriC 78.

ARCE Y ROLLET, Rafael (d.1931), lawyer
  LM 136-37; RepM 210, ill.

ARCE SANTIAGO, Petra (1904-
1925), artisan
   San 24-25.

ARCELAY, María Luisa (1893-
1981), industrialist, politician
   A 145; DiDHM 25; DiHBC 51;
   EGMPR 1:71, ill., 2:11-12,
   ill.; GrEPR 14:20, ill.;
   MujPu 235-36, ill.; PQ 24;
   PriC 78; QEQ (1936-37) 23,
   (1941-42) 23, (1948-49)
   185.

ARCELAY, Rafael (b.1889), bus
company manager
   QEQ (1936-37) 23, (1941-42)
   23-24.

ARCILAGOS, Pedro (1860-1922),
composer
   GrEPR 7:270; MusMP 217-18;
   Sil 79-83.

ARCHILLA, Gustavo (b.1887),
teacher
   Tri 1:269-73.

ARCHILLA CABRERA, Angel (1892-
1954), author, Superintendent
of Presbyterian Church
   A 69; DiLP 2, pt.1:111-12;
   GenB 380-81, ill.; GrEPR 6:
   311; Nues 66-68, ill.; QEQ
   (1936-37) 23-24, (1941-42)
   24, (1948-49) 14.

ARCHILLA CABRERA, José (1881-
1958), author
   DiLP 2, pt.1:112-13.

ARCHILLA LAUGIER, Luis A.,
politician
   GrEPR 14:21.

ARGUINSONI, Germán, musician
   MusMP 248.

ARIAS, Antonio S. (1880-1963),
banker
   AlHP 481, ill.

ARIAS, Mercedes, composer,
music teacher
   MusMP 245.

ARISTA DE SOBREMONTE, Marcos
(d.1681), bishop
   Hi de la Ig 90-91.

ARISTEGUI VELEZ, Rafael de

(b.1794), governor, soldier
   BeHNPR 2:47-50, ill.; DiDHM
   26; DiHBC 452; EnsB 71-78.

ARIZMENDI Y DE LA TORRE, Juan
Alejo de (1757*-1814), bishop
   BeHNPR 1:375-79; BiP 33-34;
   BrECP 34; CiBPI 46(ill.),53-
   55; DiDHM 26, ill.; ECPR 6:
   401; GrEPR 6:257(ill.), 258-
   59; HisD 9-10; LPR 962, 963,
   964; PRFAS 23, ill.; PuI 33-
   36.

ARJONA SIACA, Rafael, politician
   GrEPR 14:21.

ARMADA, Angel M., banker
   GrEPR 1:xvii, ill.

ARMAIZ ALGARIN, Jesús (1887-
1939), doctor
   CaM 34-35; QEQ (1933-34) 23-
   24, (1936-37) 24; Tri 2:277-
   81.

ARMSTRONG, Carlos, businessman
   Crom 76; Ver 285.

ARMSTRONG, Herminio, businessman
   Ka 16.

ARMSTRONG, Peter L. (1804?-
1855), doctor
   CaM 36.

ARMSTRONG, TOMAS (b.1800?),
doctor
   CaM 36-37.

ARMSTRONG TORO, Thomas (1840-
1907), businessman
   AlHP 333; Crom 21-22.

ARNALDO MEYNERS, José (b.1904),
journalist, poet
   DiHBC 93; DiLP 2, pt.1:117-
   118; Esb 2:137-40; GrEPR 14:
   21; QEQ (1933-34) 178, (1936-
   37) 24, (1941-42) 24, (1948-
   49) 14.

ARNALDO SEVILLA, Alfredo (1868-
1935), lawyer
   GenB 347-48, ill.; HoIPR 11,
   ill.; RepM 265, ill.

ARNALDO SEVILLA, Enrique, pharmacist
   CaF 25-26; GenB 355, ill.

ARNALDO SEVILLA, Patricio (1873-

1944), poet, journalist
   DiLP 2, pt.1:118-19.

ARNAU DE RUIZ GANDIA, Isaura
(1844-1903), teacher
   DiHBC 93; EGMPR 1:241-42,
   ill.; MujDPR 47-49, ill.;
   MujPu 45-48.

AROCENA Y RODON, José Francisco Gonzalo (b.1893), soldier
   BoHP 158-59, ill.

AROCHO DEL TORO, Gonzalo
(1898-1954), dramatist, journalist
   DiLP 2, pt.1:120-22; GrEPR
   14:21.

AROCHO RIVERA, Minerva (b.
1931), poet
   And 194-95; DiLP 2, pt.1:
   119-20.

AROSTEGUI Y HERRERA, Gonzalo
(18th-19th cent.), governor
   DiDHM 27; DiHBC 450.

ARTEAGA, Gaspar de (1619-
1674), governor
   GrEPR 14:22; Hi de P 181-
   86.

Arteaga, Genoveva see Arteaga
Torruella, Genoveva

ARTEAGA, Julio C. de (1867-
1923), musician, composer,
teacher
   AlHP 404; CiBPI 77(ill.),
   170-72; Co 1; Crom 90; ECPR
   6:402; EPI 3:228, 229; Gr-
   EPR 7:257(ill.), 258-60; L
   74-75; Mus en P 115-16;
   MusMP 72-77; Sil 85-89.

ARTEAGA TORRUELLA, Genoveva de
(b.1898*), musician, teacher
   DiHBC 101; EGMPR 4:37-39,
   ill.; GrEPR 14:22; L 78-79;
   MujDPR 252-54, ill.; QEQ
   (1933-34) 179, (1936-37)
   25-26.

ARTIGAS, José María, doctor
   CaM 41-42.

ARZOLA, Marina (b.1939), poet
   CaE 643.

ARZUAGA, Pedro, philanthropist

HoIPR 12, ill.

ARZUAGA E IZAGUIRRE, Ignacio
(d.1911), philanthropist
   Esp 71-73.

ARRAIZA, Manuel Fermín (b.1937),
poet
   DiLP 2, pt.1:122-23.

ARRARAS, José Enrique (b.1937),
lawyer, politician, educator
   GrEPR 14:21, ill.

ARRECHE PRADOS, Cándido (b.1906),
journalist
   QEQ (1936-37) 24, (1941-42)
   24.

ARREDONDO, Gaspar de (17th
cent.), governor
   DiDHM 27; GrEPR 14:21; Hi de
   P 200-203.

ARRIETA, Francisco (b.1862),
administrator
   Esp 117-20.

ARRIGOITA, Luis M. de (b.1933),
author
   DiLP 2, pt.1:123-24; PRFAS
   24.

ARRILLAGA, María (b.1940), poet,
teacher
   CaE 641-42.

ARRILLAGA, Víctor Manuel (b.
1914), poet, actor
   DelMu 30-34, ill.; DiLP 2,
   pt.1:124-25.

ARRILLAGA GARCIA, Noemí (b.
1916), chemist
   QEQ (1941-42) 24-25.

ARRILLAGA GARCIA, Rafael (1852-
1919), pharmacist, politician
   Añas 44-46; Nues 24-26, ill.

ARRILLAGA GAZTAMBIDE, Alberto (b.
1915), soldier, government
official
   Añas 101.

ARRILLAGA GAZTAMBIDE, Francisco
A. (b.1913), lawyer, politician
   A 85; Añas 98-101.

ARRILLAGA ROQUE, Juan Bautista
(1866*-1912*), author, pharmacist, politician

CaF 27; DiLP 2, pt.1:125-27; DiM 33-35; GrEPR 14:22; HisD 10; HoIPR 12, ill.

ARRILLAGA ROQUE, Rafael (1877*-1933), doctor
Añas 87-95, ill.; CaF 27; CaM 38; DiM 35-36; QEQ (1933-34) 15, (1936-37) 15.

ARRILLAGA TORRENS, Rafael (b. 1918*), doctor, author, politician
DiDHM 27; DiHBC 96-97; DiM 35; DiLP 2, pt.1:127-28; GrEPR 14:22; QEQ (1948-49) 186.

ARRILLAGA URRUTIA, Rafael P. (1879-1933), lawyer, politician
Añas 96-101.

ARRIVI, Francisco (b.1915), author, literary historian
BiP 34-35; BrECP 39-40, ill.; CaE 642; DiDHM 27-28; DiLP 2, pt.1:128-33; DicC 8-9; ECPR 6:401-2; GrEPR 14:22, ill.; PRFAS 24.

ARROYO, Angel Manuel (b.1908), poet, journalist
DiLP 2, pt.1:133-35.

ARROYO, Anita (b.1914), author, professor
DirAS 3:18.

ARROYO, José María, doctor
CaM 38-40.

ARROYO, Rafael (b.1892), engineer
QEQ (1933-34) 24, (1936-37) 24-25, (1948-49) 14-15.

ARROYO DE COLON, María (b. 1907), teacher, politician
AntHistCag 264-65; BiP 36-37; EGMPR 1:243-44, ill., 2:13, ill.; GrEPR 14:22; PQ 25; PRFAS 24-25; SobM 18-20, 25-27.

ARROYO GELY, Rafael (d.1935), painter
GrEPR 8:196.

ARROYO MOTTA, Pedro, doctor
CaM 40.

ARROYO RIOS, Rafael Antonio (b. 1904), lawyer
QEQ (1933-34) 178-79, (1936-37) 25, (1941-42) 25.

ARROYO Y SANTANA, Pedro (1866-1914), politician
GrEPR 14:22.

ARRUZA PEREZ, Juan (b.1902), doctor
QEQ (1933-34) 24-25, (1936-37) 25, (1941-42) 25.

ASCENCION, Alfredo, businessman
Crom 101.

ASENCIO, Víctor, businessman
A 123, ill.

ASENCIO CAMACHO, Fernando (b. 1907), doctor
CaM 42; QEQ (1936-37) 26, (1941-42) 25-26, (1948-49) 15.

ASENJO, Conrado (1881-1964), author, journalist
DiLP 2, pt.1:135-36; Hor 318-20; QEQ (1933-34) 25, (1936-37) 26-27, (1941-42) 26-27, (1948-49) 16-17.

ASENJO, Conrado Federico (b. 1908), engineer
QEQ (1936-37) 26, (1941-42) 26, (1948-49) 15-16.

ASENJO Y ARTEAGA, Federico (1831-1893), author, journalist
BiP 37-38; BrECP 41; DeADeA 87-101; DiDHM 28; DiHBC 111-13; DiLP 2, pt.1:136-38; ECPR 6:402-3; GenB 340-41; GenP 90; GrEPR 14:23; HoIPR 12, ill.; HoRPR 164-70; PlE 1: 314; Por 221-22; PRFAS 25; PuI 181-85.

ASENJO Y CARBO, Francisco J. (d.1894), pharmacist
CaF 27.

ASENJO DE SANTIAGO, Mercedes (b. 1891), secretary
SobM 62-65, 224-26.

Asenjo y Del Valle, Conrado see Asenjo, Conrado

ASHFORD, Bailey K. (1873-1934), doctor, scientist

AlHY 139-40; BiP 38-39;
BrECP 41-42, ill.; CaM 42;
CiBPI 224(ill.), 244-46;
DiDHM 28; DiHBC 113-14;
DicAB suppl.1:32-33; ECPR
6:405; GrEPR 14:23, ill.;
HisD 10-11; HoDMT 84-97;
Por 183-86, 193; PRFAS 25;
QEQ (1933-34) 25-26, (1936-
37) 15.

ASHFORD, Mahlon (b.1900),
secretary
QEQ (1936-37) 27.

ASHFORD DE LEE, Margarita (b.
1906), secretary, civic works
EGMPR 4:145-47.

ASPIROZ CARNERO, María D.
"Lolita" (1884-1962), musician
Añas 112-16, ill.; Orig
302, 304.

ASTOL, Eugenio (1843-1904),
actor
Orig 283(ill.), 284-90.

ASTOL, Eugenio (1868*-1948),
author, journalist, orator
Algo 34-39; AntHistCag 249-
50; BiP 41-42; CaDeT 276,
ill.; CaE 643; DiLP 2, pt.
1:138-40; ECPR 6:403-4;
GenB 342-44, ill.; GenP 91-
93, ill.; GrEPR 14:23; Ho-
IPR 16, ill.; HoYMPR 174-
83, ill.; Hi de M 128; Hor
287-91; Ka 175-76; Per 97-
99, ill.; PlE 2:153-62,
ill.; PriC 46; QEQ (1936-
37) 27, (1941-42) 27-28,
(1948-49) 17-18; Vida 51-
55.

ASTOL ARTES, Félix (1813-1901)
singer, composer
BiP 39-41; BrECP 42; DiDHM
29; ECPR 6:404; Esp 79-84,
ill.; GrEPR 14:23; Hi de M
213-14; HoIPR 13-16, ill.;
PRFAS 25-26; VerOr 13-15,
17, 37, 39, 41, 63.

ASTOR, Manuel (b.1895), doctor
CaM 42-43.

ATILES GARCIA, Guillermo
(1882-1955), author, journalist
DiLP 2, pt.1:150-51; QEQ
(1941-42) 233, (1948-49)

18.

ATILES MOREU, Guillermo (b.
1901), lawyer
QEQ (1941-42) 28, (1948-49)
18.

ATILES MOREU, Rafael (b.1900),
lawyer, journalist
QEQ (1933-34) 27, (1936-37)
27, (1941-42) 28; Tri 2:
199-203.

ATILES Y PEREZ, Ramón (1804-
1875), painter
GrEPR 14:33-34.

AUBREY Y FERNANDEZ, José, doctor
RepM 241, ill.

AUDINOT, Julio R. (1867-1910),
doctor, politician
CaM 44; GrEPR 14:23; HoIPR
16, ill.; RepM 247, ill.

AUDINOT DE COTTO, Julio (b.
1830?), doctor
CaM 43-44.

AUGER MARTINEZ, Alfonso, politician
GrEPR 14:24.

AVELLANET BALAGUER, José (1860?-
1900?), author, journalist
DiLP 2, pt.1:151-52; GenB
309-11; Nuestr 114-17.

AVELLANET DE ROSARIO, Ana (b.
1895), teacher, civic leader
EGMPR 4:147-48.

AVENDAÑO, José Joaquín de (19th
cent.), doctor
CaM 44-45.

AVILA, Ignacio "El Aguila"
(1823-1848), criminal
BeHNPR 2:64-66; GrEPR 14:
24; Hi de CR 144-45.

AVILA MEDINA, Carmelo (b.1919),
lawyer, politician
GrEPR 14:24; QEQ (1948-49)
186.

AVILA ROMAN, Víctor M. (b.1922),
politician
LiPR 121, ill.

AVILES, Angel, architect
GrEPR 114.

AVILES, Juan (b.1905), poet
CaE 646; DiLP 2, pt.1:152-
53; Port 79, 80(ill.)

AVILES, Máximo (b.1855), musician, composer
Hi de CR 196-98.

AVILES BORRERO, Jacinto, doctor
CaM 45; DiM 37.

AVILES CORDERO, Mariano (b.
1902), teacher, agronomist
QEQ (1948-49) 18.

AVILES IRIZARRY, Serapio (b.
1884), orator
EstCR 2:13-14.

AXTMAYER RODRIGUEZ, Shirley
(b.1935), hotel manager
EGMPR 3:35-36, ill.

AYALA, Benigno "Benny" (b.
1951), baseball player
PRUSA 2, ill.

AYALA, Castor, artist
PaG 44-46.

AYALA, Rafael T. de (19th
cent.), politician
ArH 403.

Ayala de García, Elena see
Ayala Pérez, Elena

AYALA DEL VALLE, Luis M. (b.
1933), lawyer, politician
GrEPR 14:24; LiPR 33, ill.

AYALA MOURA, Eladio, novelist
GrEPR 14:24.

AYALA PEREZ, Elena (b.1924),
author
DiLP 2, pt.1:153-54; EGMPR
1:97-99, ill.; PRFAS 26-27.

AYALA Y TOMAS, Esteban de
(1778-1838), government official
HisD 11; PuI 52-53.

AYBAR DE ACUÑA, Dolores (1844-
1924), philanthropist, civic
leader
DiHBC 133; MujDPR 84-88,
ill.

AYBAR MEDRANO, Julio, labor

leader, politician
GrEPR 14:24.

AYERRA SANTA MARIA, Francisco
de (1630-1708), priest, poet
BiP 42-44; BrECP 47; CiBPI
39-41; DiDHM 29; DiHBC 133-
34; DiLP 2, pt.1:154-57;
ECPR 6:405; GrEPR 14:24;
HisD 11-12; PRFAS 27; PuI
16-17.

AYESA Y LAMI, Gabriel (1763-
1840), lawyer
BeHNPR 2:35-36; HisD 12;
PuI 40-41.

AYMAMON (16th cent.), Taíno
Indian chief
GrEPR 14:24.

AYUSO VALDIVIESO, Antonio (1899-
1969), lawyer, journalist
BiP 44-45; ECPR 6:405; GrEPR
14:24; PRFAS 27; QEQ (1933-
34) 27, (1936-37) 27-28,
(1941-42) 28, (1948-49) 18-19.

AZAUSTRE, José (b.1929), painter
GrEPR 8:391.

AZIZE, Yamila (b.1953), author,
professor
DirAS 3:23.

AZMAY MIRANDA, Juana (b.1870),
Catholic nun, pharmacist
EGMPR 3:317; MujPu 150.

B

BABCOCK, Lewis C. (1871-1947),
doctor
CaM 46-48; QEQ (1933-34) 27,
(1936-37) 28, (1941-42) 28.

BABEL, Tomás (19th cent.),
pharmacist
CaF 28-30; GrEPR 14:25.

BABIN, María Teresa (b.1910),
author, critic
BiP 45-46; BrECP 49; CaE
648; ConA 107:36; DiDHM 31;
DiHBC 142; DiLP 2, pt.1:
158-61; DicC 9; DirAS 3:24;
ECPR 6:405-6; EGMPR 1:245-
46, ill.; GrEPR 14:25; PQ 25;
PRFAS 29.

BACHMAN, Alberto (b.1901),
businessman

QEQ (1936-37) 28, (1941-42) 29.

BACHMAN, George (William) (b. 1890), parasitologist
QEQ (1941-42) 29, (1948-49) 186.

BACO SORIA, Carlos, pharmacist
CaF 30.

BACON, Emeterio, musician, homeopath
CaM 48-49; GenB 348-49.

BADILLO, Hernán (b.1929), politician, lawyer
AntHistCag 428-29, ill.; CuB 1971:17-19, ill.; DiDHM 31; EPI 1:141-42, ill., 2:166-67; ECPR 6:406; GrEPR 14:25; Port 13, 14 (ill.); PRUSA 2, ill.

BADILLO HERNANDEZ, Antonio (d. 1889), preacher, philanthropist
Apu 40.

BADRENA Y CUEBAS, Manuel, consul
GenB 275.

BAEZ, Fernando Luis (b.1941), weight lifter
ECPR 6:406-7.

BAEZ, Francisco (b.1932), politician
GrEPR 14:25.

BAEZ, José María (1805*-1880*), poet
DiLP 2, pt.1:161-63; EnsB 199-205.

BAEZ, Juan R. (1875-1929), police official
HoIPR 17, ill.

BAEZ, Myrna (b.1931), artist
BrECP 49; EGMPR 4:9-10, ill.; GrEPR 8:224, ill.; PaG 208-9; PQ 26; PRFAS 29.

BAEZ, Ramón (b.1858), doctor, professor
CaM 49.

BAEZ DE SILVA, Rosa (b.1873), teacher, civic works
EGMPR 4:217-18.

BAEZ GARCIA, Eudaldo (b.1907), lawyer, politician
GrEPR 14:25; QEQ (1948-49) 19.

BAEZ RODRIGUEZ, Enrique (b.1896), engineer
QEQ (1936-37) 28, (1941-42) 29.

BAEZ ROSARIO, Jaime (b.1908), businessman, politician
GrEPR 14:25.

BAGAANAME, María, Taína Indian
GrEPR 14:26.

BAGUE Y RAMIREZ, Jaime (1890-1969), veterinarian
BiP 46; PRFAS 29-30; QEQ (1933-34) 27-28, (1936-37) 28, (1941-42) 29; Tri 2:40-46.

BAGUES Y VESTARO, Jorge Ventura (19th cent.), doctor
CaM 50.

BAHAMON DE LUGO, Francisco (16th cent.), governor
DiDHM 31-32; GrEPR 14:26; Misc 26-28.

BAHR, Carlos F., politician
GrEPR 14:26.

BAIGES GOMEZ, Pedro (1889-1948), lawyer, politician
Añas 124-26; GrEPR 14:26.

BAIZ, Juan R., insurance agent. interpreter
RepM 104, ill.

BAJANDAS, Juan G., doctor
RepM 319, ill.

BALASQUIDE, Lorenzo A. (b.1899), doctor
DiM 38; Med ix.

BALBAS CAPO, Vicente (1864-1926), journalist
DiLP 2, pt.1:163-64; GrEPR 14:26, ill.; HoIPR 17, ill.; RepM 107, ill.

BALBUENA, Bernardo de (1568*-1627*), priest, poet
BeHNPR 1:235-40; BiP 46-47; CiBPI 25(ill.), 35-37; DiDHM 32; DiHBC 144; ECPR 6:407; GrEPR 6:254-56, ill.; Hi de

la Ig 64-70; HisD 12; Misc
38-46; PRFAS 30.

BALDONI PEREZ, Dolores, author
ArH 459-60, 520.

BALDORIOTY DE CASTRO, Román
(1822-1889), journalist, educator, politician, abolitionist
AlHP 68-69, ill.; BeHNPR 2:
199-209, ill.; BgP facing
p.70, ill.; BiP 48-50; Br-
ECP 49-51, ill.; CaE 651;
CiBPI 69(ill.), 100-103;
Desd 151-54; DiDHM 32-33,
ill.; DiHBC 145-47; DiLP 2,
pt.1:164-66; ECPR 6:407-9,
ill.; EPI 1:96(ill.), 97-
98; GenP 31-32; GrEPR 14:
27, ill.; HePR 36-45, ill.;
Hi de CR 186-87; HisD 12;
HoIPR 17-18, ill.; HoDMT 9-
19; HoRPR 21-27; LPR 966,
967-68, 969, 971, ill.; Ma
49-51; MeO 85-143; Mem 69-
71; Nuestr 134-36; Orad 27;
PaI 53-68, ill.; Por 230-
32; Proc 11-100, ill.;
PRFAS 30-31, ill.; PuI 85-
95; VPR 49-59, 166.

BALDRICH Y PALAU, Gabriel
(1814-1885), governor
CiBPI 94-97; DiDHM 33; Di-
HBC 454; GrEPR 14:27, ill.

BALESTIER, Eugenio S., Freemason, master builder
Ka 87-88.

BALOSSI, John (b.1931), professor, sculptor
GentI 101-6; GrEPR 8:228,
ill.

BALSAC, José Eleuterio (d.
1889), clerk
Nuestr 148.

BALSEIRO, Aurea "Puchi", composer
GrEPR 7:140.

BALSEIRO, José A., (b.1900),
author, critic, journalist,
professor
BiP 52-53; BrECP 51; CaE
652-53; ConA 81-84:30-31;
DiDHM 33-34; DiLP 2, pt.1:
166-72, 14:28; Ind 40-43;

Oro 8-24, ill.; PlE 2:297-99,
ill.; PRFAS 31-32; QEQ (1936-
37) 28, (1941-42) 29-30,
(1948-49) 19; Tri 1:251-59;
Vida 7-10.

BALSEIRO, Juan Ramón (1897-1973),
musician, composer
GrEPR 7:131-32, 133(ill.)

BALSEIRO, Miguel (19th cent.),
soldier, farmer
BeHNPR 1:321.

BALSEIRO DAVILA, Rafael (1867-
1929), composer
ArH 530-31; BiP 50-51; BrECP
51-52; Co 2; DiDHM 34, ill;
ECPR 6:409; GrEPR 14:30, ill.;
HoIPR 18, ill.; MusMP 218-20;
Mus en P 116-17; PRFAS 31,
ill.

BALSEIRO DE GIORGETTI, Aurea,
philanthropist
DiHBC 147-48; MujDPR 140-43,
ill.

BALSEIRO MARIN DE ASTOR, María,
poet
PoA 54-58, ill.

Balseiro y Ramos, José A. see
Balseiro, José A.

BALSEIRO Y ZENO, José Julián
Benigno (1838-1895*), author
DiLP 2, pt.1:172-73; PlE 1:
105-15, ill.; PoA 7-12, ill.

BALZAC, Alberto F., insurance
agent
QEQ (1933-34) 28, (1936-37)
28, (1941-42) 30, (1948-49)
19.

BALZAC, Ricardo, businessman
Tri 1:261-67.

BAQUERO OQUENDO, Jenaro (b.
1931), economist, professor
GrEPR 14:28.

BARALT Y GRECO, José María
(19th cent.), doctor
CaM 52.

BARASORDA, Antonio (b.1945),
singer
GrEPR 14:29.

BARBARIKA, Freda, artist,
teacher
    GrEPR 8:431.

BARBOSA, José Celso (1857-
1921), doctor, politician,
journalist
    AlHP 345, ill.; BiP 53-54;
    BrECP 52; CaM 53; CiBPI 176
    (ill.), 203-16; ComA 105-
    26; DiDHM 34-35, ill.; Di-
    HBC 153-56; DiLP 2, pt.1:
    173; DiM 38-46; ECPR 6:
    410-12, ill.; EPI 1:200-
    202, ill.; GenP 39-41; Gr-
    EPR 14:29, 30(ill.); HePR
    99-109, ill.; HisD 13; Ho-
    IPR 19, ill.; HoRPR 124-31;
    HoYMPR 112-25, ill.; Imp
    269-72, 277-80; LPR 1024,
    1025-29, ill.; Orad 179-80;
    PaP 67-109; Por 242-43;
    PriC 38, ill.; PRFAS 32-33,
    ill.; QuR 3-31, ill.; RepM
    20, ill.

BARBOSA, Pedro (b.1945), scientist
    PRUSA 3.

BARBOSA SANCHEZ, Carmen Belén
(b.1886), musician, teacher
    EGMPR 4:11-12; MujPu 146-
    47; MusMP 245-46.

BARBOSA SANCHEZ, Pedro Juan
(b.1892), journalist, politician
    GrEPR 14:29; PriC 99(ill.),
    100.

BARBOSA SEPULVEDA, María Ester
(b.1921), designer
    EGMPR 4:13-14.

BARBOUR, William Richard (b.
1890), forester
    QEQ (1933-34) 28, (1936-
    37) 28-29, (1941-42) 30.

BARBUDO, María de las Mercedes
(b.1780), patriot
    DiDHM 35; DiHBC 156; EGMPR
    1:45-51, ill.; GrEPR 14:
    29; PRFAS 33-34.

BARCELO, Antonio R. (1868-
1938), lawyer, politician,
author, orator
    And 140-43; BiP 54-56; Ci-
    BPI 223(ill.), 246-48;
    DelRB 29-31; Desd 59-62,

289-92; DiDHM 35-36, ill.;
    ECPR 6:412; GenP 64; GrEPR
    14:30, 31-32(ill.), HisD 13;
    HoDMT 29-40; HoIPR 19, ill.;
    HoRPR 49-64, ill.; Hor 257-
    59; Orad 323-25; PaP 113-20;
    PriC 37, ill., 57-58, ill.;
    PRFAS 34-35, ill.; Se 127-
    35; Tri 2:163-72.

BARCELO DE ROMERO, Josefina (b.
1901), politician
    EGMPR 4:267-68, ill.; PQ 27.

BARCELO OLIVER, José B., politician
    GrEPR 14:33.

BARDALES, Eugenio, industrialist
    Tri 2:205-10.

BAREA, Justa (1891-1978), teacher, journalist
    S 88.

BARLETTA, Vicente B. (b.1885),
accountant
    QEQ (1933-34) 28, (1936-37)
    29, (1941-42) 30-31.

BARNES, Francisco (d.1904),
businessman
    Crom 78; PonY 68.

BARNES, Joaquín, fire fighter
    Ver 190, ill.

BARNES VALLENILLA, Juan, inventor, businessman
    PonY 67.

BARTOLOMEI, Clemente (1889-
1955), farmer, veterinarian
    AlHP 351.

BARREIRO, Joaquín E. (1877?-
1927), journalist
    DiLP 2, pt.1:175-76.

BARRERA, Héctor (1922-1956),
author
    DiLP 2, pt.1:176-77.

BARRERAS IBAÑEZ, Francisco (b.
1911), politician
    GrEPR 14:33; PriC 101(ill.),
    102.

BARRERAS Y PADRO, José (1865-
1937), doctor, politician
    CaM 54-55; GrEPR 14:33, ill.;
    QEQ (1933-34) 28, (1936-37)

29; RepM 225, ill.

BARRETO, Eli, artist
   GrEPR 8:431.

BARRETO PEREZ, Ramón (b.1898),
politician
   GrEPR 14:30; QEQ (1941-42)
   233, (1948-49) 20.

BARRIONUEVO, Francisco de
(16th cent.), colonist
   GrEPR 14:33.

BARRIOS SANCHEZ, Ramón, labor
leader, politician
   GrEPR 14:33.

BARRIOS SOLER, Justo, banker
   RepM 153, ill.

BASCARAN DUEÑO, Carmelo (19th
cent.), engineer
   GenB 325-26.

BASCARAN QUINTERO, Juan, mus-
keteer, governor of La Mona
Island
   GenB 326; Hi de M 203.

BASORA, Francisco (1832-1903),
doctor, revolutionary
   GenB 332; DiM 46-48; Hi de
   M 208.

BASORA, José, boxer
   EPI 1:345, ill.

BASORA, José Luis, architect
   GrEPR 9:13.

BASORA DEFILLO, Juan (b.1930),
doctor
   QEQ (1936-37) 29, (1941-42)
   31, (1948-49) 20.

BASSO, Ana Margarita, artist
   GrEPR 8:392.

BASTARD TIZOL, Jaime, musician, teacher
   MusMP 284.

BASTIDAS Y RODRIGUEZ, Rodrigo
de (1498?-1570), bishop
   BeHNPR 1:209-14; DiDHM 36;
   DiHBC 160-61; GrEPR 6:254,
   14:34; HisD 14; Hi de la
   Ig 37-39.

BATISTA, Teófilo (b.1940),
artist
   GrEPR 8:393.

BATISTA, Tomás (b.1935), pro-
fessor, sculptor
   BrECP 53-54; DiDHM 36-37;
   GrEPR 8:232, ill.

BATISTA, Tomás L. (1899?-1929),
journalist, author
   DiLP 2, pt.1:177-78.

BATISTA MARTINEZ, Armando (b.
1940), politician
   GrEPR 14:34.

BATISTA MONTAÑEZ, Armando (b.
1940), politician
   LiPR 41, ill.

BAUERMEISTER, Fernando, politician
   GrEPR 14:34.

BAUZA, Guillermo (b.1916),
author
   CiuP 109-10; DiLP 2, pt.1:
   178-80; GrEPR 14:34.

BAUZA GONZALEZ, Miguel (b.1890),
lawyer
   QEQ (1941-42) 31, (1948-49)
   20.

BAUZA GONZALEZ, Obdulio (b.1907),
poet, lawyer
   BiP 56-57; BrECP 54; CaE
   654-55; CiuP 43-44; DiLP 2,
   pt.1:180-81; ECPR 6:412;
   GrEPR 14:34; PRFAS 35; SobM
   121-23.

Bayoán see Urayoán

BAYONET JIMENEZ, Natalio (1909-
1963), doctor
   CaM 57; QEQ (1936-37) 29,
   (1941-42) 31.

BAYOUTH, Edward (b.1917), businessman
   GenB 431-32, ill.

BAYRON TORO, Fernando (b.1941),
politicial scientist, author
   DirAS 1:40.

BEAUCHAMP, Eduvigis (19th cent.),
revolutionary
   MujDPR 45-46.

BEAUCHAMP, Elías, revolutionary
  GrEPR 14:35.

BEAUCHAMP Y GONZALEZ, Ramón
(b.1868), pharmacist, politician
  CaF 31-32; GrEPR 14:39.

BEAUMONT, Felipe de (d.1626),
governor
  DiDHM 37; GrEPR 14:35; Hi
  de Pu 86-88.

BECERRA, Juan M., doctor
  AlDJ 147, ill.

BECERRA, Luis Antonio (1821-
1872), lawyer
  BeHNPR 2:269-73, ill.; Di-
  HBC 530.

BECERRA AGUIRRE, Francisco A.
(b.1910), teacher
  QEQ (1936-37) 29, (1941-
  42) 31.

BECERRA GARCIA, Juan Bautista
(b.1823), lawyer, politician
  GrEPR 14:35.

BECERRA MUÑOZ, Diego (b.1856),
government official
  QEQ (1933-34) 28-29, (1936-
  37) 29, (1941-42) 32.

BECCERIL GELPI, Joaquín A. (b.
1880), Freemason, journalist
  GrEPR 14:35, ill.; QEQ
  (1933-34) 29, (1936-37)
  29-30, (1941-42) 32,
  (1948-49) 20-21.

BECHARA, Antonio (b.1932),
artist
  GrEPR 8:431.

BECHARA, José A., agronomist,
radio station owner
  A 114-15.

BEHN, Hernand (1880-1933),
telephone company president
  QEQ (1933-34) 179-81,
  (1936-37) 15.

BEHN, Sosthenes (1882-1957),
telephone company executive,
businessman
  CuB 1947:40-42, ill.; Di-
  HBC 166-68; DicAB suppl.6:

43-45; QEQ (1933-34) 180,
  (1936-37) 30, (1941-42) 32,
  (1948-49) 21.

BEIRO, Fernando, businessman
  Ka 107.

BELAND, Guillermo, inventor
  HisD 14.

BELAVAL, Emilio, singer
  GrEPR 14:35.

BELAVAL, Emilio S. (1903-
1973), author, judge
  A 47-48; BiP 57-59; BrECP 55-
  56; CaE 656-57; DiDHM 37;
  DiHBC 168; DiLP 2, pt.1:181-
  87; DicC 12; ECPR 6:412-13;
  GrEPR 4:94-100, ill., 14:35,
  ill.; PlE 2:389-98, ill.;
  PRFAS 35; QEQ (1933-34) 29-
  30, (1936-37) 30, (1941-42)
  32-33, (1948-49) 21-22; VPR
  125-30, 168-69.

BELAVAL, Germánico S. (b.1883),
dentist
  QEQ (1936-37) 30.

BELAVAL, José S. (b.1879),
doctor
  CaM 58-59; QEQ (1936-37) 30,
  (1941-42) 33, (1948-49) 22.

BELAVAL MARTINEZ, Eugenio S.,
politician
  GrEPR 14:36.

BELISARIO LOPEZ Y CARLO, Ramón
(1842-1906), newspaper founder
  HoIPR 21, ill.

BELPRE, Pura (1899-1982), author
  ConA 73-76:51, 109:41; Port
  105, 106(ill.)

BELLBER GONZALEZ, Rosario (b.
1881), teacher, suffragette
  DiHBC 168; EGMPR 4:273-74;
  GrEPR 14:36; MujDPR 179-80,
  ill.; QEQ (1933-34) 30,
  (1936-37) 30-31, (1941-42)
  33, (1948-49) 22.

BELLO, Edwin L. (b.1932), lawyer,
politician
  GrEPR 14:36.

BENAVENTE, Julio, politician
  GrEPR 14:36.

BENEBE GUZMAN, Juan (b.1926),
politician
    LiPR 123, ill.

BENEDICTO Y GEIGEL, José (b.
1880), lawyer, professor
    LM 131-32.

BENEDICTO Y GEIGEL, José E.
(d.1915), lawyer
    LM 114; RepM 98, ill.

BENET COLON, José (b.1875),
lawyer, judge
    GrEPR 14:36; QEQ (1933-34)
    30-31, (1936-37) 31, (1941-
    42) 33-34, (1948-49) 22-23.

BENET DE NEWTON, Milagros
(1885-1945), teacher, suffragette, feminist
    EGMPR 4:239-40; GrEPR 14:
    36; PQ 1-2; QEQ (1933-34)
    199- 200, (1936-37) 110,
    (1941-42) 34-35.

BENET VALDES, Juan, doctor
    CaM 60; RepM 336, ill.

BENIQUEZ, Juan (b.1950), baseball player
    PRUSA 3.

Benítez, Alejandrina see
Benítez de Arce de Gautier,
Alejandrina

Benítez, Celeste see Benítez
Rivera, Celeste

BENITEZ, Jaime (b.1908), educator, author, Resident Commissioner
    A 18-21, ill.; BiP 60-62;
    BrECP 56-57; DiDHM 38-39;
    DiLP 2, pt.1:187-90; ECPR
    6:413; GrEPR 14:38(ill.),
    39; HisD 14; PRFAS 36;
    PRUSA 3; QEQ (1948-49) 23-
    24.

BENITEZ, José (18th-19th
cent.), soldier
    BeHNPR 1:272-73.

BENITEZ, José A., journalist
    A 79.

BENITEZ, Lucecita, singer
    GentI 24-40.

BENITEZ, María Bibiana (1783-
1873), poet, dramatist
    BiP 62-64; BrECP 57; CaE 659-
    60; CiBPI 89-90; DiDHM 39;
    DiHBC 169; DiLP 2, pt.1:190-
    93; ECPR 6:413; EGMPR 1:53,
    ill.; EPI 3:176, 177, 181,
    182; GrEPR 3:9-10, 6:76-81;
    HisD 14; MujDPR 24-30; MujP
    115-16; MujPu 9-14; PQ 3;
    PRFAS 36.

BENITEZ, Salvador (b.1930),
artist
    GrEPR 8:431; PaG 213.

BENITEZ, Wilfredo (b.1959),
boxer
    PRUSA 3, ill.

BENITEZ CASTAÑO, Eugenio (1878-
1918), poet, journalist, politician
    BiP 59-60; DiLP 2, pt.1:196-
    97; HoIPR 21, ill.; LPR 1048,
    1050, 1051; PRFAS 35-36; RepM
    72, ill.

BENITEZ CASTAÑO, Jesús (b.1874),
engineer, politician
    GrEPR 14:37; QEQ (1933-34)
    180-81, (1936-37) 31-32,
    (1941-42) 35, (1948-49) 23.

BENITEZ CASTAÑO, Regalado (b.
1880), accountant
    QEQ (1933-34) 31, (1936-37)
    32, (1941-42) 35.

BENITEZ DE ARCE DE GAUTIER,
Alejandrina (1819-1879), poet
    BiP 64-65; CiBPI 69(ill.),
    90-91; DiDHM 38, ill.; Di-
    HBC 169; DiLP 2, pt.1:193-
    96; ECPR 6:413; EGMPR 1:101-
    3, ill.; EPI 3:177, 182; GenB
    339; GenP 46-47; GrEPR 3:11-
    13; HisD 15; HoIPR 21, ill.;
    MujDPR 31-37, ill.; MujP 116;
    MujPu 17-26; PlE 1:73-82,
    ill.; PQ 3; PRFAS 37, ill.

BENITEZ DIAZ, José J. (1864-
1947), sugar mill owner, politician
    GrEPR 14:37; PriC 39, ill.

BENITEZ FLORES, Manuel (1882-
1970), author, journalist,
lawyer
    Desd 89-93; DiLP 2, pt.1:

197-99; GrEPR 14:37, ill.;
QEQ (1936-37) 179, (1941-
42) 36, (1948-49) 23; SobM
146-48.

BENITEZ GORBEA, Rafael (b.
1945), journalist
GrEPR 1:xvi-xvii, ill.

BENITEZ LUGO, Jesús M. (b.
1893), businessman
QEQ (1936-37) 32, (1941-
42) 36, (1948-49) 24.

BENITEZ REXACH, Enrique M. (b.
1891), engineer, soldier
QEQ (1933-34) 31, (1936-
37) 32.

BENITEZ REXACH, Félix (1887-
1975), engineer
GrEPR 14:37; QEQ (1948-
49) 24.

Benítez Rexach, Jaime see
Benítez, Jaime

BENITEZ RIVERA, Celeste (b.
1935), politician, professor
DiDHM 38; EGMPR 3:87-88,
ill.; GrEPR 14:39; PQ 28.

BENVENUTTI, Jesús (b.1899),
poet, teacher
AlHY 229.

BENVENUTTI, Julio, politician
AlHY 224, ill.

BERGA Y PONCE DE LEON, Pablo
(b.1883), judge
ProA 67, ill.; QEQ (1933-
34) 31-32, (1936-37) 32-
33; Tri 2:121-26.

BERIO, Aida, public servant
PRUSA 4.

BERIO RODRIGUEZ, Francisca (b.
1935), journalist
EGMPR 3:281-82, ill.

BERIO SUAREZ, María Teresa (b.
1925), doctor
EGMPR 3:137-38, ill.

BERLINGERI DE FUSTER, María
Luisa, government official
EGMPR 3:89-90, ill.

BERMUDEZ, Cundo (b.1914),
artist
GrEPR 8:306, ill.

BERMUDEZ Y HERNANDEZ, Juan (b.
1887), politician
QEQ (1936-37) 33, (1941-42)
36.

BERMUDEZ RIVERA, Efraín (b.1936),
lawyer, politician
GrEPR 14:39.

BERMUDEZ SANCHEZ, Juan (b.1884),
consul
QEQ (1936-37) 33, (1941-42)
36-37, (1948-49) 24.

BERNABE, Rafael (b.1890),
doctor
CaM 61; DiM 48; GrEPR 14:39;
QEQ (1933-34) 32-33, (1936-
37) 33, (1941-42) 37, (1948-
49) 24-25.

BERNAL, Isabel (b.1935*), artist
GrEPR 8:392; PaG 210.

BERNAL, Joaquín, doctor
CaM 61-62.

BERNAOLA, Pedro (b.1919), poet
DiLP 2, pt.1:199-200.

BERNARDINI DE LA HUERTA, Tomás
(1871-1936), lawyer, politician,
author
AlHY 212; GrEPR 14:40, ill.;
Guay 278-79; LM 128-29; QEQ
(1936-37) 33, (1941-42) 37-
38; RepM 101, ill.

BERTODANO, Alberto de (18th
cent.), governor
GrEPR 14:42.

BERTRAN, Juan Manuel (b.1897),
engineer
QEQ (1933-34) 34, (1936-37)
34-35, (1941-42) 39, (1948-
49) 25.

BERRETEAGA PEREZ, Miguel (b.
1888), police inspector
QEQ (1941-42) 38.

BERRIOS, ANGEL O. (b.1940),
engineer, politician
LiPR 118, ill.

BERRIOS, José L., politician
GrEPR 14:40; RepM 320, ill.

BERRIOS, Pedro María (1838-
1919), priest
  HoIPR 22, ill.; LPR 990,
  992, 993; Nuestr 151-53.

BERRIOS, Rubén (b.1939), politician, lawyer
  BrECP 57-58; DiDHM 39-40,
  ill.; ECPR 6:413-14; GrEPR
  14:40, ill., 41(ill.);
  HisD 15; PRFAS 37-38, ill.

BERRIOS, Víctor C. (1892-1941)
doctor
  CaM 63-64.

BERRIOS AMARO, Aurelio (b.
1916), lawyer
  QEQ (1948-49) 25.

BERRIOS BERDECIA, José (1888-
1960), politician
  GrEPR 14:40.

BERRIOS BERDECIA, José Nicasio
(1890-1959), politician
  GrEPR 14:40; QEQ (1933-34)
  33, (1936-37) 34, (1941-42)
  38, (1948-49) 25.

BERRIOS BERDECIA, Ramón (1895-
1947), doctor
  CaM 63; QEQ (1933-34) 33,
  (1936-37) 34, (1941-42) 38.

BERRIOS BERDECIA, Tomás (b.
1888), government official,
politician
  QEQ (1933-34) 33-34, (1936-
  37) 34, (1941-42) 38-39.

BERRIOS COLON, Manuel (b.1881)
businessman
  QEQ (1933-34) 34, (1936-37)
  34, (1941-42) 39.

BERRIOS GIRONA, Pepita, singer
  MusMP 172-73.

Berríos Martínez, Rubén see
Berríos, Rubén

BERRIZBEITIA, Carlos (b.1899),
author, journalist
  QEQ (1936-37) 34.

BERROCAL, José E. (b.1896),
chemist
  QEQ (1933-34) 34, (1936-37)
  34, (1941-42) 39, (1948-49)
  25.

BESOSA, Harry F. (b.1881),
lawyer
  QEQ (1933-34) 34-35, (1936-
  37) 35, (1941-42) 39-40,
  (1948-49) 25-26; RepM 301,
  ill.

BESOSA, Manuel (b.1870), politician
  DiHBC 169; GrEPR 14:41, ill.

BESOSA, Pedro Juan, politician
  GrEPR 14:41.

BESOSA DE CASTRO, Mima (19th
cent.), seamstress
  DiHBC 169; GrEPR 14:42, ill.

BESOSA SILVA, Gertie Yolanda (b.
1923), architect
  EGMPR 3:139-40; QEQ (1948-
  49) 26.

BESOSA WORDEN, Celendonio (b.
1895), businessman, secretary
  QEQ (1936-37) 35, (1941-42)
  40.

BESSELL, William Weston, Jr. (b.
1901), soldier, engineer
  QEQ (1948-49) 26-27.

BETANCES, Ramón Emeterio
(1827-1898), doctor, author,
political activist, abolitionist
  AlHP 332, ill.; BeHNPR 2:
  221-40, ill.; BiP 65-68; Br-
  ECP 58-59, ill.; CaM 64-65;
  CiBPI 70(ill.), 113-18; Desd
  143-46; DiDHM 40-41, ill.;
  DiHBC 169-71; DiLP 2, pt.1:
  201-3; DiM 48-57; ECPR 6:
  414-15; EPI 1:109-14, ill.;
  GenB 251-52; GenP 60-61; Gr-
  EPR 14:42, 43(ill.); HePR 46-
  54, ill.; Hi de CR 157-69,
  ill.; Hi de M 199-200, ill.,
  277-93, ill.; HisD 15; HisP
  73-77, 79-87, 106-7, 109,
  133-37, 154; HoIPR 22, ill.;
  HoRPR 53-57; LPR 976, 977-78,
  979, 981; Nuestr 57-59; PaI
  69-86, ill.; Por 237-38;
  PRFAS 38, ill.; PRP 56-58;
  PuI 136-39; Se 61-71, ill.

BETANCES FERNANDEZ, Manuel (b.
1862), apothecary, politician
  CaF 33; GrEPR 14:42.

BETANCES JAEGER, Clotilde (b.
1890), journalist, author

DiLP 2, pt.1:203-5.

BETANCOURT, Marcos, actor
DelMu 36-40, ill.

BETANCOURT POMAR, Efigenio (b.
1921), engineer
QEQ (1948-49) 27.

BETANZOS, Amalia, government
official
Port 123, 124(ill.)

BEVERLEY, James R. (1894-
1965), governor, lawyer
Desf 109-12, ill.; DiDHM
41; DiHBC 438; GrEPR 14:
44; QEQ (1933-34) 35,
(1936-37) 35, (1941-42) 40,
(1948-49) 27.

BIAGGI, Arturo (b.1848), de-
tist
CaM 65.

BIAGGI, Julio (b.1940), artist
GrEPR 8:431.

BIAGGI, Virgilio (b.1913),
biologist, professor
BrECP 59-60; GrEPR 14:44;
PRFAS 39.

BIAGGI Y SANCHEZ, Robustiano
(1849-1912), lawyer
GenB 266; RepM 267, ill.

BIAGGI Y SANCHEZ, Tomás Virgilio (1848-1886), doctor
CaM 65-66; DiM 57-60; Med
23-24; Ver 171.

BIAMON SILVA, Luis (1906-
1964), doctor
CaM 66; DeADeA 229-32.

BIASCOECHEA, Diego A. (b.
1892), doctor
A 107; QEQ (1936-37) 35,
(1941-42) 40.

BIASCOECHEA MORALES, Esther A.
(b.1915), secretary, philanthropist
EGMPR 4:187-88, ill.

BIERLEY, John Robert (b.1908),
doctor
QEQ (1941-42) 40.

BIGAS MOLINS, Juan (1863-

1934), businessman
AlHP 282, ill.

BIRD, Rafael (b.1884), soldier
QEQ (1948-49) 28.

BIRD ARIAS, Enrique (1873-1917),
sugar mill owner
GrEPR 14:44.

BIRD ELIAS, Agustín, businessman
Guay 280.

BIRD FERNANDEZ DE ALVAREZ,
María T., teacher, travel agent
EGMPR 3:319-20, ill.

BIRD LEON, Modesto (1833-1918),
sugar mill owner
Guay 279-80; HoIPR 23, ill.

BIRD LOPEZ, Enrique (b.1895),
businessman, politician
GrEPR 14:44; QEQ (1941-42)
40-41.

BIRD LOPEZ, Esteban (1905-1969),
economist
GrEPR 14:44; QEQ (1941-42)
41, (1948-49) 27-28.

BIRD LOPEZ, Jorge, politician,
baseball club owner
GrEPR 14:44, ill.; PRUSA 4.

BISHOP, Adam (b.1878), doctor,
soldier, auditor
DiHBC 176.

BISHOP, Ella Morgan, educator
QEQ (1936-37) 35-36.

BITHORN, Hiram G. (1916-1951),
baseball player
DiDHM 41; EPI 1:332, ill.;
GrEPR 14:44; PRFAS 39.

BLADUELL ROBERTS, Héctor A. (b.
1904), doctor
QEQ (1933-34) 35-36, (1936-
37) 36, (1941-42) 41,
(1948-49) 28.

BLANCO, Antonio Nicolás (1887-
1945), author, journalist
BiP 68-69; BrECP 63; CaE 661;
DiLP 2, pt.1:224-26; HoIPR
76, ill.; PlE 2:237-44, ill.;
PRFAS 40.

BLANCO, Eloy (b.1933), artist
    Port 107, 108(ill.)

BLANCO, Enrique T. (b.1886),
historiographer
    DiHBC 177; DiLP 2, pt.1:
    226-27; QEQ (1933-34) 181-
    82, (1936-37) 37, (1941-
    42) 42.

BLANCO, Felipe (1877-1939),
policeman
    AlHP 240, ill.; QEQ (1933-
    34) 181; (1936-37) 36-37,
    (1941-42) 41-42, (1948-49)
    28-29.

BLANCO, Juan P. (b.1885),
teacher
    QEQ (1933-34) 37, (1936-37)
    37, (1941-42) 42-43, (1948-
    49) 29.

BLANCO, Julián E. (1830-1905),
author, journalist, politician
    BiP 69-70; BrECP 63-64; Ci-
    BPI 180-82; DiDHM 41-42;
    DiHBC 177-78; DiLP 2, pt.1:
    227-28; ECPR 6:415-16; GenP
    27; GrEPR 14:45, ill.; HisD
    15; HoIPR 24, ill.; HoRPR
    57-63; LPR 982, 984, 985,
    987; PRFAS 40; PuI 166-72.

BLANCO, Miguel, engineer
    A 125.

BLANCO, Tomás (1900*-1975),
author, historian, doctor
    BiP 70-71; BrECP 64-65; CaE
    662; DiDHM 42; DiHBC 178;
    DiLP 2, pt.1:228-32; DiM
    61-62; ECPR 6:416; GrEPR 5:
    58-61; Ind 43-44; Per 58-
    60, ill.; PIE 2:463-76,
    ill.; PRFAS 40.

BLANCO CID, Julián W. (b.
1883), businessman, government
official
    QEQ (1933-34) 36-37, (1936-
    37) 36.

BLANCO FERNANDEZ, Antonio (b.
1878), journalist, author
    DiLP 2, pt.1:232-34.

BLANCO MORALES, Heliodoro (b.
1889), engineer
    QEQ (1933-34) 37, (1936-37)
    37, (1941-42) 43.

Blanco Sosa, Julián see Blanco,
Julián

BLANES JUAN, Antonio (b.1828),
philanthropist
    GenB 328-29, Hi de M 206.

BLANES MANGUAL, Antonio (b.
1885), doctor
    CaM 68; QEQ (1933-34) 37-
    38, (1936-37) 37.

BLASCO PAGAN, Alfredo (b.1870),
lawyer
    LM 135; RepM 260, ill.

BLASINI, Francois José (b.1901),
doctor
    CaM 68; QEQ (1933-34) 38,
    (1936-37) 37, (1941-42) 43.

BLASINI, Jeannette (b.1941),
painter
    GrEPR 8:393.

BLASINI CABASA, Domingo, designer
    AlHY 241, ill.

BLASQUEZ ACOSTA, Manuel, doctor
    RepM 220, ill.

BLASSINI, Francisco (d.1913),
musician
    MusMP 285.

BLENK, Jaime Humberto (1856-
1917), priest, bishop
    GrEPR 6:266-67, ill., 14:45.

BLISS ALLEN, Peggy Ann (b.1940),
journalist, photographer
    EGMPR 4:205-6, ill.

BLOCH, Peter, author, musicolo-
gist
    PaG 250.

BLOCK, Claudio Federico (19th
cent.), doctor
    CaM 69.

BLOISE ANGLADE, José G. (b.
1896), engineer, government
official
    A 60; Nues 72-75, ill.

BLONDET, Carlos Honoré (b.1866),
politician
    GrEPR 14:166; Guay 250; QEQ
    (1936-37) 37-38, (1941-42)
    43.

BLONDET, Carmen Inés (b.1945), artist
GrEPR 8:431, 14:45.

Bobb, Maggie see Brandsness de Bobb, Maggie

BOBE ACEVEDO, Melanio (b. 1930), social worker, politician
LiPR 121.

BOCANEGRA LOPEZ, Susano (b. 1876), lawyer
QEQ (1933-34) 182, (1936-37) 38, (1941-42) 43-44, (1948-49) 29.

BOFILL Y CORREA, Rafael, journalist
GenB 254; Nuestr 31-33.

BOLAÑOS, Juan de (17th cent.), governor
Hi de Pu 96-97.

BOLIVAR ALVAREZ, Pedro (1865-1933), businessman
QEQ (1933-34) 38.

BONAFOUX Y QUINTERO, Luis (1855-1918), author, critic, journalist
BiP 71-72; BrECP 65; CaE 663-64; DiDHM 42-43; DiHBC 181: DiLP 2, pt.1:234-38; ECPR 6:416-17; GrEPR 14:46; Guay 250-51; HoIPR 24, ill.; Ind 44-45; LPR 1020, 1021-22, 1023; PRFAS 41.

BONELLI, Pablo M., doctor
Guay 280.

BONET SANTOS, Domingo (b. 1884), politician
GrEPR 14:46; QEQ (1941-42) 233-34.

BONETA, Luis C. (1886-1941), doctor
CaM 71-72; RepM 307, ill.

BONILLA, Antonia (b.1910), Catholic nun
EGMPR 3:321-22, ill.; EPI 2:229-31; MujP 231-33, ill.

BONILLA, Frank (b.1925), educator
Port 171, 172(ill.)

BONILLA CUEBAS, Eugenio (1865?-1910), author, journalist, dentist
DiLP 2, pt.1:238; GenB 299; HoIPR 24, ill.; Nuestr 82-83; RepM 211, ill.

BONILLA DIAZ, Jacob (b.1905), lawyer
QEQ (1941-42) 44, (1948-49) 29-30.

BONILLA NORAT, Félix (b.1912), artist, critic
GrEPR 8:308, ill., 14:46.

BONILLA RYAN, José, painter
GrEPR 8:431.

BONILLA Y TORRES, José Antonio (1770-1855), priest, author
BeHNPR 2:75-81; DiDHM 43; DiLP 2, pt.1:238-41; EPI 1:70; EnsB 95-100; HisD 16; PuI 42-45.

BONNET BENITEZ, Juan Amedée (b. 1899), engineer
QEQ (1933-34) 38, (1936-37) 38, (1941-42) 44, (1948-49) 30.

BONNET BENITEZ, Luis C. (b. 1912), biologist
QEQ (1941-42) 44-45.

BONNIN, Francisco, businessman
A 140.

BONNIN, Gaspar (19th cent.), businessman
Crom 99-100.

BONNIN ARMSTRONG, Ana Inés (b. 1902), author
CaE 664; DiLP 2, pt.1:241-43; EGMPR 1:105-6, ill.; PRFAS 41.

BONNIN FUSTER, Pedro Juan (1877-1948), businessman
AlHP 351, ill.

BONO DE QUEJO, Juan (15th-16th cent.), shipowner
GrEPR 14:46.

BOOTHBY ROUSSET, Thomas (b. 1883), businessman
GenB 390-91, ill.

BORDONADA GONZALEZ, Jesús (b.

1905), accountant
    QEQ (1948-49) 30-31.

BORGES LOPEZ, Pedro (b.1900),
politician
    GrEPR 14:46.

BORGOS MILLAN, José D. (b.
1887), professor, government
official
    QEQ (1936-37) 179, (1941-
    42) 45.

BORIA FUENTES, Felicia (b.
1901), secretary, government
employee
    EGMPR 3:91-92, ill.; QEQ
    (1936-37) 38, (1941-42) 45.

BOSCANA, Lucy, actress
    DelMu 48-51, ill.; EGMPR
    4:17-19, ill.; PQ 29.

BOSCIO, Juan Luis (b.1895),
businessman, philanthropist
    A 124; And 144-47.

BOSCH, Francisco (1875-1934),
businessman
    AlHP 351.

BOSCH, Pedro, teacher
    Tri 1:287-94.

BOSCH ESPINOS, Joaquín (19th
cent.), doctor
    CaM 73-74.

BOSCH Y PUIG, Wenceslao
(1858-1920), lawyer
    DiDHM 43; HoIPR 25, ill.

BOTELLO, Andrés (17th cent.),
soldier
    GrEPR 14:47.

BOTELLO, Angel (1913-1986),
artist
    GrEPR 8:310, ill.

BOTHWELL, Samuel C. (b.1864),
lawyer
    LM 133; RepM 332, ill.

BOU, Blas L. (b.1929), politician
    GrEPR 14:47.

BOU LEDESMA, Aurelia (b.1911)
wife of Gov. Piñeiro
    EGMPR 4:353.

BOUET, Carmen H. (b.1948),
painter
    GrEPR 8:431.

BOURASSEAU, Arturo (b.1945),
painter
    GrEPR 8:431.

BOURET, Emilio F. (b.1893),
doctor
    QEQ (1936-37) 38, (1941-42)
    45.

BOURET, Juan Pedro (b.1882),
businessman
    QEQ (1936-37) 38-39, (1941-
    42) 45.

BOURET, Pedro, businessman
    RepM 149, ill.

Bourne, Dorothy see Dulles de
Bourne, Dorothy

BOURNE, James Russell (b.1897),
federal employee
    QEQ (1936-37) 39.

BOVER, BARTOLOME (b.1903),
professor, music critic
    GrEPR 14:47.

BOYSEN MONSERRAT, Federico Alberto (1860-1915), priest
    Jes 144-47.

BOZELLO Y GUZMAN, Carmen (1859?-
1885), author
    DiLP 2, pt.1:243; EGMPR 1:
    107, ill.; MujDPR 52-53, ill.

BRACETTI, Mariana (1840?-1904*),
heroine of Grito de Lares
    Añas 16-23, ill.; BiP 72-73;
    BrECP 68; CiBPI 71(ill.),
    130-32; DiDHM 43, ill.; DiHBC
    184; ECPR 6:417; EGMPR 1:59-
    60; GenB 327; GrEPR 14:47;
    Hi de M 204, ill.; HisD 17;
    MujDPR 41-43, ill.; MujP 120-
    21; PQ 4; PRFAS 41-42, ill.

BRACER, Israel (b.1913), accountant
    QEQ (1948-49) 31.

BRAEGGER, Víctor (b.1890), insurance representative
    QEQ (1933-34) 182, (1936-37)
    39, (1941-42) 45-46, (1948-
    49) 31.

BRANDI DE SEIJO, Antonia (b. 1894), teacher
QEQ (1948-49) 31.

BRANDSNESS DE BOBB, Maggie, journalist
EGMPR 4:207-8, ill.

BRASCHI, Juan (1874?-1934), journalist, author
DiDHM 44; DiLP 2, pt.1:243-44; GrEPR 14:47; Ind 45-46; PRFAS 42.

BRASCHI, Manuel (19th cent.), politician
Ka 88.

BRASCHI, Mario (1840-1891), journalist
BiP 74; DiDHM 44, ill.; Di-HBC 184-85; DiLP 2, pt.1:244-46; ECPR 6:417; GenB 313-15; GrEPR 14:47; HoIPR 25-26, ill.; HoRPR 180-83; Mem 126; Nuestr 121-24; PaP 201-14; Pin 38-39; PRFAS 42-43, ill.; PuI 233-37.

BRASCHI, Wilfredo (b.1918), author, professor
BrECP 68-69; DiDHM 44-45; DiLP 2, pt.1:246-48; GrEPR 14:47; PRFAS 43.

BRAU, Salvador (1842-1912), author, historian, statesman
Ant 155-66; BgP facing p. 76, ill.; BiP 74-76; BrECP 69, ill.; CaE 667-68; CiBPI 174(ill.), 189-91; Cre 19-23; DiDHM 45, ill.; DiHBC 185-87; DiLP 2, pt.1:248-54; ECPR 6:417-18; EPI 1:156, ill.; GenP 72, 285-86; GrEPR 5:61-64, 14:47, 48 (ill.); Hi de CR 130-32, ill.; HisD 17; HoIPR 26, ill.; HoRPR 72-78; Ind 46-48; LPR 1000, 1001, 1002, 1003, ill.; MeO 35-84; PlE 1:309-25, ill.; Por 225-26; PRFAS 43-44, ill.; Sd 97-122.

BRAU CABRERA, Kermit (b.1909), doctor
QEQ (1936-37) 39, (1941-42) 46.

BRAU DEL TORO, Herminio (b. 1922), chemist

GrEPR 14:49.

BRAU DELGADO, Herminio (b.1881), musician, composer
EstCR 2:30-34, ill.; GrEPR 14:47; Hi de CR 227-28.

BRAU GONZALEZ, Fermín (b.1886), pharmacist
QEQ (1936-37) 39, (1941-42) 46.

BRAU Y GONZALEZ, Oscar (b.1882), engineer, businessman
DeTUP 31-34.

BRAU GONZALEZ, Salvador (b.1880), pharmacist
QEQ (1933-34) 39, (1936-37) 39, (1941-42) 46.

BRAU ZUZUARREGUI, Mario (1871-1941), artist, journalist, poet
DiLP 2, pt.1:254-55; GrEPR 8:139-40; LPR 788, 790, 791.

BRAVO, Rodolfo, industrialist, farmer
A 110.

BRAVO CABASSA, Leopoldo (b. 1908), politician, accountant
QEQ (1948-49) 31-32.

BRAVO DE RIVERO, Esteban (18th cent.), governor
DiDHM 46; DiHBC 187-88; Gr-EPR 14:49.

BRAVO Y GONZALEZ, Oscar Federico (b.1882), engineer, businessman
GenB 394-95, ill.; QEQ (1933-34) 39-40, (1936-37) 39, (1941-42) 46-47, (1948-49) 32.

BRAVO PARDO, Luis (1836-1906), businessman
GenB 258-62, ill.; Hi de M 196; Nuestr 60-61.

BRENNAN, Dan, artist
GrEPR 8:431.

BRENNAN, Flora, artist
GrEPR 8:394.

BRINDLE, William, Jr. (b.1901), pharmacist, teacher
QEQ (1941-42) 47.

BRISTOL SABATER, Arnaldo (b.

1945), athlete
  GrEPR 14:49.

BRITTON, Elizabeth Gertrude
(1858-1935), botanist
  QEQ (1933-34) 182-83,
  (1936-37) 15.

BRITTON, Nathaniel Lord
(1859-1935), botanist
  QEQ (1933-34) 183, (1936-
  37) 15.

BROOKE, John Rutter (1838-
1926), soldier, governor
  Desf 1-4, ill.; DiDHM 46;
  DiHBC 188-89; GrEPR 14:49,
  ill.

BROWN, Everett D. (b.1883),
teacher
  QEQ (1936-37) 39-40, (1941-
  42) 47.

BROWN, J. Henri, lawyer
  RepM 55, ill.

Broyoán see Urayoán

BRUCKMAN, Mathías (19th
cent.), revolutionary
  GrEPR 14:50(ill.), 51; Hi
  de M 193-94, ill.; HisD 17.

BRULL, Pedro Juan (b.1901),
poet, teacher
  DiLP 2, pt.1:255-56.

BRULL NATER, Jorge (b.1918),
pharmacist
  CaF 37.

BRUMBAUGH, Martin Grove (1862-
1930), educator
  BioD 1:194-95; DiHBC 189;
  GrEPR 14:51.

BRUNET DEL VALLE, Lorenzana
(b.1882), teacher, author
  DiHBC 189; DiLP 2, pt.1:
  256-57; EGMPR 1:109-10,
  ill.; MujDPR 200-201, ill.

BRUNET MALDONADO, Virgilio (b.
1901), lawyer, politician
  QEQ (1948-49) 32.

BRUNO, Francisco (b.1807?),
pharmacist
  CaF 37-38.

BRUNO, Francisco G. (d.1930),
dentist
  Guay 252; Ka 96.

BRUNO, José Antonio, engineer
  Guay 252-53.

BRUNO DE CAÑELLAS, Cecilia,
singer
  MusMP 173-74.

BRUNO DOMINGUEZ, Carlos (1867?-
1892), journalist
  Guay 251-52.

BRUNO LUZUNARIS, Angel F. (b.
1904), lawyer, judge
  QEQ (1941-42) 47.

BRUSELAS, Gerónimo de (16th
cent.), settler
  GrEPR 14:51.

BRUSI ALVAREZ, Alberto, lawyer,
judge
  RepM 313, ill.

BRYAN Y SOUFFRONT, Tomás (b.
1874), lawyer
  LM 129; ProA 36; RepM 139,
  ill.

BUENO RIVERA, Manuel (b.1898),
Boy Scout official
  QEQ (1933-34) 40, (1936-37)
  40, (1941-42) 47, (1948-49)
  32.

BUESO, Andrés, artist
  GrEPR 8:394.

BUITRAGO, Alejandro, doctor,
politician
  Guay 253.

BUJOSA MOLINA, Alfonso (b.1907),
politician, labor activist
  GrEPR 14:51; QEQ (1948-49)
  32-33.

BULBENA MASFERRER, César A. (b.
1887), painter, decorator
  QEQ (1936-37) 40.

BULL, Ernest M. (b.1875),
businessman
  QEQ (1933-34) 40, (1936-37)
  40, (1941-42) 48.

BUNKER, Franklin H. (1879-
1955), tobacco expert
  AntHistCag 338-39, 340, ill.;

QEQ (1933-34) 40, (1936-37) 40, (1941-42) 48, (1948-49) 33.

BUNKER, Oscar L. (b.1904), architect
AntHistCag 300-301; QEQ (1941-42) 48, (1948-49) 33.

BURE, Perfecto, notary public
Ka 111.

BURES, Antonio S. (b.1890), engineer
QEQ (1941-42) 48-49, (1948-49) 33-34.

BURGOS, Gloria E. (b.1925), poet
AntHistCag 250-51; AntPoe-Cag 231-33.

BURGOS, Julia de (1917*-1953), poet
BiP 76-77; BrECP 69-70, ill.; CaE 669-70; CiBPI 230(ill.), 302-4; DiDHM 46-47, ill.; DiHBC 192-93; DiLP 2, pt.1:257-60; ECPR 6:418-19; EGMPR 1:111-13, ill.; EPI 1:242-43, ill., 2:223-29; Esb 2:70-71; GrEPR 14:51; MujP 217-24, ill.; Not 122-24; Per 23-25, ill.; PQ 4-5; PRFAS 44, ill.

BURGOS RIVERA, Agustín (b.1896), politician, government official
GrEPR 14:51; QEQ (1948-49) 34.

BURSET MASFERRER, Joaquín A. (b.1881), music teacher, politician
GrEPR 7:209(ill.), 210-11, 14:51; MusMP 285; QEQ (1933-34) 41, (1936-37) 40, (1941-42) 49, (1948-49) 34.

BURSET MASFERRER, Víctor, lawyer, politician
RepM 160, ill.

BUSCAGLIA, José (b.1938), sculptor
BiP 77-78; BrECP 70; DiDHM 47; ECPR 6:419; GrEPR 8:312, ill.; PRFAS 45.

BUSCAGLIA RIVERA, Rafael (b.

1902), lawyer, government official
GrEPR 14:51; QEQ (1948-49) 34.

BUSQUETS Y SOLER, Jaime (1852-1914), farmer, Freemason
GenB 311-12; Hi de M 191-92, ill.; Nuestr 118-20.

BUSTAMANTE, María Rosario (18th-19th cent.), took vaccine to Cuba
EGMPR 1:57; MujDPR 19; MujPu 7.

BUSTELO, Manuel, newspaper publisher
Port 57, 58(ill.)

BUSTELO, Miguel A., politician
GrEPR 14:51.

BUTTE, George Charles (b.1877), lawyer, acting governor
QEQ (1933-34) 41, (1936-37) 40-41.

BUTTE, Woodfin Lee (b.1908), lawyer
QEQ (1933-34) 41-42, (1936-37) 41.

BUXEDA DE VALLE, Teresa (b.1875), author
ArH 520; MujPu 151-54.

BUXEDA VELEZ, Fernando Luis (b.1917), doctor
QEQ (1948-49) 34.

BYRNE, Edwin Vincent (1891-1963), Catholic bishop
GrEPR 6:285, 14:52, ill.; QEQ (1933-34) 42, (1936-37) 41, (1941-42) 49, (1948-49) 35.

BYROADE, George L. (1871-1936), soldier
QEQ (1933-34) 42, (1936-37) 15.

C

CABALLER, Luis (1867-1947), journalist
AlHP 137, ill.

CABALLERO, Celso, politician
GrEPR 14:53.

CABALLERO, Juan (18th cent.),
soldier
   GrEPR 14:53.

CABALLERO, Mariano A., doctor
   Tri 2:273-76.

CABALLERO, Ramón C. F. (b.
1820?), author
   DiLP 2, pt.1:260-62; GrEPR
   14:53.

CABALLERO BALSEIRO, Josefa (b.
1890), novelist
   DiLP 2, pt.1:262-64; GrEPR
   14:53; Ind 48-49.

CABALLERO LOPEZ, Pedro (b.
1894), teacher
   QEQ (1936-37) 179, (1941-
   42) 49, (1948-49) 186.

CABAN, Florencio (d.1951),
artist
   PaG 37, 38-39.

CABAN, Roger (b.1944), photographer
   PRUSA 4.

CABAN FERNANDEZ, Leopoldo (b.
1905), Lutheran minister
   QEQ (1936-37) 41, (1941-42)
   49-50.

CABAN Y ROSA, Juan Tomás,
politician
   BoHP 143(ill.), 144.

CABAN ROSAS, Ketty (b.1929),
composer, businesswoman
   EGMPR 4:15-16.

CABANILLAS, Isabel (b.1905),
poet, journalist
   DiLP 2, pt.1:264-65; EGMPR
   1:115-16.

CABANILLAS DE RODRIGUEZ, Ber-
ta (b.1894), home economist,
teacher
   EGMPR 1:247-49, ill.

CABASSA, Hiram David (b.
1915), engineer
   QEQ (1948-49) 35.

CABASSA, Leopoldo, landowner,
sugar industrialist
   RepM 312, ill.

CABASSA DE FAJARDO, Antonia

(1881-1973), politician
   EGMPR 2:15, ill.; GenB 378-
   79, ill. GrEPR 14:53; PriC
   72, ill.

CABASSA TUA, Ramiro (b.1896),
politician
   DiDHM 49.

CABASSA Y TUA, Regino (b.1896),
businessman, civic leader
   GenB 440-41, ill.

CABEZUDO, Lourdes, singer
   L 138-47.

CABEZUDO, Paulina, singer
   L 138-40.

CABEZUDO, Santa, singer
   L 138-47.

CABRAL Y BAEZ, Pablo (b.1883),
consul
   QEQ (1933-34) 183, (1936-37)
   179.

CABRANES, José (b.1940), judge
   PRUSA 4, ill.

CABRER, Juan, businessman
   Crom 28; Esp 113-16; GrEPR
   14:53.

CABRERA, Angela, politician
party official, civic works
   Port 169, 170(ill.); PQ 30.

CABRERA, Carlos (b.1857), poli-
tician, sugar mill owner
   DeTUP 17-18; GrEPR 14:53;
   Ka 164-65; Ver 166.

CABRERA, Domingo (b.1835), pharmacist
   CaF 39; CaM 82; GrEPR 14:53.

CABRERA, Enrique, political
activist
   Ver 168-69, ill.

CABRERA, Ernesto (b.1934),poli-
tician
   GrEPR 14:53.

CABRERA, Francisco Manrique (b.
1908), author, professor
   BiP 78-79; BrECP 71-72; CaE
   784; DiHBC 200; DiLP 2, pt.1:
   265-68; ECPR 6:419; EsbCrit
   19-23; GrEPR 14:54; PRFAS
   47.

CABRERA, Gabriel Pilar (19th cent.), doctor
CaM 82-83; DiM 63-64.

CABRERA, Miguel (b.1790), poet
DiLP 2, pt.1:268-69.

CABRERA TORRES, Rafael (b. 1888), banker
QEQ (1936-37) 41, (1941-42) 50.

CABRERA VAZQUEZ, Alba Raquel (b.1928), journalist
EGMPR 3:283-84, ill.

CABRERA VAZQUEZ DE IBARRA, Palmira (b.1910), politician
EGMPR 1:251-52, ill., 2:17, ill.; GrEPR 14:54; PriC 75-76, ill.

CABRERO Y ECHEANDIA, Manuel Joaquín, businessman, accountant
BoHP 141, 143(ill.)

CABRERO Y ECHEANDIA, Severiano, businessman
BoHP 144-45, 146(ill.)

CACERES, Alonso de (16th cent.), church employee
GrEPR 14:54.

CACERES, Víctor M. (b.1934), politician
GrEPR 14:54.

CACIMAR (d.1514), Taíno Indian chief
CiBPI 14-17; GrEPR 14:54.

CADIERNO Y RODRIGUEZ, Segundo (b.1872), businessman
QEQ (1933-34) 42, (1936-37) 42, (1941-42) 50, (1948-49) 35.

CADILLA, Arturo (b.1895), author, journalist, doctor
DiLP 2, pt.1:269-70; DiM 64-65; GrEPR 14:54; PoA 61-63, ill.; QEQ (1933-34) 43, (1936-37) 42, (1941-42) 50-51; Vida 63-64.

CADILLA, Carmen Alicia (b. 1908), poet, journalist
ArH 524-25; BiP 80-81; Br-

ECP 72; CaE 674; DiDHM 49; DiLP 2, pt.1:270-73; ECPR 6:420; EGMPR 1:121-23, ill.; GrEPR 14:54; Ind 50-51; PRFAS 48; QEQ (1936-37) 179-80, (1941-42) 51.

CADILLA, Francisco M. (b.1894), author, historian
DiLP 2, pt.1:273-75; QEQ (1933-34) 43, (1936-37) 42, (1941-42) 51.

CADILLA DE MARTINEZ, María (1886*-1951), author, historian, folklorist, painter
ArH 520-21; BiP 79-80; BrECP 72; CiBPI 223(ill.), 275-78; DiDHM 49; DiHBC 203; DiLP 2, pt.1:275-77; ECPR 6:419-20; EGMPR 1:117-19, ill.; EPI 3:179, 180, 184, 185; GrEPR 14:54; HoYMPR 230-38, ill.; Ind 49-50; MujDPR 174-76, ill.; MujP 125-26; Not 129-30; PlE 2:181-98, ill.; PoA 73-75, ill.; PQ 5; PRFAS 47-48; QEQ (1933-34) 183-84, (1936-37) 42, (1941-42) 52, (1948-49) 35-36; Vida 43-46.

Cadilla de Ruibal, Carmen Alicia see Cadilla, Carmen Alicia

CADILLA DE TIO, María de los Angeles (d.1977), musician, teacher
GrEPR 14:54.

CADILLA MATOS, Arturo (1867-1896), poet
DiLP 2, pt.1:277-78.

CADIZ MARTINEZ, Ernesto (b.1893), doctor, politician
GrEPR 14:55; QEQ (1948-49) 36-37.

CAGUAX (16th cent.), Taíno Indian chief
GrEPR 14:55.

CAICOYA, José Manuel, actor
DelMu 54-57, ill.

CAJIGA, Luis Germán (b.1934), artist
BrECP 74; DiDHM 50; GrEPR 8:236, ill.; PaG 201; PRFAS 48.

CAJIGAS, Avilio, artist
GrEPR 8:396.

CAJIGAS, Tomás (b.1894), doctor
CaM 84; QEQ (1933-34) 43-44, (1936-37) 42-43, (1941-42) 52, (1948-49) 186-87.

CAJIGAS Y SOTOMAYOR, Zoilo (d.1961), artist
PaG 39-40.

CALDERIN, Delia (b.1928), singer, teacher
GrEPR 14:55.

CALDERON, Antonio (16th cent.), bishop
Hi de la Ig 43-44.

CALDERON, César A. (b.1915), engineer
QEQ (1948-49) 37.

CALDERON, Eugene (b.1919), educator
Port 159, 160(ill.)

CALDERON, Gil, sea captain
GrEPR 14:55.

CALDERON, Manuel R., businessman
RepM 193, ill.

CALDERON APONTE, José (1838-1909?), author, journalist
Cre 63-64; DiLP 2, pt.1:278-79; GrEPR 14:55.

CALDERON CEPEDA, Pablo, real estate agent
A 163, ill.

CALDERON DE GONZALEZ, Sila, government official
EGMPR 3:93-94, ill.

CALDERON ESCOBAR, Juan (1902-1942), author, journalist
CaE 675; DiLP 2, pt.1:279.

CALDERON LASEN, Enrique (b. 1906), accountant
QEQ (1933-34) 44, (1936-37) 43.

CALDERON MOLINARY, Andrés (b. 1902), teacher
QEQ (1948-49) 37.

CALDWELL, William Grant (b. 1905), soldier
QEQ (1933-34) 44, (1936-37) 180.

CALERO JUARBE, Calixto (b. 1937*), politician, lawyer
GrEPR 14:55; LiPR 28, ill.

CALIMANO, F. (b.187?), businessman
RepM 257, ill.

CALOCA Y CUETO, Juan (19th-20th cent.), landowner, politician
RepM 135, ill.

CALOR MOTA, Candelario (b.1898), engineer, professor
QEQ (1941-42) 53, (1948-49) 37; Tri 2:61-65.

CALVO, Angel, industrialist
A 145, ill.

CALZADA, Sergio E. (b.1936), politician
LiPR 118, ill.

CALLEJO, Fernando (1862-1926), musician, composer
BrECP 74-75; Co 3; GrEPR 14:55; HoIPR 29, ill.; PRFAS 48.

CALLEJO, Margarita, singer
DiHBC 207.

CALLEJO, Sandalio (1833-1883), composer, educator
GrEPR 14:55; MusMP 221-23.

CAMACHO, María Teresa, business college owner, teacher
DiHBC 207; EGMPR 1:253-55, ill.; MujDPR 230-33, ill.; QEQ (1936-37) 43, (1941-42) 53.

CAMACHO, Paul (b.1929), painter
GrEPR 8:314, ill.

CAMACHO BOTET, Luis F. (b.1937), lawyer, politician
GrEPR 14:56.

CAMACHO Y MARCO(S), Gabriel (19th cent.), doctor
CaM 85-87.

CAMARA, Andrés, radio station manager
A 113.

CAMARA SANDINI, Elena (19th cent.), teacher
DiHBC 209; EGMPR 1:257-58, ill.; MujDPR 95-97, ill.

CAMBERO, Jorge (d.1656?), priest, teacher
DiHBC 210.

CAMBLOR GONZALEZ, Manuel (b. 1869), businessman
QEQ (1936-37) 180, (1941-42) 53-54.

CAMEJO, Rafael W. (b.1898), poet, journalist
DiLP 2, pt.1:279-81.

CAMINERO MILAN, Joaquín (b. 1937), poet
AlHY 176-77.

CAMPBELL, Bruce R. (b.1879), Protestant minister
QEQ (1936-37) 43, (1941-42) 54.

CAMPECHE Y JORDAN, José (1752*-1809), painter
BeHNPR 1:336-42, ill.; BiP 81-83; BrECP 75, ill.; CiBPI 45(ill.), 50-52; Desd 76-79; DiDHM 50-51, ill.; DiHBC 212-13; Eco 158-64; ECPR 6:420-21; EnsB 13-24; EPI 1:69, ill.; Exp 86-95; GrEPR 8:7-13, 18-27, 240, ill.; HisD 18; LPR 787-88, 789, 962, 963, ill.; PaG 47-56; Por 200-202; PRFAS 49, ill.; PuI 29-32.

CAMPI, Josefa A. (b.1835), poet
Hi de CR 127-29.

CAMPILLO Y ABRAMS, Luis (b. 1871), lawyer
LM 129; RepM 71, ill.

CAMPOS AYALA, Guillermo (b. 1921), politician
LiPR 30, ill.

CAMPOS DEL TORO, Enrique (b. 1900), lawyer, government official
DiHBC 213; GrEPR 14:56, ill.; PRFAS 49-50; QEQ (1941-42) 54, (1948-49) 37-38.

CAMPOS Y ESPINOSA, Alonso de (d. 1678), soldier, governor
Hi de P 187-89.

CAMPOS PARSI, Héctor (b.1922), composer, professor
BiP 83-84; BrECP 75-76, ill.; DiDHM 51; DiHBC 213-14; ECPR 6:421; GrEPR 1:xii-xiii, ill., 7:311-17, ill., 14:65-67, ill.; L 101; Mus en P 152-53; PRFAS 50; PRUSA 5.

CAMPRUBI, José (b.1879), journalist, engineer
QEQ (1933-34) 44, (1936-37) 43, (1941-42) 54.

CAMPRUBI DE JIMENEZ, Zenobia (1887-1956), translator
EGMPR 4:195-97, ill.

CAMUÑAS CREUX, Manuel (1853-1927), politician
GrEPR 14:58, ill.; RepM 88, ill.

CAMUÑAS MONGE, Jorge (b.1915), accountant
QEQ (1948-49) 38.

CAMUÑAS PEREZ, José F. (b.1907), lawyer
QEQ (1941-42) 54.

CANALES, Desiderio, lawyer
Ka 24-25.

CANALES, Nemesio R. (1878-1923), author, journalist, critic, lawyer
AlDJ 23-24, 79-89, ill.; BiP 84-86; BrECP 76-77, ill.; CaE 676-77; CiBPI 223(ill.), 258-61; Desd 56-58; DiDHM 51-52, ill.; DiHBC 215; DiLP 2, pt.1:282-86; ECPR 6:421-22; GrEPR 5:64-66, 14:58, ill.; HoDMT 41-51; HoYMPR 212-28, ill.; Ind 51-52; PlE 2:165-78, ill.; PRFAS 50-51, ill.; RepM 203, ill.; VPR 99-110, 168.

CANALES, Rosario, politician
AlDJ 14, ill.

CANALES TORRESOLA, Mario
(1899-1962), politician
    AlDJ 42-43, ill.; GrEPR 14:
    59; QEQ (1948-49) 187.

CANALES VALLDEJULY, Julio,
industrialist
    AlHP 470, ill.

CANALS, José Antonio, engineer
    RepM 136, ill.

CANALS SALDAÑA, José Manuel
(b.1899), engineer
    QEQ (1933-34) 44, (1936-
    37) 43, (1948-49) 38.

CANCEL MIRANDA, Rafael (b.
1929), revolutionary
    GrEPR 14:59.

CANCEL NEGRON, Ramón (b.1937),
author, lawyer
    DiLP 2, pt.1:286-88.

CANCEL RIOS, Juan J. (b.
1925), lawyer, politician
    GrEPR 14:59, ill.; PriC
    103-4, ill.

CANCIO, Francisco, pharmacist
    Crom 61-62.

CANCIO Y CORES, José Luis (b.
1896), lawyer
    QEQ (1933-34) 44-45, (1936-
    37) 44, (1941-42) 54.

CANCIO Y CORES, Miguel M.,
pharmacist
    BoHP 198.

CANCIO ORTIZ, Juan (1854*-
1951), farmer, politician
    RepM 278, ill.; S 91; Tri
    1:349-55.

CANCIO RODRIGUEZ, Miguel M.,
pharmacist
    CaF 40.

CANCHANI, Nemesio (b.1946),
artist, teacher
    GrEPR 8:395.

CANDAL, Norma, actress
    DelMu 60-65, ill.; EGMPR
    4:21-23, ill.; GentI 132-
    38.

CANINO, Espiridión, doctor

RepM 242, ill.

CANINO SALGADO, Marcelino J.
(b.1943), professor, author
    BrECP 77; GrEPR 1:xvii-
    xviii, ill., 14:60, ill.;
    PRFAS 51.

CANSINO, García Alonso (16th
cent.), sea captain
    GrEPR 14:60.

CANTERO Y SCHWARZ, José Laureano
(b.1917), industrialist
    Desd 308-10.

CAPARROS PEREZ, Jenaro (b.1899),
pharmacist
    QEQ (1933-34) 45, (1936-37)
    44, (1941-42) 55.

CAPELLA, Antonio, pharmacist
    Ka 128-29.

CAPELLA, María A., designer
    EGMPR 4:25-26.

CAPESTANY OLLER, Rogelio (b.
1866), engineer
    QEQ (1936-37) 44, (1941-42)
    55.

CAPETILLO, Luisa (1880*-1922),
suffragette, feminist, labor
leader, author
    ArH 520; BrECP 78; DiDHM 52;
    DiLP 2, pt.1:290-92; EGMPR
    4:275-77; GrEPR 14:61; PQ 6;
    PRFAS 51-52.

CAPLLONCH, Vicente, businessman
    Ka 45.

CAPO, José Mariano, notary, sugar
mill owner
    Ka 83.

CAPO, Bobby, singer, composer
    ECPR 6:487; GrEPR 7:139-40,
    ill.; L 129-37; Port 25,
    26(ill.)

CAPO, Félix Manuel (b.1922),
musician, composer
    Com 2.

CAPO CINTRON, Eduardo (b.
1822), lawyer, politician
    GrEPR 14:61; QEQ (1933-34)
    185, (1936-37) 44, (1941-42)
    55.

CAPO DE ANTONSANTY, Teresa
(b.1840), civic leader
    DiHBC 231; EGMPR 1:73-74,
    ill.; GrEPR 14:61; MujDPR
    97-100, ill.

CAPO MATRES, Luis (b.1868),
lawyer
    RepM 194, ill.

CARABALLO, José, painter
    PaG 238.

CARABALLO, Rafael (b.1940),
painter
    GrEPR 8:432.

CARABALLO GORDILS, Daisy (b.
1925), professor
    GrEPR 1:x, ill., 14:61.

CARABALLO NEGRON, José (b.
1914), labor leader
    PRFAS 52.

CARBALLEIRA CAÑELLAS, Ignacio
(1879-1936), judge, politician
    QEQ (1933-34) 45, (1936-
    37) 15.

CARBIA, Vilma, radio and television hostess, actress
    EGMPR 4:29-30, ill.

CARBIA BURT, Ramón (b.1880),
architect
    QEQ (1936-37) 44, (1941-
    42) 55.

CARBIA DE CHAVES, Awilda (b.
1938), actress
    EGMPR 4:27-28, ill.

CARBONELL TORO, Celedonio,
politician
    GrEPR 14:61; RepM 248, ill.

CARBONELL TORO, Salvador
(1841-1909*), doctor, politician, abolitionist
    CaM 92-93; DiM 66-71; GenB
    252, ill.; GenP 108-9,
    ill.; Hi de CR 234-43; Hi
    de M 190-91; HisD 20;
    Nuestr 13-15; PuI 245-53.

CARDE Y PERUYERO, José G.,
dentist
    BoHP 167, ill.

CARDENAS, Pedro de (16th
    cent.), colonist

GrEPR 14:61.

CARDENAS HEMLOCK, Lupe, charity
work, fund raiser
    Port 5, 6(ill.)

CARDONA, Alice, community
activist
    Port 149, 150(ill.)

CARDONA, Francisco de (16th
cent.), treasurer of San Juan
    GrEPR 14:61; HisD 20.

CARDONA, José Aracelio (b.1912),
educator, minister
    GrEPR 1:xii, ill., 14:62,
    ill.

CARDONA, Néstor de, doctor
    A 108.

CARDONA DE QUIÑONES, Ursula
(1836-1875), poet
    DiLP 2, pt.1:292-93; EGMPR
    1:125-27; MujDPR 38-39, ill.;
    Muj Pu 30-44.

CARLO ORTIZ, Simón (1882-1943),
engineer
    GenB 442-43, ill.

Carmelita, Sister see Bonilla,
Antonia

CARMOEGA Y MORALES, Enrique R.
(b.1888), engineer
    QEQ (1933-34) 45, (1936-37)
    44, (1941-42) 55, (1948-49)
    38.

CARMOEGA MORALES, Rafael (1884-
1968), architect
    GrEPR 9:75-76; PriC 220, ill.

CARMONA RIVERA, Gumersindo (b.
1932), politician
    LiPR 39, ill.

CARO COSTAS, Aída R. (b.1924),
historian
    DiHBC 233-34; DiLP 2, pt.1:
    293-94; EGMPR 1:259-60, ill.

CARO COSTAS, Salvador V. (b.
1914), engineer
    QEQ (1941-42) 56.

CARO RAMOS, Ceferino (b.1936),
politician
    LiPR 124, ill.

CARPEGNA, Ramón (19th cent.),
Spanish soldier
DiHBC 235.

CARTAGENA COLON, Demetrio (b.
1904), teacher
QEQ (1948-49) 41.

CARTAGENA MARTINEZ, Juan
(1891?-1956), artisan
San 31-35.

CARUANA, Jorge José (b.1882),
bishop
DiHBC 239; GrEPR 6:270-71,
ill.; QEQ (1948-49) 41.

CARVAJAL, Francisco Andrés de
(d.1586), bishop
Hi de la Ig 39-40.

CARRASQUILLO, Pedro (1910-
1964), poet
DiLP 2, pt.1:295-96.

CARRASQUILLO QUIÑONES, Ernesto (b.1901), politician, labor
leader
GrEPR 14:62, 63(ill.); PriC
105(ill.), 106.

CARRASQUILLO HERPEN, Manuel
(b.1902), lawyer, professor
QEQ (1936-37) 45, (1941-
42) 56, (1948-49) 38-39.

CARRAZA, Diego de (16th cent.)
governor
DiDHM 52; GrEPR 14:61.

CARREÑO, José (18th cent.),
acting governor
GrEPR 14:63.

CARRERAS, Carlos N. (1895-
1959), journalist, author
And 220-21; BiP 86-88; Ci-
BPI 290-91; DiDHM 52-53;
DiLP 2, pt.1:296-99; Per
155-57; PRFAS 52; QEQ
(1936-37) 45, (1941-42)
56-57, (1948-49) 39.

CARRERAS, Francisco J. (b.
1932*), educator
DiDHM 53; GrEPR 14:63, ill.

CARRERAS ANGLADA, Francisco
Isidoro (b.1883), chemist
QEQ (1941-42) 56, (1948-
49) 39.

CARRERAS CAMACHO, Miguel (b.
1900), police official
QEQ (1941-42) 56.

CARRERAS Y DELGADO, Gerónimo
(1856-1921), doctor
CaM 96-97; RepM 251, ill.

CARRERAS RODRIGUEZ, Juan (b.
1892), teacher
QEQ (1933-34) 45-46, (1936-
37) 45, (1941-42) 57.

CARRERO, Alberto (b.1948),
tennis player
ECPR 6:422.

CARRERO, Jaime (b.1931), author,
teacher
Añas 3-7; BrECP 79; DiLP 2, pt.
1:299-300; GrEPR 5:66-68, 8:
316, ill.; Ind 52-53; PRFAS 53.

CARRION, Diego (b.1883), insurance agent
QEQ (1933-34) 46, (1936-37)
45, (1941-42) 57.

CARRION, José Luis (b.1924),
banker
GrEPR 14:64.

CARRION DE MALAGA, Pablo Benigno (1798-1871), bishop
DiDHM 53-54; DiHBC 235; EnsB
155-62; GrEPR 6:260-61, ill.

CARRION GAGO, Antonio (b.1896),
accountant
QEQ (1933-34) 46, (1936-37)
45, (1941-42) 57, (1948-49)
39.

CARRION MADURO, Tomás (1870-
1920), journalist, poet, orator
AlHP 133-34, ill.; BiP 88-
89; CaE 682; DiDHM 54, ill.;
DiLP 2, pt.1:300-302; ECPR
6:422-23; GrEPR 14:64, ill.;
Imp 305-7; LPR 1048, 1049;
PRFAS 54-55, ill.; RepM 289,
ill.

CARRION Y PACHECO, Arturo L.
(b.1893), doctor
CaM 98; QEQ (1936-37) 45-
46, (1941-42) 57-58, (1948-
49) 39-41.

CARRION Y PACHECO, Rafael (1891-
1964), banker

PRFAS 53-54; QEQ (1936-37) 46, (1941-42) 58, (1948-49) 41.

CARRO, John (b.1927), lawyer, judge
Port 77, 78(ill.)

CARRO RIVERA, Felipe (b.1896), agronomist, politician
GrEPR 14:65; QEQ (1936-37) 46, (1941-42) 58.

CASABLANCA, Pedro P. (b.1894), educator
QEQ (1936-37) 46, (1941-42) 58-59.

CASABLANCA, Ramón C. (b.1902), public relations officer
QEQ (1941-42) 234.

CASABLANCA DE LA CUERDA, Rosario, school administrator
GenB 354, ill.

CASAL PEITEADO, Ricardo (b. 1876), bookkeeper
QEQ (1936-37) 46-47, (1941-42) 59, (1948-49) 187.

CASAL VALDES, Ulpiano (b. 1892), lawyer
A 121; QEQ (1936-37) 47, (1941-42) 59, (1948-49) 41.

CASALDUC, Ismael (1900-1958), poet, journalist
DiLP 2, pt.1:302.

CASALDUC, José Eduardo, businessman
QEQ (1936-37) 46, (1941-42) 59, (1948-49) 41-42.

CASALDUC Y COLON, Eduardo (19th cent.), doctor, politician
CaM 99.

CASALDUC GOICOECHEA, Felipe, lawyer, politician
RepM 233, ill.

CASALS, Alfredo, businessman
Crom 82.

CASALS, Luis, businessman
Crom 17; Ka 41.

CASALS, Pablo (1876-1973), musician, composer

BiP 89-90; ConA 93-96:84-87; CuB 1950:82-84, ill., 1964: 71-74, ill., 1973:452; DiDHM 55, ill.; ECPR 6:423; GrEPR 14:65, ill., 66-68(ill.); HisD 22; L 104-19; PRFAS 55, ill.

CASANOVA, Felipe, teacher
Tri 2:15-22.

CASANOVA, Rosita, pianist
L 97-98, 100(ill.)

CASANOVA DUPERROIX, Carlos (1856*-1904*), author, orator, journalist, musician
DiLP 2, pt.1:302-3; GenB 288-90, ill.; GenP 79-80; Hi de M 128, 192-93, ill.; HoIPR 32, ill.; Ind 54; MusMP 246-47; Nuestr 51-52; PIE 1: 480-81.

CASANOVA PRATS, Abelardo (b. 1903), lawyer, politician
GrEPR 14:68; QEQ (1941-42) 59.

CASANOVA PRATS, Teobaldo (b. 1894), mathematician, teacher
GenB 434, ill.; QEQ (1948-49) 42.

Casanovas Duperroi, Carlos see Casanova Duperroix, Carlos

CASAÑAS DE O'CONNOR, Aida, lawyer
EGMPR 3:141-42.

CASAS, Bartolomé de las (1474-1566), historian, Defendor of the Indians
DiDHM 55; GrEPR 14:68; HisD 27.

CASAS, Myrna (b.1934), dramatist, director
BrECP 80; DiLP 2, pt.1:304-6; EGMPR 4:31-32, ill.; GrEPR 14:68; PRFAS 55-56.

CASASUS MARTI, Carmen G. (b. 1893), teacher
Añas 143-45.

CASELLAS, Juan, businessman, politician
AlDU 8, 14, 81, ill.

CASENAVE, Luis de (1901-1976), photographer

GrEPR 14:69, ill.

CASIANO, Angel, painter
GrEPR 8:432.

CASIANO, Félix (b.1900), educator
QEQ (1933-34) 46, (1936-37)
47, (1941-42) 59.

CASIANO JUSINO, Lorenzo (b.
1890), agronomist, bookkeeper
QEQ (1933-34) 46-47, (1936-
37) 47, (1941-42) 59-60,
(1948-49) 42.

CASIANO OLMEDA, Juan (1910-
1944), poet
AlHY 166-68, 221-22; DiLP
2, pt.1:306-7.

CASIANO VARGAS, Ulises (b.
1933), bishop
GrEPR 6:287.

CASO Y SOTO, Luis (1858-1932),
pharmacist, journalist
ArH 541.

CASTAGNET, Francisco N.,
businessman
A 128.

CASTAING, Horacio (d.1935),
painter
AlHP 339, ill.; GrEPR 8:
148.

CASTAÑO GUADALUPE, Jesús M.
(b.1906), politician
GrEPR 14:69.

CASTAÑO ORTIZ, Carlos L. (b.
1933), politician
LiPR 128, ill.

CATEJON HERNAIZ, Gabriel (b.
1878), lawyer, judge
QEQ (1933-34) 47, (1936-
37) 47, (1941-42) 60.

CASTELAR, Emilio, abolitionist
DiHBC 244-45.

CASTELLANOS, Diego, educator,
television host
PRUSA 5, ill.

CASTELLANOS, Juan de (ca.1475-
1550), treasurer
DiHBC 245-46; GrEPR 14:70.

CASTELLANOS, Juan de (1522-
1607), priest, poet
BrECP 80; DiDHM 56; DiHBC
245; HisD 22; PRFAS 56.

CASTELLANOS, Miguel (16th
cent.), government oficial
GrEPR 14:70.

CASTELLON FLORES, Roberto (b.
1893*), pharmacist, politician
CaF 42; GrEPR 14:70; QEQ
(1933-34) 47, (1936-37)
47, (1941-42) 60.

CASTILLO, Braulio Rafael (b.
1933), actor, singer
DelMu 68-73, ill.; GentI 85-
90; GrEPR 14:70, 71(ill.)

CASTRO, Baltasar de (16th
cent.), factor
GrEPR 14:71.

CASTRO, Carlos Manuel de (b.
1893), doctor, politician
CaM 102; DiM 71; QEQ (1936-
37) 181, (1941-42) 76.

CASTRO, Julio P., landowner,
politician
RepM 181, ill.

CASTRO, Pedro Adolfo de (1895-
1936), architect
GrEPR 9:78-81.

CASTRO BLANCO, David, architect
Port 87, 88(ill.)

CASTRO CASANOVA, Salvador,
musician
MusMP 247-48.

CASTRO GONZALEZ, Rafael, businessman
RepM 63, ill.

CASTRO Y GUTIERREZ, Ramón de
(d.1810), governor, soldier
BeHNPR 1:269-96, ill.; Di-
DHM 56.

CASTRO LUND, Arturo (b.1900),
newspaper manager
QEQ (1948-49) 42.

CASTRO MACHUCA, Luis A. (b.
1885), lawyer
QEQ (1933-34) 47, (1936-37)
47, (1941-42) 60.

CASTRO MARTINEZ, Oscar (b. 1884), accountant, auditor
  GenB 387, ill.

CASTRO QUESADA, Luis (1909?-1955), journalist, poet
  DiLP 2, pt.1:308-9.

CASTRO RIOS, Andrés (b.1942), poet
  BrECP 80-81; DiLP 2, pt.1: 309-11; GrEPR 14:71; PRFAS 56.

CASTRO RIVERA, Oscar (b.1914), lawyer
  A 84; QEQ (1948-49) 43.

CATALA, Luis F., veterinarian
  AlHP 337, ill.

CATALA COLLAZO, Felicidad R., social worker
  EGMPR 3:143-45, ill.

CATALA MATTEI, Luis Enrique (b.1917), farmer, politician
  GrEPR 14:71.

CATAÑO, Hernando de (16th cent.), doctor
  CaM 102-3, 476; GrEPR 14: 71.

CATINCHI, Antonio (b.1895), electrician
  QEQ (1948-49) 43.

CAUTIÑO INSUA, Eduardo, politician
  EntP 193-201; GrEPR 14:72; LM 132; RepM 112, ill.

CAUTIÑO INSUA, Jenaro (1882-1948), politician
  GrEPR 14:72, ill.; Guay 254-55; Ka 125; PaGa 223-30, ill.; QEQ (1936-37) 47, (1941-42) 60.

CAUTIÑO VAZQUEZ, Genaro, businessman
  Guay 254.

CAUZOS, Ana de (17th cent.), philanthropist, nun
  EGMPR 1:43-44; EPI 3:133, 134, 135; GrEPR 14:72; MujDPR 17-18; MujP 48-49; MujPu 6.

CEBOLLERO, Pedro A. (b.1896),

poet, teacher
  BoHP 122-23, 129(ill.); DiLP 2, pt.1:311-13; PRFAS 56; QEQ (1933-34) 48-48, (1936-37) 48, (1941-42) 60.

CEDEÑO, Blanca (b.1921), municipal government official
  Port 55, 56(ill.)

CEDEÑO, Norberto (b.1889), artisan
  San 35-38.

CEDO ALZAMORA, Federico (b. 1939), poet
  DiLP 2, pt.1:313.

CEDO Y RODRIGUEZ, Darío (b. 1919), businessman
  GenB 408, ill.

CEIDE, Amelia (b.1908), author, journalist
  CaE 684-85; DiLP 2, pt.1: 313-15; EGMPR 1:129-31, ill.; PRFAS 57; QEQ (1948-49) 43.

CELIS AGUILERA, José de (1827-1893), landowner, political activist
  BiP 90-91; CiBPI 72(ill.), 111-13; ECPR 6:423-24; GenP 29; GrEPR 14:72; HisD 23-24; HoIPR 32, ill.; HoRPR 32-35; LPR 972, 974, 975; Pin 32-33; PRFAS 57; PuI 121-26.

CENTENO RIVERA, Pablo (b. 1947), politician
  LiPR 119, ill.

CEPEDA, Martín (19th cent.), iron worker
  CiBPI 175(ill.), 218-20.

CEPEDA, Orlando (b.1937), baseball player
  CuB 1968:83-86, ill.; ECPR 6: 424; EPI 1:335-36, ill.; PRUSA 6.

CEPEDA GARCIA, Samuel (b.1937), politician
  LiPR 40, ill.

CEPEDA TABORCIUS, Francisco (1846-1910), author, political activist
  DiDHM 56-57; DiLP 2, pt.1: 315-17; GrEPR 14:72-73, ill.; Mem 23-26, 137-64; Ver 156-57.

CEPERO BREWER, Frank (b.1911),
engineer
   QEQ (1948-49) 43.

CEPERO CEPERO, Pedro (1941-
1963), basketball player
   AlHP 427, ill.

CERDA PALOU, Juan, cattle and
dairy owner
   A 148-49.

CERDEIRA VELOSO, Francisco
(b.1887), author, journalist
   ProA 64-65, ill.; QEQ
   (1948-49) 43-44.

CERECEDO, Javier H. (b.1893),
engineer, consultant
   QEQ (1933-34) 48, (1936-
   37) 48, (1941-42) 61,
   (1948-49) 44.

CERECEDO, Leopoldo, chemist
   Tri 2:157-61.

CEREZO, Benny Frankie, lawyer,
politician
   GrEPR 14:73.

CERON, Juan (15th-16th cent.),
governor
   DiDHM 57; GrEPR 14:73;
   HisD 24.

CERVANTES DE LOAYZA, Iñigo
López (16th cent.), governor
   GrEPR 14:73.

CERVONI BRENES, Fran (b.1913)
painter, poet, professor
   BrECP 83-84; DiLP 2, pt.1:
   331-33; GrEPR 8:395; PaG
   199; PRFAS 57.

CERVONI GELY, Francisco
(1879-1933), author, lawyer,
politician
   DiLP 2, pt.1:333-34; GrEPR
   14:74; Guay 280-81.

CERRA DETISHMAN, María del
Pilar, fencer
   MujP 242.

CESPEDES, Juan de (16th
cent.), governor
   DiDHM 58; GrEPR 14:74.

CESTERO, Ferdinand R. (1864-
1945), poet

BiP 91-93; BoBP 15-17; CaE
685; DiDHM 58; DiHBC 261;
DiLP 2, pt.1:334-36; ECPR
6:424; GrEPR 14:74, ill.;
HoIPR 32-33, ill.; HoYMPR
162-72, ill.; Per 17-19,
ill.; PlE 2:139-49, ill.;
PRFAS 58, ill.; QEQ (1936-
37) 180, (1941-42) 61-62.

CESTERO DE RUIZ ARNAU, Celia
(b.1879), teacher
   DiDHM 58; DiHBC 261; EGMPR
   1:75-76, ill.; GrEPR 14:74;
   MujDPR 156-57, ill.; QEQ
   (1933-34) 48-49, (1936-37)
   48, (1941-42) 61.

CESTERO Y MOLINA, Nicolás Rafael
(1869-1910), doctor
   CaM 104.

CESTERO MONCLOVA, Luis (1882-
1925), pharmacist, author
   ArH 484.

CESTERO PADILLA, Rafael (b.1900),
poet
   DiLP 2, pt.1:336-37.

CIANCHINI, Luis F. (b.1892),
engineer, soldier
   QEQ (1933-34) 185, (1936-
   37) 48.

CIFRE DE LOUBRIEL, Estela (b.
1910), historian, professor
   DiDHM 58-59; EGMPR 1:261-
   62, ill.

CINTRON, José Manuel, painter
   GrEPR 8:432.

CINTRON, Miguel Angel, painter
   GrEPR 8:432.

CINTRON, Petra, painter
   GrEPR 8:432.

CINTRON ANTONSANTI, William (b.
1941), politician
   LiPR 128, ill.

CINTRON CARDONA, Wilfredo (b.
1917), author, journalist
   DiLP 2, pt.1:338-39.

CINTRON Y CINTRON, José Facundo
(ca.1846-1901), lawyer, political
activist
   PuI 312-15.

CINTRON MOSCOSO, Isabel (b. 1945), journalist
EGMPR 3:287, ill.

CINTRON MOTTA, Julio (1873-1945), doctor
CaM 105.

CINTRON RAMOS, Juan (b.1889), pharmacy clerk
GenB 439.

CINTRON VALLDEJULY, Guillermo (1887-1952), journalist, poet
AlHP 131-32, ill.; BiP 94; BoBP 29-31; DiLP 2, pt.1: 337-38; ECPR 6:424-25; GenB 369-71, ill.; GrEPR 14: 74; HoIPR 33, ill.; PRFAS 58; QEQ (1948-49) 44-45.

CIRIA, Antonio de, government official
Exp 292-93, ill.

CLAUDIO, Francisco "Pacheco", artisan
San 38-41.

CLAUSELLS ARMSTRONG, Pedro (1867-1955), agricultural engineer
AlHP 330, ill.; QEQ (1936-37) 48, (1941-42) 62.

CLAVELL, Jaime (1880-1952), farmer, politician
AlHP 331, ill.

CLAVELL, Salustio (1849-1911), teacher
AlHP 349.

CLEMENTE, Roberto (1934-1973), baseball player
CuB 1972:76-78, ill., 1973: 452; DiDHM 59; ECPR 6:425; EPI 1:335(ill.), 336-37; GrEPR 14:76, PRFAS 59.

CLETOS NOA, Amalia, teacher, painter
GrEPR 8:33; MujPu 53-54.

CLETOS NOA, Juan, painter, teacher
GrEPR 8:30, 33.

CLIVILLES VALENCIA, José Zoila (1866-1914), poet, businessman
Ka 121; PoA 83-85, ill.

COBALLES GANDIA, Lorenzo (1888-1955), politician, poet
DiLP 2, pt.1:339-40; GrEPR 14:76; Hor 179-84; PRFAS 59.

COBAS, Amador (b.1910), educator, physicist
A 86-87; GrEPR 14:76.

COBAS, Antonio, businessman
Ka 79-80.

COBIAN RIVERA, José, politician
GrEPR 14:76; RepM 330, ill.

COCA NAVAS, Rafael (b.1933), politician
GrEPR 14:76; LiPR 39, ill.

COCHRAN, Herman L. (b.1875), banker, lottery director
QEQ (1936-37) 48, (1941-42) 62, (1948-49) 45; RepM 75, ill.

COFRESI, Roberto (1791-1825), pirate
BeHNPR 2:27-30; CiBPI 86-89; DiDHM 59; DiHBC 267; EstCR 2: 82-89; GrEPR 14:76; Hi de CR 110-24; HisD 26; HisP 39-41; Por 308.

COIRA, Francisco, politician
GrEPR 14:76.

COLBERG, Cindy, tennis player
MujP 241.

COLBERG, Juan Enrique (1917-1964), author, journalist
BiP 95-96; DiLP 2, pt.1: 340-42; ECPR 6:425; Per 83-85; PRFAS 59-60.

COLBERG, Rebekah, athlete
EGMPR 4:279-82, ill.; MujP 241-42.

COLBERG DE RODRIGUEZ, Blanca (b 1918), politician
EGMPR 2:19-20, ill.; GrEPR 14: 77; PriC 79.

COLBERG PABON, Pedro F. (b.1870), pharmacist, politician
Hi de CR 226-27.

COLBERG RAMIREZ, Elisa (b.1905), teacher, Girl Scout leader
EGMPR 4:283-85, ill.

COLBERG RAMIREZ, Severo (b.
1924), politician
    DiDHM 59-60; GrEPR 14:77,
    ill.; LiPR 26-27, ill.;
    PRFAS 60.

COLBERG RAMIREZ, Wilson P. (b.
1902), lawyer
    QEQ (1933-34) 49, (1936-37)
    48-49, (1941-42) 62, (1948-
    49) 45.

COLE, Benjamín (b.1920), politician
    GrEPR 14:77; LiPR 125, ill.

COLE, Roberto (b.1915), composer, musician
    Com 2; GrEPR 7:133, 135,
    ill.

COLEMORE, Charles Blayney (b.
1879), Episcopalian bishop
    QEQ (1933-34) 49, (1936-37)
    49, (1941-42) 63, (1948-49)
    45.

COLOM, Ulpiano R. (1861-
1906), politician
    GrEPR 14:80; HoIPR 34, ill.

COLOM MARIN, Ulpiano E. (b.
1905), agronomist
    QEQ (1948-49) 46.

COLOM MARTINEZ, José Enrique
(b.1889), engineer
    DelRB 35-39; QEQ (1933-34)
    49-50, (1936-37) 49,
    (1941-42) 63-64.

COLOM MARTINEZ, José Luis (b.
1905), Pan American Union
official
    QEQ (1933-34) 49, (1936-37)
    49, (1941-42) 63, (1948-49)
    45-46.

COLOM MUÑIZ, Juan (b.1883),
politician
    GrEPR 14:80; QEQ (1933-34)
    50, (1936-37) 50, (1941-
    42) 64.

COLOMBANI, Leslie (b.1939),
sculptor
    GrEPR 8:396.

COLOMO, Juan José (18th cent.)
governor
    GrEPR 14:80.

COLON, Aberano, musician, composer
    MusMP 248-49.

COLON, Ana (b.1947), fashion
designer
    PRUSA 6, ill.

COLON, Cristóbal (1446-1506),
explorer
    BeHNPR 1:1-161, ill.; DiHBC
    272; HisD 27.

COLON, Diego (ca.1480-1526),
governor of the Indies
    HisD 27; Por 50-54.

COLON, Emilio M., educator
    A 90.

COLON, Evangelina, opera singer
    PRUSA 6, ill.

COLON, Gilbert (b.1944), federal
employee
    PRUSA, ill.

COLON, Marcos A. (1892-1964),
poet, journalist
    DiLP 2, pt.1:342-43; Hor
    187-90.

COLON, Miriam, actress
    EGMPR 4:33-34, ill.; EPI 2:
    209-10; Port 43, 44(ill.);
    PQ 31; PRUSA 7, ill.

COLON, Roberto (b.1899), businessman
    QEQ (1936-37) 51, (1941-42)
    66, (1948-49) 187.

COLON BAERGA, Enrique (b.1877),
journalist
    QEQ (1936-37) 50, (1941-42)
    64.

COLON BATALLA, Juan de Diós
(1882-1962), businessman
    AlHP 330, ill.

COLON BONFIGLIO, José Vicente
(1843-1869), author
    DiLP 2, pt.1:343-44; PoA 97-
    101.

COLON CASTAÑO, Ramiro L. (b.
1904), politician
    A 57-58, ill.; GrEPR 14:
    80; PriC 107-8, ill.

COLON CASTRO, Luis (b.1893), pharmacist
QEQ (1936-37) 180-81, (1941-42) 64.

COLON COLON, Isidoro (1863-1928), educator, author
AlHP 328; Crom 53.

COLON COLON, Ramiro (1859-1935), educator
AlHP 273-74, ill.

COLON COLLAZO, Jesús M. (b. 1940), politician
LiPR 124.

COLON DELGADO, Oscar (1889-1968), painter, teacher
ArH 576-77; BiP 96; BrECP 97; GrEPR 8:148-50, 320, ill.; PaG 170; PRFAS 60.

COLON DIAZ, Felipe, politician
GrEPR 14:80.

COLON FRIAS, Edmundo D. (b. 1890), agronomist
BiP 97-98; GrEPR 14:82; PRFAS 60-61; QEQ (1933-34) 50, (1936-37) 50, (1941-42) 64-65, (1948-49) 46; Tri 1: 357-63.

COLON FRIAS, Isidoro Alberto (b.1891), engineer, professor
A 97, ill.; GrEPR 14:82; QEQ (1933-34) 186, (1936-37) 50, (1941-42) 65, (1948-49) 46-47; Tri 1: 357-63.

COLON GARCIA, Ennio M. (b. 1927), lawyer, professor
DirAS 4:97.

COLON MARTINEZ, Noel (b.1927), lawyer, judge
BrECP 97-98; GrEPR 14:82; PRFAS 61.

COLON MELENDEZ, Efraín (b. 1920), politician
GrEPR 14:82.

COLON MORALES, Rafael (b.1941) artist, professor
GrEPR 8:322, ill.; PaG 215.

COLON OLIVIERI, Angel Alberto (b.1915), chemist, professor
QEQ (1948-49) 47.

COLON OLIVIERI, Isidoro Alfonso (b.1917), chemist, professor
QEQ (1948-49) 47-48.

COLON PAGAN, Pedro (b.1901), engineer
QEQ (1936-37) 50, (1941-42) 65-66.

COLON PELLOT, Carmen María (b. 1911), author, journalist
DiLP 2, pt.1:344-45; EGMPR 1:263-64, ill.; QEQ (1948-49) 48.

COLON Y RAMIREZ DE ARELLANO, Juan José (1847-1889), educator
ArH 291-98.

COLON REVERA, Antonio (b.1870), farmer
QEQ (1936-37) 51, (1941-42) 66.

COLON RIVERA, Víctor A. (b. 1914), dentist, politician
GrEPR 14:82.

COLON VAZQUEZ, Cristino R. (b. 1893), lawyer, judge
QEQ (1933-34) 50-51, (1936-37) 51.

COLON VELAZQUEZ, Luis A. (b. 1915), lawyer, politician
GrEPR 14:82; PriC 109-10, ill.; QEQ (1948-49) 48.

COLON WARREN, Hemeterio (1839-1889), educator
AlHP 276, ill.; Hi de Cay 234-35; PuI 223-26.

COLORADO, Antonio Julio (b. 1903), journalist, author, translator
A 88, ill.; BiP 98-99; ConA 17-20R:152; DiLP 2, pt.1: 345-46; ECPR 6:426; GrEPR 14: 82, 83(ill.); PRFAS 61.

COLORADO D'ASSOY, Rafael (b. 1868), photographer
QEQ (1948-49) 48.

COLTON, George R. (1865-1916), governor, customs expert
Desf 50-56, ill.; DiDHM 60; DiHBC 438; DicAB 2:322-23;

GrEPR 14:83, ill.; RepM 7,
ill.

Columbus, Christopher see
Colón, Cristóbal

COLL, Edna (b. 1906), author,
professor
    DiDHM 61; DiLP 2, pt.1:346-
    49; PRFAS 62.

COLL Y BRITAPAJA, José (1840-
1904), author, journalist
    DiLP 2, pt.1:349-51; PlE 1:
    114; PoA 107-12, ill.

COLL Y CUCHI, Cayetano (1881-
1961), lawyer, politician, author, journalist
    DiDHM 61-62; DiLP 2, pt.1:
    351-52; GrEPR 14:78, ill.;
    PoA 123-38, ill.; PRFAS 62;
    RepM 61, ill.; Vida 41-42.

COLL CUCHI, José (1877-1960),
politician, author
    ArH 518-19; BrECP 96, ill.;
    CaF 44; Desd 33-36, 237-41;
    DiLP 2, pt.1:352-53; GrEPR
    14:79, ill.; Ind 55-56;
    PRFAS 62; RepM 62, ill.

COLL Y CUCHI, Víctor (1885-
1961), doctor, author
    DiLP 2, pt.1:353-54; DiM
    72.

COLL PUJOLS, Víctor A. (b.
1910), lawyer
    QEQ (1941-42) 70, (1948-49)
    48-49.

COLL Y TOSTE, Cayetano (1850-
1930) doctor, historian, author
    BgP facing p.98, ill.; BiP
    217-19; BrECP 96-97, ill.;
    CaE 687-88; CaM 107-8; Ci-
    BPI 174(ill.), 197-200;
    Desd 84-88, 184-89; DiDHM
    60-61, ill.; DiHBC 275-78;
    DiLP 2, pt.1:354-58; DiM
    72-79; ECPR 6:425-26; EPI
    1:156, ill.; GenP 33-37;
    GrEPR 14:78, ill.; HisD 27;
    HoIPR 34-35, ill.; HoRPR
    63-72; PaH 1:426-29; Per
    91-92, ill.; PlE 1:445-57,
    ill.; PoA 145-46, ill.; Por
    226; PRFAS 63, ill.; PuI
    vii-xvii, ill.; RepM 60,
    ill.; Tri 2:127-33; VPR 87-

93, 167.

COLL Y VIDAL, Antonio (b.1898),
journalist, author
    BiP 100-101; CaE 688; CiuP
    13-14; DiLP 2, pt.1:358-62;
    GrEPR 14:77; PlE 2:333-40,
    ill.; PRFAS 63-64; QEQ (1933-
    34) 185, (1936-37) 49, (1941-
    42) 62-63, (1948-49) 49.

COLL Y VIDAL, José (1892-1970),
journalist
    BiP 102-4; DiLP 2, pt.1:362-
    63; GrEPR 14:77, ill.; Per
    129-31; PRFAS 64; QEQ (1933-
    34) 185-86, (1936-37) 49,
    (1941-42) 63; Tri 2:46-52.

COLLADO MARTELL, Alfredo (1900-
1930), author
    BiP 99-100; BrECP 95-96; Di-
    HBC 278; DiLP 2, pt.1:363-65;
    GrEPR 14:80; PlE 2:395; PRFAS
    64; Tri 2:291-95.

COLLAZO, Néstor R. (b.1930),
engineer, politician
    GrEPR 14:80; LiPR 35, ill.

COLLAZO, Oscar (b.1914), revolu-
tionist
    GrEPR 14:80.

COLLAZO COLLAZO, Francisco (b.
1900), educator
    Hi de Cay 244; QEQ (1948-49)
    187.

COLLAZO DE CALAF, Concepción
(1860-1906), charity work
    MujPu 57-58.

COLLAZO DE CARRANZA, Paulina (b.
1917), journalist, poet
    DiLP 2, pt.1:365-67.

COLLINS, James Lawton (b.1882),
Army officer
    QEQ (1941-42) 234.

COMAS GUERRA, Eliseo (b.1905),
journalist
    QEQ (1936-37) 181, (1941-42)
    66, (1948-49) 49.

COMAS PAGAN, Juan Ezequiel
(1870-1928), poet, dramatist
    DiLP 2, pt.1:368; GrEPR 14:
    83; Hi de CR 213-14, 220-21,
    ill.; PlE 1:110.

COMAS RITTER, Juan Francisco
(1837)-1903), poet
    DiLP 2, pt.1:367-68; GrEPR
    14:83; Hi de CR 191-92;
    PlE 1:110.

COMAS ROIG, Juan (b.1798),
businessman
    Esp 85-88; Hi de CR 191.

Compostela see Vázquez Díaz,
Francisco

COMPTE, Josefa (b.1876), poet,
teacher, feminist
    DiHBC 288; EGMPR 1:265,
    ill.; MujDPR 154-55, ill.;
    MujPu 148-49.

CONCEPCION, Ernesto, actor,
director
    DelMu 76-79, ill.

CONCEPCION DE GRACIA, Gilberto
(1909-1968), lawyer, politician
    BrECP 98-99; DiDHM 62; Gr-
    EPR 14:83, 84-85(ill.)

CONCEPCION DE GRACIA, Herminio
(b.1913), lawyer, politician
    GrEPR 14:86.

CONCEPCION VAZQUEZ, Angel de
la (1790-1841), priest, educator
    BeHNPR 2:31-33; DiDHM 202;
    EnsB 51-56; HisD 28; PuI
    59-61.

CONCHILLOS, Lope de (16th
cent.), Secretary of Council
of the Indies
    GrEPR 14:86.

CONDE, Emilia, singer, musician
    L 148-71.

CONDE, Pedro (1898-1955),
doctor, minister
    CaM 109-10.

CONESA, Hamlet Pedro (b.1903),
engineer
    QEQ (1936-37) 51, (1941-
    42) 66, (1948-49) 49.

CONESA, Miguel, painter
    GrEPR 8:432.

CONTRERAS MARTINEZ, Juan (19th

cent.), soldier, governor
    DiDHM 62; GrEPR 14:86, ill.

CONTRERAS RAMOS, José (1865-
1908), author, journalist, orator
    DiLP 2, pt.1:373-74; LPR
    1042, 1043.

CONTY, Rafael (d.1814), soldier
    BeHNPR 1:318; DiHBC 293.

COOK, Donald H. (b.1891), chemist,
professor
    QEQ (1936-37) 51, (1941-42)
    66.

COOK, Melville Thurston (b.
1869), botanist
    QEQ (1933-34) 51, (1936-37)
    51, (1941-42) 66-67, (1948-
    49) 49-50.

COOK, Paul, customs official
    RepM 84, ill.

COOPER, Alexander T. (1884*-
1949), military doctor
    CaM 110-11; QEQ (1948-49)
    50.

COOPER, Robert A. (b.1874),
judge
    QEQ (1936-37) 51-52, (1941-
    42) 67, (1948-49) 50.

CORA VEGA, Néstor (b.1906),
barber, novelist
    Ind 56-57.

CORA Y VIRELLA, José Horacio
(b.1903), lawyer, politician
    GrEPR 14:86; QEQ (1933-34)
    51, (1936-37) 52, (1941-42)
    67.

CORCHADO COLON, Vicente (b.
1923), journalist, politician
    GrEPR 14:86.

CORCHADO CRUXENT, Eugenia (b.
1868), teacher
    EGMPR 4:219.

CORCHADO Y JUARBE, Manuel (1840-
1884*), author, orator, lawyer
    BeHNPR 2:253-62, ill.; BgP
    facing p.104, ill.; BiP 104-
    5; CaE 690; DiDHM 62-63, ill.;
    DiHBC 300-302; DiLP 2, pt.1:
    378-81; ECPR 6:426-27; EnsB
    263-76; GenP 23; GrEPR 14:
    86, ill.; HisD 29-30; HoIPR

35, ill.; HoRPR 45-49; Ind 57-58; LM 117; LPR 998, 999, 1001, ill.; Nuestr 24-25; Orad 93; PlE 1:304; Por 240-41; PRFAS 64-65; PuI 227-32; Se 83-96, ill.; VPR 37-44, 165-66.

CORCHADO JUARBE, Martín R. (1839-1898), doctor
CaM 111; Crom 46-47; DiM 80-85; GenP 22; Med 33-35; Mem 92-93; MueYV 140-48; Ver 167, 168(ill.)

CORDERO, Angel (b.1942), jockey
CuB 1975:90-92, ill.; Port 197, 198(ill.); PRUSA 7, ill.

CORDERO, Ernesto (b.1946), composer
GrEPR 7:324-25.

CORDERO, Félix R. (b.1931), painter
PaG 213; Port 183, 184 (ill.)

CORDERO, Francisco H. (1852-1907), actor
Orig 298-300, ill.

CORDERO, Mario, soldier
QEQ (1933-34) 51-52, (1936-37) 52.

CORDERO, Rafael (1790-1868), teacher
BiP 106-8; BioD 1:312-13; BrECP 103-4; CiBPI 65(ill.) 81-84; ECPR 6;427; EPI 1: 115, ill.; EnsB 141-53; GrEPR 14:87, ill.; HePR 31-35, ill.; HisD 30; HoIPR 35, ill.; LPR 964, 965, 966, 967; Ma 39-40; Por 258-59; PRFAS 66.

CORDERO, Virgilio N. (b.1893), Army officer
DiHBC 302-3; QEQ (1936-37) 52, (1948-49) 187-88.

CORDERO BAEZ, Francisco "Paquito" (b.1931), television and musical producer
GrEPR 14:88, ill.

CORDERO DAVILA, César (1904-1965), Army officer

GrEPR 14:88, ill.; QEQ (1941-42) 67-68, (1948-49) 50-51.

CORDERO DEL ROSARIO, Loaiza (1887*-1957), teacher, founder of school for the blind
Añas 117-23, ill.; BiP 106; DiHBC 302; EGMPR 1:77-78, ill.; GrEPR 14:88; LPR 818, 819, 820; MujDPR 194-96, ill.; PQ 7; PRFAS 65; Tri 1: 105-11.

CORDERO FUERTES, Antonio (1850-1934) Freemason
Nues 39-41, ill.

CORDERO LOPEZ, José R., businessman
CaDeT 244-46, ill.

CORDERO MATOS, Ramón (1875-1927), teacher
AlHP 275, ill.

CORDERO MOLINA, Celestina (18th cent.), teacher
DiHBC 302; EGMPR 1:267-68; GrEPR 14:88; MujDPR 23-24.

Cordero Molina, Rafael see Cordero, Rafael

CORDERO RODRIGUEZ, Modesto (1858-1940), poet
AlHY 161-62, 209; DiLP 2, pt. 1:382-83; Ka 173; QEQ (1936-37) 52.

CORDOVA, Carlos A. (b.1940), banker
Port 95, 96(ill.)

CORDOVA, Pedro Tomás de (1785-1869), priest, author
DiLP 2, pt.1:384-86; HisD 30.

CORDOVA CHIRINO, Carmen, civic works
EGMPR 4:157-58, ill.

CORDOVA CHIRINO, Jacobo (1901-1955), journalist
DiLP 2, pt.1:386-87; Per 121-23.

CORDOVA CHIRINO, William, politician
GrEPR 14:88, 89(ill.)

CORDOVA DAVILA, Félix (1878*-1938*), judge, poet, Resident

Commissioner
  BiP 108; DiDHM 63, DiLP 2,
  pt.1:387-88; ECPR 6:427;
  GrEPR 14:88, 89(ill.); Imp
  117-19; PRFAS 66-67; QEQ
  (1936-37) 52; RepM 232,
  ill.

CORDOVA DAVILA, Rafael, politician
  GrEPR 14:90.

CORDOVA DAVILA, Ulpiano, S.,
doctor
  DiM 85-87.

CORDOVA DE BRASCHI, Julita (b.
1912), professor
  EGMPR 1:269-70, ill.

CORDOVA DIAZ, Jorge Luis (b.
1907), lawyer, judge, Resident
Commissioner
  DiDHM 63-64; GrEPR 14:90;
  HisD 30: PRUSA 7, ill.;
  QEQ (1948-49) 51.

CORDOVA LANDRON, Arturo (1883-
1959), journalist, essayist
  DiLP 2, pt.1:388; Per 109-
  11.

CORDOVES ARANA, Rafael (b.
1896), lawyer
  QEQ (1933-34) 187, (1936-
  37) 52, (1941-42) 68,
  (1948-49) 51.

CORDOVES Y BERRIOS, José
(1847-1906), teacher, civil
servant
  PuI 320-21.

CORDUA, Carla (b.1925), professor, philosopher
  DirAS 4:101.

COREY, Merton Leroy (b.1883),
lawyer
  QEQ (1933-34) 187, (1936-
  37) 181, (1941-42) 68.

CORONAS Y FERNANDEZ, Eusebio
(1857-1925), doctor
  DiM 88-89; GenP 24; Ka 181-
  82; Med 27-29; Mem 96-97.

CORTADA, Juan (18th-19th
cent.), politician
  GrEPR 14:91; PriC 39, ill.

CORTES, Fernando, actor

DelMu 83-85, ill.

CORTES, Mapi, actress
  DelMu 82-85, ill.

CORTES GONZALEZ, Francisco
(1875-1950), composer, conductor,
musician
  ArH 544-45; GrEPR 7:262-63;
  Mus en P 117-18; MusMP 223-
  24; QEQ (1936-37) 53, (1941-
  42) 69, (1948-49) 51-52.

CORTES MENDIALDUA, Aurelio,
industrialist
  A 146.

CORTES MORALES, Marcelino
(1885-1954), artisan
  San 42-44.

CORTES QUIÑONES, Jenaro (1867-
1934), journalist, politician
  GrEPR 14:91; QEQ (1933-34)
  53, (1936-37) 15.

CORTON, Antonio (1854-1913),
author, journalist
  BiP 108-10; BrECP 106; CaE
  691; DiDHM 65; DiHBC 313;
  DiLP 2, pt.1:392-95; ECPR 6:
  428; GrEPR 14:91; HisD 31;
  HoRPR 170-76; Mem 62-68; PlE
  1:275-88, ill.; PRFAS 67;
  PuI 337-44.

CORUJO, José Ignacio, politician
  ArH 578.

CORUJO COLLAZO, Juan (b.1933),
lawyer, politician
  GrEPR 14:91; LiPR 40, ill.

CORRADA DEL RIO, Alvaro (b.1896),
politician
  QEQ (1936-37) 53, (1941-42)
  68.

CORRADA DEL RIO, Baltasar (b.
1935), lawyer, politician,
Resident Commissioner
  DiDHM 64; GrEPR 14:91; LiPR
  112-13, ill.; PRUSA 6, ill.

CORREA, Antonio de los Reyes,
"El Capitán Correa" (d.1758),
soldier
  ArH 36-41; BeHNPR 1:241-49;
  BiP 128-29; Desd 107-10; Di-
  DHM 64; DiHBC 305-5; ECPR 6:
  484-85; GrEPR 14:295, ill.;
  PRFAS 80-81; PuI 18-21.

CORREA RIVERA, Francisco (b.
1901), sports commentator
QEQ (1948-49) 51.

CORRETJER, Antonio, Jr.,
(1893-1945), dentist, educator
AlHP 259, ill.; QEQ (1936-
37) 53, (1941-42) 68-69.

CORRETJER, Juan Antonio (1908-
1985), author, critic, politician
BiP 110-11; BrECP 104-5;
CaE 691; DiDHM 64-65, ill.;
DiLP 2, pt.1:388-91; DicC
29-30; ECPR 6:428; GrEPR
14:90, ill.; PRFAS 67-68,
ill.

COSME Y CALVO, Antonio (b.
1882), engineer
QEQ (1936-37) 53.

COSS SERRANO, Frank (b.1921),
businessman, politician
GrEPR 14:91.

COSTA, Antonio, landowner,
farmer
RepM 118, ill.

COSTA MANDRY, Oscar (b.1898),
doctor, professor
CaM 114-16; GrEPR 14:92;
QEQ (1936-37) 53-54, (1941-
42) 69-70, (1948-49) 52.

COSTAS, Orlando E. (b.1942),
author, minister
ConA 101:123-24.

COSTAS DIAZ, Jaime Francisco
(1881-1950), doctor
AlHP 283, ill.

COSTAS PURCELL, Enrique (1892-
1947), doctor
AlHP 248, ill.

COTONER Y CHACON, Fernando
(19th cent.), governor
DiDHM 65; DiHBC 453.

COTTES DE LAZARO, Obdulia
(1860-1931), teacher, journalist
EGMPR 3:37-38, ill.; MujDPR
115-16, ill.

COTTO, Esteban de (19th cent.),
pharmacist
CaF 45-46.

COTTO, Juan Agustín (19th
cent.), pharmacist
CaF 45.

COTTO, Juan Ruberto (19th
cent.), pharmacist
CaF 46-47.

COTTO, Miguel de (19th cent.),
doctor
CaM 117.

COTTO THORNER, Guillermo (b.
1916), novelist
CaE 692; DiLP 2, pt.1:416-
17; GrEPR 5:69-70; Ind 59-
60; PRFAS 68.

COWLES, Henry T. (b.1887),
educator
QEQ (1941-42) 70, (1948-49)
188.

COYCA, Elvira, sculptress
GrEPR 8:397.

CRESPO CONTI, Pedro (b.1908),
poet
DiLP 2, pt.1:417-18.

CRESPO GOMEZ, José R. (b.1852),
journalist, poet, politician,
pharmacist
Añas 47-48.

CRESPO PEREZ, Agapito (b.1916),
politician
GrEPR 14:92.

CRILLEY, A. Cyril (b.1902),
federal government employee
QEQ (1941-42) 70.

CROSAS FERRAL, Andrés (1845-
1913), businessman, volunteer
soldier
GrEPR 14:92, ill.; HoIPR 36,
ill.; RepM 87, ill.

CROSAS Y GRAHAM, Andrés B. (b.
1877), lawyer
RepM 176, ill.

CRUZ, Alejandro (b.1938),
politician
LiPR 121, ill.

CRUZ, Domingo (1864-1934), musician
AlHP 244, ill., 404; MusMP
285-86.

CRUZ, Héctor (b.1953), baseball player
    PRUSA 8.

CRUZ, José (b.1947), baseball player
    PRUSA 8, ill.

CRUZ, Miriam, politician,
government official
    PQ 32.

CRUZ, Rubén, television host
    PRUSA 9.

CRUZ, Wilnelia Merced, model,
beauty queen
    AntHistCag 775-80, ill.;
    GrEPR 14:92, 93(ill.)

CRUZ APONTE, Ramón A. (b.
1928*), educator
    DiDHM 66; PRFAS 68-69.

CRUZ COLON, Eliasim (b.1949),
painter
    GrEPR 8:398.

CRUZ DISDIER, Silvestre (b.
1888), lawyer
    QEQ (1941-42) 70-71.

CRUZ HORTA, Manuel (b.1904?),
lawyer
    Tri 1:239-43.

CRUZ JIMENEZ DE NIGAGLIONI,
Olga (b.1933), lawyer, politician, feminist
    EGMPR 2:21-22, ill.; GrEPR
    14:94.

CRUZ LOPEZ, David (b.1909),
educator, author
    BrECP 113-14; GrEPR 14:92;
    PRFAS 69.

CRUZ MANZANO, Juan A. (b.
1948), politician, lawyer
    LiPR 123.

CRUZ MONCLOVA, Lidio (1899-
1983), historian, professor
    BiP 111-12; BrECP 114-15,
    ill.; DiDHM 65-66; DiHBC
    314; DiLP 2, pt.1:445-48;
    ECPR 6:428; GrEPR 14:94;
    HisD 31; PlE 2:373-86,
    ill.; PRFAS 69-70; QEQ
    (1933-34) 54, (1936-37) 54,
    (1941-42) 71.

CRUZ MUÑOZ, Cruz, politician
    CaDeT 173-74, ill.

CRUZ Y NIEVES, Antonio (1907-
1967), journalist, author
    DiLP 2, pt.1:448-49; PRFAS
    70.

CRUZ OLMO, Ramón Ariosto (1886-
1923), musician, composer
    ArH 532-33, 543.

CRUZ QUIJANO, Bernardo (b.1908),
accountant
    QEQ (1948-49) 52.

CRUZ ROMAN, Tomás (d.1878), sea
captain
    ArH 249, 250, 261.

CRUZ VIDAL, Mercedes Esperanza
(b.1932), doctor
    EGMPR 3:147-48.

CRUZADO SILVA, Gustavo, lawyer
    HoIPR 36, ill.; QEQ (1936-
    37) 54, (1941-42) 71, (1948-
    49) 52-53.

CUBERO, Ramón, politician
    ProA 34.

CUBIÑA, Alfredo, artist
    GrEPR 8:398.

CUCURELLA, Jaime (1876-1936),
poet
    AntPoeCag 37-39.

CUCHI ARNAU, Felipe (b.1868),
lawyer
    ArH 515-16; LM 123; RepM
    137, ill.

CUCHI ARNAU, José (1858*-1936),
painter
    ArH 535; GrEPR 8:39.

CUCHI COLL, Isabel (b.1904),
author, critic
    ArH 521-23, 541-42: CaE 693;
    DiDHM 66, ill.; DiLP 2, pt.
    1:449-51; EGMPR 3:289-90,
    ill.; GrEPR 14:94; Ind 60;
    PRFAS 70-71, ill.

CUCHI COLL, Luis Felipe, civic
works
    Tri 1:341-48.

Cuebas, Eduardo see Cuevas
Morales, Eduardo

CUEBAS ARREDONDO, Eugenio
(1840-1907), landowner, businessman
GenB 308-9.

CUEBAS ARREDONDO, Felipe (d.
1908), political leader
GenB 306-7; Nuestr 111-13.

CUEBAS BRACETTI, Maximino,
educator
GenB 321-22; Hi de M 197;
Nuestr 146-47.

CUERDA GARCIA, Francisco de
la (18th cent.), bishop
Hi de la Ig 151-70.

CUERDA Y GARCIA, Tomás (1819-
1894), doctor
CaM 119-21; GenB 351-52,
ill.

CUESTA MENDOZA, Antonio
(1887-1949), historian
DiLP 2, pt.1:456-57.

CUETO, Adrián (d.1914), doctor, political leader
AlDU [99], ill.

CUETO Y RODRIGUEZ, José M.
(19th cent.), doctor
CaM 121.

CUEVAS, Carmen Leila, author
EGMPR 4:181-83, ill.; SobM
49-52.

CUEVAS, Clara (b.1933), author, journalist
BrECP 120; ConA 57-60:147;
DiLP 2, pt.1:457-58; GrEPR
14:94; PRFAS 71.

CUEVAS, Thomas, businessman
Port 127, 128(ill.)

CUEVAS ABOY, Juan, educator
AlHP 348.

CUEVAS Y BACENER, Manuel Sergio (1822-1897), educator
PuI 101.

CUEVAS DE MARCANO, Concepción
(b.1929), educator
PRFAS 72.

CUEVAS MORALES, Eduardo
(1852-1912), singer, composer,

conductor
GrEPR 7:270; MusMP 174-75;
Orig 295-98.

CUEVAS SOTILLO, Fabricano, educator, political leader
Guay 281-82.

CUEVAS ZEQUEIRA, Rafael (1883-
1957*), politician, author
DiLP 2, pt.1:458-59; GrEPR
14:94; HoIPR 37, ill.; QEQ
(1936-37) 54, (1941-42) 71-
72, (1948-49) 53.

CUEVAS ZEQUEIRA, Sergio (1862*-
1926), author, professor, orator
BiP 112-14; DiDHM 67; DiLP
2, pt.1:459-61; ECPR 6:429;
HoIPR 37, ill.; PRFAS 72.

CUEVILLAS HERNANDEZ, Hilario,
lawyer
LM 113.

CULPEPER, Samuel B. (b.1907),
teacher
QEQ (1936-37) 55, (1941-42)
72, (1948-49) 53.

CUMPIANO, Emilio, doctor, poet
And 190-93.

CUNEO, Miguel de (15th cent.),
sailor
GrEPR 14:94.

CUPERES VAZQUEZ, Pedro José
(1857-1957), artisan
San 44-45.

CUPRILL RIVERA, Ramón Fundador
(b.1885), accountant
QEQ (1948-49) 188.

CURBELO, Guillermo (1857-1933),
doctor
CaM 122-23; DiM 89-90.

CURET DE DE ANDA, Miriam (b.
1918), educator, critic
PRFAS 73.

CURRY, James Edward (b.1907),
lawyer
QEQ (1948-49) 188.

CUYAR, Luis C. (b.1885), auditor
QEQ (1936-37) 55, (1941-42)
72.

CUYAR GATELL, Luis Federico (b.

1914), lawyer
   QEQ (1948-49) 53.

CHABERT, Augusto de, engineer
   Ka 67.

CHACON, Iris, entertainer
   GentI 68-72.

Chanca, Diego Alvarez de see
Alvarez Chanca, Diego de

CHARDON, Carlos E. (1897-
1965), scientist
   BiP 114-15; BrECP 84; DiDHM
   69; DiHBC 320-21; DiLP 2,
   pt.1:461-64; ECPR 6:429;
   GrEPR 14:95, ill.; HisD 24-
   25; HoPP 21-45, ill.; Oro
   110-16, ill.; PRFAS 75; QEQ
   (1933-34) 54-55, (1936-37)
   55, (1941-42) 72-73, (1948-
   49) 53-54; Tri 1:61-64.

CHARDON, Félix, clerk
   Crom 92.

CHARDON, Fernando (b.1907),
agronomist, sportsman
   DiHBC 321-22; GrEPR 14:95.

CHARDON Y GERALDINO, Carlos
L., office clerk
   Ka 137.

CHAULON DE NEVARES, Giselle
(b.1927), researcher
   EGMPR 3:285-86, ill.

CHAVES ESTRADA, José (b.1899),
doctor
   CaM 123; QEQ (1936-37) 55,
   QEQ (1941-42) 73, (1948-
   49) 55.

CHAVEZ, David (b.1922), lawyer, judge
   QEQ (1948-49) 189.

CHAVIER AREVALO, Arístides
(1867*-1942), musician, composer, teacher
   BiP 115-16; BrECP 84; Co 4;
   DiHBC 323; ECPR 6:429-30;
   EPI 3:228, 229; GrEPR 7:
   255-58, ill., 14:94; HoIPR
   38, ill.; Mus en P 119-20;
   MusMP 78-89; PRFAS 75-76,
   ill.; QEQ (1933-34) 55-57,
   (1936-37) 56, (1941-42)
   73-74.

CHEVREMONT, Rosendo (1911-
1960), essayist
   DiLP 2, pt.1:464-65.

CHIESA, Wilfredo (b.1952),
painter
   GrEPR 8:318, ill.

CHIESA DE PEREZ, Carmen (b.1914),
teacher, author
   DiDHM 69; DiLP 2, pt.1:465-
   66; Ind 60-61; PRFAS 76.

CHIQUES CARRION, Carlos V. (b.
1882), dentist
   CaDeT 178-79, ill.; QEQ
   (1933-34) 57, (1936-37)
   56, (1941-42) 74.

CHIQUES MARTI, Francisco, educator
   CaDeT 51, ill.

CHIQUES MARTI, Miguel, educator
   CaDeT 63, ill.; RepM 227,
   ill.

CHOUDENS, José M., pharmacist,
politician
   RepM 252, ill.

D

DABAN Y RAMIREZ DE ARELLANO,
Antonio (b.1844), governor,
soldier
   Exp 277-81, ill.

DABAN Y RAMIREZ DE ARELLANO,
Luis (19th cent.), governor
   DiDHM 71; GrEPR 14:97, 98
   (ill.)

DAEN, Lindsay (b.1923), sculptress
   GrEPR 8:324, ill.

DAGUAO, Taíno Indian chief
   GrEPR 14:96.

DALEY, Edmund L. (b.1883),
Army officer
   QEQ (1941-42) 74-75.

DALMAU CANET, Sebastián (1884-
1937), author, journalist
   CaE 694; DiHBC 324; DiLP 2,
   pt.1:466-68; GrEPR 14:97;
   HoIPR 38, ill.; QEQ (1936-
   37) 57.

DALMAU DE BLANCO, Manuela (b. 1889*), teacher
    EGMPR 1:271-72, ill.; QEQ (1933-34) 57, (1936-37) 57, (1941-42) 75.

Dalta, Luis see Sierra, Pedro

DANFORTH, Stuart T. (b.1900), educator, scientist
    QEQ (1936-37) 57.

DANIO GRANADOS, Francisco (18th cent.), governor
    GrEPR 14:97.

DAPENA, Ramón (1798-1888), doctor
    CaM 124-26.

DAPENA LAGUNA, José N. (b. 1912), lawyer, politician
    GrEPR 14:97; PriC 111-12, ill.

DAPENA QUIÑONES, Conchita (b. 1914), wife of Gov. Sánchez Vilella
    EGMPR 4:357-58, ill.

DAPENA VIDAL, Ramón E. (b. 1928), insurance agent, politician
    GrEPR 14:97.

DAUBERCIES DE MORAN, Alison (b.1931), painter
    GrEPR 8:399.

DAUBON, José Antonio (1840-1922), author, journalist
    BiP 118-19; BrECP 127; CaE 694; Cre 73-74; DiDHM 72; DiLP 2, pt.1:468-69; ECPR 6:430; GrEPR 14:100; PRFAS 77.

DAUBON Y DUPUY, Antonio (1769-1835), sea captain
    BeHNPR 1:319-21, ill.

DAVID, Simplicio (19th cent.), musician, composer
    ArH 578.

DAVILA, Basilio, doctor
    A 92-93.

DAVILA, Carlos V. (b.1914), lawyer, judge
    GrEPR 14:100.

DAVILA, Edwin (b.1942), artist
    AlDJ 155-56, ill.

DAVILA, Héctor "Tato", doctor, amateur athletics
    AntHistCag 476.

DAVILA, Horace E. (b.1918), banker
    DiHBC 324-25; GrEPR 14:100.

DAVILA, Jorge V. (b.1899), engineer
    QEQ (1936-37) 57.

DAVILA, José, politician
    RepM 258, ill.

DAVILA, José Antonio (1899*-1941), poet, critic, doctor
    BiP 119-20; BrECP 127; CaE 694-95; DiLP 2, pt.1:469-71; DiM 91-93; ECPR 6:430; GrEPR 14:100; Per 13-15, ill.; PlE 2:423-27, ill.; PRFAS 77-78; VPR 157-64, 169.

DAVILA, José Jacinto (1845?-1875?), teacher, poet
    DiLP 2, pt.1:471-72; GrEPR 14:100.

DAVILA, Virgilio (1869-1943), poet, teacher, politician
    BiP 122-24; BrECP 127-29, ill.; CaE 695; CiBPI 222(ill.), 248-51; DiDHM 72, ill.; DiLP 2, pt.1:472-75; ECPR 6:430-31; GrEPR 14:100; HoDMT 117-33; HoIPR 38, ill.; Hor 306-8; PlE 2:89-98, ill.; PRFAS 78, ill.; QEQ (1936-37) 57-58, (1941-42) 75-76; Tri 2: 227-33.

DAVILA CRIADO, Naida R. (b. 1939), actress, producer
    EGMPR 4:35-36.

DAVILA DE PIZZINI, Nereida, civic works
    EGMPR 4:175-76.

DAVILA DIAZ, Juan (b.1892), politician
    GrEPR 14:100; QEQ (1948-49) 55.

DAVILA HERNANDEZ, Norberto (b. 1900), chemist
    QEQ (1948-49) 55.

DAVILA MONSERRATE, José M.
(b.1905), lawyer, politician
    GrEPR 14:100; QEQ (1948-
    49) 55.

DAVILA Y RAMIREZ, Rodolfo
(1851-1919), journalist, political activist
    Hi de CR 147-49.

DAVILA RICCI, José (b.1904),
journalist
    A 79-80; BiP 121-22; GrEPR
    14:100; PRFAS 78; QEQ
    (1936-37) 57, (1941-42) 75,
    (1948-49) 55-56.

DAVILA SEMPRIT, José (1902-
1958), author
    DiLP 2, pt.1:475-76.

DAVIS, George Whitefield
(1839-1918), governor, Army
officer
    Desf 9-12, ill.; DiDHM 72-
    73; DicAB 3:115-16; GrEPR
    14:99(ill.), 101.

DAVIS, James Peter (b.1904),
Catholic bishop
    GrEPR 6:279, 14:101; QEQ
    (1948-49) 56.

DEFENDINI, Josefina E.,
teacher
    AlHP 396, 397(ill.)

DEFILLO, José R. (d.1887),
music teacher
    Nuestr 71-73.

DEFILLO AMIGUET DE CASALS,
Pilar (1853-1931), Pablo
Casal's mother
    ECPR 6:432; EGMPR 4:287-
    89; EPI 3:178, 183; HoYMPR
    68-83, ill.; MujP 122; PQ
    7.

DEGETAU GONZALEZ, Federico
(1862-1914), author, statesman, Resident Commissioner
    AlHP 243, ill.; BgP facing
    p.262, ill.; BiP 125-26;
    BrECP 132, ill.; CaE 695-
    96; CiBPI 213-15, 229
    (ill.); DeADeA 265-74; Di-
    DHM 74-75, ill.; DiHBC
    325-28; DiLP 2, pt.1:481-
    83; ECPR 6:432-33; EntP
    145-63; GenP 102-3; GrEPR
    5:71-72, 14:101, ill.;

HisD 32; HoIPR 39, ill.; Ho-
    RPR 158-64; Ind 64-66; LPR
    1012, 1013, 1015, ill.; Lie
    75-79, ill.; Mem 62-68; Orad
    253-55; PlE 1:391-401, ill.;
    PRFAS 79, ill.; PuI 363-70;
    RepM 82, ill.

DELANO, Irene, artist
    GrEPR 8:400.

DELANO, Jack (b.1914), photographer, artist
    GrEPR 14:101(ill.), 102.

DE LA O, Eva, singer
    Port 109, 110(ill.)

DELGADO, Cecilio (b.1897),
engineer
    QEQ (1936-37) 58, (1941-42)
    78, (1948-49) 59.

DELGADO, Emilio R. (1940-1967),
poet, journalist
    CaE 696-97; DiLP 2, pt.1:
    483-85; PRFAS 79.

DELGADO, Manuel (b.1842), soldier
    Exp 283-85.

DELGADO, Olimpia (1876-1957),
civic works, political activist
    S 85.

DELGADO, Osiris (b.1920), artist,
educator
    BiP 127-28; BrECP 133; DiDHM
    75; GrEPR 1:xiii, ill., 8:
    244, ill., 14:102-3; PaG 199-
    200; PRFAS 82.

DELGADO, Ramón H., politician
    GrEPR 14:103, ill.; RepM 89,
    ill.

DELGADO, Rubén, architect
    Port 121, 122(ill.)

DELGADO CARBONELL, Sandalio (d.
1914), pharmacist
    Hi de M 213.

DELGADO CINTRON, Carmelo (b.
1940), lawyer, author, educator
    BrECP 132-33; DiDHM 75; GrEPR
    1:ix, ill., 14:102.

DELGADO DE TORRES, Alma, lawyer
    EGMPR 3:149-50, ill.; S 90.

DELGADO DE VOTAW, Carmen, author, feminist
    PQ [62], ill.; PRUSA 9.

DELGADO GONZALEZ, Ismael (b. 1919), poet
    DiLP 2, pt.1:485-87.

DELGADO MARQUEZ, Rafael (b. 1905), engineer
    QEQ (1941-42) 78.

Delgado Mercado, Osiris see Delgado, Osiris

DELGADO NEGRONI, Antonio Manuel (b.1886), businessman
    QEQ (1936-37) 58.

DELGADO PASAPERA, Germán (b. 1928), historian, author
    DirAS 1:179.

DELGADO RAMOS, Ramón (b.1903), poet
    AntHistCag 251; AntPoeCag 139-41.

DELGADO RIVERA, Francisco (1891-1971), photographer, artist
    Guay 282-83.

DELGADO RODRIGUEZ, José Antonio, politician
    LiPR 126.

DELIZ, Monserrate (1896-1969), music teacher
    EGMPR 1:273-74; ProA 39-40; QEQ (1941-42) 234-35.

DELIZ MENDEZ, Luis A. (b. 1890), engineer
    QEQ (1936-37) 58-59, (1941-42) 78-79.

DEL MAR, Roland H. (b.1908), Army officer
    DiHBC 598-600.

Demar, Carmen see Porrata Doria de Aponte, Carmen

DE PASS, George P. (b.1887), federal employee
    QEQ (1936-37) 60, (1941-42) 76-77, (1948-49) 57.

DE'PREY, Juan (1904-1962), artist
    PaG 171-74.

DERKES,Eleuterio (1836-1883), teacher, author
    DiDHM 76; DiLP 2, pt.1:487-88; EnsB 255-61; GrEPR 14: 104; Guay 255-56; PRFAS 82.

DESCARTES, Pedro María (19th cent.), politician
    GrEPR 14:104; Ver 235-36, ill.

DESCARTES ANDREU, Sol Luis (b. 1911), educator
    DiDHM 76; DiHBC 330-31; GrEPR 14:104; QEQ (1948-49) 59-60.

DESPUJOLS Y DUSSAY, Eulogio (19th cent.), governor
    DiDHM 76-77; DiHBC 454-55; GrEPR 14:104.

DESSUS, Luis Felipe (1875-1920), poet, journalist
    AlHP 135, ill.; BiP 129; CaE 703-4; DiLP 2, pt.1:488-89; ECPR 6:433; Guay 283; PaGa 137-50, ill.; PRFAS 82.

DE VEGA, Leonardo (b.1943), hair stylist, make-up artist
    Port 185, 186(ill.)

DEXTER, Edwin Grant (b.1868), educator
    QEQ (1936-37) 182.

DEXTER, Francis (b.1867), lawyer
    RepM 35, ill.

DEXTER LARRIÑAGA, Donald R. (b. 1907), lawyer
    QEQ (1936-37) 60.

DEYNES SOTO, Miguel A. (b.1936), politician
    GrEPR 14:104; LiPR 31, ill.

DIAGO RODRIGUEZ, Gonzalo (b. 1885), businessman, government official
    QEQ (1941-42) 235.

DIAZ, Alba Nydia, actress
    DelMu 89-92, ill.

DIAZ, Arturo, accountant, contractor
    GrEPR 14:104.

DIAZ David (b.1942), television newscaster
    Port 167, 168(ill.)

DIAZ, Domingo, photographer
CaDeT 61, ill.

DIAZ, Francisco (18th cent.),
soldier
BeHNPR 1:302-3; HisD 33.

DIAZ, Horacio, architect
GrEPR 9:120, 125-26.

DIAZ, José (d.1797), soldier
BeHNPR 1:300-301.

DIAZ, José (1774-1812), soldier
BeHNPR 1:301, 311-12.

DIAZ, José Francisco, educator, Freemason
Nues 30-32, ill.

DIAZ, José J., doctor, politician
CaM 130; RepM 189, ill.

DIAZ, Julio, industrialist
A 154.

DIAZ, Justino (b.1940), opera
singer
BiP 132-33; BrECP 150; ECPR
6:433; EPI 2:218-20; GentI
47-52; GrEPR 7:347, ill.,
14:105; Mus en P 156-57;
PRFAS 83; PRUSA 10, ill.

DIAZ, Luis Felipe (b.1938),
politician
GrEPR 14:105.

DIAZ, Manuel, social worker
Port 111, 112(ill.)

DIAZ, Marie (b.1949), painter
GrEPR 8:432.

DIAZ, Miguel (16th cent.),
colonist, government official
GrEPR 14:105.

DIAZ ALFARO, Abelardo (b.
1920), author, social worker
AntHistCag 251-52; BiP 129-
31; BrECP 149-50, ill.; CaE
704-5; DiDHM 77; DiHBC 337-
38; DiLP 2, pt.1:489-93;
DicC 34; ECPR 6:434; GrEPR
14:105; PRFAS 82-83.

DIAZ CANEJA, Ignacio (1845?-
1903?), journalist, author
DiLP 2, pt.1:493-96.

DIAZ CANEJA, Luis (1886-1923),
journalist, dramatist
DiLP 2, pt.1:496-97.

DIAZ CINTRON, Rafael (b.1884),
lawyer
QEQ (1933-34) 59, (1936-37)
60, (1941-42) 79.

DIAZ COLLAZO, Román (b.1891),
lawyer
QEQ (1936-37) 60-61, (1941-
42) 79.

DIAZ CORDERO, Antonio A. (b.
1893), architect
QEQ (1933-34) 59-60, (1936-
37) 61, (1941-42) 79.

DIAZ DE CABRERA, Francisco (17th
cent.), bishop
Hi de la Ig 59-60.

DIAZ DE COLLAZO, Adaljisa (b.
1932), lawyer
EGMPR 3:153-54.

DIAZ DE SOTO, Mercy (b.1938),
educator
EGMPR 4:325-26, ill.

DIAZ DE TAPIA, Rosario, teacher
Ma 46-48.

DIAZ DIAZ, Pedro E., politician
GrEPR 14:105; PriC 172, ill.

DIAZ GARCIA, Manuel (1894-1940),
doctor
BiP 131-32; CaM 131; GrEPR
14:105; HoIPR 39, ill.;
PRFAS 83.

DIAZ GARCIA, Silvino (b.1890),
accountant
QEQ (1941-42) 79, (1948-49)
189.

DIAZ GONZALEZ, Elisa, social
worker
EGMPR 3:95-97, ill.

DIAZ MARCHAND, Francisco, politician
GrEPR 14:105.

DIAZ MONTERO, Aníbal (b.1911),
author, journalist
BiP 133-34; DiDHM 77-78,
ill.; DiLP 2, pt.1:497-98;
GrEPR 5:72-73; Ind 66-68;
PRFAS 83-84, ill.

DIAZ MORALES, Abelardo M.
(1885-1950), teacher, journalist, Baptist minister
    AlHP 187, ill.; AntHistCag
    287-89; CaDeT 196-97, ill.;
    Per 171-73; QEQ (1933-34)
    60, (1936-37) 61, (1941-42)
    79-80, (1948-49) 60.

DIAZ NADAL, Roberto (b.1912),
author, journalist
    DiLP 2, pt.1:499-500.

DIAZ NAVARRO, Herminio (1860*-
1918), politician
    Crom 15-16; DiDHM 78-79;
    DiHBC 338-39; EntP 98-116,
    182-92; GenP 20; GrEPR 14:
    105-6, ill.; HoIPR 39,
    ill.; LM 121-22; LPR 1038,
    1039-40, 1041; Mem 95-96;
    Orad 239-40; PaP 161-69;
    PRFAS 84; RepM 90, ill.

DIAZ NEVAREZ, Gilberto (b.
1955), politician
    LiPR 127, ill.

DIAZ PEREIRA, Olimpio (b.
1891), teacher, National Guard
    QEQ (1941-42) 80.

DIAZ PONCE DE LEON, Humberto
(b.1915), lawyer
    QEQ (1941-42) 80.

DIAZ RIVERA, Francisco (b.
1924), accountant, politician
    GrEPR 14:106.

DIAZ RIVERA, José Inés (b.
1940), politician
    LiPR 126, ill.

DIAZ RIVERA, Lope Max (b.
1942), artist
    GrEPR 8:326, ill.

DIAZ RIVERA, Rurico (b.1914),
doctor
    QEQ (1941-42) 80, (1948-
    49) 189.

DIAZ RODRIGUEZ, Juan, artist
    GrEPR 8:432.

DIAZ SANTOS, Julio (b.1932),
artist
    GrEPR 8:328, ill.

DIAZ SOLER, Carmelo (1882-
1942), conductor, musician

BrECP 150-51; GrEPR 14:106;
    HoIPR 40, ill.; MusMP 249;
    PRFAS 84-85.

DIAZ SOLER, Luis M. (b.1916),
historian, professor
    BiP 134-36; DiHBC 339; DiLP
    2, pt.1:500-501; GrEPR 14:
    106; PRFAS 85.

DIAZ TIRADO, Miguel (b.1930),
politician
    LiPR 120, ill.

DIAZ VALCARCEL, Emilio (b.1929),
author
    BrECP 151-52, ill.; CaE 707;
    DiDHM 78; DiLP 2, pt.1:501-
    4; DicC 35; GrEPR 5:73-77,
    14:106, ill.; Ind 68; PRFAS
    85.

DIAZ VASQUEZ, Arturo, landowner,
politician
    RepM 209, ill.

DIEGO, José de (1866*-1918),
author, lawyer, politician
    And 54-58, 84-91, 165-66,
    186-89; BiP 136-39; BrECP
    129-31, ill.; CaE 707-8;
    CiBPI 179(ill.), 215-18; Cre
    47-49; DiDHM 73-74, ill.; Di-
    HBC 339-40; DiLP 2, pt.1:504-
    15; ECPR 6:434-35; EntP 89-
    97; EPI 1:154-55, ill.; GenB
    317-20, ill.; GenP 69-71,
    ill., 297; GrEPR 14:107, 108
    (ill.); HePR 110-13; Hi de M
    179-87, 188, 327-41; HisD
    33; HoIPR 40-41, ill.; LM
    126-27; LPR 1042, 1043-48,
    1049, ill.; Mem 135-36;
    Nuestr 144-45; Orad 305-8; PaI
    135-48, ill.; PlE 2:31-49,
    ill.; Por 243-45; ProA 11-12;
    Proc 231-99, ill.; PRFAS 86,
    ill.; QuR 65-89, ill.; RepM
    30, ill.; SobM 184-86; VPR
    69-85, 167.

DIEGO, Pedro de, businessman
    Ka 89.

DIEGO, Pedro R. de (1875-1924),
poet, journalist
    DiLP 2, pt.1:515-16; PRFAS
    86.

DIEGO-PADRO, José Isaac de
(1896*-1974), author, journalist
    AlHY 229; BiP 139-41; BrECP

131-32; DiHBC 340-41; DiLP
2, pt.1:516-19; ECPR 6:434;
GrEPR 5:77-79, 14:109,
ill.; Ind 61-63: PlE 2:321-
30; PRFAS 87.

DIEZ DE ANDINO, Juan (b.1889),
author
Desd 11-14; DiLP 2, pt.1:
520-22; Hor 11-14; Vo 13-
16.

DIEZ DE ANDINO, Rafael, politician
HoIPR 42, ill.

DIEZ LOPEZ, Federico (d.1918),
businessman
CaDeT 52, ill.

DI MARTINO, Rita, manager
Port 191, 192(ill.)

DIMAS, Marcos (b.1924), artist
GrEPR 8:432.

DIMAS ARUTI, Federico Matías
(b.1897), dentist
QEQ (1933-34) 60, (1936-37)
182, (1941-42) 235-36.

Diplo see Ortiz de Rivero,
Ramón

Dirube see López Dirube, Rolando

DISDIER, Edmundo (b.1927),
composer
GrEPR 7:145.

DIX, Benjamín R., government
official
RepM 64, ill.

DOBAL Y GIULIANI, José M.
(1916-1957), medical technolo-
gist, artist
Vo 85-88.

DOLAN, Joseph M. (b.1903),
teacher
QEQ (1948-49) 60.

DOMENECH, Gloria E., glove
manufacturer
A 149, ill.

DOMENECH, Manuel, architect
Crom 74.

DOMENECH, Manuel (b.1942),

social researcher
GrEPR 1:xii, ill.

DOMENECH, Manuel V. (b.1873),
engineer, politician
GrEPR 14:109; Ka 177-79;
QEQ (1936-37) 182-83, (1941-
42) 80-81.

DOMENECH HERNANDEZ, Luis, author
BoHP 123, 131(ill.)

DOMINGUEZ, Camilo, businessman
A 122, ill.

DOMINGUEZ, César (b.1896),
doctor
QEQ (1933-34) 60-61, (1936-
37) 61, (1941-42) 81, (1948-
49) 60.

DOMINGUEZ, Jorge V. (b.1883),
judge
RepM 85, ill.

DOMINGUEZ, José A. (d.1947),
doctor
HoIPR 43, ill.

DOMINGUEZ, José de Jesús (1843-
1898), doctor, author, politician
Añas 36-40, ill.; BrECP 152;
CaE 709; CaF 53; CaM 132-33;
DiLP 2, pt.1:522-24; DiM 96-
98; GenB 254, ill.; GrEPR
14:109; Hi de M 128, 195-
96; HoIPR 42, ill.; Nuestr
28-30; PlE 1:354-55; PRFAS
87; PuI 258.

DOMINGUEZ, Pilar (1800-1894),
teacher
ArH 457.

DOMINGUEZ GOMEZ, Celestino (d.
1927), pharmacist, politician
GrEPR 14:110; Guay 256-57.

Domínguez Gómez, José de Jesús
see Domínguez, José de Jesús

DOMINGUEZ RUBIO, Celestino (d.
1964), lawyer
Guay 257; Ka 95.

DOMINGUEZ VALENTIN, Alejandro
(1868-1941), author, musician
Añas 69-74, ill.

DONES, Salomón (1850-1913),
journalist

GrEPR 14:110, HoIPR 42,
ill.

DONES PADRO, Adolfo (b.1887),
lawyer, politician
GrEPR 14:110; QEQ (1936-37)
183.

DONES ROSARIO, Adolfo S. (b.
1913), lawyer, politician
LiPR 35, ill.

DONNELLY DE ROMERO BARCELO,
Kate (b.1939), wife of Gov.
Romero Barceló
EGMPR 4:365-66, ill.

DOOLEY, Eliza Bellows King (b.
1880), federal government
official
QEQ (1936-37) 61, (1941-42)
81.

DRAKE, Francis (c1543-1596),
British admiral, pirate
DiHBC 346; GrEPR 14:110,
ill.; HisD 34.

DRAUGHON, Donald A. (b.1898),
engineer
QEQ (1936-37) 61.

DREW, Jaime L. (1876-1948),
teacher, engineer
AlHP 246-47, ill.; Ka 109-
10.

DRURY, Marion Richardson (b.
1849), Protestant minister
QEQ (1933-34) 61.

DUCHESNE, Casimiro (d.1906),
musician, composer
MusMP 224-26.

DUCHESNE, Rafael (b.1890),
musician, teacher
GrEPR 14:110.

DUEÑO, Aurelio, musician
MusMP 250.

DUEÑO, Manuel (b.1880), doctor
DiM 99-100; RepM 273, ill.

DUEÑO COLON, Braulio (1854-
1934), composer, musician
BiP 141-43; BrECP 157; Ci-
BPI 75(ill.), 155-57; Co
5; DiHBC 346; ECPR 6:435;
EPI 3:228, 229; GrEPR 7:
203-6, ill., 14:110, ill.;

HoDMT 134-48; HoIPR 43, ill.;
L 40; Mus en P 90-100; PRFAS
87-88; QEQ (1933-34) 61,
(1936-37) 15.

DUEÑO Y DUEÑO, Belén, musician
MusMP 286.

DUEÑO PAGANI, Europa (d.1932),
singer, actress
Orig 305-6.

DUFRESNE, José (18th cent.),
governor
DiDHM 79.

DULIEVRE, Francisco, musician
MusMP 286.

DULLES DE BOURNE, Dorothy (b.
1893), social worker, educator
DiHBC 346-47; QEQ (1933-34)
38-39, (1936-37) 61.

DUMOND, José Armand (19th
cent.), pharmacist
CaF 53-54.

DUMONT Y DUFRESNE, José Enrique
(d.1878), doctor
AlHY 138-39; CaM 134-40.

DUNSCOMBE, William Colby (b.
1881), doctor
QEQ (1941-42) 82.

DURAN, Ana Luisa (b.1939?),
author
CaE 710.

DURAND LOPEZ, Pedro Jaime (b.
1914), doctor
QEQ (1948-49) 60-61.

DURAND MANZANAL, Rafael (b.
1921), economist
DiHBC 348-49; GrEPR 14:110.

DURAND MARTIN, Nicolás (b.1890),
teacher, politician
QEQ (1936-37) 61-62.

Duval, Armando see Monteagudo
Rodríguez, Joaquín

E

ECHAGUE, Rafael de (19th cent.),
governor
DiDHM 81.

ECHEANDIA, Getulio (20th cent.),

politician
  GrEPR 14:111.

ECHEANDIA FONT, Marcianita,
chemist, feminist
  GrEPR 14:111; QEQ (1948-49)
  61.

ECHEVARRIA, Cesareo, tobacco
industrialist
  A 32.

ECHEVARRIA, Juan Manuel
(1813?-1866), author
  DiLP 2, pt.1:524-26; GrEPR
  14:111; Ind 68-69.

ECHEVARRIA, Lydia, actress
  DelMu 94-98, ill.

ECHEVARRIA DE LA ROSA, Arturo
Luis (b.1899), doctor
  QEQ (1933-34) 62, (1936-37)
  62, (1948-49) 61.

ECHEVARRIA DIAZ, Andrés (1877-
1946), priest
  HoIPR 43, ill.

ECHEVARRIA MORALES, Moisés
(1888-1941), labor leader,
politician
  AlHP 137, ill.; GrEPR 14:
  111; QEQ (1933-34) 62,
  (1936-37) 62, (1941-42) 82.

EGOZCUE Y CINTRON, Manuel
(1855-1906), politician
  GrEPR 14:111; PuI 350-52.

EGURBIDA, Leonardo (b.1945),
musician, teacher
  GrEPR 14:111.

ELIAS HERREROS, José (19th
cent.), doctor
  CaM 144.

ELMENDORF, Colton R. (1878-
1927), businessman, Freemason
  Nues 51-53, ill.

ELVIRA, Pablo, opera singer
  PRFAS 89; PRUSA 10, ill.

ELZABURU Y VIZCARRONDO, José
de, politician
  GrEPR 14:111.

ELZABURU Y VIZCARRONDO, Manuel
(1851-1892), politician, lawyer, author, journalist

Ant 143-52; BgP facing p.126,
  ill.; BiP 143-44; BrECP 171,
  ill.; CaE 711; CiBPI 77(ill.),
  153-55; DiDHM 81, ill.; DiHBC
  362; DiLP 2, pt.1:559-62;
  ECPR 6:435-36; GrEPR 14:112,
  ill.; HisD 34; HoIPR 44,
  ill.; HoRPR 131-36; LM 115-16;
  LPR 1010, 1012, 1013; Orad
  123-24; Por 224-25; PRFAS 89,
  ill.; PuI 329-36.

ELLIS CAMBIASO, Federico, doctor
  A 94-95.

EMANUELLI RIVERA, Luis Rafael
(b.1901), pharmacist
  QEQ (1933-34) 62, (1936-37)
  62.

EMMANUELI, Miguel, businessman
  Crom 60.

EMMANUELLI, Rafael (1888-1961),
soldier
  Desd 181-83.

ENAMORADO CUESTA, José (b.1892),
author, journalist, political
activist
  AlHY 170-71, 216-17; DiLP 2,
  pt.1:562-65; GrEPR 14:113,
  ill.; PRFAS 90; QEQ (1948-49)
  61.

ENCARNACION VEGA, Natalio (b.
1905), pharmacist
  CaF 56-58; GrERP 14:113.

ENRIQUEZ, Juan (17th cent.),
Spanish army officer
  GrEPR 14:114.

ENRIQUEZ DE SOTOMAYOR, Enrique
(17th cent.), governor
  DiDHM 82; GrEPR 14:114; Hi de
  Pu 91-92.

ERGUI, Martín (b.1876), government official
  QEQ (1948-49) 189-90.

ERN, Henri (1863-1933), musician, teacher
  GrEPR 7:228(ill.), 229, 14:
  114.

ESCABI, Jorge A. (b.1915),
engineer
  QEQ (1948-49) 61-62.

ESCABI, Rodolfo (b.1909),

pharmacist, professor
    CaF 58-59; GrEPR 14:114.

ESCALERA, Alfredo, boxer
    PRUSA 10.

ESCALERA ORTIZ, Juan (b.
1952), professor, author
    DirAS 3:150.

ESCALONA, Bernardo (b.1830),
Freemason
    Nues 22-23, ill.

ESCALONA DE NIN, Rosita (b.
1909), concert pianist,
teacher
    EGMPR 4:41-42, ill.; QEQ
    (1941-42) 82-83, (1948-49)
    62.

ESCALONA VINCENTY, Nelson (b.
1920), politician
    GrEPR 14:114.

ESCOBAR, José (b.1899), engineer
    QEQ (1933-34) 62-63,
    (1936-37) 62.

ESCOBAR, Sixto (b.1913), boxer
    ECPR 6:436; EPI 1:338-40,
    ill.; PRUSA 10.

ESCORIAZA DE CARDONA, José
Eurípedes (1828*-1921), politician, Spanish government
official
    BeHNPR 2:281-83, ill.;
    ECPR 6:436; GrEPR 14:114;
    HisD 35; PuI 148-52.

Escoriaza y Cardona, José
Pascasio see Escoriaza de
Cardona, José Eurípides

ESCUDERO MIRANDA, Juan (1860?-
1925?), poet
    DiLP 2, pt.1:566-67.

ESCUDERO TORRUELLAS, Antonio
(b.1914), accountant
    QEQ (1941-42) 236, (1948-
    49) 62.

ESPADA, Angel, cigar manufacturer
    Ka 116.

ESPADA, Tiburcio (1794-1852),
sculptor, bookbinder
    BeHNPR 1:250-52; CiBPI 55-

57; S 83.

ESPADA MARRERO, José (b.1892),
author
    DiLP 2, pt.1:567.

ESPADA REVERA, Julio (b.1955),
fashion designer
    PRUSA 11.

ESPADA RODRIGUEZ, José (b.1893),
author
    AlHY 168, 229-30; DiLP 2, pt.
    1:567-69; GrEPR 14:114.

ESPAILLAT, José María (1777-
1850), doctor
    CaM 145-46; DiHBC 372;
    GrEPR 14:114.

ESPENDEZ, Ricardo (1851-193?),
builder
    Guay 258-59.

ESPENDEZ NAVARRO, Juan (b.
1902), educator
    Guay 257-58; QEQ (1941-42)
    236, (1948-49) 62.

ESPINOSA, José Gregorio, author
    Nuestr 99-103.

ESPINOSA, Susana, artist
    GrEPR 8:401.

ESPINOSA, Victoria (b.1922),
theater director, critic, professor
    EGMPR 4:43-44, ill.; PRFAS
    90-91.

ESTEVA, Armando (1882-1916),
author
    HoIPR 44, ill.

ESTEVA, Carlos (b.1906), agricultural engineer
    QEQ (1936-37) 62-63, (1941-
    42) 83.

ESTEVA, Ilka, painter
    GrEPR 8:432.

ESTEVE, Gil (b.1798), bishop
    BeHNPR 2:115-17, ill.

ESTEVES, Buenaventura (b.1884?),
lawyer, judge
    BoHP 191-92, ill.; ProA 49,
    ill.

ESTEVES, José de Jesús (1882-

1918), poet, critic, judge
ArH 484; BiP 144-45; BrECP
192-93; CaE 712-13; DiLP 2,
pt.1:569-71; GrEPR 14:115;
HoIPR 44, ill.; PlE 2:125-
35, ill.; ProA 13, ill.;
PRFAS 91.

ESTEVES, Luis Raúl (1893-
1958), Army officer, author
DiLP 2, pt.1:571-72; ProA
50; QEQ (1933-34) 63-64,
(1936-37) 63, (1941-42)
83-84, (1948-49) 62-63.

ESTEVES GOMEZ, Juan (b.1896),
politician
GrEPR 14:115; QEQ (1933-34)
64-65, (1936-37) 63.

ESTEVES VOLCKERS, Guillermo
(b.1888), engineer
DelRB 7-25, ill.; GrEPR 14:
115; ProA 48; QEQ (1933-34)
64, (1936-37) 63-64, (1941-
42) 84-85, (1948-49) 63-64;
Tri 1:55-60.

ESTEVES VOLCKERS, René (b.
1903), engineer
QEQ (1936-37) 183.

ESTHER MARY, Sister, Catholic
nun, social worker
AlHP 168, ill.

ESTRADA, Erik (b.1950), actor
PRUSA 11, ill.

ESTRADA, Noel (1918-1979),
composer
BrECP 193; Com 3: DiDHM 82;
DiHBC 376; GrEPR 7:132-33;
PRFAS 91-92.

ESTRADA FORNET, Eloy (b.1886),
educator
QEQ (1933-34) 189, (1936-
37) 64, (1941-42) 85.

ESTURIO, José Damián, musician, composer
MusMP 226.

EULATE SANJURJO, Carmela or
Carmen (1861*-1933*), author,
biographer
BiP 145-46; DiDHM 189; Di-
LP 2, pt.1:582-87; ECPR 6:
437; EGMPR 1:135, ill.; Gr-
EPR 5:80-82, 14:115; Ind
69-70; MujDPR 131-33, ill.;

MujP 123-24; MujPu 119-24;
PaF 79-80; PlE 1:282-83; PQ
8; PRFAS 92; QEQ (1936-37)
183-84.

EXCLUSA RODRIGUEZ, Rafael G.
(b.1904), politician
GrEPR 14:115; QEQ (1948-49)
64.

F

FABIAN, Rafael (b.1860), busi-
nessman
Esp 107-11; HoIPR 45, ill.;
RepM 67, ill.; Tri 1:69-75.

Fagot, Altamira see Matienzo
Román, Amelia

FAGOT, Emilio (1883-1946),
politician
AlHP 283, ill.

FAGUNDO, Juan (d.1847), artist,
teacher
GrEPR 8:30.

FAIRBANK, Miles H. (b.1898),
lawyer
QEQ (1941-42) 85.

FAJARDO CARDONA, Mateo (1862*-
1933), politician
GenB 284-86; HoIPR 46, ill.;
RepM 190, ill.

FAJARDO CARDONA, Pascasio (b.
1859), lawyer, politician
RepM 235, ill.

FALCON ELIAS, Ramón (b.1863),
lawyer, politician
LM 137.

FANO MARXUACH, Francisco L.
government official, translator
QEQ (1933-34) 65, (1936-37)
184.

FANTAUZZI, José Manoutau, businessman
Tri 2:139-44.

FARIA LUGO, María Dolores (b.
1906), teacher
EGMPR 1:275-76.

FARRULLA, Angel (d.1930), actor
Orig 305.

FAS ALZAMORA, Juan Antonio (b.

1948), lawyer, politician
LiPR 31, ill.

FASSIG, Oliver Lanard (b.
1860), meteorologist
QEQ (1936-37) 64.

FAURA Y CLADELLAS, Juan, doctor
CaM 148-50.

FEBUS, Sixto, painter
GrEPR 8:401, 14:117.

FELICE DE OTERO, Matilde (b.
1885), author
EGMPR 4:241-42.

FELICES, Jorge (b.1917), author, journalist
CaE 714; DiLP 2, pt.1:587-
88; GrEPR 14:117; Ind 71;
PRFAS 93; Vida 49-50.

FELICES, Salvador (b.1923),
Air Force officer
PRUSA 11, ill.

FELICI, Alicia, singer
MusMP 175-76.

FELICIANO, Carlos Ricardo,
artist
GrEPR 8:433.

FELICIANO, José, singer
PRUSA 11, ill.

FELICIANO FABRE, Mariano (b.
1928), educator
PRFAS 93-94.

FELICIANO LOPERENA, Jesús (b.
1946), artist
GrEPR 8:433.

FELICIANO MENDOZA, Ester (b.
1917), author, teacher
BiP 146-48; BrECP 195-96;
CaE 715, 802; DiDHM 83; Di
HBC 379-80; DiLP 2, pt.1:
588-91, ill.; GrEPR 14:117;
PRFAS 93.

FELICIANO VELAZQUEZ, Lino (b.
1893), teacher, inspector
QEQ (1933-34) 65, (1936-37)
64, (1941-42) 85.

FELIU PESQUERA, José Luis (b.
1918), politician
GrEPR 14:117, 118(ill.);

QEQ (1933-34) 65-66, (1936-
37) 64, (1948-49) 64.

FELIU SERVERA, Leopoldo (b.
1883), lawyer, politician
GrEPR 14:119; PriC 40, ill.

FELIX DE SANTANA, Lydia H. (b.
1932), teacher
EGMPR 4:255-56, ill.

FERNANDEZ, Ariel (b.1949),
artist
GrEPR 8:433, 14:119.

FERNANDEZ, Atilano, businessman
A 131, ill.

FERNANDEZ, Benito, businessman
Port 113, 114(ill.)

FERNANDEZ, Dolores, teacher,
philanthropist
PaF 81-82.

FERNANDEZ, Jesse, painter
GentI 80-85.

FERNANDEZ, José A. (1901-1975),
architect
GrEPR 9:116-17, 14:119.

FERNANDEZ, Luis J. (b.1864),
doctor
ProA 48-49, ill.

FERNANDEZ, Manuel, businessman
A 134.

FERNANDEZ, Rufo Manuel (1790-
1855), educator, priest
BeHNPR 2:84-93, ill.; BgP
facing p.140, ill.; BiP 152-
54; BrECP 333; CiBPI 65
(ill.), 80-81; DiDHM 84-85,
ill.; ECPR 6:437-38; EnsB
103-12; Esp 43-57; GrEPR 14:
119; LPR 850, 851, 852, ill.;
PRFAS 95-96.

FERNANDEZ, Ruth (b.1919?),
singer, politician
BiP 154-55; DiDHM 85; ECPR
6:438; EGMPR 2:25-26, 4:47-
49, ill.; GentI 118-26; Gr-
EPR 7:156-57, ill., 14:119,
ill.; L 122-28; PQ 33; PRFAS
96.

FERNANDEZ, Victoriano M. (1884*-
1964), author
DiLP 2, pt.1:591-92; Nues

69-71, ill.

FERNANDEZ BLANCO, Luis (b. 1892), businessman
QEQ (1933-34) 66, (1936-37) 64, (1941-42) 86.

FERNANDEZ CARBALLO, Joaquín (b.1892), dentist
QEQ (1936-37) 64, (1941-42) 86.

FERNANDEZ CARBALLO, R. (b. 1897), dentist
QEQ (1933-34) 66, (1936-37) 65.

FERNANDEZ COLON, Agustín (b. 1888), farmer
QEQ (1933-34) 66, (1936-37) 65.

FERNANDEZ CORONAS, José F. (b. 1872), lawyer
RepM 200, ill.

FERNANDEZ CUYAR, Francisco (b. 1908), lawyer
QEQ (1936-37) 65, (1941-42) 86.

FERNANDEZ CUYAR, Luis (b. 1907), engineer
QEQ (1941-42) 86.

FERNANDEZ DE AREVALO, Juan (16th cent.), priest
DiDHM 83-84; GrEPR 14:119.

FERNANDEZ DE LEWIS, Carmen Pilar "Piri", (b.1922), author
BrECP 196; DiLP 2, pt.1: 597-98; GrEPR 14:122, ill.; PRFAS 96.

FERNANDEZ DEL ARROYO, Arcadio (1870-1951), Jesuit priest
Jes 147-48.

FERNANDEZ FRANCO DE MEDINA, Juan (1646?-1698), soldier, governor
Hi de P 203-6.

FERNANDEZ GARCIA, Benigno (1887-1944), politician
GrEPR 14:120, ill.; Hi de Cay 242; QEQ (1936-37) 65, (1941-42) 86-87.

FERNANDEZ GARCIA, Eugenio (1888-1946), doctor, politician
CaM 152; DiHBC 383; DiM 106; GrEPR 14:120; HoIPR 46, ill.; Tri 1:309-17.

FERNANDEZ GARCIA, Luis Jorge (b.1894), doctor
ProA 48-49, ill.

FERNANDEZ GARZOT, Rogelio (b. 1910), lawyer
QEQ (1936-37) 184, (1941-42) 87, (1948-49) 64.

FERNANDEZ JUNCOS, Manuel (1846-1928), author, journalist, politician
Ant 9-14; BgP facing p.132, ill.; BiP 148-51; BrECP 196-98, ill.; CaE 716-17; CiBPI 179(ill.), 193-95; Cre 13-18; DeADeA 243-64; DiDHM 84, ill.; DiLP 2, pt.1:592-97; ECPR 6:438-39; GrEPR 14: 120-22, ill.; HisD 36; HoIPR 46-47, ill.; Ind 73; MeO 11-34; PlE 1:423-42, ill.; Por 227-29; Pro 303-59, ill.; PRFAS 94, ill.; RepM 105, ill.; Tri 1:5-12.

FERNANDEZ KNIDEL, Miguel (b. 1888), telegraph operator
QEQ (1933-34) 66-67, (1936-37) 65, (1941-42) 87.

FERNANDEZ LOPEZ, Martín, journalist
GenB 315-16; Nuestr 125-27.

FERNANDEZ MARCHANTE, Ramón (b. 1910), doctor
DiM 106-7; QEQ (1941-42) 87.

FERNANDEZ MARINA, Ramón (b. 1909), doctor, author
ConA 41-44R:214-15; DiM 107; GentI 138-45.

FERNANDEZ MARTINEZ, José Ramón (19th cent.), politician
GrEPR 14:122.

FERNANDEZ MASCARO, Guillermo (1872-1960), doctor, revolutionary
DiM 107-8; GrEPR 14:122-23.

FERNANDEZ MENDEZ, Eugenio (b. 1924), author, anthropologist, professor
BiP 151-52; CaE 717; DiDHM

83; DiHBC 383-84; DiLP 2,
pt.1:598-601; ECPR 6:439;
GrEPR 14:123; PRFAS 94-95.

FERNANDEZ MENDEZ, Lionel (b.
1915), lawyer, politician
A 58-59; GrEPR 14:123,
ill.; PriC 113-14, ill.

FERNANDEZ MUÑOZ DE ELZABURU,
María Manuela (1866*-1903),
author, translator
DiHBC 384; DiLP 2, pt.1:
601-2; EGMPR 1:137, ill.;
GrEPR 14:123; MujDPR 56-57,
ill.; MujPu 59-60.

FERNANDEZ NATER, Amparo, feminist, author
EGMPR 4:259-60, ill.; Muj-
DPR 136-38, ill.; MujPu
134-37.

FERNANDEZ NATER, Manuel (1873-
1934), doctor, politician
CaM 153-55; GrEPR 14:123;
QEQ (1933-34) 15, 67; RepM
205, ill.

FERNANDEZ NATER, Ramón, police
official
RepM 294, ill.

FERNANDEZ ORTIZ, Angel (b.
1892), pharmacist, lawyer
CaF 60-61; QEQ (1933-34)
67, (1936-37) 65, (1941-42)
87.

FERNANDEZ RAMIREZ, Rodolfo,
architect
GrEPR 9:126, 129.

FERNANDEZ SANCHEZ, Angel (b.
1903), author
DiLP 2, pt.1:602-4.

FERNANDEZ SANZ, Fabiola (b.
1923), transportation executive
EGMPR 4:327-28, ill.

Fernández Schulze, Victoriano
M. see Fernández, Victoriano
M.

FERNANDEZ VANGA, Epifanio
(1880-1961), lawyer, author,
journalist
BiP 155-56; Desd 94-97; Di-
LP 2, pt.1:604-5; ECPR 6:
439; GenP 98; GrEPR 14:123;

LM 135; Per 70-72; PRFAS 97.

FERNOS, Antonio (b.1944),
lawyer, professor
DirAS 4:155.

FERNOS ISERN, Antonio (1895-
1974), doctor, politician,
Resident Commissioner
DiDHM 86; DiM 108-9; GrEPR
14:124-25, ill.; PriC 115-16,
ill.; PRFAS 97-98; QEQ (1933-
34) 67-68, (1936-37) 65-66,
(1941-42) 87-88, (1948-49) 64-
65; SobM 82-85.

FERRA, Margot, painter
GrEPR 8:402.

FERRACANE, Gerardo (b.1943),
professor
DirAS 3:157.

FERRAN, Alfredo, doctor
RepM 337.

FERRAN, Joaquín (d.1943), philanthropist
AlHP 353, ill.; Crom 32.

FERRAND, Edward A., scientist
Port 59, 60(ill.)

FERRARI, José Rafael, pharmacist
A 100-101; ProA 38.

Ferré, Isolina see Ferré
Aguayo, María Isolina

FERRE, Maurice (b.1935), engineer, politician
GrEPR 14:125; PRUSA 13, ill.

FERRE AGUAYO, Carlos (1906-
1958), engineer
AlHP 455, ill.; QEQ (1941-
42) 88.

FERRE AGUAYO, José Antonio (b.
1902), industrialist
QEQ (1936-37) 66, (1941-42)
88, (1948-49) 65.

FERRE AGUAYO, Luis A. (b.1904),
politician, governor, arts
patron, industrialist
A 50, ill.; BiP 157-58; Br-
ECP 198-99; CuB 1970:134-
36, ill.; DiDHM 86-87, ill.;
DiHBC 284-85; ECPR 6:440-41;
EPI 1:224-29, ill.; GrEPR 14:

125, 126-28(ill.); HisD 36;
HoPP 127-33, ill.; LiPR 64-
65, ill.; PaG 177-79; Pon
89; PRFAS 98, ill.; PRUSA
12, ill.; QEQ (1948-49) 65.

FERRE AGUAYO, María Isolina
(b.1914), nun, social worker
DiDHM 87; PRUSA 12, ill.

FERRE BACALLAO, Antonio (1877-
1959), industrialist
AlHP 454-55, ill.; PonY
133.

FERRE RAMIREZ DE ARELLANO, Antonio Luis (b.1934), manager,
civic leader
GrEPR 14:125.

FERREIRO, Luciano, businessman, politician
Ka 46.

FERRER, José (b.1912), actor
A 72; BiP 159-61; CuB 1944:
202-5, ill.; DiDHM 88; Di-
HBC 385; ECPR 6:441; EPI 1:
174-76, ill., 2:206, 207-
9; GentI 7-11; GrEPR 14:
129; Port 1, 2(ill.); PRFAS
99; PRUSA 13, ill.; QEQ
(1948-49) 65-66.

FERRER, Julio, doctor
Ka 19; RepM 187, ill.

FERRER, Miguel (b.1886), engineer
QEQ (1933-34) 189-90,
(1936-37) 66, (1941-42) 88,
(1948-49) 66.

FERRER, Miguel, architect
DiHBC 387-88; GrEPR 9:107-
10, 14:125.

FERRER, Rafael (1885*-1951),
critic, essayist, journalist
CaE 720; DiLP 2, pt.1:605-
6; Lie 7-10, 247-54, ill.

FERRER, Rafael (b.1933), pro-
fessor, sculptor
GrEPR 8:248, ill., 14:129;
PaG 204.

FERRER, Susi (b.1940), artist
GrEPR 8:330, ill., 14:125;
PaG 210-11; PQ 34.

FERRER CANALES, José (b.1913),

author, professor
BiP 158-59; DiDHM 88-89;
DiLP 2, pt.1:606-8; PRFAS
98-99.

Ferrer Cintrón, José see
Ferrer, José

FERRER DE RIVERA, Ardillie (b.
1927), lawyer
EGMPR 3:155-56.

FERRER HERNANDEZ, Gabriel
(1847*-1900*), doctor, politician, author
CaE 720; CaM 156-57; DiDHM
87-88; DiHBC 385-86; DiLP 2,
pt.1:608-9; DiM 109-15; GrEPR
14:129; HoRPR 176-80; PRFAS
99-100; PuI 322-24.

FERRER OTERO, Monserrate (1885-
1966), composer
DiHBC 387; EGMPR 4:51-52,
ill.; GrEPR 7:263-65, 266
(ill.), 14:129; MujDPR 196-
200, ill.; MujP 123; MusMP
227-28.

FERRER SANTANA, Rafael E. (b.
1907), doctor
QEQ (1948-49) 66.

FIDALGO DIAZ, José (1910-195?),
businessman, author
Esb 3:106-8; QEQ (1941-42) 88-
89, (1948-49) 66-67.

FIDDLER, Earle Thomas (b.1887),
lawyer
QEQ (1941-42) 89, (1948-49)
67.

FIGARELLA ORSINI, Néstor (b.
1912), weight lifter
ECPR 6:441-42.

FIGUERAS Y CHIQUES, José María
(1852-1910), lawyer, judge
LM 117; RepM 204, ill.

FIGUEROA (Family), musicians
BiP 219; BrECP 199-200, ill.;
DiHBC 397-98; GrEPR 7:236-
43, ill.; L 79-80; Mus en P
157-59.

FIGUEROA, Antonio S. (b.1909),
judge
Port 51, 52(ill.)

FIGUEROA, Carmelina (b.1911),

musician, music teacher
  GrEPR 7:240-41, 14:134.

FIGUEROA, Eduardo (b.1948),
baseball player
  PRUSA 13, ill.

FIGUEROA, Edwin (b.1925), author
  BiP 161-62; CaE 721-22; Di-
  HBC 398; DiLP 2, pt.1:609-
  12; ECPR 6:442; GrEPR 14:
  129; PRFAS 100.

FIGUEROA, Gabino, teacher
  PaE 60-66.

FIGUEROA, Guillermo, musician,
composer
  BrECP 200; DiHBC 397-98;
  GrEPR 7:242.

FIGUEROA, Ivonne, musician
  PQ 35.

FIGUEROA, Jaime "Kachiro" (b.
1910), musician
  GrEPR 7:242; QEQ (1936-37)
  67-68; Tri 1:303-7.

FIGUEROA, Jesús (1878-1971),
musician, composer
  BrECP 199; Co 6; DiHBC 397;
  ECPR 6:443; GrEPR 7:269,
  ill., 14:133; Mus en P 157-
  59; PRFAS 101, ill.; QEQ
  (1933-34) 68, (1936-37) 66-
  67.

FIGUEROA, José "Pepito" (b.
1905), musician
  BrECP 199-200; DiHBC 397;
  GrEPR 7:236(ill.), 238-39,
  14:134; QEQ (1936-37) 68-
  69; Tri 2:217-21.

FIGUEROA, José J. (b.1892),
businessman
  QEQ (1941-42) 236, (1948-
  49) 69.

FIGUEROA, José Víctor, politician
  GrEPR 14:129.

FIGUEROA, Leonor Isabel (1908-
1915), musician
  DiHBC 397; EGMPR 4:53-54;
  GrEPR 7:241-42; QEQ (1936-
  37) 69.

FIGUEROA, Loida (b.1917), author, historian
  AlHY 175-76; BrECP 200-201;
  ConA nr9:166; DiDHM 89-90;
  DiLP 2, pt.1:612-13; DirAS
  1:230; GrEPR 14:129; Ind
  73-74; PRFAS 101-2.

FIGUEROA, Luis de (16th cent.),
priest
  GrEPR 14:131.

FIGUEROA, Narciso (b.1909),
composer, musician
  BrECP 200; DiHBC 397; GrEPR
  14:130(ill.), 131; QEQ
  (1936-37) 69.

FIGUEROA, Pablo (b.1938),
author, film maker
  ConA 61-64:193-94; Port 61,
  62(ill.)

FIGUEROA, Pedro Juan, actor
  DelMu 100-104, ill.

FIGUEROA, Rafael, musician
  BrECP 200; DiHBC 398; GrEPR
  7:243.

FIGUEROA, Sotero (1863?-1923),
author, journalist, orator
  BiP 163-67; CiBPI 168-70;
  DiDHM 90, ill.; DiLP 2, pt.
  1:613-15; ECPR 6:442; EnsB
  vii-xiv, ill.; GrEPR 14:131,
  ill.; PRFAS 102, ill.

FIGUEROA BENITEZ, Efrén (b.
1926), politician
  GrEPR 14:132.

Figueroa Berríos, Edwin see
Figueroa, Edwin

FIGUEROA CARRERA, Leopoldo
(1884*-1969), doctor, lawyer,
politician
  BiP 162-63; DiDHM 89; DiHBC
  398-99; DiM 115; ECPR 6:442-
  43; GrEPR 14:132-33, ill.;
  HisD 37; HoPP 135-36; PriC
  189, ill.; PRFAS 100-101;
  QEQ (1933-34) 190, (1936-37)
  67, (1948-49) 67-68; Tri 1:
  365-71.

FIGUEROA Y CASTILLA, Baltasar
(17th cent.), governor
  Hi de P 187.

FIGUEROA CORDERO, Andrés (b.
1923), revolutioanry
GrEPR 14:133.

FIGUEROA CHAPEL, Ramón (b.
1935), author, professor
ConA 45-48:158; DirAs 3:
159.

FIGUEROA DE CARDENAS, Javier
(b.1946), historian, professor
GrEPR 1:xviii, ill.

FIGUEROA DE CIFREDO, Patria
(b.1918*), teacher, author
DiDHM 90; EGMPR 1:279-80.

FIGUEROA Y FIGUEROA, Manuel
Oscar (b.1877), lawyer
LM 129.

FIGUEROA HERNANDEZ, Luis Alberto (b.1952), politician
LiPR 36, ill.

Figueroa Iriarte, Jesús see
Figueroa, Jesús

FIGUEROA Y JIRAU, Manuel,
doctor
CaM 158-62.

Figueroa Mercado, Loida see
Figueroa, Loida

FIGUEROA MONTOYA, José Luis
(b.1923), businessman
QEQ (1948-49) 69.

FIGUEROA MORALES, Doris (b.
1938), lawyer
EGMPR 3:157.

FIGUEROA RIVERA, Juan (b.
1906), lawyer
QEQ (1933-34) 68, (1936-
37) 67.

FIGUEROA RODRIGUEZ, Plácido
(b.1900), accountant, politician
GrEPR 14:133.

Figueroa Sanabia see Figueroa

FILARDI, Carmelo (b.1900),
caricaturist
AlHY 236-37, ill.; DiDHM
90-91.

FINKENBINDER, Frank (b.1898),
Pentecostal minister

QEQ (1936-37) 69-70.

FIOL NEGRON, Julio (b.1895),
teacher
QEQ (1933-34) 190-91, (1936-
37) 70, (1941-42) 89; Tri 2:
9-13.

FIOL RODRIGUEZ, Rosa E. (b.
1927), doctor
EGMPR 3:159-60, ill.

FIRPO Y SUAREZ DE MENDOZA, Gonzalo, politician
Apu 47-48.

FIZ JIMENEZ, Epifanio (b.1886),
labor leader, politician
GrEPR 14:134; QEQ (1933-34)
191, (1936-37) 70.

FLEYTAS COLBERG, José Antonio
(1870-1925), pharmacist, politician
Hi de CR 228-33, ill.; HoIPR
47, ill.; RepM 328, ill.

FLINTER, George Dawson (19th
cent.), Spanish soldier
DiHBC 399.

FLORES, Angel (b.1900), author,
translator, professor
ConA 103:143; DiLP 2, pt.1:
615-19.

FLORES, Gilberto (b.1952),
baseball player
PRUSA 14, ill.

FLORES, Irving (b.1926), revolutionary
GrEPR 14:134.

FLORES, Pedro (1894*-1979),
composer
BiP 167-68; BrECP 201, ill.;
Com 3; DiDHM 91; DiHBC 399;
ECPR 6:443; EPI 2:213-15;
GrEPR 7:130-31, ill.; L 58-
59; PRFAS 102-3.

FLORES DE PADILLA, Hylda (b.
1915), teacher
EGMPR 1:281-82, ill.

FLORES LOPEZ, Andrés (b.1878),
politician
QEQ (1933-34) 68, (1936-37)
70.

FLORIT, Gloria, artist

GrEPR 8:402.

FONFRIAS, Ernesto Juan (b. 1909), author, politician
BiP 168-69; BrECP 202; CaE 722; DiHBC 400; DiLP 2, pt. 1:635-39; ECPR 6:443-46; GrEPR 5:82-85, 14:135; Hor 106-7; Ind 74-79; PRFAS 103; QEQ (1941-42) 89-90, (1948-49) 69-70.

FONFRIAS, Francisco "Paquito" (b.1926), composer, agent
GrEPR 7:142, 145, 148(ill.)

FONSECA JIMENEZ, Angel (b. 1923), politician
GrEPR 14:135.

FONT, Agustín E. (b.1891), lawyer, author, orator
A 84-85; BoHP 189; DiLP 2, pt.1:639-40; GrEPR 14:135.

FONT, Gilberto M. (b.1902), engineer
QEQ (1936-37) 184, (1941-42) 90, (1948-49) 190.

FONT, Juan Higinio (b.1895), doctor
CaM 166; GrEPR 14:135; QEQ (1933-34) 69, (1936-37) 70, (1941-42) 90, (1948-49) 70.

FONT, Luz Odilia, actress
DelMu 106-10, ill.

FONT, Manuel (b.1888), author
DiLP 2, pt.1:640-41; Hor 309-10.

FONT, Miguel T. (b.1878), pharmacist
BoHP 165-66; QEQ (1933-34) 69, (1936-37) 70.

FONT,Nydia Elena (b.1927), teacher, musician
DiDHM 92; GrEPR 14:135.

FONT, Pablo, pharmacist
Ka 109.

FONT GIMENEZ, Manuel (b.1888), engineer, Army officer
GenB 395-96, ill.

FONT Y GUILLOT, Eliseo (1856-1923), doctor
CaM 164-65; DiM 116-17;

GenB 28, 276-77, ill.; GenP 43, 73-76, ill.; GrEPR 14: 136; Hi de M 188-89, ill.; HoIPR 47, ill.; LPR 1022, 1023-24; PRFAS 103; VerOr 119.

FONT SALDAÑA, Jorge (b.1907), journalist, politician
DiLP 2, pt.1:641-43; GrEPR 14:135; Hor 295-98; QEQ (1948-49) 70-71.

FONT SUAREZ, Eugenio (b.1895), lawyer, poltician
GrEPR 14:136; QEQ (1948-49) 190.

FONTANEZ, Carmelo (b.1945), artist, professor
GrEPR 8:332, ill.

FONTANEZ, Rosa María, federal official
PRUSA 14.

FOOTE, Charles E. (b.1873), judge
QEQ (1933-34) 69-70, (1936-37) 70-71; RepM 65, ill.

FORASTIERI BRASCHI, Eduardo (b. 1942), author, educator
DirAS 3:166.

FORASTIERI LONGO, José (b.1898), doctor
CaDeT 217, ill.; QEQ (1933-34) 70, (1936-37) 71.

FORES, Santiago, businessman
Crom 68.

FORES Y MORAZO, Benito, lawyer
RepM 132, ill.

FORESTIER DOUBLET, Teodoro (1833-1911), politician
GenB 296-97; Hi de M 206-7; Nuestr 78-79.

FORESTIER GREGORY, Emilio (b. 1895), poet
DiLP 2, pt.1:643-44.

FORNARIS, Fernando B. (1900-1961), lawyer
AlHP 280, ill.

FORNIZ, Zoila Luz, pianist
GrEPR 14:136.

FORT, Gustavo (1880-1924),

author
    Desd 260-66; DiLP 2, pt.1:
    644-45; Lie 105-7, ill.

FORTUÑO SELLES, Francisco (b.
1892), engineer
    QEQ (1933-34) 70, (1936-37)
    71, (1941-42) 90-91; Tri 1:
    407-12.

FORTUÑO SELLES, Ramón (1889-
1952), politician, author
    AlHP 136, ill.; DiLP 2, pt.
    1:645; GrEPR 14:136; QEQ
    (1936-37) 71, (1941-42) 91,
    (1948-49) 71; Tri 2:291-95.

FORREST Y VELEZ, Gerardo
(1859-1918), pharmacist, political activist
    BoHP 114, 115(ill.); CaF
    63; GrEPR 14:136.

FOURNIER, Pedro, politician,
orator
    AlHP 350.

FOURNIER MARQUEZ, Ramón (b.
1891), doctor, veterinarian,
embalmer
    QEQ (1936-37) 71, (1941-42)
    92, (1948-49) 71.

FOXA Y LECANDA, Narciso de
(1822-1883), author
    BiP 169-70; CaE 724-25; Di-
    LP 2, pt.1:645-47; ECPR 6:
    446; PRFAS 104.

FRADE, Ramón (1875-1954),
artist
    BiP 170-71; BrECP 202-3;
    DiHBC 419; GrEPR 8:150-85,
    252, ill.; Hi de Cay 239-
    41; PaG 164-65; PRFAS 104.

FRAGOSO, Víctor (1944-1982),
author, producer, professor
    DiDHM 92.

FRANCESCHI, Edgardo, painter
    GrEPR 8:433.

FRANCESCHI CABALLERO, Francisco (b.1898), doctor, navigator
    A 91-92, ill.; DiM 117-20.

FRANCIA PONCE DE LEON, Benito,
military doctor
    CaM 169; DiM 120-23.

FRANCO, Idalia Margarita

"Beba" (b.1946), beauty queen
    GrEPR 14:136-38, ill.

FRANCO, María Judith, actress
    DelMu 112-16, ill.

FRANCO LOPEZ, Gabriel, economist, professor
    A 87-88, ill.

FRANCO MORALES, José, artist
    ArH 536-37.

FRANCO OPPENHEIMER, Félix (b.
1912), author, professor
    BiP 171-73; BrECP 203; CaE
    725-26; DiDHM 92-93; DiLP 2,
    pt.1:647-51; ECPR 6:447;
    GrEPR 14:138; PRFAS 104.

FRANCO ORTIZ, Angel (1848-1891),
doctor
    CaM 170.

FRANCO SOTO, Carlos (b.1876),
politician, lawyer, judge
    GrEPR 14:138, ill.; LM 134;
    ProA 66; RepM 161, ill.

FRANCO SOTO, José Angel (1875-
1959), doctor, author
    BoHP 196, ill.; CaM 171;
    DiLP 2, pt.1: 651-52; DiM
    123-25; QEQ (1936-37) 71;
    RepM 215, ill.

FRANKLIN, Eduardo (b.1886),
journalist
    QEQ (1936-37) 72, (1941-42)
    92, (1948-49) 190-91.

FRANKLIN, Eduardo E. (b.1909),
manager
    QEQ (1936-37) 184-85, (1941-
    42) 92, (1948-49) 191.

FRANQUI, Sylvia I. (b.1949),
artist
    GrEPR 8:433.

FRANQUI ACOSTA, Pedro (b.
1928), politician
    LiPR 117, ill.

FRANQUIZ, José A. (b.1906), author, educator
    AlHY 168-70, 220-21; DiLP 2,
    pt.1:652-55; QEQ (1941-42)
    91-92; Vida 37-40.

FRASQUERI FORESTIER, Luisa
(b.1852), music teacher

EGMPR 1:283, ill.; GenB
357-58, ill.

FREYRE BARBOSA, Luis (b.1864),
lawyer
LM 131; QEQ (1936-37) 72.

FREYRE DE LA SIERRA, José
Ramón (b.1868), lawyer
LM 129-30.

FREYRE DIAZ, Luis (b.1901),
accountant
QEQ (1933-34) 70, (1936-
37) 72.

FREYRE Y RIVAS, Ildefonso (d.
1885), artist
GenB 297-98; Nuestr 80-81.

FREYRE Y RIVAS, José Ramón
(1840-1873), journalist, politician
Desd 205-9; DiDHM 93; DiLP
2, pt.1:655-56; EO 163-69;
GenB 253; GrEPR 14:138; Hi
de M 127, ill., 202; Nuestr
19-21; Por 211-12; RepM
282, ill.

FRONTERA FOUGERAT, Roberto C.
(1894-1914), author
PoA 197-203, ill.

FUENTE, Alfonso de la (16th
cent.), purser of San Juan
GrEPR 14:138.

FUENTE, Fidel de la (1902-
1961), priest
AlHP 163, ill.

FUENTE, Luis R., businessman,
inventor
A 39, ill.

FUERTES, Esteban Antonio
(1838-1903), engineer, professor
BioD 1:488-89; CiBPI 122-
23; LPR 988, 989-90, 991;
PRFAS 104-5.

FULLANA SERRA, Francisco,
architect
A 98.

FULLANA SERRA, Jaime, engineer, businessman
A 98-99, ill.

FUSTER, Jaime L., doctor

A 95.

FUXENCH DE SAN MIGUEL, Haydée
(b.1910), government
official
EGMPR 3:99-100; QEQ (1948-
49) 157.

G

GADEA, Ramón E. (1862?-1900),
pharmacist, author
AlHP 227, ill.; CaF 65; Crom
56.

GADEA PICO, Ramón A., (1898-
1975), author, journalist, lawyer
DiLP 2, pt.1:657-58.

GAETAN BARBOSA, Manuel (b.
1875), teacher, lawyer
QEQ (1933-34) 70, (1936-37)
72.

GALAN, Gilda, actress
DelMu 118-23, ill.

GALBREATH, William Robert
(1886*-1946), doctor
CaM 173-74; QEQ (1936-37)
72.

GALIÑANES, Julio C. (b.1906),
businessman
QEQ (1941-42) 93, (1948-49)
72.

GALIÑANES, Rosa, musician,
teacher
MusMP 251-52.

GALIÑANES SANCHEZ, José (1875-
1949), teacher, manager
HoIPR 48, ill.

GALUZZO, Manuel (d.1887), doctor
Nuestr 86-87.

GALVEZ OTERO, Julio (1883-
1940), journalist
HoIPR 49, ill.

GALLARDO, Carlos (b.1886),
secretary
QEQ (1933-34) 70, (1936-37)
72, (1941-42) 93.

GALLARDO, Félix Francisco (b.
1830), pharmacist
CaF 67-68.

GALLARDO DIAZ, Fernando (b.

1900), lawyer, politician
GrEPR 14:139: QEQ (1936-
37) 72, (1941-42) 93, SobM
173-76.

GALLARDO DIAZ, José Arturo (b.
1909), doctor
QEQ (1941-42) 93, (1948-
49) 72.

GALLARDO GARCIA, José Miguel
(b.1897), educator
GrEPR 14:139, ill.; QEQ
(1941-42) 93, (1948-49)
72-73; Tra 56-57.

GALLARDO LARA, Juan G. (b.
1888), government official
QEQ (1933-34) 71, (1936-37)
72 ; Tri 1:65-67.

GALLART, José, landowner
Mem 173.

GALLEGO, Laura Matilde (b.
1924), poet
CaE 726-27; DiLP 2, pt.1:
658-59; EGMPR 1:139-41,
ill.; PRFAS 107.

GALLISA, Carlos (b.1933),
lawyer, politician
GrEPR 14:139, ill.

GAMA, Antonio de la (16th
cent.), judge
GrEPR 14:140.

GAMIR MALADER, José, acting
governor
DiHBC 454.

GANDARA, José N. (1907-1954),
doctor
AlHP 245, ill.; BiP 173-74;
PRFAS 107.

GANDARA, Raúl (b.1910), author, head of fire fighting
service
DiLP 2, pt.1:659-60; GrEPR
14:140; PRFAS 107.

GANDIA CORDOVA, Ramón (b.
1863), engineer
ArH 515; QEQ (1936-37) 185.

GANDIA CORDOVA, Ramón, politician
GrEPR 14:140.

GANDIA FANTAUZZI, Oscar A. (b.

1898), stenographer
QEQ (1948-49) 73.

GANDIA VILA, Ernesto (b.1911),
politician
GrEPR 14:140.

GANDIA VILA DE CANTERA, Iris,
engineer
EGMPR 3:161-62, ill.

GARCIA, David, evangelist
AlHP 198, ill.

GARCIA, Domingo (b.1930*), artist
GrEPR 8:334, ill.; PaG 203-4.

GARCIA, Emilio Isaac (b.1887),
politician
QEQ (1933-34) 72, (1936-37)
73.

GARCIA, Francisco A., politician
GrEPR 14:140.

GARCIA, Isidoro "Danny" (1917-
1963), baseball player, teacher
AlHP 427, ill.

GARCIA, José M. (1887-1971),
artist, architect
GrEPR 8:434.

GARCIA, Manuel Osvaldo (b.
1886), poet
DiLP 2, pt.1:660-61.

GARCIA, Mildred (b.1951),
painter
PaG 239.

GARCIA, Norberto (b.1881),
politician
QEQ (1933-34) 72, (1936-37)
74.

GARCIA, Osvaldo, artist
GrEPR 8:403.

GARCIA, Ramón, artisan
San 45-46.

GARCIA, Robert (b.1917), politician
Port 17, 18(ill.); PRUSA 14,
ill.

GARCIA ABREU, José (b.1889),
government official
QEQ (1948-49) 73.

GARCIA AYALA, Brunilda Elena
(b.1947), singer, director
EGMPR 4:55-56, ill.

GARCIA BENITEZ, José Miguel,
engineer
A 40.

GARCIA CABRERA, Esteban (1854-
1913), doctor
CaM 177-78; HoIPR 49, ill.

GARCIA CABRERA, José (b.1903),
dentist
QEQ (1933-34) 71, (1936-37)
72.

GARCIA CABRERA, Manuel (b.
1905), lawyer
QEQ (1948-49) 73-74.

GARCIA CABRERA, Rafael (d.
1929), teacher
S 86.

GARCIA CAMBA, Andrés (19th
cent.), governor
DiHBC 453; GrEPR 14:141.

GARCIA CAPELLA, Estrella (b.
1907*), lawyer
EGMPR 4:213-14, ill.; QEQ
(1933-34) 71, (1936-37) 72-
73, (1941-42) 94.

GARCIA CARABALLO, Ramón (b.
1927), politician
LiPR 121, ill.

GARCIA CUERVO, Emilio (b.
1866), lawyer
LM 125.

GARCIA DE ESCAÑUELA, Bartolomé (17th cent.), bishop
Hi de la Ig 84-89.

GARCIA DE GUADIANA, Francisco
(16th cent.), priest
GrEPR 14:157.

GARCIA DE LA TORRE, Félix
(1882-1962?), doctor
CaM 179-80; DiM 126-27;
Eco 109-20; RepM 322, ill.

GARCIA DE QUEVEDO, Pedro Tomás
(1865-1936), pharmacist, politician
Añas 64-68, ill.; QEQ
(1933-34) 71-72, (1936-37)
73.

GARCIA DE QUEVEDO, Rafael,
pharmacist
A 101.

GARCIA DE QUEVEDO DEL RIO,
Manuel (1890-1947), doctor
Añas 127-34, ill.

GARCIA DE SAINT-JUST, Enrique
(b.1765), soldier
BeHNPR 1:318-19.

GARCIA DIAZ, Julio (1898-1970),
professor
BrECP 205; GrEPR 14:141;
PRFAS 107-8.

GARCIA DIAZ, Manuel (b.1903),
author
DiLP 2, pt.1:661-63.

GARCIA DUCOS, Juan (1883-1943),
politician, newspaper owner
GrEPR 14:141; PriC 40, ill.;
ProA 42-43; QEQ (1936-37) 73.

GARCIA FARIA, Felipe (1892-
1937), doctor, politician
CaM 179; DiM 126; GrEPR 14:
141; QEQ (1933-34) 72,
(1936-37) 73.

GARCIA FONTEBOA, Manuel, artist
GrEPR 8:403.

GARCIA GARCIA, Ramón H. (b.
1893), poet
PoA 207-10, ill.

GARCIA GENZEL, John (b.1917),
Lutheran minister
Port 47, 48(ill.)

GARCIA GONZALEZ, Celso A. (b.
1889), engineer
QEQ (1936-37) 73-74, (1941-
42) 94.

GARCIA GONZALEZ, Miguel (b.
1894), lawyer
CaDeT 191; QEQ (1936-37)
74, (1941-42) 94.

GARCIA LAGO, Ramón (19th cent.),
businessman
ArH 414.

GARCIA LASCOTT, Eulalio (b.
1878), doctor
RepM 230, ill.

GARCIA MELENDEZ, Carlos Mario

(b.1913), politician
GrEPR 14:141.

GARCIA MELENDEZ, Pascasio (d.
1964), politician
GrEPR 14:141.

GARCIA MENDEZ, Juan B. (b.
1896), lawyer, politician
A 83-84; BoHP 191; GrEPR
14:141; ProA 34; QEQ (1936-
37) 74, (1941-42) 95.

GARCIA MENDEZ, Manuel A.,
lawyer, politician
A 83; GrEPR 14:141; ProA
37.

GARCIA MENDEZ, Miguel (b.
1888), engineer, author
DiLP 2, pt.1:663-64; QEQ
(1933-34) 72, (1936-37) 74,
(1941-42) 95.

GARCIA MENDEZ, Miguel Angel
(b.1902), lawyer, politician
BiP 174-75; ECPR 6:447,
449; GrEPR 14:142-43(ill.),
144; HisD 38; HoPP 111-26:
PriC 95-96, ill.; ProA 38,
ill.; PRFAS 108; QEQ
(1933-34) 191, (1936-37)
74, (1941-42) 95.

GARCIA MOLINARI, Ovidio (b.
1914), scientist, author
QEQ (1948-49) 74.

GARCIA MORIN, Manuel (b.1917),
scientist, professor
BrECP 205; GrEPR 14:144;
PRFAS 108.

GARCIA OLIVERO, Carmen Sylvia
(b.1936), social worker
EGMPR 3:163-65, ill.

GARCIA ORTIZ, José A. (b.
1946), politician
LiPR 31, ill.

GARCIA PACHECO, Leandro (b.
1900), educator, lawyer
QEQ (1941-42) 95, (1948-
49) 75.

GARCIA PASSALACQUA, Juan M.
(b.1937), lawyer, author,
journalist
DiDHM 95; DiHBC 426; GrEPR
14:144.

GARCIA PELICCIA, Francisco
(b.1896), dentist
GrEPR 14:144; QEQ (1933-34)
72-73, (1936-37) 74, (1941-
42) 95-96, (1948-49) 75.

GARCIA PERAZA, Juanita "Mita"
(1897-1970), religious leader
DiDHM 95; EGMPR 3:323-24,
ill., 348-68.

GARCIA PORTELA, Carlos (b.
1921), lawyer, politician
GrEPR 14:144; PriC 117-18,
ill.

GARCIA QUEVEDO, Jacinto R. (b.
1896), doctor
QEQ (1933-34) 73, (1936-37)
74-75, (1941-42) 236.

GARCIA QUEVEDO, Orlando C. (b.
1893), doctor
QEQ (1948-49) 75.

GARCIA QUIÑONES SINGALA, María,
teacher
CaDeT 180.

GARCIA RIGAU, Joaquín, businessman
A 153.

GARCIA RIVERA, Oscar (b.1900),
lawyer, politician
GenB 363-65, ill.

GARCIA RUIZ, Santos (b.1912),
engineer, politician
QEQ (1941-42) 236, (1948-49)
191.

GARCIA SAINT LAURANT, Diego
(1861-1904), politician
GenB 493; HoIPR 50, ill.;
VerOr 118.

GARCIA SALGADO, Octavio (b.
1849), politician
GrEPR 14:145; RepM 120, ill.

GARCIA SEGOVIA, Juan M. (b.
1934), artist
GrEPR 8:404.

GARCIA SOLTERO, Armando (b.
1893), doctor
Guay 283-84; QEQ (1941-42)
96.

GARCIA SORIANO MENTRIE, Antonio
(b.1898), musician

QEQ (1933-34) 73, (1936-37)
75, (1941-42) 96.

GARCIA TAÑON, José (b.1934),
politician
GrEPR 14:145.

GARCIA TORRES, Manuel A. (b.
1942), politician
LiPR 123.

GARCIA Y TROCHE Y PONCE DE
LEON, Juan (ca.1525-1590),
chronicler
CiBPI 23(ill.), 32-34; Di-
DHM 95-96; DiLP 2, pt.2:
1250-53; GrEPR 14:275,
ill.; HisD 38; PuI 1-5.

GARCIA URRUTIA, Juan, artist
GrEPR 8:404.

GARCIA VALDEDIOS, Pablo (b.
1896), educator
QEQ (1941-42) 96-97.

GARCIA VEVE, Adolfo, politician
GrEPR 14:145, ill.; QEQ
(1941-42) 97.

GARCIA VEVE, Angel (b.1854),
lawyer, judge
LM 130; RepM 144, ill.

GARCIA VEVE, Luis (b.1897),
optometrist
GrEPR 14:145; QEQ (1936-
37) 74, (1941-42) 97.

GARCIA YANGUAS, Aurelio (b.
1894), lawyer
QEQ (1941-42) 97.

GARFFER, Raymond W., businessman
A 146, ill.

GARVEY, William J., industrialist
QEQ (1933-34) 191-92.

GARRASTEGUI, Anagilda (b.
1932), poet
CaE 731; DiLP 2, pt.1:664-
65; PRFAS 109.

GARRASTEGUI, Luis A. (b.1924),
lawyer, novelist
Ind 80.

GARRIDO, Juan (16th cent.),

slave
GrEPR 14:145.

GARRIDO COLLAZO, José (b.
1902), doctor
QEQ (1936-37) 75, (1941-42)
97.

GARRIDO MORALES, Eduardo (1898-
1953), doctor
CaM 185-86; QEQ (1933-34)
73-74, (1936-37) 75.

GARRIGA REGUERO, María Mercedes
(b.1908), author
AntHistCag 252; AntPoeCag
145-46; DiLP 2, pt.1:665-67;
EGMPR 1:143-45, ill.

GATELL, Rafael (b.1893*), author
DiLP 2, pt.1:667-68; GrEPR
14:145; Ind 81.

GATELL, Rafael A. (1862-1916),
doctor
CaM 187; Hor 366-69.

GATELL DE RODRIGUEZ, Palmira
(b.1890), doctor
CaM 186-87; EGMPR 3:167-68,
ill.; QEQ (1936-37) 75.

GATELL Y GARCIA DE QUEVEDO,
Federico (1859-1906), pharmacist, politician
CaF 69-71; GenB 287-88; GrEPR
14:145; Nuestr 49-50.

GAUDIER, Martín (b.1892), author, industrialist
GenB 423-24, ill.; VerOr 99-
100.

GAUDIER Y PARELLA, José Antonio
(b.1813), piano teacher
GenB 359-60.

GAUDIER Y TEXIDOR, Benito (1859-
1936), doctor
CaM 187-92; DiM 128; GenB
255-58, ill.; GenP 26; HoIPR
50, ill.; VerOr 254-57, ill.

GAUDIER TEXIDOR, Francisco (b.
1852), music teacher
GenB 346-47, ill.

GAUTHIER, Emilio E. (b.1908),
agricultural engineer
QEQ (1941-42) 97.

GAUTHIER, Jorge, politician

GrEPR 14:145.

GAUTHIER, Luis, lawyer
Crom 29.

GAUTHIER, Pascasio M. (b.
1895), advertising agent
QEQ (1936-37) 75-76.

GAUTIER BENITEZ, José (1848*-
1880), poet
AntHistCag 252-54; AntPoe-
Cag 13-15; BgP facing p.
148, ill.; BiP 176-80; Br-
ECP 206; CaDeT 164-65,
ill.; CaE 732-33; CiBPI 75
(ill.), 146-49; DeADeA 212-
26; DiDHM 96, ill.; DiHBC
427; DiLP 2, pt.1:668-74;
ECPR 6:448(ill.), 449; EPI
1:151, ill.; EnsB 207-16;
GrEPR 14:145; HisD 38; Ho-
IPR 50-51, ill.; HoRPR 106-
15; LPR 1008, 1010, 1011,
ill.; MeO 145-88; Pin 40-
43; PlE 1:139-51, ill.; Por
217-19; PRFAS 109, ill.;
PuI 325-28.

GAUTIER DAPENA, Jenaro (d.
1924), politician
GrEPR 14:145.

GAYA BENEJAM, Raúl (b.1904),
engineer
QEQ (1948-49) 75.

GAYOL, Manuel, musician,
teacher
GrEPR 14:146.

GAZTAMBIDE, Francisco (1895-
1976), author
Per 75-77.

GAZTAMBIDE ARRILLAGA, Mario
(b.1917), politician
GrEPR 14:146.

GAZTAMBIDE ARRILLAGA, Rubén,
politician
GrEPR 14:146.

GEIGEL ARROYO, Juan Enrique
(b.1911), lawyer
QEQ (1936-37) 185.

GEIGEL DE GANDIA, Luisa (b.
1916), artist, professor
A 73; DiHBC 427-28; EGMPR
4:57-58; GrEPR 8:336, ill.

GEIGEL POLANCO, Vicente (b.
1904), author, lawyer, politician
A 49-50; And 216-19; BiP 180-
81; CaE 733-34; ConA 85-88:
205; DiDHM 97; DiHBC 428; Di-
LP 2, pt.1:674-78; ECPR 6:
449; Esb 41-46; GrEPR 14:146,
147(ill.); Hor 173-75; PRFAS
109-10; QEQ (1933-34) 74,
(1936-37) 76, (1941-42) 98,
(1948-49) 75-76; Tri 2:187-
93.

GEIGEL SABAT, Fernando J. (1881-
1964), lawyer, author
DiLP 2, pt.1:678-79; GrEPR 14:
146; QEQ (1933-34) 74, (1936-
37) 76, (1941-42) 98, (1948-
49) 191.

GEIGEL Y ZENON, José (1841-1892),
author, journalist, politician
DiLP 2, pt.1:679-82.

GELPI, Sergio Guillermo (b.
1898), lawyer
A 84; QEQ (1941-42) 236,
(1948-49) 76; Tri 1:373-78.

GELPI, William R. (b.1904),
doctor
QEQ (1941-42) 99.

GELPI BOSCH, José Rosario (d.
1961), politician
GrEPR 14:146.

GEORETTI Y FERNANDEZ, Eduardo
(1866-1937), businessman, politician
DiDHM 97; GenP 99-100; GrEPR
14:146, ill.; HoIPR 51, ill.;
PriC 37, ill.; QEQ (1933-34)
75, (1936-37) 76-77; RepM
39, ill.; Tri 1:47-53.

GERALDINO, Alejandro (1455-1525),
bishop
Ver 273.

GERENA BRAS, Gaspar (b.1909),
author
And 154-56; CiuP 79-80; DiLP
2, pt.1:682; PRFAS 110; SobM
28-30.

GERHART, George Albert (b.
1905), forest technician
QEQ (1936-37) 76.

GIGANTE, Arturo (b.1890), author, journalist
    DiLP 2, pt.1:682-83; GenB
    361-63, ill.; PRFAS 110.

GIGANTE DAVILA, Arturo (b.
1869), businessman, manager
    HoIPR 52, ill.

GIL, Juan (16th cent.), government official
    GrEPR 14:148.

GIL, Pedro (b.1894), teacher
    Tri 1:223-29.

GIL DE LAMADRID, Jesús (b.
1896), poet, journalist
    DiLP 2, pt.1:683-84; PoA
    235-40, ill.

GIL DE LAMADRID, Joaquín
(1893*-1955), poet
    AlHP 128-30, ill.; DiLP 2,
    pt.1:684-85; PoA 223-27,
    ill.

GIL DE LAMADRID, Josefa,
humanitarian
    DiHBC 431; MujDPR 51-52;
    MujPu 49-50.

GIL ROSIO, Pedro (b.1892),
educator
    QEQ (1933-34) 74-75.

GILORMINI, Mihiel (b.1918),
Air Force officer
    AlHY 58-59, ill.

GILL, Martin Edward (b.1870),
judge
    RepM 44, ill.

GIMENEZ, Juan Francisco (1783-
1851), priest
    EnsB 87-93.

GIMENEZ AGUAYO, José (b.1902),
lawyer
    QEQ (1941-42) 99.

GIMENEZ DE LA ROSA, Rafael (b.
1903), accountant, National
Guard officer
    QEQ (1936-37) 76, (1941-
    42) 99, (1948-49) 76-77.

GIMENEZ MORENO, Alfredo (b.
1875), pharmacist
    QEQ (1936-37) 185.

GIMENEZ Y MORENO, Eduardo (1820-
1865), doctor, pharmacist
    BeHNPR 2:153-54; CaF 71-72;
    CaM 195-96.

GIMENEZ NUSSA, Nicolás (1871-
1913), doctor
    CaM 198-99; GenB 299-300; Ho-
    IPR 53, ill.; Nuestr 90-91;
    RepM 206, ill.

GINORIO, Emigdio S. (1867-
1959), author, lawyer
    DiLP 2, pt.1:685; LM 130-31;
    QEQ (1941-42) 99, (1948-49)
    77.

GINORIO, Manuel M. (1869-1929),
lawyer, politician
    GrEPR 14:148; HoIPR 53, ill.

GINORIO, Ulises (d.1886), pharmacist, educator
    ArH 548; CaF 72.

GIOL TEXIDOR, Alejandro, doctor,
politician
    CaM 200; GrEPR 14:148; RepM
    298, ill.

GIORGETTI, Carlos Q. (1878-
1953), musician, author
    AlHP 134, ill.

Giorgetti, Eduardo see Georgetti
y Fernández, Eduardo

GIRON, Socorro (b.1919), author,
professor
    And 65-71; Desd 222-26; DiLP
    2, pt.1:686-87; EGMPR 1:147-
    48, ill.

GIRONA, Matilde, musician,
teacher
    MusMP 287.

GIULIANI, Salvador (1886-1929),
doctor, pathologist
    CaM 200-201; DiHBC 431.

GIUSTI DE GIUSTI, María (1879-
(1879-1933), businesswoman
    EGMPR 3:325-26, ill.; Muj-
    DPR 148-50, ill.

GLINES, Walter Ashley (1880-
1947), doctor
    CaM 201; QEQ (1936-37) 77.

GODREAU GUERRERO, Elías Pablo

(b.1905), engineer
   QEQ (1948-49) 77.

GODREAU GUERRERO, Francisco (b.
1899), engineer
   QEQ (1948-49) 77.

GODREAU GUERRERO, Miguel Florencio (b.1906), doctor
   QEQ (1936-37) 77.

GODREAU MANATOV, Guillermo,
politician
   GrEPR 14:148.

GOENAGA, Esteban A. de (b.
1882), dentist
   QEQ (1933-34) 75-76, (1936-
   37) 77, (1941-42), 100,
   (1948-49) 78.

GOENAGA, José Vicente de (19th
cent.), liberal activist
   GrEPR 14:148.

GOENAGA Y OLZA, Francisco R.
de (1855-1937), doctor
   CaM 201-3; DiM 129-33; Ho-
   IPR 53-54, ill.; QEQ (1936-
   37) 181; RepM 108, ill.

Goico see Goyco

GOICOCHEA, Francisco, singer
   MusMP 177-78.

GOICOECHEA, José María, lawyer
   Crom 58.

GOICOECHEA, Martín (1832-
1896), priest
   Jes 150.

GOITIA MONTALVO, Darío, politician
   GrEPR 14:148.

GOMEZ, Luis F. (b.1931),
judge
   PRUSA 15.

GOMEZ, Rubén (b.1927), baseball player
   EPI 1:333, ill.

GOMEZ, Wilfredo, boxer
   PRUSA 15, ill.

GOMEZ ACEVEDO, Labor, professor, author
   GrEPR 1:vii, ill., 14:148.

GOMEZ ALDEA DE ALVAREZ, Virginia, civic-religious works
   EGMPR 3:327-28, ill.

GOMEZ BERRIOS, Nélida (b.1935),
government official
   EGMPR 3:39-40, ill.

GOMEZ BRIOSO, José (1854-1930),
doctor, politician
   CaM 208; DiM 133-36; GrEPR
   14:149.

GOMEZ CINTRON, Ramón (b.1881),
soldier, Freemason
   Nues 63-65, ill.

GOMEZ COSTA, Arturo (b.1895),
poet, critic, editor
   BiP 181-82; CaE 735; DiLP
   2, pt.1:687-90; PRFAS 110;
   SobM 177-80.

GOMEZ Y CUEBAS, Gerónimo (1850-
1900), doctor
   BoHP 141-42, 143, ill.; CaM
   206-7; DiM 136; GenB 262-63,
   ill.; Nuestr 64-65.

GOMEZ DE MARCHAN, Encarnación,
singer, musician
   MusMP 178.

GOMEZ GARRIGA, María Libertad
(1898-1961), politician,
teacher
   EGMPR 2:27, ill., 3:41-42,
   ill.; GrEPR 14:149; PriC 78.

GOMEZ HERNANDEZ, Sotero (b.
1914), politician
   GrEPR 14:149.

GOMEZ PULIDO, Ramón (19th
cent.), governor
   GrEPR 14:149.

GOMEZ TEJERA, Carmen (1890-
1973), educator, author
   BiP 182-84; DiHBC 461; DiLP
   2, pt.1:690-94; ECPR 6:449-
   50; EGMPR 1:285-86, ill.;
   GrEPR 14:149; MujDPR 222-
   23, ill.; PQ 36; ProA 39;
   PRFAS 110-11; QEQ (1933-34)
   76, (1936-37) 77.

GOMEZ TIZOL, Manuel (1842-1914),
musician, teacher
   MusMP 253-54.

GONZALEZ, Antonio C., politician
   GrEPR 14:149, ill.; RepM
   237, ill.

GONZALEZ, Antonio J. (b.1921),
economist, politician
   BrECP 212; DiDHM 97-98,
   ill.; GrEPR 14:150, ill.;
   PRFAS 111-12, ill.

GONZALEZ, Carlos, painter
   PaG 240.

GONZALEZ, Enrique, dentist,
politician
   Crom 73; Ka 98.

GONZALEZ, Fernando, politician
   GrEPR 14:150; RepM 314,
   ill.

GONZALEZ, Fernando (b.1950),
baseball player
   PRUSA 15.

GONZALEZ, Fernando L. (b.
1887), businessman
   QEQ (1936-37) 78.

GONZALEZ, José Emilio (b.
1918), author, critic, professor
   BiP 189; BrECP 213-14,
   ill.; CaE 736-37; DiDHM 98;
   DiLP 2, pt.1:694-96; ECPR
   6:450; GrEPR 1:ix, ill.,
   14:150; PRFAS 114.

GONZALEZ, José Felipe, doctor
   A 108-9, ill.

GONZALEZ, José Ismael, engineer
   A 38.

GONZALEZ, José Luis (b.1926),
author
   BiP 187-89; BrECP 214; Di-
   DHM 98; DiHBC 461; DiLP 2,
   pt.1:696-700; GrEPR 5:85-
   87, 14:151, ill.; Ind 81-
   83; PRFAS 113.

GONZALEZ, José Vicente (d.
1896), political activist
   Nuestr 53-54.

GONZALEZ, Josefina, artist
   GrEPR 8:434.

González, Josemilio see González, José Emilio

GONZALEZ, Juan (16th cent.),
colonist
   DiHBC 463; GrEPR 14:151; HisD
   39.

GONZALEZ, Julio, government
official
   Ka 111-12.

GONZALEZ, Manuel A., educator
   Port 173, 174(ill.)

GONZALEZ, Manuel María (19th
cent.), revolutionary
   GrEPR 14:151.

González, Nilda see González
Monclova, Nilda

GONZALEZ, Rafael A. (b.1922),
professor, author
   DirAS 3:195.

GONZALEZ, Rosa A. (b.1891),
nurse
   DiHBC 462-63; EGMPR 3:173-
   74, ill.; GrEPR 14:151; Muj-
   DPR 216-18, ill.

GONZALEZ, Santiago (1837-1903),
teacher
   AlHP 240, ill.

GONZALEZ ALBERTY, Fernando (b.
1908), poet
   CaE 738; DiLP 2, pt.1:700.

GONZALEZ ANGEL, José Manuel (b.
1908), lawyer
   QEQ (1941-42) 100.

GONZALEZ BLANES, Héctor, politician
   GrEPR 14:152.

GONZALEZ CARBO, Alfonso (b.
1901), poet
   DiLP 2, pt.1:700-701.

GONZALEZ CEPEDA, José Máximo (b.
1915), dentist
   QEQ (1948-49) 78.

GONZALEZ CORDOVA, José Angel
Plácido (b.1919), architect
   QEQ (1948-49) 78-79.

GONZALEZ CORREA, Ernesto (1893-

1904), pharmacist
   Añas 148-50, ill.

GONZALEZ CORREA, María de los
Angeles (b.1901), poet
   PoA 245-49, ill.

GONZALEZ CRUZ, Héctor (b.
1947), economist, politician
   LiPR 37, ill.

GONZALEZ CUYAR, Luis R. (b.
1887), engineer
   QEQ (1936-37) 79, (1941-
   42) 102, (1948-49) 79.

GONZALEZ CHAPEL, Milagros (b.
1908), teacher, politician
   EGMPR 2:29, ill.; GrEPR 14:
   152; PriC 78.

GONZALEZ CHAVEZ, Juan (1820-
1865), book binder, printer
   BiP 184-85; DiDHM 98-99;
   Esp 65-70; EnsB 121-27; Gr-
   EPR 14:152; PRFAS 112.

GONZALEZ DE COLL VIDAL, Rosa,
educator, museum director
   EGMPR 1:287-88.

GONZALEZ DE DEGETAU, Consuelo
(b.1838), Federico Degetau's
mother
   DiHBC 461; MujDPR 88-89,
   ill.

GONZALEZ DE LINARES, Francisco,
governor
   DiDHM 99; DiHBC 450-51;
   HisD 39.

GONZALEZ DE TOLEDO, Rosa (b.
1891), social worker
   DiHBC 461; EGMPR 4:291-93,
   ill.; MujDPR 237-39, ill.;
   QEQ (1936-37) 77.

GONZALEZ FAGUNDO, Francisco
(b.1875), lawyer, politician
   GrEPR 14:152; QEQ (1933-34)
   76, (1936-37) 77-78, (1941-
   42) 100; Tri 2:173-79.

GONZALEZ FLORES, Carlos G. (b.
1906), pharmacist
   CaF 74.

GONZALEZ FLORES, Enrique A.
(b.1908?), pharmacist
   CaF 74.

GONZALEZ GARCIA, Matías (1866-
1938), author, journalist
   BiP 185-87; BrECP 212-13;
   CaE 739; DiDHM 99; DiHBC
   461-62; DiLP 2, pt.1:702-4;
   ECPR 6:450; GrEPR 5:87-89,
   14:152, ill.; HoIPR 54,
   ill.; Ind 83-87; PlE 1:595-
   613, ill.; PRFAS 112-13; QEQ
   (1933-34) 76-77, (1936-37)
   78; Tri 1:193-99.

GONZALEZ GARCIA, Pedro, lawyer
   RepM 287, ill.

GONZALEZ GARCIA, Sebastián
(1908-1967), professor, author
   A 86; DiDHM 99-100.

GONZALEZ GINORIO, José (1879-
1940), educator, author
   ArH 519; DiLP 2, pt.1:704-6;
   GrEPR 5:89-90, 14:152; HoIPR
   55, ill.; Ind 87-88; Nues
   54-57, ill.; PRFAS 113; QEQ
   (1936-37) 78-79, (1941-42)
   100-101; Tri 1:395-400.

GONZALEZ GONZALEZ, Carlos (b.
1888), doctor, politician
   CaM 209; QEQ (1933-34) 77,
   (1936-37) 79.

GONZALEZ GONZALEZ, Eugenio (b.
1886), pharmacist, doctor
   CaF 74-75.

GONZALEZ GONZALEZ, José Felipe
(b.1892), doctor
   QEQ (1941-42) 101, (1948-49)
   79.

GONZALEZ GONZALEZ, Julio César
(1878-1963), notary public
   Hor 223-25; ProA 52, ill.;
   RepM 290, ill.

GONZALEZ HERNANDEZ, José (b.
1907), lawyer
   A 24-25; QEQ (1941-42) 101,
   (1948-49) 191.

GONZALEZ LAMAS, Antonio (b.
1887), lawyer
   QEQ (1933-34) 77-78, (1936-
   37) 79, (1941-42) 101-2,
   (1948-49) 191-92; Tri 1:275-
   79.

GONZALEZ LAMELA, Juan M. (b.
1945), professor
   DiDHM 100.

GONZALEZ MALDONADO, Edelmira
(b.1923), educator, author
   DiLP 2, pt.1:706; PRFAS
   114.

GONZALEZ MALDONADO, Rafael A.
(b.1904), lawyer, judge
   QEQ (1941-42) 237, (1948-
   49) 81.

GONZALEZ MAÑON, Jacinto (b.
1916), doctor
   QEQ (1948-49) 79.

GONZALEZ MARTINEZ, Isaac
(1871-1954), doctor
   AlDU [91], ill.; BrECP 251-
   53; GrEPR 14:153, ill.; Ho-
   DMT 98-107; HoIPR 55, ill.;
   PRFAS 115; QEQ (1933-34)
   192-93, (1936-37) 79-80,
   (1941-42) 102-3, (1948-49)
   79-80; RepM 142, ill.; Tri
   1:319-25; Una 37-39.

GONZALEZ MARTINEZ, Manuel
(1862-1944), businessman
   HoIPR 56, ill.; Ka 167; QEQ
   (1941-42) 236-37.

GONZALEZ MAS, Ezequiel (b.
1919), professor, critic
   DirAS 3:196.

GONZALEZ MENA, América (b.
1911), teacher
   QEQ (1941-42) 103.

GONZALEZ MENA, Enrique (b.
1882), politician, lawyer
   GrEPR 14:153, ill.; Ka
   [194]; LM 134; ProA 32-33;
   QEQ (1933-34) 78, (1936-37)
   80-81, (1941-42) 103-4;
   RepM 340, ill.; Tri 2:235-
   40.

GONZALEZ MONCLOVA, Nilda (b.
1929), professor, drama critic
   BrECP 215; EGMPR 1:289-91,
   ill.; GrEPR 14:154; PRFAS
   115.

GONZALEZ MUÑOZ, Andrés (b.
1841), governor, soldier
   DiDHM 100; Exp 285-87.

GONZALEZ OLIVER, Wallace (b.
1925), lawyer
   GrEPR 14:154.

GONZALEZ PAZ, Elsie E. (b.

1913), teacher, author
   ConA 45-48:191-92.

GONZALEZ PEDROSO, Eduardo
(1822-1862), author, journalist,
translator
   DiLP 2, pt.1:706-7; GrEPR
   14:154.

GONZALEZ PEREZ, Aníbal (b.1956),
professor, author
   DirAS 3:196.

GONZALEZ POLA, Julio (b.1870?),
sculptor
   GrEPR 8:434.

GONZALEZ PORRATA, Esmeraldo (b.
1905), politician
   QEQ (1948-49) 81.

GONZALEZ QUIARA, José (1860?-
1902), author, journalist
   DiLP 2, pt.1:707-8; GrEPR
   14:154; Hi de M 200; Ind
   88-89; MueYV 166-70; Nuestr
   139.

GONZALEZ-WIPPLER, Migene (b.
1936), author
   ConA 109:157.

GONZALEZ QUIÑONES, Manuel (b.
1897), agricultural engineer
   QEQ (1936-37) 81, (1941-42)
   105.

GONZALEZ RAMON, Rafael Antonio
(b.1890), engineer
   QEQ (1933-34) 78-79, (1936-
   37) 81, (1941-42) 104.

GONZALEZ RAMOS, Pedro (b.1935),
educator
   DiDHM 101; GrEPR 14:154.

GONZALEZ REICHARD, Noel (b.
1912), lawyer
   QEQ (1941-42) 104.

GONZALEZ REYES, María Isabel
(b.1933), lawyer
   EGMPR 3:169-70.

GONZALEZ RIVERA, Santiago (b.
1890), teacher
   QEQ (1936-37) 81, (1941-42)
   105.

GONZALEZ RIVERO, Ciriaco (1861-
1911), agriculturalist
   AlHP 349.

GONZALEZ RIVERA, José, industrialist
   A 36.

GONZALEZ ROMAN, Silma, social
worker
   EGMPR 3:171-72, ill.

GONZALEZ SALICRUP, Ramón (b.
1878), engineer, painter
   QEQ (1933-34) 79, (1936-37)
   81.

GONZALEZ SANCHEZ, Heriberto
(b.1949), artist
   GrEPR 8:405.

GONZALEZ SEIJO, Gilberto,
artist
   ArH 538-39: GrEPR 8:118-19.

GONZALEZ SUAREZ, Antonio
(1881-1930), politician
   Añas 102-5, ill.

GONZALEZ TORRES, José Antonio
(b.1927), politician
   GrEPR 14:154.

GONZALEZ TORRES, Rafael Antonio (b.1922), journalist,
author
   GrEPR 14:154; Ind 89-90;
   PRFAS 115-16.

GONZALEZ VILLAMIL, Diana C.
(b.1955), equestrienne
   GrEPR 14:154-55.

GORBEA NAVEDO, Manuel (b.1867)
teacher
   QEQ (1933-34) 79, (1936-37)
   81.

GORBEA PLA, Juan I. (b.1890),
accountant
   QEQ (1933-34) 79-80, (1936-
   37) 81, (1941-42) 105,
   (1948-49) 81.

GORDILS VASSALLO, José (1868-
1932), poet, journalist
   DiLP 2, pt.1:708-10; GrEPR
   14:155; Hor 123-28; PRFAS
   116.

GORE, Robert H. (1886-1972),
governor
   ConA 89-92:206; Desf 113-
   16, ill.; DiDHM 101; DiHBC
   438; QEQ (1933-34) 193,
   (1936-37) 82; Tra 124-28.

GORRITZ, Carmelo J., politician
   GrEPR 14:155.

Gosnell, Patria see Arán de
Gosnell, Patria

GOTAY, Consuelo (b.1949), artist
   GrEPR 8:405.

GOTAY, Modesto (1875-1973),
author
   Per 179-81.

GOULD, Alice Bache, historian
   DiHBC 143.

Goyco, Agustín Osvaldo see Goyco,
Osvaldo A.

GOYCO, Felipe Rosario "Don Felo"
(b.1899), musician, composer
   GrEPR 7:125-26, 14:155, ill.

GOYCO, Osvaldo A. (1887-1963),
doctor
   AlHP 370, ill.; QEQ (1933-34)
   80, (1936-37) 82, (1941-42)
   106.

GOYCO, Pedro Gerónimo (1808-
1890), doctor, politician
   BiP 190-91; CaM 203-4; CiBPI
   69(ill.), 91-93; Desd 115-18;
   DiDHM 101; DiM 137-43; ECPR
   6:450-51; EPI 1:94(ill.), 95;
   GrEPR 14:155; HisD 38-39;
   HoIPR 52, ill.; PRFAS 116;
   PuI 62-66.

GOYCO, Ramón G. (b.1893), politician
   GrEPR 14:155; QEQ (1936-37)
   82.

GOYCO DAUBON, José Antonio (b.
1914), chemist, pharmacist
   QEQ (1948-49) 81.

GOYENA, Joaquín J. (ca.1765-1834),
painter
   GrEPR 8:27-28.

GOYENO O'DALY, Francisco (ca.
1785-1855), painter
   GrEPR 8:30.

Graham, Lessie see Spencer de
Graham, Sarah Isabel

GRAHAME, Laurence Hill, government official
   RepM 16, ill.

Granados, Francisco see Danio
Granados, Francisco

GRANADOS NAVEDO, José (b.
1946), politician
    GrEPR 14:156; LiPR 33, ill.

GRAND COURT, Grivot, scientist
    Hi de M 209.

GRANT, Chapman, soldier, her-
patologist
    DiHBC 463.

GRANT CHACON, Pedro (b.1920),
labor leader
    GrEPR 14:156, ill.

GRANT PARDO, Arturo (b.1886),
educator
    QEQ (1933-34) 193-94,
    (1936-37) 82.

GRAÑA DE IRIARTE, Mercedes,
artist
    GrEPR 8:434.

GRAÑA LAVIOSSA, Manuel (b.
1860), banker
    RepM 133, ill.

GRAU ARCHILLA, Raúl (b.1910),
poet
    CaE 740-41; DiLP 2, pt.1:
    710-11.

GRENVILLE, Richard (1542-
1591), English naval officer
    DiHBC 463-65; GrEPR 14:156.

GRAY, Richard W. (b.1874),
meteorologist
    QEQ (1936-37) 82, (1941-42)
    106.

GREGORY SANTIAGO, Linda,
painter, educator
    GrEPR 8:406.

GREVI BELLAGAMBA, Francisco,
politician
    GrEPR 14:157.

GRIFFITTS, Thomas H. D. (b.
1878), doctor
    QEQ (1941-42) 106.

GRIFO MONSERRATE, Luisa, singer
    MusMP 178-79.

GRILLASCA SALAS, Andrés, poli-

tician
    GrEPR 14:156.

GRILLASCA SALAS, Lucy (1895-
1944), teacher
    AlHP 325, ill.

GRIMALDO, Juan Francisco de
(16th cent.), banker
    GrEPR 14:157.

GRIMALDO, Nicolao (16th cent.),
banker
    GrEPR 14:157.

GROMER, Samuel David, educator,
government official
    RepM 17, ill.

GROVAS, Rafael (b.1905), Catholic bishop
    GrEPR 6:287; QEQ (1948-49)
    81-82.

GRUENING, Ernest (b.1887), newspaper manager
    QEQ (1936-37) 82-83.

GUAL DEVARIE, Alfonso, politician
    Imp 213-15.

GUANINA (16th cent.), Taína Indian
    GrEPR 14:157.

GUARDIOLA ALMODOVAR, Justo A.
(b.1895), politician
    GrEPR 14:157; QEQ (1948-49)
    82.

GUARIONEX (16th cent.), Taíno
Indian chief
    GrEPR 14:157.

GUASP CERVERA, Ignacio (1810?-
1874), author
    DiDHM 102; DiLP 2, pt.1:
    711-12; GrEPR 14:157.

GUASP VERGARA, Ignacio (1887-
1962), author, journalist
    BoBP 51-54; Desd 302-7; DiLP
    2, pt.1:713-15.

GUAYAMA (16th cent.), Taíno
Indian chief
    GrEPR 14:157.

GUERRA MONDRAGON, Miguel (1880-
1947), politician, author
    BiP 191-92; CaE 741; DiDHM
    102; DiLP 2, pt.1:715-17;

ECPR 6:451; GrEPR 14:157-58, ill.; HoIPR 57, ill.; LM 135-36; Lie 113-16, ill.; PRFAS 116-17; QEQ (1941-42) 106-7; RepM 299, ill.

GUERRERO, Pedro, musician
MusMP 254.

GUEVARA, María Teresa (b. 1896), educator, nun
EGMPR 4:223-24; GrEPR 14:158.

GUEVARA CASTAÑEIRA, Josefina (b.1918), journalist, author
BiP 192-93; DiLP 2, pt.1: 717-20; EGMPR 1:149-51, ill.; GrEPR 5:90-91; Ind 90-91; PRFAS 117.

GUIJARRO COBIAN, Antonio (b. 1897), doctor
QEQ (1933-34) 80, (1936-37) 83, (1941-42) 107.

GUILLEN, Miguel (19th cent.), musician, teacher
MusMP 287-88.

GUILLERMETY QUINTERO, Fidel, pharmacist, politician
CaF 76-77, 187-88.

GUILLERMETY ROSALES, Rafael (b.1881?), lawyer
RepM 288, ill.

GUISCAFRE ARRILLAGA, Jaime (b. 1911), coffee expert
QEQ (1936-37) 83, (1941-42) 107-8, (1948-49) 82-83.

GUISCAFRE ARRILLAGA, Rosario (b.1919*), poet, journalist
DiLP 2, pt.1:720-21; EGMPR 3:291-91, ill.

GUTIERREZ, Natividad (b.1940), artist
GrEPR 8:406; PaG 210.

GUTIERREZ DE COS, Pedro (1750-1833), priest, bishop
BeHNPR 2:7-10, ill.; EnsB 43-49.

GUTIERREZ DE RIVAS, Gabriel (d.1703), governor
GrEPR 14:158.

GUTIERREZ DEL ARROYO, Isabel (b.1907), historian, educator
BrECP 222-23; DiHBC 475-76; DiLP 2, pt.1:721-23; EGMPR 1:293-94, ill.; GrEPR 14: 159; PRFAS 117.

GUTIERREZ Y ESPINOSA, Felipe (1825-1900), composer
BiP 193-94; BrECP 223; Co7; DiHBC 476; ECPR 6:451; EPI 3: 228; GrEPR 7:185-88, ill., 14:159; Mus en P 121-22; MusMP 101-16; PRFAS 118; PuI 173-74.

GUTIERREZ FRANQUI, Víctor (1908-1963), politician
GrEPR 14:159, ill.; QEQ (1948-49) 83.

GUTIERREZ IGARAVIDEZ, Pedro (1871-1935), doctor
CaM 219; DiHBC 476; DiM 143-45; GrEPR 14:159; HoIPR 57, ill.; RepM 140, ill.

GUTIERREZ MORALES, Guillermo (b.1928), poet
DiLP 2, pt.1:723-24.

GUTIERREZ ORTIZ, Víctor (1872-1956), doctor, politician
CaM 220; DiM 145-47; GrEPR 14:159; HoIPR 58, ill.; QEQ (1933-34) 80-81, (1936-37) 83.

GUZMAN, Carmen Isabel (b.1946), painter
GrEPR 8:407.

GUZMAN, Julio Víctor (1901-1965), teacher
S 88.

GUZMAN, Miguel Angel (b.1939), painter, sculptor
PaG 221-24.

GUZMAN BENITEZ, José de, politician
Crom 70; GrEPR 14:160, ill.; RepM 47, ill.

GUZMAN BENITEZ, Juan de (1868?-1934), lawyer, politician
GenP 19; GrEPR 14:160, ill.; HoIPR 58, ill.; RepM 77, ill.

GUZMAN DE CAPO, Rosa (b.1891), teacher
EGMPR 4:173-74, ill.

GUZMAN DE FONT, Aida (b.1932),
psychiatrist
EGMPR 3:101-2, ill.

GUZMAN DE GOMEZ, Milagros (b.
1928), personnel officer
EGMPR 3:103-4, ill., 4:
329-30, ill.

GUZMAN DE PEREZ, Inés Julia
(b.1920), teacher
EGMPR 1:295-96.

GUZMAN RODRIGUEZ, Manuel
(1863-1932), doctor, author,
politician
Añas 54-63, ill.; CaM 221-
22; DiLP 2, pt.1:724-26;
DiM 147-52; GenB 323-24,
ill.; Hi de M 191; HoIPR
58, ill.; PaF 84-85.

GUZMAN RODRIGUEZ, Manuel
(1892-1971), doctor, author
Añas 140-42, ill.; CaM 223-
24; DiM 147; GenB 376-77,
ill.

GUZMAN SOTO, José L. de (1884-
1941), doctor
CaM 220-21; QEQ (1936-37)
185, (1941-42) 108.

H

HABA BRUNET, Gabriel de la (b.
1896), lawyer
QEQ (1933-34) 57, (1936-37)
58, (1941-42) 76, (1948-49)
56-57.

HABA Y TRUJILLO, Abelardo de
la (1865-1923), doctor
HoIPR 59, ill.

HADLEY, Evan Worth (b.1898),
forester
QEQ (1941-42) 108.

HALL, Elizabeth, teacher
Ma 65-67.

HALL, Wilfred M. (b.1894),
engineer
QEQ (1941-42) 108.

HARLAN, James S., lawyer
MueYV 176-85.

HARO, Andrés de (16th cent.),
Royal Treasurer
GrEPR 14:161.

HARO, Juan de (d.1631), governor
BeHNPR 1:231-33; DiDHM 103;
GrEPR 14:161; Hi de Pu 89-91.

HARTWELL, Frank Eugene (b.
1873), meteorologist
QEQ (1933-34) 81, (1936-37)
83-84.

HARTZNELL, Charles (b.1861),
lawyer
LM 135; RepM 36, ill.

HARRIS, John William (b.1876),
missionary, lawyer
GrEPR 14:161; QEQ (1933-34)
81, (1936-37) 83; Tri 1:
121-26.

HAWKINS, John (1532-1595),
English naval officer
GrEPr 14:161.

HENDRICKZS, Boudewijn (17th
cent.), sailor
GrEPR 14:161.

HENNA, José Julio (1848-1924),
doctor, politician
CiBPI 75(ill.), 149-52; DiM
153-54; EPI 1:135-40, ill.;
3:21-57; GenP 104; GrEPR 14:
162; HisD 46; HisP 125-26,
141-44; HoIPR 59, ill.; Med
39-42.

HENNA, Joseph, pharmacist
Ver 164, ill.

Henna, Julio see Henna, José
Julio

HENRIQUEZ, Miguel (18th cent.),
sailor
GrEPR 14:162.

HENRIQUEZ, Tito (b.1920), musician, composer
Com 4; GrEPR 7:140-41, ill.

HENRY, Guy V. (1839-1899), governor
Desf 5-8; DiDHM 103-4; GrEPR
14:162, ill.; Hi de Cay 60-
61.

HERNAIZ LOPEZ, Juan (1850-1930),
lawyer, politician
GrEPR 14:162; HoIPR 60, ill.

HERNAIZ VERONNE, Luis (1876-
1929), politician

GrEPR 14:162; HoIPR 60,
ill.

HERNANDEZ, Alberto (b.1903),
engineer
QEQ (1941-42) 108, (1948-
49) 83.

HERNANDEZ, Demetrio (b.1840),
government official
BoHP 156-67, ill.

HERNANDEZ, Diego (b.1934),
Navy commander, pilot
PRUSA 16, ill.

HERNANDEZ, José P. H. (1892-
1922), poet, pharmacist,
musician
BiP 197-99; BrECP 227-28;
CaE 751; DiDHM 104; DiHBC
480-81; DiLP 2, pt.1:726-
29: ECPR 6:451-53, ill.:
GrEPR 14:162; HoYMPR 240-
56, ill.; PlE 2:411-20,
ill.; PRFAS 120-21.

HERNANDEZ, Marife, government
employee
PRUSA 16, ill.

HERNANDEZ, Pedro (19th cent.),
doctor
Crom 97-98.

HERNANDEZ, Rafael (1892*-
1965), composer
BiP 200-202; BrECP 228-29,
ill.; CiBPI 225(ill.), 285-
87; Com 4-5; DiDHM 481-82;
ECPR 6:453, 454(ill.); EPI
1:172-73, ill., 2:210-13;
GrEPR 7:127-29, 131, ill.,
14:162; HisD 46; L 44-59;
Per 46-48, ill.; PRFAS 121-
22, ill.

HERNANDEZ, Roberto (b.1939),
author
DiLP 2, pt.1:729-30.

HERNANDEZ ACEVEDO, Manuel (b.
1921), artist
GrEPR 8:338, ill.; PaG 199.

HERNANDEZ ACOSTA, Enrique,
manager
QEQ (1936-37) 84.

HERNANDEZ AGOSTO, Miguel (b.
1927), politician
DiDHM 105; GrEPR 14:163,

ill.; LiPR 24-25, ill.

HERNANDEZ AQUINO, Luis (b.1907),
author, professor
BiP 194-95; BrECP 225-26;
CaE 752-53; CiuP 65-66; DiDHM
105; DiLP 2, pt.1:730-36;
ECPR 6:453; GrEPR 5:91-94,
ill., 14:163; Ind 91-93;
PRFAS 119.

Hernández Araújo, Carmen see
Hernández de Araújo, Carmen

HERNANDEZ ARBIZU, Juan Antonio (1825-1889), lawyer
BeHNPR 2:285-87, ill.; BoHP
113, 115, ill.; LM 112.

HERNANDEZ COLON, Miguel,
politician
GrEPR 14:163.

HERNANDEZ COLON, Rafael (b.
1936), politician, governor
BrECP 226-27; CuB 1973:183-
85, ill.; DiDHM 105-6; Di-
HBC 479-80; GrEPR 14:164
(ill.), 165; HisD 46; LiPR
66-67, ill.; Pon 89-90; PRFAS
120; PRUSA 16, ill.

HERNANDEZ CRUZ, Luis (b.1935),
artist
BiP 196-97; BrECP 227; DiHBC
480; GrEPR 8:256, ill.; PaG
214; PRFAS 120.

HERNANDEZ CRUZ, Víctor (b.1949),
poet, teacher
CaE 754.

HERNANDEZ DE ARAUJO, Carmen
(1832-1877), author
BiP 195-96; CaE 756; DiDHM
106; DiHBC 480; DiLP 2, pt.1:
736-37; ECPR 6:453, 455;
EGMPR 1:153-54, ill.; EPI 3:
177, 178, 182, 183; GrEPR 14:
163; MujDPR 40-41; MujP 116-
17; MujPu 27-29; PlE 1:197-
205, ill.; PRFAS 119.

HERNANDEZ DE LEON, Efraín (b.
1953), painter
GrEPR 8:434.

HERNANDEZ DE MEDINA, Pepita,
civic works
AlDJ 137, 139, 141, 143, ill.

HERNANDEZ DEL VALLE, Pedro (b.

1899), doctor
    QEQ (1936-37) 84.

HERNANDEZ FERRER, Juan (b.
1933), politician
    LiPR 127, ill.

HERNANDEZ GONZALEZ, Neftalí
(b.1936), lawyer, politician
    GrEPR 14:165.

HERNANDEZ HERNANDEZ, Francisco
José (1882*-1940), doctor
    CaM 227; QEQ (1933-34) 81,
    (1936-37) 84.

HERNANDEZ HERNANDEZ, Luis G.
(b.1891), chemist
    QEQ (1933-34) 81-82, (1936-
    37) 84.

HERNANDEZ JIMENEZ, Domingo A.,
artist
    A 75, ill.

HERNANDEZ LOPEZ, Juan (1859*-
1943), lawyer, politician
    DiHBC 481; EntP 141-44;
    GenP 21; GrEPR 14:165,
    ill.; LM 117-18; Lie 239-
    43; Orad 209-12; PaP 123-
    57; QEQ (1933-34) 82-83,
    (1936-37) 84-85, (1941-42)
    108-9; RepM 38, ill.; VisC
    29-60.

HERNANDEZ LOPEZ, Rodulfo
(1846-1907), newpaper publisher
    Apu 60-61.

HERNANDEZ MARTINEZ, Antonio R.
(b.1879), accountant
    QEQ (1933-34) 83, (1936-37)
    85, (1941-42) 109, (1948-
    49) 83.

HERNANDEZ Y MARTINEZ, Francisco Jorge (1816*-1885), doctor
    CaM 226; DiHBC 482; DiM
    154-61.

HERNANDEZ ROSA, Manuel (1892-
1958), businessman
    A 171; Añas 135-39, ill.

HERNANDEZ SALGADO, Francisco
Jorge (1816-1885), doctor,
political activist
    Eco 165-71; EnsB 277-84;
    GrEPR 14:166.

HERNANDEZ SANCHEZ, Jesús (b.
1929), author
    DiLP 2, pt.1:738-39.

HERNANDEZ SANCHEZ, Jesús (b.
1939), politician
    GrEPR 14:166.

HERNANDEZ Y SANTIAGO, José
Conrado (1849*-1932), lawyer,
judge
    HoIPR 35, ill.; LM 114-15;
    RepM 25, ill.

HERNANDEZ TRABAL, José (b.1954),
painter
    GrEPR 8:434.

HERNANDEZ USERA, José (b.1880),
lawyer
    LM 131; QEQ (1936-37) 85,
    (1941-42) 109-10.

HERNANDEZ USERA, Rafael (1888-
1946), lawyer, author
    DiLP 2, pt.1:739-41; QEQ
    (1936-37) 85, (1941-42) 110.

HERNANDEZ VALES, Pedro H.
(1899-1957), dentist
    AlDU 57, [101], ill.; QEQ
    (1936-37) 85, (1941-42) 110.

HERNANDEZ VARGAS, Francisco (b.
1914), author, lawyer
    CaE 755-56; DiDHM 106-7; Di-
    LP 2, pt.1:742; PRFAS 122.

HERRERA, Antonio de (1549-1625),
chronicler
    HisD 46.

HERRERA, Joaquín (19th cent.),
doctor
    CaM 230-31.

HERRERA COTAL, Pedro (b.1943),
politician
    LiPR 39, ill.

HERRERA Y GEIGEL, Luis (b.1879),
dentist
    QEQ (1933-34) 83, (1936-37)
    86.

HERRERO, Blas (b.1895), doctor,
politician
    CaM 231; DiM 161; GrEPR 14:
    166.

HERRERO, Juan N., government
official

Tri 2:145-50.

HERRERO, Susana (b.1945),
artist, professor
GrEPR 8:340, ill.

HERRERO RAMIREZ, Juan M. (b.
1888), lawyer
QEQ (1933-34) 83-84, (1936-
37) 86, (1941-42) 110-11.

HERRICK, Philip F. (b.1909),
lawyer
QEQ (1941-42) 237, (1948-
49) 83.

HIDALGO, Hilda, educator,
civic works
PQ 37.

HIDALGO CESTERO, Carlos A. (b.
1925), physiotherapist, athlete
CaM 232-33.

HIDALGO DIAZ, Antonia (b.1918)
lawyer, politician
EGMPR 2:31, ill.; GrEPR 14:
166.

HILERA Y MORA, Félix R. (b.
1890), accountant
QEQ (1933-34) 84, (1936-37)
86, (1948-49) 83-84.

HILL, Charles F. (b.1885?),
government official
RepM 119, ill.

HINCKLEY, Robert (b.1853),
artist
QEQ (1933-34) 84, (1936-37)
185.

HITA VAZQUEZ, Vicente (b.
1901), politician, pharmacist,
lawyer
CaF 79; GrEPR 14:166; QEQ
(1933-34) 84-85, (1936-37)
86, (1941-42) 111, (1948-
49) 84.

HITCHMAN, Jackson C. (b.1873),
engineer
QEQ (1936-37) 86, (1941-42)
111.

HOFFMAN, William Albert (b.
1874), scientist, professor
QEQ (1936-37) 87, (1941-42)
111.

HOHEB or HOHELE, Carlos Benjamín (1845-1898), doctor
CaM 233-34.

HOLMES, Frederick Charles (b.
1870), businessman
QEQ (1933-34) 85, (1936-37)
87, (1941-42) 111; Tri 1:
389-94.

HOLLAND, Vilma G., artist
EGMPR 4:59-60, ill.; GrEPR
8:434.

HOMAR, Lorenzo (b.1913), artist
BiP 202-3; BrECP 237; DiDHM
107; DiHBC 496-97; GrEPR 8:
260, ill.; PaG 192-93; PRFAS
122; PRP 251.

HONORE, Carmelo (b.1885),
government official
Tri 1:141-47.

HONORE, Sabas (b.1894), doctor
QEQ (1933-34) 85, (1936-37)
87.

HONORE BLONDET, Carlos, politician
GrEPR 14:166; QEQ (1936-37)
87.

HORD, Henry F., lawyer
RepM 34, ill.

HOSTOS, Eugenio Carlos de (b.
1879), Army officer
QEQ (1933-34) 86, (1936-37)
87-88, (1941-42) 112-13,
(1948-49) 85-86.

HOSTOS, Adolfo J. de (1887-1982),
historian, author
DiDHM 108; DiHBC 499-502;
DiLP 2, pt.1:755-57; GrEPR
14:168; HisD 47; PRFAS 122-23;
QEQ (1933-34) 85-86, (1936-
37) 87, (1941-42) 112, (1948-
49) 84-85.

HOSTOS, Eugenio María de (1839-
1903), author, educator, political activist
BgP facing p.266, ill.; BiP
203-5; BioD 2:669-70; BrECP
238-40, ill.; CaE 757-58;
CiBPI 73(ill.), 124-27; Di-
DHM 107-8, ill.; DiHBC 503-
10; DiLP 2, pt.1:757-64;
ECPR 6:455-56; EPI 1:106-8,
ill.; GenB 241-44, ill.; GenP

48-50, ill.; GrEPR 5:94-97,
14:167(ill.), 168; HePR 73-
81, ill.; Hi de M 198,
ill., 311-20; HisD 47; Ho-
IPR 61, ill.; HoRPR 35-45;
Ind 94-96; LPR 992, 993-97,
999; MueYV 171-76; Orad 73-
74; PaE 49-54; PaI 101-18,
ill.; PaP 33-38; PlE 1:209-
26, ill.; Por 234-37; PRFAS
123-24, ill.; PuI 218-22;
VPR 61-67, 166.

HOSTOS, Luisa Amelia de, author
    EGMPR 4:221; MujDPR 219-20,
    ill.

HOSTOS BRUNET, Eugenio María
de (b.1917), doctor
    DiHBC 502.

HOSTOS DE AYALA, Filipo Luis
de (b.1890), businessman
    A 120, ill.; DiHBC 502-3;
    QEQ (1933-34) 86-87,
    (1936-37) 88, (1941-42)
    113, (1948-49) 86-87.

HOYOS GOMEZ, Cándido (b.1898),
baseball player
    AlHP 432-33, ill.

HOYT, Henry M., lawyer
    RepM 15, ill.

HUCUYOA (16th cent.), Taíno
Indian chief
    GrEPR 14:168.

HUEL, Abraham (17th-18th
cent.), settler
    GrEPR 14:168.

HULL, Harwood (b.1885), journalist
    QEQ (1936-37) 87, (1941-
    42) 113-14, (1948-49) 87.

HUNT, William H. (1857-1949),
governor
    Desf 19-25, ill.; DiDHM
    108; DiHBC 437; GrEPR 14:
    169; QEQ (1936-37) 185-86;
    RepM 9, ill.

HUNTINGTON, Susan, teacher
    Ma 68-69.

HURST, Lillian, actress
    DelMu 134-38, ill.

HUTCHINSON, Henry (b.1915),
musician
    GrEPR 14:169.

HUTCHINSON, Henry (b.1950),
musician
    GrEPR 14:169.

HUTCHINSON DE PEDREIRA, Mary
Alice (b.1907), music teacher
    EGMPR 1:297.

HUTCHISON, Harvey M. (b.
1878), judge
    QEQ (1933-34) 87, (1936-37)
    88.

HUYKE, Bernardo (b.1881), educator
    QEQ (1936-37) 88-89, (1941-
    42) 114.

HUYKE, Emilio Enrique (b.1912),
journalist, sports writer
    AlHP 419, ill.; BrECP 241,
    ill.; DiDHM 109; GrEPR 14:
    169; PRFAS 124; QEQ (1936-
    37) 186, (1941-42) 114,
    (1948-49) 87.

HUYKE, Juan B. (1880-1961), author, politician
    BiP 205-6; DiHBC 516; Desd
    98-102; ECPR 6:456; GrEPR
    14:169, ill.; Hor 328-39;
    Ind 96-97; Por 275-76; PRFAS
    124; QEQ (1933-34) 87-88,
    (1936-37) 89, (1941-42) 114,
    (1948-49) 87-88; Tri 1:3-4.

I

ICKES, Harold Le Clair (1874-
1952), lawyer, author
    DicAB suppl.5:341-44; QEQ
    (1936-37) 89, (1941-42) 115.

IGARAVIDEZ, Leonardo (19th
cent.), sugar mill owner, politician
    DiHBC 517; EnsB 288-89; Gr-
    EPR 14:171.

IGARAVIDEZ, Leonardo, doctor
    RepM 308, ill.

IGARAVIDEZ GUTIERREZ, Enrique
(b.1898), lawyer
    QEQ (1936-37) 89, (1941-42)
    115, (1948-49) 88.

IGARTUA AVILES, Víctor, judge
BoHP 199; QEQ (1933-34) 88,
(1936-37) 89, (1941-42)
115-16.

IGLESIAS, Olga, singer
DiHBC 518; EGMPR 4:61-62;
GrEPR 14:171.

IGLESIAS, Santiago (1903-
1966), architect
GrEPR 9:95.

IGLESIAS DE LA CRUZ, José A.
(b.1902), lawyer
QEQ (1941-42) 237-38,
(1948-49) 88.

IGLESIAS FONT, Jaime (19th
cent.), politician
AlDU 13.

IGLESIAS GENEBREIRA, Juan
(1851-1899*), doctor, politician
Añas 41-43, ill.; CaM 237-
38; Crom 18; DiM 180-82;
Med 45-48; Mem 93.

IGLESIAS PANTIN, Santiago
(1870-1939), labor leader,
Resident Commissioner
BiP 206-7; BrECP 243; CiBPI
222(ill.), 238-41; CuB
1940:421, ill.; DiDHM 111,
ill.; DiHBC 518-19; DicAB
suppl.2:331-32; ECPR 6:
456-57; EPI 1:203-4; GrEPR
14:171, 172-73(ill.); HisD
47-48; HoIPR 61, ill.; Ho-
PP 139-53, ill.; LuO 77,
80-82, ill.; PriC 41, ill.;
PRFAS 125, ill.; PRP 129-
30; QEQ (1933-34) 88,
(1936-37) 89-90.

IGLESIAS PEREZ, Roberto (b.
1930), politician
LiPR 118, ill.

IGLESIAS SILVA, Santiago
(1895-1968), politician
GrEPR 14:171.

IMBERT, Fred, businessman
A 166, ill.

INCE, John Henry, government
official
RepM 83, ill.

INCLAN, Serafín, tobacco industrialist
A 31.

INES, Doña (16th cent.), Agüey-
baná's mother
EGMPR 1:37; MujDPR 11-12.

INFANTE, Isidoro (1897-1969),
doctor
QEQ (1933-34) 88, (1936-37)
90, (1948-49) 88; SobM 31-33.

INFANTE DIAZ DE OTAZU, Eduardo
(1878-1961), teacher
AlHP 397, ill.

IRIARTE MIRO, Celestino (1887-
1967), politician
A 46; And 170-72; GrEPR 14:
174; PriC 189; QEQ (1936-37)
90, (1941-42) 116, (1948-49)
88-89.

IRIZARRY, Carlos (b.1938),
artist
GrEPR 8:342, ill.; PaG 215.

IRIZARRY, Epifanio (b.1915),
artist
AlHP 340-41, ill.; BrECP 259;
GrEPR 8:344, ill.; PaG 197-
98; Pon 63; PRFAS 125-26.

IRIZARRY, Ivan (b.1933), banker
Port 177, 178(ill.)

IRIZARRY, José M. (b.1902),
pharmacist
QEQ (1933-34) 88-89, (1936-
37) 90.

IRIZARRY, Marcos (b.1936), artist
GrEPR 8:346, ill.

IRIZARRY ACARON, Edilberto (b.
1938), author
DiLP 2, pt.1:780-81.

IRIZARRY DE PUIG, Adolfina (b.
1893), teacher
EGMPR 1:229-30.

IRIZARRY YUNQUE, Carlos J. (b.
1922), lawyer, judge
GrEPR 14:174.

ISALES, Darisabel, singer
GrEPR 14:174.

ISERN APONTE, Lorenzo (b.1880),

politician
  CaDeT 199-200, ill.; GrEPR
  14:174; QEQ (1941-42) 241,
  (1948-49) 182.

ISERN GIMENEZ, Emigdio (b.
1868), engineer
  QEQ (1948-49) 89.

ISSASI, Francisco Arnaldo de
(d.1661), bishop
  Hi de la Ig 81.

Istomin, Marta see Montañez,
Marta

ITURRINO, Raúl G. (b.1941),
professor
  DirAS 4:256.

IZCOA DIAZ, Evaristo (1855-
1901), journalist
  AlHP 344, ill.

IZCOA MOURE, Jesús (b.1908),
politician
  GrEPR 14:174.

IZQUIERDO MORA, Luis (b.1931),
doctor, politician
  GrEPR 14:174.

IZQUIERDO STELLA, José G. (b.
1936), lawyer, politician
  GrEPR 14:174.

J

JANER ARIAS, Felipe (1880-
1935), lawyer
  QEQ (1933-34) 89, (1936-37)
  15.

JANER PALACIO, Ana (1888-1973)
psychiatrist
  CaM 242, 482; EGMPR 3:175-
  76, ill.

JANER SOLER, Felipe (1855-
1929), educator, author
  BiP 207-8; DiLP 2, pt.1:
  781-82; HoIPR 62, ill.; Ma
  59-62; PRFAS 127.

JANER Y SOLER, Rafael (1852-
1910), educator
  PuI 296-99.

JARABO, José R. (b.1944), lawyer, politician
  GrEPR 14:175; LiPR 33, ill.

JASPARD or JASPART, Carlos Car-
ville (19th cent.), doctor
  CaM 243.

JAUREYBO (16th cent.), Taíno
Indian chief
  GrEPR 14:175.

JENSEN, Herminio C. (b.1898),
businessman
  QEQ (1936-37) 90, (1941-42)
  116.

JEREZ, Hernando, colonist
  GrEPR 14:175.

JESUS, Agustín de, politician
  GrEPR 14:175.

JESUS, Angel R. de (b.1891),
judge
  QEQ (1948-49) 56.

JESUS, Esteban de (b.1951),
boxer
  PRUSA 9.

JESUS, Francisco Rafael de (b.
1891), doctor
  QEQ (1936-37) 58, (1941-42)
  76, (1948-49) 56.

JESUS, Iván de (b.1953), baseball player
  PRUSA 9.

JESUS, Salvador M. de (1927-
1969), author
  CaE 762; DiLP 2, pt.1:782-
  84; GrEPR 14:175; PRFAS 127.

JESUS CASTRO, Tomás de (1902-
1970), author, critic, journalist
  BiP 208-10; BoBP 87-90; DiLP
  2, pt.1:784-88; Ind 66; PRFAS
  127.

JESUS LOPEZ, Antonio de, pharmacist, political activist
  RepM 310.

JESUS RIVERA, Luis Gonzalo de
(b.1936), politician
  LiPR 35, ill.

JETT, Thomas Leland, government
official
  RepM 97, ill.

JIMENEZ, Francisco P. (b.1903),

poet, journalist, teacher
AntHistCag 254-55; AntPoe-
Cag 111-13; BiP 210-11; CaE
763; DiLP 2, pt.1:788-89;
PRFAS 128.

JIMENEZ, J. del C., doctor
RepM 305, ill.

JIMENEZ, Justo (19th cent.),
Hi de CR 189-90.

JIMENEZ, Manuel "Canario"
(1895-1975), composer, singer
Com 5; EPI 2:215-18; GrEPR
7:73, ill.

JIMENEZ CRUZ, Julio (b.1896),
politician
GrEPR 14:176; QEQ (1933-34)
89, (1936-37) 90.

JIMENEZ CRUZ, Manuel (d.1918),
doctor, educator
CaDeT 62, ill.; RepM 157,
ill.

JIMENEZ DE BETANCOURT, Nellie
(b.1924), businesswoman
EGMPR 3:43-44, ill.

JIMENEZ DE CASIANO, Nora (b.
1934), businesswoman
EGMPR 4:331-32, ill.

JIMENEZ Y DURAN, Juan Francisco (1783-1851), priest
BeHNPR 2:69-73, ill.

JIMENEZ GARCIA, Juan (d.1938),
businessman
CaDeT 60, ill.

JIMENEZ GARCIA, Lorenzo, lawyer
RepM 178, ill.

JIMENEZ HERNANDEZ, Adolfo (b.
1910), author
DiLP 2, pt.1:789-91.

JIMENEZ LOPEZ, Jorge L. (b.
1908), engineer
QEQ (1936-37) 90, (1941-42)
116, (1948-49) 192.

JIMENEZ LOPEZ, Juan B. (b.
1899), pharmacist
QEQ (1933-34) 89, (1936-37)
90.

JIMENEZ LUGO, Angel (b.1910),

poet, journalist
DiLP 2, pt.1:791-92; QEQ
(1948-49) 89.

JIMENEZ MALARET, René (b.1903),
author, journalist, critic
CaE 764; DiLP 2, pt.1:792-
95; PRFAS 128.

JIMENEZ MATTA, Teresa (1903-
1975), businesswoman
EGMPR 3:329-30, ill.

JIMENEZ MELENDEZ, Gaspar (b.
1936), politician
LiPR 36, ill.

JIMENEZ MENDEZ, Baltazar (b.
1931), politician
LiPR 118, ill.

Jiménez Moreno, Eduardo see
Giménez Moreno, Eduardo

JIMENEZ Y MORENO, Eleuterio (d.
1861), lawyer
BeHNPR 2:119-32, ill.

JIMENEZ OTERO, Víctor Rafael,
social worker
QEQ (1941-42) 116-17.

JIMENEZ PEREZ, Manuel (1772-
1781), bishop
BeHNPR 1:261-68, ill.; DiDHM
113; EnsB 1-12; Hi de la Ig
138-47; HisD 87.

JIMENEZ PREVIDI, Mila Rosa (b.
1949), painter
PaG 216.

JIMENEZ SANJURJO, Gabriel (ca.
1850-1909), doctor
CaDeT 232-33.

JIMENEZ SERRA, Buenaventura,
doctor
ProA 17-18.

JIMENEZ SERRA, Manuel, politician
ProA 17.

JIMENEZ SICARDO, Gustavo (b.
1888), lawyer, dramatist
DiLP 2, pt.1:795-96; GrEPR
14:176; Hor 370-73.

JIMENEZ SOLA, Enrique (b.1903*),
poet
AntHistCag 255; AntPoeCag

199-200; DiLP 2, pt.1:796-800.

JIMENEZ VAN HOY, María, advertising director, civic works
Port 131, 132(ill.)

JOGLAR CACHO, Manuel (b.1898), poet
BiP 211-12; BrECP 261; Di-DHM 113; ECPR 6:457; GrEPR 14:176; PlE 2:363-70, ill.; PRFAS 128.

JOHNSON, Harrison (1877-1965), politician
AntHistCag 337-38, 340 (ill.); RepM 80, ill.

JONES, William Ambrose (1865-1921), Catholic bishop
GrEPR 6:268-70.

JONES, William Atkinson (1849-1918), lawyer, politician
PriC 15.

JORDAN, Octavio, doctor, politician
CaM 245; DiM 183.

JOVET, Carmen Elda (b.1947), television reporter and newscaster
EGMPR 4:333-35, ill.

JUANCHO, Francisco (16th cent.), colonist
GrEPR 14:176.

JUBERT, José, industrialist
A 25-26.

JUDICE SUSONI, José (b.1869), police official
QEQ (1941-42) 117.

JULIA, Mario (1899-1956), doctor
CaM 246; QEQ (1936-37) 91, (1941-42) 117, (1948-49) 89.

JULIA, Raúl (b.1940), actor
CuB 1982:187-90, ill.; Port 41, 42(ill.); PRUSA 17, ill.

JULIA GARCIA, Ramón C. (b.1896), lawyer
QEQ (1933-34) 89, (1936-37)

91, (1941-42) 117.

JULIA MARIN, Ramón (1878-1917), author
BiP 212-14; CaE 765; DiLP 2, pt.1:800-804; ECPR 6:457; GrEPR 5:98-100, 14:176; Ind 98-99; PRFAS 128-29.

JUMACAO, Taíno Indian chief
GrEPR 14:176.

JUNGHANNS, Robert A., collector
DiHBC 562.

JUSTICIA, Andrés (b.1891), businessman
Tri 2:211-15.

JUVENAL ROSA, Pedro (b.1897), lawyer, author
Ind 99-100.

K

Kadosh, A. see Quiñones, Francisco Mariano

KAVETSKY, Roy (b.1946), artist
GrEPR 8:434.

KENRICK, Gleason Willis (b.1901), physicist, professor
QEQ (1941-42) 117-18, (1948-49) 89-90.

KERN, Howard Lewis (b.1886), lawyer
QEQ (1936-37) 186.

KLUMB, Henry (1905-1984), architect
GrEPR 9:97-106; Tra 290-91.

KNEIPPLE, Elizabeth (b.1902), poet, educator
EGMPR 4:225-26; Tri 1:89-96.

KOPPISCH DE CARDONA, Enrique (b.1904), pathologist, professor
CaM 247-48; DiHBC 564; QEQ (1936-37) 91, (1941-42) 118, (1948-49) 90.

KRUG, Frederick (b.1893), engineer
QEQ (1933-34) 89-90, (1936-37) 91.

KRUG, Julius A. (b.1907), federal official

QEQ (1948-49) 90.

KUCHNO, Paul, artist
    GrEPR 8:434.

KUSCHKE, Carl Gustav Paul (b.
1880), professor
    QEQ (1936-37) 91, (1941-42)
    118, (1948-49) 90-91.

L

LABADIE EURITE, Juan (b.1915),
professor
    QEQ (1948-49) 91.

LABARTHE, Pedro Juan (1906*-
1966), author, professor
    BiP 214-15; CaE 766-67;
    DiLP 2, pt.2:805-10; ECPR
    6:457; Ind 100; PRFAS 131;
    QEQ (1933-34) 90, (1936-37)
    186, (1941-42) 119, (1948-
    49) 91-92.

LABIOSA, Wilfredo (1937),
artist
    GrEPR 8:435.

LABOY, Luis, politician
    A 47; GrEPR 14:179.

LABRA, Rafael María de (1841-
1918), lawyer, journalist,
abolitionist
    BgP facing p.290, ill.; BiP
    215-17; DiDHM 115, ill.;
    GrEPR 14:179; HisD 50;
    PRFAS 131, ill.

LABRADA GREGORICH, Consuelo
(b.1926), pharmacist
    EGMPR 4:209-10, ill.

LACOMBA, Luis H., musician,
composer
    ArH 574-75.

LACOMBA ARANA, Manuel Eladio,
musician, composer
    ArH 574.

LA COSTA E IZQUIERDO, Ricardo
(b.1872), lawyer
    LM 125.

LACOT, Eduardo, doctor
    Crom 23-24.

LACROIX, Carlos Elío, author,
political activist

Ver 163-64, ill.

Lago, Genoveva see Storer de
Lago, Genoveva

LAGO, Jesús María (1873*-
1929*), poet, painter
    BiP 222-23; BrECP 263; CaE
    767; DiDHM 115, ill.; DiLP
    2, pt.2:810-12; ECPR 6:457-
    58; GrEPR 14:179, ill.; Ka
    30-31; PaH 414-17; PlE 2:
    75-86, ill.; PRFAS 132.

LAGUERRE, Enrique A. (b.1906),
author, educator
    BiP 224-27; BrECP 263-65,
    ill.; CaE 768-69; DiDHM 116,
    ill.; DiHBC 565-66; DiLP 2,
    pt.2:812-20; DicC 58; ECPR
    6:458; GrEPR 5:100-106, 14:
    180, ill.; Ind 100-106; PRFAS
    132-33, ill.; Vida 15-17.

LAGUNA DAPENA, Darío (1844-
1905), naval officer
    Guay 259-60.

LAIR, Clara (1895?-1973), poet
    BiP 227-29; BrECP 265; DiDHM
    145, ill.; DiLP 2, pt.2:
    1065-67; EGMPR 1:183-84, ill.;
    GrEPR 14:247; Per 31-34,
    ill.; PlE 2:431-41, ill.; PQ
    9; PRFAS 133, ill.; Vo 104-7.

LAKE, Mary O. (1876-1934), Baptist missionary
    AlHP 184, ill.

LALLANDE, Joseph G. (b.1893),
businessman
    QEQ (1936-37) 91, (1941-42)
    119-20.

LAMOUTTE, Beltrán Elías (b.1837?),
doctor, politician
    CaF 85; CaM 251-52; DiM 184;
    GrEPR 14:180.

LAMOUTTE, Sylvia María (b.1935),
musician
    GrEPR 14:180.

LANAUZE ROLON, José A. (1893-
1951), doctor, author
    AlHP 244, ill.; DiM 184-85.

LANDING, Jorge Luis, politicial
activist
    GrEPR 14:180

LANDIS, Walter K., Post Office
official
    RepM 54, ill.

LANDO, Francisco Manuel de
(16th cent.), governor
    GrEPR 14:180; HisD 50.

LANDRON BOU, Iris M., journalist
    EGMPR 3:293.

LANDRON Y LANDRON, Rafael (b.
1880), labor leader, Methodist
minister
    QEQ (1936-37) 91-92, (1941-
42) 120.

LANDRON OTERO, Enrique, politician
    GrEPR 14:180.

LARGE AQUILI, Simón (b.1872),
lawyer
    LM 129.

Lanzos, Ana de see Cauzos, Ana
de

LARRINAGA, Tulio (1847-1917),
politician, Resident Commissioner, orator
    CiBPI 176(ill.), 195-97;
    DiDHM 117; DiHBC 567-68;
    DicAB 6:8-9; Exp 289-92,
    ill.; GenP 77; GrEPR 14:
    180(ill.), 181; HisD 51;
    HoIPR 63, ill.; LPR 1006,
    1008, 1009, 1011; PuI 316-
    19; RepM 28, ill.

LARROCA, Eduardo (b.1895),
administrator
    A 170; QEQ (1933-34) 90-91,
    (1936-37) 92, (1941-42)
    120, (1948-49) 92.

LARROCA PIERRET, Eduardo (b.
1870), government official
    QEQ (1936-37) 92.

LASA DIAZ, Gladys (b.1911),
lawyer
    EGMPR 3:177-78.

LASALLE DEL VALLE, Beatriz (b.
1881*), teacher, feminist,
author
    DiHBC 569; EGMPR 4:295-98,
    ill.; MujDPR 170-72, ill.;
    MujPu 155; PQ 9.

LASALLE DOVAL, Francisco (b.
1858), judge
    RepM 277, ill.

LASSISSE LIZANA, Alfredo (1857-
1933), medical clerk
    GenB 352-53, ill.

LASSISSE RIVERA, Alfredo (1885-
1945), doctor
    CaM 254-55; GenB 416-17,
    ill.; HoIPR 63, ill.

LASSISSE RIVERA, Enrique (b.
1890), doctor
    CaM 255-56; GenB 417-18,
    ill.; QEQ (1936-37) 92,
    (1941-42) 120, (1948-49) 92-
    93.

LASTRA CHARRIEZ, Rafael Alonso
(1887-1946), politician
    GrEPR 14:181; HoIPR 63-64,
    ill.; Per 148-50.

LATONI RIVERA, Raúl (b.1937),
politician
    GrEPR 14:181.

LAUGIER, Agustín R. (b.1889),
doctor
    QEQ (1933-34) 194, (1936-37)
    92, (1941-42) 120, (1948-49)
    93.

LAUGIER, Juan Ramón (1891-1942),
doctor
    QEQ (1936-37) 92-93, (1941-
42) 121.

LAVANDERO, Ramón (1887-1953),
doctor, author
    A 93; CaM 257-58; DiLP 2, pt.
    2:820-22.

LAZARO, José M. (b.1909), author,
professor
    DiLP 2, pt.2:822-24.

LEAHY, William (1875-1959),
governor
    CuB 1941:501-2, ill., 1959:
    250; Desf 122-25, ill.; Di-
    DHM 117; DiHBC 438; DicAB
    suppl.6:373-74; GrEPR 14:182;
    QEQ (1941-42) 121, (1948-49)
    93-94.

LEAKE, Harry P. (b.1875), lawyer
    RepM 300.

LEAL SOLEY, Gloria, journalist
EGMPR 4:227.

LEBRON, José Ramón (b.1916),
Baptist leader
QEQ (1933-34) 91.

LEBRON, Lolita (b.1919), revolutionary
GrEPR 14:181, ill.

LEBRON, Santos, shoemaker
Ka 94.

LEBRON RODRIGUEZ, Ramón (1868-
1959), author
DiLP 2, pt.2:824-25; QEQ
(1933-34) 91, (1936-37) 93,
(1941-42) 121, (1948-49)
94; Vida 59-60.

LEBRON VELAZQUEZ, José R. (b.
1916), Evangelist minister
QEQ (1936-37) 93, (1941-42)
121, (1948-49) 94.

LECCIA, Luis, poet
Ver 189.

LE COMPTE, Eugenio (b.1886),
educator, lawyer
QEQ (1933-34) 91-92, (1936-
37) 93, (1941-42) 121-22,
(1948-49) 93.

LECOMPTE, Luisa, musician
MusMP 255.

LECOMPTE, Sergio (d.1912),
musician, teacher
MusMP 255.

LEDESMA DAVILA, Sylvia, manager, author
EGMPR 3:45-46, ill.; Hor
344-48.

LEDRU, André Pierre (1761-
1825), naturalist
ECPR 6:458; HisD 51.

LEE, Albert Edward (b.1873),
businessman
QEQ (1936-37) 93-94, (1941-
42) 122.

LEE, Atherton, agronomist
QEQ (1936-37) 94, (1941-42)
123.

LEE, Muna(1895-1965), author,

wife of Gov. Muñoz Marín
ConA 25-28R:419; Not 413-14;
QEQ (1933-34) 92, (1936-37)
94, (1941-42) 123, (1948-49)
94-95; Tra 100, 106, 114-15.

LEE Y TAPIA, Waldemar F. (b.
1906), businessman
QEQ (1933-34) 194, (1936-37)
94, (1948-49) 95.

LEE Y TAPIA, William E. A. (b.
1898), businessman
QEQ (1936-37) 94.

LEFEBRE, Enrique (1880-1942),
author, critic, lawyer
BiP 229; BoBP 35-38; DiLP 2,
pt.2:825-26; Guay 260; PRFAS
133-34; Una 179-82.

LEFRANC, Eugenio (b.1862), engineer
QEQ (1936-37) 94.

LEGRAND, Adolfo F. (b.1894),
pharmacist
QEQ (1936-37) 94, (1941-42)
123-24.

LEGRAND, J. Federico (1858-1928),
pharmacist, scientist
AlDU 19; HoIPR 64, ill.

LEMERY, José (b.1811), governor
BeHNPR 2:109-13, ill.; DiDHM
117; DiHBC 453; GrEPR 14:182.

LEON, José M. de, priest
AlDJ 145, ill.

LEON, Rafael, lawyer
Crom 51.

LEON, Vicente (b.1900), politi-
cian
AlDJ 7-8, ill.; GrEPR 14:182;
QEQ (1941-42) 124.

LEON GELABERT, Mario (b.1921),
author
QEQ (1948-49) 95-96.

LEON Y LUGO, Sergio (b.1882),
lawyer
QEQ (1933-34) 92-93, (1936-
37) 95, (1941-42) 124.

LEON PARRA, Manuel (1877-1950),
lawyer
AlHP 259, ill.

LESPIER, Edelmiro (1855-1957),
journalist
    GenB 366-67, ill.

LEVIS BERNARD, José Elías
(1871-1942), painter, author,
journalist
    BiP 229-31; Cre 57-61; Di-
    LP 2, pt.2:826-28; GrEPR
    5:106-7, 8:119-21, ill.,
    14:182; HoIPR 64, ill.; Ind
    107-8; PlE 1:270; PRFAS
    134; QEQ (1933-34) 93,
    (1936-37) 95, (1941-42)
    124.

LEWIS, Oscar (1914-1970), author, sociologist
    ConA P1:378-79; DiHBC 570-
    71.

LEZCANO, Sixto (b.1953), baseball player
    PRUSA 17, ill.

LICIAGA JUARBE, Manuel Epifanio (1837-1900), doctor
    BoHP 113-14, 115(ill.)

LIENAU, Ernesto H., politician
    ProA 26, ill.

LIENAU, Oscar, politician
    ProA 7-8.

LIMON DE ARCE, José (1877-
1940), author, journalist
    BoBP 21-25; CaE 771; DiLP
    2, pt.2:835-37; GrEPR 14:
    182; PRFAS 134; Una 191-97.

LINDSAY, Samuel McCune (b.
1869), educator
    QEQ (1936-37) 186-87.

LINDSTROM, L. L. (b.1893), engineer
    QEQ (1933-34) 93, (1936-37)
    95, (1941-42) 125.

LIPPITT, William Fontaine
(1865-1958), doctor
    CaM 262-63; Nues 42(ill.),
    43-44; QEQ (1933-34) 93-94,
    (1936-37) 95-96, (1941-42)
    125, (1948-49) 96.

LIS DE CHAVIER, Hilda de (b.
1922), lawyer
    EGMPR 3:151-52.

LIVINGSTONE, Clara E. (b.1900),
aviator
    EGMPR 4:215-16, ill.; QEQ
    (1936-37) 96, (1941-42)
    125-26.

LIZANA, Francisco de (16th cent.)
pharmacist
    CaF 87, 171-72; GrEPR 14:182.

LIZAUR, Francisco de (16th
cent.), accountant
    DiHBC 587-88; GrEPR 14:182.

Lomar, Martha see López de
Victoria de Reus, María

LOMBA, José María, author
    Esp 101-6.

LOMBA GUERRERO, Ignacio (b.
1883), businessman
    QEQ (1933-34) 94-95, (1936-
    37) 96.

LONGO, Florentino, businessman
    A 30-31.

LOPEZ, Adalberto (b.1943),
historian, author
    ConA 103:297.

LOPEZ, Antonio, fashion illus-
trator, designer
    Port 193, 194(ill.)

LOPEZ, Domingo (b.1942), painter
    GrEPR 8:407; PaG 214-15.

LOPEZ, Eddie (1940-1971), author, journalist
    GrEPR 14:183.

LOPEZ, Frutos, Army officer
    DeADeA 474-80.

LOPEZ, Julio César (b.1926),
author
    DiDHM 117-18; DiLP 2, pt.2:
    837-38.

López, Magda see López de Victoria, Magdalena

LOPEZ, Pedro, painter
    GrEPR 8:435.

LOPEZ, Ramón B., journalist
    CiBPI 173(ill.), 182-85.

LOPEZ AGUSTO DE LA MATA, Juan

(17th cent.), bishop
  Hi de la Ig 70-72.

LOPEZ ANTONGIORGI, José A.
(1881-1938), doctor
  CaM 267; HoIPR 64, ill.;
  QEQ (1933-34) 194, (1936-
  37) 96.

LOPEZ ANTONGIORGI, Pascual (b.
1890), Army officer
  QEQ (1936-37) 187.

López Baños see López de Baños

LOPEZ BARALT, José (b.1906),
author
  QEQ (1941-42) 126.

LOPEZ CABALLERO, Adair (b.
1916), teacher
  QEQ (1948-49) 96-97.

LOPEZ CARLO, Ulises, businessman
  RepM 229, ill.

LOPEZ CEPERO BONANO, Mariana
F. (b.1893), charity work
  EGMPR 3:331-32, ill.

LOPEZ COLON, Antonio L. (b.
1886), lawyer
  QEQ (1941-42) 126.

LOPEZ CRUZ, Esteban, author
  DeADeA 215-16.

LOPEZ CRUZ, Francisco (b.
1909), musician, composer
  BiP 231-32; BrECP 273,
  ill.; DiDHM 118; GrEPR 14:
  183; PRFAS 135.

LOPEZ CUADRA, Antonio, businessman, political activist
  RepM 125, ill.

LOPEZ CHAAR, Alfonso (b.1939),
politician
  LiPR 120, ill.

LOPEZ DE BAÑOS, Miguel (19th
cent.), governor
  DiDHM 118; DiHBC 451-52;
  GrEPR 14:183.

LOPEZ DE HARO, Damián (1581-
1648), bishop, author
  DiDHM 118-19; DiLP 2, pt.2:
  839-42; GrEPR 6:256, 258;

Hi de la Ig 74-80.

LOPEZ DE LA ROSA, Leandro (b.
1889), doctor
  CaM 268; QEQ (1936-37) 187,
  (1941-42) 126, (1948-49) 97.

LOPEZ DE RAMOS CASELLAS, Ricarda
(1879-1968), feminist, suffragette, teacher
  EGMPR 4:243-44, ill.; MujDPR
  177-79, ill.

LOPEZ DE VELEZ, Ana (b.1867?),
feminist, suffragette, teacher
  DiHBC 589; EGMPR 4:245-46,
  ill.; GrEPR 14:183; MujDPR
  134-36, ill.

LOPEZ DE VICTORIA, Anastasio,
businessman
  Nuestr 128-30.

LOPEZ DE VICTORIA, José (ca.1869-
1939), artist
  GrEPR 8:126-27.

LOPEZ DE VICTORIA, Juan de Dios
(b.1868), priest
  GrEPR 6:289.

LOPEZ DE VICTORIA, Magdalena (b.
1900), poet, painter
  AlHY 172, 226-27; BiP 232-
  33; CaE 777; DiLP 2, pt.2:
  852-55; EGMPR 1:155-57, ill.;
  PRFAS 135; QEQ (1941-42)238,
  (1948-49) 99.

LOPEZ DE VICTORIA, Nicolás (19th
cent.), journalist, politician
  GenB 325; Hi de M 199; Nuestr
  41-42.

LOPEZ DE VICTORIA, Pelegrín
(1850-1942), author, journalist
  AlHY 227-28; DiLP 2, pt.2:
  851-52.

LOPEZ DE VICTORIA DE REUS, María
(b.1893), author, feminist
  DiHBC 589; DiLP 2, pt.2:855-
  57; DiDHM 119-20; EGMPR 1:
  159-60, ill.; GrEPR 14:183;
  MujDPR 223-35, ill.; PRFAS
  135.

López de Victoria Fernández,
Magda see López Fernández,
Magda

LOPEZ DEL CAMPO, Rafael (b. 1936), sculptor
GrEPR 8:348, ill.; PaG 211.

LOPEZ DEL VALLE, A., lawyer, landowner
RepM 184, ill.

LOPEZ DEL VALLE, Federico (b. 1891), farmer
A 151; QEQ (1933-34) 95, (1936-37) 96, (1941-42) 126.

LOPEZ DEL VALLE, Manuel F. (b. 1890), doctor
CaM 268; QEQ (1936-37) 96.

LOPEZ DIAZ, Enrique (b.1920), lawyer
RepM 271, ill.

LOPEZ DIRUBE, Rolando (b. 1928), artist
GentI 162-66; GrEPR 8:350, ill.

LOPEZ DOMINGUEZ, Francisco A. (b.1890), engineer, author
A 67; QEQ (1933-34) 194-97, (1936-37) 96-98, (1941-42) 126-28, (1948-49) 97-99; Tri 1:421-28.

LOPEZ GARCIA, José (b.1940), lawyer, politician
GrEPR 14:184; LiPR 40, ill.

LOPEZ IRIZARRY, Ramón (b. 1897), pharmacist
GrEPR 14:184; QEQ (1933-34) 95, (1936-37) 98, (1941-42) 128-29.

LOPEZ Y JIMENEZ, Esteban (b. 1845?), doctor
CaM 265.

LOPEZ Y JUBES, José Antonio (1903-1956), doctor, painter
DiM 204.

LOPEZ LANDRON, Rafael (1863-1917), lawyer, politician
Desd 213-21; DiLP 2, pt.2: 842-43; GrEPR 14:184-85, ill.; HoIPR 65, ill.; LM 120; Orad 273-75; RepM 141, ill.; SobM 117-20.

LOPEZ LOPEZ, Joaquín (1900-

1942), author
BiP 233-34; BrECP 273-74; CaE 776; DiDHM 119; DiLP 2, pt.2:843-45; GrEPR 14:185; Guay 260; PRFAS 135-36.

LOPEZ MARTINEZ, Orlando (b.1921), politician
LiPR 126, ill.

LOPEZ MEDRANO, Andrés (19th cent.), doctor
CaM 263-64.

LOPEZ MELGAREJO, Juan (16th cent.), governor
DiDHM 119; GrEPR 14:185.

LOPEZ MOLINA Y LOPEZ CEPERO, Jesús María (b.1892), accountant
QEQ (1933-34) 96, (1936-37) 98, (1941-42) 129.

LOPEZ MONTANO, J. Isaac, businessman
RepM 284, ill.

LOPEZ MUÑOZ, Gustavo (b.1904), chemist
QEQ (1948-49) 99.

LOPEZ NUSSA, Rafael (1885-1943*), doctor
AlHP 277, ill.; CaM 268-69; QEQ (1933-34) 96, (1936-37) 98-99.

LOPEZ QUIÑONES, Eurípides, doctor
RepM 286, ill.

LOPEZ PACHECO, Olaguibeet A. (b.1915), veterianarian
QEQ (1948-49) 99-100.

LOPEZ RAMIREZ, Benigno (1896-1965), artisan
San 46-48.

LOPEZ RAMIREZ, Jorge Emilio (b.1921), engineer, educator
QEQ (1948-49) 100.

LOPEZ RIVERA, Florence (b.1911), pharmacist, hospital administrator
EGMPR 3:333-34.

LOPEZ RODRIGUEZ, Carlos (b. 1903), educator
QEQ (1948-49) 100.

LOPEZ ROIG, Lucy, clinical psychologist, personnel officer
    EGMPR 3:105-6, ill.

LOPEZ SANABRIA, Martín (b. 1908), engineer, author
    QEQ (1948-49) 100.

LOPEZ SANCHEZ, Dionisio (19th cent.), doctor
    CaM 264.

LOPEZ SANCHEZ, Francisco (1883-1950), author
    DiLP 2, pt.2:845-46; QEQ (1933-34) 96, (1936-37) 99, (1941-42) 129, (1948-49) 100-101; Vida 20-28.

LOPEZ SANTORI, Maica, artist
    GrEPR 8:435.

LOPEZ SICARDO, Rafael (1875-1937), doctor, politician, author
    CaM 269-70; DiM 204-6; Ho-IPR 65, ill.; QEQ (1936-37) 99.

LOPEZ SOBA, Elías (b.1927), musician, teacher
    BrECP 274; GrEPR 14:185; Mus en P 155-56; PRFAS 136.

LOPEZ SOTO, Danny (b.1941), politician
    GrEPR 14:185; LiPR 32, ill.

LOPEZ SURIA, Violeta (b.1926), author
    BrECP 274-75; CaE 776-77; DiLP 2, pt.2:846-51; DicC 60; EGMPR 1:161-63, ill.; GrEPR 14:185; PQ 38; PRFAS 136.

LOPEZ TIZOL, Eduardo (b.1883), lawyer
    QEQ (1941-42) 129.

LOPEZ VEGA, José (b.1900), politician, businessman
    GrEPR 14:185.

LORAND DE OLAZAGASTI, Adelaida, educator, author
    PRFAS 137.

LORENZI, Santiago F. (b.1865),

businessman
    DeTUP 21-24.

LOUBRIEL RIVERA, Oscar (b.1900), educator
    QEQ (1941-42) 129-30, (1948-49) 101.

LOWMAN, León (b.1950), artist
    GrEPR 8:408.

LOZADA, Justo Pastor (b.1902), translator, lawyer
    QEQ (1948-49) 101.

LOZANO, Alfredo (b.1913), sculptor
    GrEPR 8:352, ill.

LUBE DE DROZ, Josefina, author, teacher
    EGMPR 1:301-2.

LUCCA IRIZARRY, Rigoberto (b. 1951), painter
    GrEPR 8:435.

LUCCHETTI, Antonio (1888-1958), engineer
    GrEPR 14:186.

LUCIANO, José S. (b.1901), pharmacist
    A 104, ill.; QEQ (1941-42) 238, (1948-49) 101.

LUGO, Ariel E. (b.1943), author, professor
    ConA 41-42R:432-33.

LUGO, Elena (b.1910), professor
    DirAS 4:326.

LUGO, Nick (b.1902), businessman
    Port 153, 154(ill.)

LUGO, Pedro R., pharmacist
    A 103.

LUGO, Samuel (b.1905), poet
    BiP 238-39; BrECP 275; CaE 780-81; CiuP 25-26; DiDHM 120; DiLP 2, pt.2:857-61; ECPR 6:459; GrEPR 14:186; PRFAS 137-38.

LUGO BOUGAL, Delia (b.1931), lawyer, judge
    EGMPR 3:179.

LUGO QUIÑONES, Eurípides J.
(b.1979), accountant
  QEQ (1948-49) 101-2.

LUGO SILVA, Enrique, educator,
author
  AntHistCag 786, ill.

LUGO VIÑA, Eduardo, politician
  GrEPR 14:186; Guay 261-63.

LUGO VIÑA, Grace de (b.186?),
charity work
  EGMPR 4:229-30.

LUGO VIÑAS, José, doctor
  CaM 270.

LUGOVINA, Francisco (b.1940),
businessman
  Port 85, 86(ill.)

LUIS, Juan (b.1940), governor
of the Virgin Islands
  PRUSA 17, ill.

Luis de Añasco see Añasco,
Luis

LUISA ,"La Cacica" (16th
cent.), Taína Indian
  EGMPR 1:35, ill.; GrEPR 14:
  368; MujDPR 12-13.

LUKAS, Anton C. (b.1908),
teacher
  QEQ (1941-42) 130, (1948-
  49) 102.

LUNA Y LOPEZ, José de (19th
cent.), doctor
  CaM 270-71.

LLAMAS, Nestor (b.1930), civic
leader
  Port 63, 64(ill.)

LLANO, Joaquín del, printer
  ArH 519.

LLANOS, Victorio (b.1897),
poet
  Desd 293-95; DiLP 2, pt.2:
  861-62.

LLAUGER, Carlos, lawyer
  Tri 2:81-86.

LLAVAT RODRIGUEZ, Francisco,
dentist
  GenB 422-23.

LLAVERIAS Y ARRENDONDO, Federico,
Dominican diplomat, author
  QEQ (1936-37) 99.

LLENZA BUSO, Alice (b.1910),
teacher, author
  EGMPR 1:303-5.

LLENZA BUSO, Harry B. (b.1904),
lawyer
  QEQ (1933-34) 96-97, (1936-
  37) 99, (1941-42) 130,
  (1948-49) 102.

LLERAS DELGADO, Víctor L. (b.
1924), businessman
  Ka 127.

LLOBET DIAZ, Josefina (1898-
1967), politician
  EGMPR 2:33, ill.; GrEPR 14:
  187; PriC 79.

LLOBET DIAZ, Ramón (b.1893),
politician
  GrEPR 14:187.

LLOMPART, Julio V. (b.1895),
businessman
  QEQ (1933-34) 97, (1936-37)
  99, (1941-42) 130, (1948-49)
  102.

LLOREDA, Enrique, judge
  ProA 66.

LLORENS, Washington (b.1900),
author, pharmacist
  And 270-74; BiP 243-44; CaF
  89; DiDHM 121; DiHBC 592-93;
  DiLP 2, pt.2:862-67; ECPR 6:
  459; GrEPR 1:x-xi, ill.; 14:
  186; PRFAS 139-40; QEQ (1933-
  34) 97, (1936-37) 100, (1941-
  42) 131, (1948-49) 102.

LLORENS TORRES, Luis (1876-
1944), author, lawyer, politician
  And 92-96; BiP 239-43; Br-
  ECP 271-72, ill.; CaE 773-
  74; CiBPI 226(ill.), 261-64;
  DiDHM 121-22, ill.; DiHBC
  591-92; DiLP 2, pt.2:867-75;
  ECPR 6:459; GenP 95; GrEPR
  14:187, 188-89(ill.); HisD
  52; PlE 2:53-71, ill.; PRFAS
  139, ill.; QEQ (1936-37) 100,
  (1941-42) 130-32; Tri 2:53-
  59; VPR 135-38, 169.

LLORENS TORRES, Soledad (1880-1968), poet
DiDHM 122; DiLP 2, pt.2: 875-77; EGMPR 1:165-66, ill.; MujDPR 153-54, ill.

LLORT, Julio (b.1911), artist
GrEPR 8:435.

LLOVERAS SOLER, Ramón (b. 1890), businessman
QEQ (1933-34) 97, (1936-37) 100, (1941-42) 131, (1948-49) 103.

LLOVET RILDON, María (b.1859), teacher
DiHBC 593; EGMPR 1:307-8, ill.; MujDPR 57-58, ill.; MujPu 117-18.

LLOVIO DE TORRES, Antonia (b. 1908), lawyer
EGMPR 3:181.

LLUBERAS Y RODRIGUEZ, Arturo Santiago (b.1874), politician
GrEPR 14:190; QEQ (1933-34) 97-98, (1936-37) 100-101; RepM 173, ill.; Tri 1:113-19.

LLUBERAS SAVIÑON, René Bienvenido (b.1896), chemical technician, consul
QEQ (1933-34) 98, (1936-37) 187.

LLUCH, Erick R. (b.1951), painter
GrEPR 8:435.

LLUCH MORA, Francisco (b. 1924), author, professor
AlHY 159(ill.), 174-75, 224; And 205-8; BiP 244-45; CaE 774-75; DiDHM 122; DiLP 2, pt.2: 877-83; ECPR 6: 460; GrEPR 14:190; PRFAS 140.

LLUVERAS, José F., politician
GrEPR 14:190, ill.

Lluveras y Rodríguez, Arturo see Lluberas y Rodríguez, Arturo

M

MABODAMACA "Mabó El Grande"

(16th cent.), Taíno Indian chief
GrEPR 14:191.

MAC ALLISTER, María, teacher, poet
EstCR 1:53-55.

MCCASKEY, Charles Irving (b. 1877), secretary
QEQ (1936-37) 106-7.

MAC LEARY, James Harvey (b. 1845), judge
RepM 26, ill.

MCCLELAND, Thomas Brown (b. 1886), horticulturist
QEQ (1936-37) 107.

MCCONNELL, Herbert S. (b.1905), lawyer
QEQ (1948-49) 108-9.

MCCORMICK, Santiago (19th cent.), sugar industry promoter
DiHBC 616.

MACIAS CASADO, Manuel (19th cent.), soldier, governor
DiDHM 123; GrEPR 14:191, 192 (ill.)

MACJONES, Walter, politician
GrEPR 14:191, ill.

MCMANUS, James Edward (b.1900), Catholic bishop
AlHP 157, ill.; GrEPR 6:285.

MACHIAVELO BETANCOURT, José A. (1862-1902), poet
DiLP 2, pt.2:884; PoA 263-77, ill.

MACHIAVELO BETANCOURT, Nicolás (1856-1908), poet
PoA 253-55.

MACHIN, María E. (1884-1971), teacher
DiHBC 594; EGMPR 1:309-10, ill.; MujDPR 204-6, ill.; PQ 10.

MACHIN, Rafael B. (b.1929), politician
GrEPR 14:193.

MACHUCA, Felipe (b.1914), dramatist

DiLP 2, pt.2:884-85.

MACHUCA, Julio (b.1908), author, government official
BiP 245-46; DiLP 2, pt.2:
885-87; GrEPR 5:108-9; Ind
109-11; PRFAS 141.

Machuchal see Rodríguez, Adalberto

MADERA, Simón (1875-1957),
musician, composer
BiP 246-47; BrECP 177;
GenB 53; GrEPR 14:193; Mus-
MP 288-89; PRFAS 141.

MADERA Y REYES, José B. (19th
cent.), politician
GenB 300-301; Nuestr 92-93.

MADRAZO, Higenio (b.1919),
priest
AlHP 160, ill.

MADRAZO, José, businessman
A 137.

MADURO, José A. (b.1907),
artist
GrEPR 8:150.

MAGRIÑA, Ramón, banker
A 70, ill.

Malaret, Augusto see Malaret
Yordán, Augusto

MALARET, Marisol, beauty queen
GentI 11-21; GrEPR 14:193,
194-95(ill.)

MALARET YORDAN, Augusto (1878-
1967), author, lexicographer
BiP 247-49; BrECP 277; Ci-
BPI 225(ill.), 264-66; Di-
DHM 123-24; DiHBC 595; Di-
LP 2, pt.2:887-93; ECPR 6:
193, ill.; PIE 2:217-24,
ill.; PRFAS 141-42.

MALARET YORDAN, Pedro (b.
1863), doctor
CaM 274; DiM 207-9; QEQ
(1933-34) 197, (1936-37)
101; RepM 130, ill.

MALCOLM, George Arthur (b.
1881), lawyer
QEQ (1941-42) 132.

MALDONADO, Adál Adalberto,
photographer
Port 208.

MALDONADO, Alexander W. (b.
1935*), journalist
BiP 249-50; DiDHM 124; ECPR
6:460; GrEPR 14:196; PRFAS
142; SobM 34-36, 114-16, 152-
55.

MALDONADO, Antonio (b.1920),
painter
GrEPR 8:408; PaG 202.

MALDONADO, Carlos, painter
GrEPR 8:436.

MALDONADO, Ismael (1881-1963),
educator
AlHP 433-34, ill.

MALDONADO, Juan (b.1941), painter
GrEPR 8:436; PaG 236.

MALDONADO, Mariano, musician,
composer
ArH 531-32.

MALDONADO, Teófilo (1906-1963),
author, biographer
DiLP 2, pt.2:893-94; HoPP
11-14.

MALDONADO DENIS, Manuel (b.1933),
professor, author
BrECP 277-78; DiDHM 124; GrEPR
14:196; PRFAS 142.

MALDONADO MALDONADO, Salustiano
(b.1891), labor leader, politician
GrEPR 14:196; QEQ (1948-49)
103-4.

MALDONADO SANTIAGO, Rigoberto
(b.1905), pharmacist
QEQ (1941-42) 132.

MALDONADO SIERRA, Eduardo, doctor
A 104-6, ill.

MALDONADO TORRES, Juan (b.1937),
politician
GrEPR 14:228.

MANAUTOU, Gregorio (b.1886),
chemist
QEQ (1948-49) 104.

MANCEVO Y MORENO, Francisco

(1822-1875), doctor
   CaM 275.

MANES, Charles S. (b.1872),
police official
   RepM 92, ill.

MANESCAU, Narciso, businessman
   Ka 31-32.

MANESCAU Y CONDE, Miguel (b.
1889), engineer, politician
   QEQ (1936-37) 101.

MANGUAL, Ivan (b.1951), athlete
   GrEPR 14:196, ill.

MANGUAL DE CESTERO, Estela (b.
1865), poet, singer
   EGMPR 1:167-69, ill.; Muj-
   DPR 116-18, ill.; MujP 123;
   MujPu 105-9; MusMP 179-80.

MANGUAL DE CESTERO, Teresa
(1870-1930), journalist, civic
leader
   EGMPR 4:149-50.

MANRIQUE CARTAGENA, Nicolás,
industrialist
   Tri 2:283-89.

MANRIQUE GIL, Cipriano (b.
1875), businessman
   CaDeT 214-15, ill.; QEQ
   (1936-37) 187; RepM 217,
   ill.

MANRIQUE SOLA, Enrique (b.
1907), politician
   GrEPR 14:196; QEQ (1936-37)
   101.

MANSO, Alonso (d.1539), bishop
   BeHNPR 1:201-8; DiDHM 125;
   GrEPR 6:252(ill.), 253; Hi
   de la Ig 33-37; HisD 53.

MANZANEDO, Bernardino de (16th
cent.), priest
   GrEPR 14:197.

MANZANO AVIÑO, Pedro (b.1884),
author
   Guay 284; QEQ (1933-34) 99,
   (1936-37) 101.

MARANGES, Federico R. (b.
1902), chemist, engineer

QEQ (1941-42) 133.

MARCANO, Hipólito (b.1913),
lawyer, politician
   DiDHM 125; GrEPR 14:197,
   ill.; Nues 76-79, ill.; PriC
   119-20, ill.; PRFAS 142-43.

MARCANO, Luis J., chemist, businessman
   A 167.

MARCANO DE RIVERA, José Ciriaco
(1861?-1923), doctor
   CaM 276; DiM 209-10.

Marcial, Odon see Coll y Cuchí,
Cayetano

MARCIAL BURGOS, Víctor A. (b.
1924), doctor
   DiHBC 600; PRFAS 143-44.

MARCIAL DE LEON, Carmen (b.1931),
union official
   Port 97, 98(ill.)

MARCIAL QUIÑONES, José (1827-
1893), politician, teacher
   S 84.

MARCOS MORALES, Miguel (b.1886),
lawyer, politician
   GrEPR 14:197; QEQ (1933-34)
   99, (1936-37) 102, (1941-42)
   133.

MARCHAND SICARDO, Juan, businessman
   Tri 2:151-55.

MARCHANY, Sadot, (b.1937), artist
   GrEPR 8:436.

MARCHANY MERCADO, Antonio (b.
1906), lawyer
   QEQ (1941-42) 133, (1948-49)
   104.

MARCHESI, José María (19th
cent.), governor
   GrEPR 14:197.

MARGARIDA LLENZA, Guillermo,
businessman
   A 152.

MARGENAT, Alfredo (b.1907),
author
   DiLP 2, pt.2:894-96; PRFAS
   144.

MARGENAT, Hugo (1933-1957),
poet
    BrECP 278-79, ill.; CaE
    786; DiLP 2, pt.2:896-97;
    GrEPR 14:197; Per 27-29,
    ill.; PRFAS 144-45.

MARI, Esther, actress
    DelMu 140-44, ill.

MARI BRAS, Juan (b.1928*),
lawyer, politician
    BrECP 279-80; DiDHM 125-26;
    GrEPR 14:198(ill.), 199;
    PRFAS 145.

MARI MATTEI, Juan (1874-1925),
farm worker
    GenB 333, ill.

MARIANI, Pedro Domingo (1880-
1921), poet
    AlHY 211; DiLP 2, pt.2:897-
    98.

MARIANI, Domingo (b.1881),
painter
    AlHY 237, ill.

MARIANI, Xavier, businessman
    Crom 81.

MARICHAL, Carlos (1923-1969),
artist
    BiP 250-51; BrECP 280-81;
    DiDHM 126; ECPR 6:460-61;
    GrEPR 8:199-201, 354, ill.;
    PRFAS 145.

MARICHAL, Poli, painter
    GrEPR 8:436.

MARIN, Augusto, artist
    GrEPR 8:264, ill.; PaG 195-
    97.

MARIN, Calisto Buenaventura
(b.1843), pharmacist
    Apu 58-60.

MARIN, Francisco Gonzalo
(1863-1897), author, orator,
musician, typographer
    BiP 251-52; BrECP 281-82;
    CaE 827-28; CiBPI 164-68;
    DiDHM 127; DiLP 2, pt.2:
    898-901; ECPR 6:461; GrEPR
    14:199; LPR 1040, 1041;
    MeO 189-209; PlE 1:229-48,
    ill.; PRFAS 146; PuI 353-
    62.

MARIN, Gerard Paul (b.1922),
author
    DiLP 2, pt.2:901-3; GrEPR
    14:199.

Marín, Manuel see Marín Gautier,
Manuel

Marín, Ramón see Marín Solá,
Ramón

MARIN, Sabás (19th-20th cent.),
governor
    DiDHM 126.

MARIN CASTILLA, Américo, journalist, businessman
    Ver 186-87, ill.

MARIN CASTILLA, Ramón, served
in Cuban militia
    Ver 171-72, ill.

MARIN CASTILLO DE MUÑOZ RIVERA,
Amalia (1872-1957), politician
    EGMPR 2:35, ill.; GrEPR 14:
    199, ill., 200(ill.); PriC
    78.

MARIN GAUTIER, Manuel (b.1886),
pharmacist, politician
    A 102; CaF 92-94; GenB 385-
    86, ill.; GrEPR 14:200.

MARIN MARIEN, Eduardo (b.1882),
judge, author
    QEQ (1936-37) 102; RepM 171,
    ill.

MARIN MOLINA, Adolfo (1858-1914),
painter
    ArH 534-35.

MARIN MOLINARI, Santiago A.
(1825-1898), naval officer
    ArH 260-61.

MARIN SHAW, Wenceslao Tomás
(1865-1896), blacksmith, soldier
    ArH 330-39.

MARIN SOLA, Ramón (1832-1902),
author, journalist, teacher
    AlHP 346, ill.; BiP 253; CaE
    786; Crom 84; DiDHM 127; Di-
    HBC 603; DiLP 2, pt.2:903-6;
    ECPR 6:461-62; GenP 97; GrEPR
    14:200; HePR 63-72, ill.;
    HisD 54; Por 221; Pq 234-35;
    PRFAS 146; PuI 156-60.

MARQUES, Guillermo S. (b. 1931), banker
GrEPR 14:200.

MARQUES, Luis R., engineer
A 26.

MARQUES, René (1919-1979), author
BiP 254-55; BrECP 282-83, ill.; CaE 787-88; ConA 97-100:343; DiDHM 128, ill.; DiLP 2, pt.2:906-19; DicC 63; ECPR 6:462; GrEPR 5: 109-16, 14:201, ill.; HisD 54; Ind 111-13; PRFAS 147, ill.

MARQUES MUÑOZ, Luis Rogelio (b.1918), engineer
QEQ (1948-49) 104.

MARQUEZ, José L., politician
GrEPR 14:201.

MARQUEZ, Juan Luis, journalist
A 78-79, ill.

MARQUEZ, Rafael, artist
GrEPR 8:436.

MARQUEZ, Rafael, musician, composer
MusMP 256.

MARQUEZ ABRAHAMS, José Miguel (1875-1915), lawyer
LM 126; RepM 115, ill.

MARQUEZ DE DIAZ, Carmen N. (b. 1898), civic leader
EGMPR 4:151-52.

MARTE MARTINEZ, Hipólito (ca. 1866-1926), artisan
San 48-50.

MARTI, Ignacio, musician
MusMP 256.

MARTI, Mariano (d.1792), bishop
Hi de la Ig 134-38.

MARTI, Mona, actress, singer
DelMu 152-57, ill.; EGMPR 4:65-66, ill.

MARTI, Rafael (d.1931), pilot
DiHBC 604; GrEPR 14:201.

MARTI CUYAR, José (b.1864), doctor
RepM 339, ill.

MARTI NUÑEZ, Rafael (b.1932), doctor, politician
GrEPR 14:201.

MARTI RODRIGUEZ, Francisco (b. 1907), banker
QEQ (1948-49) 104-5.

MARTIN, Angel Manuel (b.1918), judge
GrEPR 14:201.

MARTIN, H. A., educator
Tri 2:195-97.

MARTIN, José Luis (b.1921), author, educator
BiP 255-56; CaE 794; ConA nr12:298; DiDHM 128; DiLP 2, pt.2:929-32; DirAs 3:342; ECPR 6:462; PRFAS 147.

MARTIN, Ramón (b.1802?), pharmacist
CaF 95.

MARTIN TELLADO, Bernabé (b. 1922), economist, banker
GrEPR 14:202.

MARTINEZ, Antonia (19th cent.), philanthropist
DiHBC 604; MujDPR 30-31, ill.; MujPu 56.

MARTINEZ, Arsenio, politician
GrEPR 14:202.

MARTINEZ, Iris, actress
DelMu 160-64, ill.; EGMPR 4: 63-64, ill.

MARTINEZ, Josefa, author
GrEPR 14:292; Ind 114.

MARTINEZ, Julio T. (1878-1953), painter, engineer, architect
GrEPR 8:136-38; QEQ (1936-37) 104-5, (1941-42) 136-37, (1948-49) 107.

MARTINEZ, Ladislao "Ladí" (1898-1979), musician, composer
Com 6; GrEPR 7:123-24.

MARTINEZ, Luis, businessman
A 169.

MARTINEZ, Martita, actress
  DelMu 166-70, ill.

MARTINEZ, Miguel O. (b.1937),
educator
  Port 73, 74(ill.)

MARTINEZ, Pura E., poet,
teacher
  Tri 1:97-103.

MARTINEZ, Ramón A. (b.1922),
artist
  GrEPR 8:436.

MARTINEZ, Ramón O., educator
  Tri 2:135-38.

MARTINEZ ACOSTA, Carmelo
(1879-1952), journalist
  AlHY 162-63, 210-11; DiLP
  2, pt.2:932-33; GrEPR 14:
  202; QEQ (1933-34) 100,
  (1936-37) 102, (1941-42)
  134, (1948-49) 105.

Martínez Acosta de Pérez
Almiroty, María see Martínez
de Pérez Almiroty, María

MARTINEZ ALVAREZ, Antonio (b.
1885), doctor, author
  CaM 281; DiLP 2, pt.2:933-
  35; DiM 210-12; Tri 1:63-
  68.

MARTINEZ ALVAREZ, Rafael
(1882-1959), author, lawyer,
professor
  BiP 257-58; CaE 794; DiLP
  2, pt.2:935-37; GrEPR 5:
  117-18, 14:202; Ind 114-15;
  PlE 2:273; PRFAS 148; QEQ
  (1936-37) 102-3, (1941-42)
  134-35, (1948-49) 105; Tri
  2:3-8; Vida 32-34.

MARTINEZ APARICIO, Manuel,
musician
  MusMP 256-57.

MARTINEZ AVILES, Emiliano,
lawyer, poet
  Hor 283-86.

MARTINEZ CAPO, Juan (b.1923),
author, journalist, critic
  BrECP 283; CaE 795; DiDHM
  129; DiLP 2, pt.2:937-39;
  GrEPR 14:202; PRFAS 148-49.

MARTINEZ COLON, Héctor M. (b.

1939), lawyer, politician
  GrEPR 14:203; LiPR 38, ill.

MARTINEZ CRUZ, Américo (b.1938),
politician
  LiPR 30, ill.

MARTINEZ DAVILA, Manuel A. (1883-
1934*), politician, author
  DiLP 2, pt.2:939-40; GrEPR
  14:203; Guay 284-85; Ind 115-
  16; PlE 2:273; QEQ (1933-34)
  100-101, (1936-37) 15.

MARTINEZ DAVILA, José, lawyer
  RepM 304, ill.

MARTINEZ DE ANDINO, Agustín (b.
1889), engineer
  QEQ (1933-34) 101, (1936-37)
  103.

MARTINEZ DE ANDINO, Gaspar (17th
cent.), governor
  GrEPR 14:202; Hi de P 193-
  200.

MARTINEZ DE ANDINO, Vicente
(1758-1837), soldier
  DiDHM 129; EPI 1:69-70, ill.;
  HisD 54; PuI 37-39.

MARTINEZ DE ANDINO FERRER, Julio
(b.1909), engineer
  QEQ (1941-42) 135, (1948-49)
  105-6.

MARTINEZ DE BERROCAL, Matilde
(1884-1972), civic leader
  EGMPR 4:159-60, ill.

MARTINEZ DE FERNANDEZ NATER, Mar-
colina, civic and social works
  DiHBC 604; MujDPR 187-89,
  ill.

MARTINEZ DE LA TORRE, Angel M.
(b.1908), engineer
  QEQ (1948-49) 106.

MARTINEZ DE ONECA, Pedro (d.
1760), bishop
  Hi de la Ig 124-34.

MARTINEZ DE PEREZ ALMIROTY,
María (b.1883), teacher, poli-
tician
  GrEPR 14:202; MujDPR 183-84;
  QEQ (1933-34) 101-2, (1936-
  37) 103, (1941-42) 135.

MARTINEZ DELGADO, Arturo (b. 1870), lawyer
   QEQ (1936-37) 103.

MARTINEZ GANDIA, Adrián (1842? -1895), educator
   PuI 254-56.

MARTINEZ GONZALEZ, Víctor Primo (b.1873), lawyer, journalist
   QEQ (1936-37) 103-4, (1941-42) 135-36; RepM 295, ill.

MARTINEZ GUASP, Joaquín, doctor
   CaM 282-83; GenB 324; Hi de M 196-97.

MARTINEZ HERNANDEZ, Ramón, manager
   QEQ (1933-34) 102, (1936-37) 104.

MARTINEZ LOPEZ, Benjamín (b. 1922), educator
   PRFAS 149-50.

MARTINEZ MARTINEZ, Frank (b. 1884), judge, politician
   GrEPR 14:203; PriC 41, ill.; QEQ (1933-34) 102-3, (1936-37) 104, (1941-42) 136, (1948-49) 106; RepM 127, ill.

MARTINEZ MASDEU, Edgar (b. 1941), educator, author
   BrECP 283-84; PRFAS 150.

Martínez Mirabel, Julio Tomás see Martínez, Julio T.

MARTINEZ MORALES, José A. (b. 1890), accountant
   QEQ (1933-34) 103, (1936-37) 105.

MARTINEZ NADAL, Rafael (1877-1941), politician, journalist, author
   BiP 258-59; BrECP 284; ComA 17-45; DiHBC 604-5; DiLP 2, pt.2:940-41; GenB 398-403, ill.; GenP 45; GrEPR 14: 203, 204-5(ill.); Hi de M 134; HisD 54; HoIPR 68, ill.; HoPP 67-136, ill.; Ind 116-17; Orad 361-63; PriC 61-62, ill.; PRFAS 150-51; QEQ (1933-34) 103,

(1936-37) 105.

MARTINEZ OHUVIÑAS, Isaac F., businessman
   GenB 263-64; Nuestr 34-35.

MARTINEZ OHUVIÑAS, Lorenzo, businessman, politician
   GenB 264-65; Nuestr 88-89.

MARTINEZ OTERO, Abelardo, educator
   A 169, ill.

MARTINEZ PARODI, Ricardo, politician
   GrEPR 14:203.

MARTINEZ PICO, Amalia (b.1929), doctor, educator
   EGMPR 3:183-85, ill.

MARTINEZ PLEE, Manuel (1861-1928), musician, journalist
   BiP 259-60; DiHBC 605; DiLP 2, pt.2:941-42; GrEPR 14: 203; MusMP 117-21; PRFAS 151; Tri 1:335-39.

MARTINEZ PLOWES, Juan (19th cent.), governor
   GrEPR 14:206.

MARTINEZ PRADE, Modesto, pharmacist
   RepM 317, ill.

MARTINEZ PUMAREJO, Ana (19th cent.), wife of revolutionary
   MujDPR 43-45, ill.

MARTINEZ QUINTERO, José E. (b. 1868), teacher, journalist
   Exp 293-94; RepM 291, ill.

MARTINEZ RIVERA, Edelmiro (b. 1901), lawyer
   QEQ (1941-42) 137.

MARTINEZ RIVERA, Ezequiel (d. 1964), doctor
   CaM 281-82.

MARTINEZ ROGER, Rafael (b. 1899), photographer
   QEQ (1948-49) 106.

MARTINEZ ROMAN, José A. (b. 1919), accountant
   QEQ (1948-49) 106-7.

MARTINEZ ROSELLO, Manuel
(1862-1931), doctor, author,
politician
    CaM 283-84; DiLP 2, pt.2:
    942-43; DiM 212-14.

MARTINEZ SCHETTINI, Aida (b.
1918), lawyer
    EGMPR 3:107-8, ill.

MARTINEZ TOLENTINO, Jaime (b.
1943), professor, author
    DirAS 3:343.

MARTINEZ URBINA, Rafael (b.
1921), politician
    GrEPR 14:206.

Martínez Vélez, Ramonita see
Marti, Mona

MARTINEZ VILAR, Aurea (b.
1926), author, social works
    EGMPR 3:335-37, ill.

MARTORELL, Antonio (b.1939),
artist
    BiP 260-61; BrECP 284-85;
    GrEPR 8:268, ill.; PaG 209;
    PRFAS 151-52.

MARTORELL, Eduardo, musician
    MusMP 257.

MARTORELL, José (19th cent.),
doctor
    CaM 285.

MARTORELL TORRENTS, Miguel (b.
1891), politician
    GrEPR 14:206; QEQ (1941-42)
    137, (1948-49) 107-8.

MARTY PEREZ, Randolfo (b.
1896), doctor, politician
    CaM 285; DiM 214; GrEPR 14:
    206; QEQ (1933-34) 103,
    (1936-37) 105.

MARVEL, Thomas Stahl, architect
    GrEPR 9:135.

MARVIN, Alexander, politician
    GrEPR 14:206.

MARXUACH Y ABRAMS, Rafael,
pharmacist, politician
    CaF 98.

MARXUACH ACOSTA, Gilberto (b.

1910), professor, lawyer
    DiHBC 605.

MARXUACH Y ECHEVARRIA, José M.
(1848-1910), doctor, politician
    DiHBC 605-6; GrEPR 14:202.

MARXUACH PLUMEY, Acisclo (b.
1892*), chemist, government
official
    CaF 97; DiHBC 606-7; QEQ
    (1933-34) 103-4, (1936-37)
    105.

MARXUACH PLUMEY, Teófilo (b.
1877), engineer, soldier
    DiHBC 607.

MARZAN CARRERAS, Isabelino, politician
    GrEPR 14:206.

MARRERO, Carmen (b.1907), author, journalist, teacher
    BiP 261-63; DiLP 2, pt.2:919-
    21; ECPR 6:462; EGMPR 3:295-
    96, ill.; GrEPR 14:201; PRFAS
    152; Vida 66-67.

MARRERO, Diego O. (1896-1959),
poet
    DiLP 2, pt.2:921-22.

MARRERO, Jacinto (b.1894),
author, journalist
    DiLP 2, pt.2:922-24.

MARRERO, José Luis "Chavito",
actor
    DelMu 146-50, ill.

MARRERO, Víctor, lawyer
    Port 129, 130(ill.); PRUSA
    18.

MARRERO DENIS, José (b.1881),
teacher, author
    QEQ (1933-34) 99-100.

MARRERO HUECA, Manuel (b.
1948), politician
    LiPR 36, ill.

MARRERO NAVARRO, Domingo (1909-
1960), author, Methodist minister
    AlHP 187, ill.; BiP 263; DiLP
    2, pt.2:924-26; PRFAS 152.

MARRERO NUÑEZ, Julio (b.1910),
author, professor
    CaE 789-90; DiLP 2, pt.2:

926-29; GrEPR 14:201; PRFAS
152-53.

MARRERO RIOS, Borínquen (b.
1899), lawyer
    QEQ (1933-34) 100, (1936-
    37) 102, (1941-42) 134,
    (1948-49) 104.

MARROIG, Miguel, teacher
    ProA 31.

MAS, Arturo, tailor, author
    Ka 174.

MAS, Maruja, actress
    DelMu 172-75, ill.

MASCARO, Juan, businessman
    A 135.

MASCARO Y HOMAR, Ignacio
(1760-1815), soldier
    BeHNPR 1:297-98.

MASFERRER Y BERRIOS, Joaquín
(1866-1900), educator, politician
    PuI 371-72.

MASSANETY Y CALDENTEY, Juan
(1819-1894), educator
    ArH 458-59.

MASSO, Gildo (b.1891), educator
    Hi de Cay 243-44; QEQ
    (1933-34) 104, (1936-37)
    105-6.

MATANZOS, Francisco, doctor
    CaM 286.

MATHEU Y DE ADRIAN, Fidela
(1852-1927), teacher, poet
    AlHY 160-61, 228; DiHBC
    612; DiLP 2, pt.2:944;
    EGMPR 1:171-73, ill.; GrEPR
    14:207; MujDPR 90-95, ill.;
    MujP 121; MujPu 87-94.

MATHEW, Alfredo, government
official
    Port 173, 174(ill.)

MATHEWS, Thomas George (b.
1925), author, professor
    ConA 49-52:358-59; DiHBC
    612; DirAS 1:505.

MATIENZO, Bienvenido (b.1888),

engineer
    QEQ (1933-34) 197, (1936-37)
    106.

MATIENZO ALMAVIZCAR, Joaquín,
businessman
    RepM 262, ill.

MATIENZO CINTRON, Rosendo (1855-
1913), lawyer, politician, orator, author
    AlHP 260, ill.; BiP 263-64;
    BrECP 285-86, ill.; CiBPI
    177(ill.), 200-203; Cre 43-
    45; Crom 45; Desd 196-200;
    DiDHM 129; DiLP 2, pt.2:944-
    47; ECPR 6:462-63; EntP 21-
    35, 56-78; GenP 62-63; GrEPR
    14:207, 208-9(ill.); HisD 54;
    HoIPR 68, ill.; HoYMPR 84-94,
    ill.; Hor 356-62; LM 122; LPR
    1012, 1014, 1015-18, 1019;
    Mem 99-100; Nues 15-21, ill.;
    Orad 163-65; PaI 119-34,
    ill.; PIE 1:515-25, ill.;
    PRFAS 153; PuI 345-48; Ver
    176(ill.), 177.

MATIENZO DE MONSERRATE, Luisa
(b.1910), designer
    EGMPR 4:67.

MATIENZO ROMAN, Amelia (b.
1913), poet
    EGMPR 1:175-76.

MATIENZO ROMAN, Carlota (b.1881),
teacher
    DiHBC 612-13; EGMPR 4:193,
    ill.; MujDPR 192-93, ill.;
    PQ 11.

MATILLA JIMENEZ, Alfredo (b.
1910), educator, author
    A 89-90, ill.; QEQ (1948-49)
    108.

MATOS, Juan N., farmer, author
    Tri 1:207-13.

MATOS AGRAIT, Antonio Rafael (b.
1895), farmer
    A 165, ill.; QEQ (1948-49)
    108.

MATOS BERNIER, Félix (1869-
1937), author, journalist
    AlHP 124-25, ill.; BiP 265-
    67; BrECP 286; CaE 797; Cre
    35-41; DiLP 2, pt.2:947-50;
    ECPR 6:463; GrEPR 14:207,
    ill.; HisD 54; Ind 117-19;

Mem 100-101; PlE 1:499-511,
ill.; PRFAS 153-54; QEQ
(1936-37) 106.

MATOS BERNIER, Rafael (1881-
1939), journalist
AlHP 126-27, ill.; BiP 267-
68; DiLP 2, pt.2:950-51;
ECPR 6:463, 465; PlE 1:503-
4; PRFAS 154.

MATOS DE PALES, Consuelo (b.
1872), poet
MujDPR 126-30, ill.

MATOS PAOLI, Francisco (b.
1915), author, politician
BiP 268-69; BrECP 286-87;
CaE 797-98, ill.; CiuP 95-
96; DiDHM 129-30; DiLP 2,
pt.2:952-55; DicC 65; ECPR
6:465; GrEPR 14:210; PRFAS
154.

MATTA, Enrique, politician
GrEPR 14:210.

MATTA, Enrique G. (b.1894?),
novelist
CaE 798.

MATTEI, José María, pharmacist
Ka 156.

MATTEI, Juan (b.1861), lawyer,
politician
RepM 192, ill.

MATTEI, Virgilio P., artist
AlHP 340, ill.

MATTEI RIVERA, José Enrique
(b.1903), businessman
QEQ (1948-49) 192.

MATTEI Y RODRIGUEZ, Andrés
(1863-1925), author
AlHY 163, 211; DiLP 2, pt.
2:955-56.

MATTEI SEMIDEI, Tito (b.1908),
doctor
QEQ (1941-42) 138, (1948-
49) 108.

MAULEON BENITEZ, Carmen Cecilia, educator
BrECP 287-88; PRFAS 155.

MAUNEZ, Santiago Z. (b.1897),
civic leader, accountant

DiDHM 130.

MAUNEZ VIZCARRONDO, Santiago
(b.1924), author, painter
DiDHM 130-31.

MAURAS, Edwin (b.1948), artist
GrEPR 8:356, ill.

MAY, David William (b.1868),
agronomist
QEQ (1933-34) 104, (1936-37)
106.

MAYMI, Carmen Rosa, federal
government official
EGMPR 3:109-10, ill.; PQ 39.

MAYMI NEVARES, José Rafael
(1903-1951), doctor
CaM 287.

MAYMON PALMER, Francisco (1870-
1954), cinema owner
GenB 424-25, ill.; HoIPR 68,
ill.

MAYOL, Bart (b.1915), artist
GrEPR 8:409.

MAYORAL, Angel M. (b.1888),
insurance agent
QEQ (1948-49) 108.

MAYORAL BARNES, Manuel (1866-
1952), journalist, author
AlHP 141, ill.

MAYORAL DE HERNANDEZ COLON, Lila
(b.1942), wife of Gov. Hernández
Colón
EGMPR 4:363, ill.

MAYORAL GARAY, Juan (d.1824),
Army officer
PonY 60, 64.

MEDIN VASSALLO, Virginia (b.
1905), work with aged, Catholic
missionary
EGMPR 4:299-301, ill.

MEDINA, Luis, sculptor
GrEPR 8:410.

MEDINA, Ramón Felipe (b.1935),
author
BrECP 291; DiLP 2, pt.2:
956-57; GrEPR 5:118-19; PRFAS
155.

MEDINA, William, federal employee
 PRUSA 18, ill.

MEDINA BEM, Vicente (b.1904), agronomist
 QEQ (1948-49) 109.

MEDINA GONZALEZ, Adolfo (1867?-1925), author, journalist
 DiLP 2, pt.2:957-58.

MEDINA GONZALEZ, Julio, artist
 GrEPR 8:129-31.

MEDINA GONZALEZ, Julio, politician
 GrEPR 14:210.

MEDINA RAMIREZ, Ramón (1892-1964), politician
 CiBPI 288-90; PaI 5-14.

MEGWINOFF GAUTHIER, Alexander (b.1900), government employee
 QEQ (1948-49) 109.

MEJIA, Francisco, politician
 AlHY 78-79; GrEPR 14:211, ill.

MELENDEZ, Concha (b.1895), author, critic, educator
 AntHistCag 255-56; AntPoe-Cag 95-96; BiP 269-71; BrECP 292, ill.; CaDeT 218; CaE 799-800; DiDHM 131-32, ill.; DiHBC 624; DicC 66-67; ECPR 6:465; EGMPR 1:311-13, ill.; MujDPR 249-51, ill.; Oro 74-82, ill.; PlE 2:445-60, ill.; PQ 40; PRFAS 156, ill.; QEQ (1936-37) 107.

MELENDEZ, Francisco Aparicio (1850-1894), printer, author
 GenB 302-3; Nuestr 104-5.

MELENDEZ, Julio (b.1924), author
 DiLP 2, pt.2:965-66.

MELENDEZ ARANA, Alfonso (b.1927), artist, professor
 GrEPR 8:358, ill.

MELENDEZ BAEZ, Juan (b.1908), politician
 GrEPR 14:211.

MELENDEZ CANO, Luis E. (b.1939), politician
 LiPR 128, ill.

MELENDEZ CRUZ, Vicente (b.1896), educator
 QEQ (1936-37) 107.

MELENDEZ MUÑOZ, Miguel (1884-1966), author, journalist,
 And 161-64; BiP 271-73; BrECP 293-94; CaE 800-801; CiBPI 227(ill.), 272-74; DiDHM 132, ill.; DiHBC 624; DiLP 2, pt.2:966-75; ECPR 6:465-66; GrEPR 5:119-23, 14:212; Hi de Cay 235-38; Ind 120-22; Por 62-64; PlE 2:201-13, ill.; PRFAS 157, ill.; QEQ (1936-37) 107, (1948-49) 109; VPR 119-23, 168.

MELENDEZ Y RUIZ, Salvador (18th-19th cent.), governor
 DiDHM 132; DiHBC 449-50.

MELENDEZ VALDES, Diego de (16th cent.), governor
 DiDHM 133.

MELERO, Jochi (b.1949), photographer
 GrEPR 1:xix, ill.

MELIA FERRER, Bartolomé (b.1866), businessman
 A 116; QEQ (1936-37) 107-8.

MELON, Esther M. (b.1933), author, professor
 BrECP 293; DIDHM 133; PRFAS 157-58.

MELTZ, Carlos B. (1855?-1900), businessman, Freemason
 Nues 27-29, ill.

MELLADO, Antonio (19th cent.), doctor
 CaM 289-91.

MELLADO, Ramón (1904*-1985), educator
 BiP 273-75; DiDHM 133-34; ECPR 6:466; GrEPR 1:xiv, ill., 14:212, ill.; PRFAS 158-59.

MENDEZ, Alfred Francis (b.1907), Catholic bishop
 GrEPR 14:212.

MENDEZ, Ana G. (b.1908), educator
EGMPR 1:315-16, ill.; PRFAS 159.

MENDEZ, Angel María, auditor
ProA 59.

MENDEZ, Antonio "Tony", politician
A1DJ 129, 131, ill.

MENDEZ, Enrique (b.1931), doctor
PRUSA 19, ill.

MENDEZ, Justo A. (b.1917), politician
GrEPR 14:212, ill.; LiPR 28, ill.; PRFAS 160.

MENDEZ, Néstor H. (b.1917), doctor
QEQ (1948-49) 110.

MENDEZ, Olga A., politician, professor
Port 69, 70(ill.)

MENDEZ, Orlando R., engineer
A 99.

MENDEZ, Rafael M. (b.1886), pharmacist
QEQ (1933-34) 197-98, (1936-37) 108, (1941-42) 139.

MENDEZ, Roger "Edris" (b. 1919), Army officer
QEQ (1948-49) 111.

MENDEZ BALLESTER, Manuel (b. 1909), dramatist, journalist
A 73-74, ill.; BiP 275-76; BrECP 293-94, ill.; CaE 801; DiDHM 134-35, ill.; DiLP 2, pt.2:975-82; DicC 9-10; ECPR 6:466-67; GrEPR 5:123-26, 14:213, ill.; Ind 122-23; PRFAS 159-60, ill.

MENDEZ CABRERO, Pablo E. (b. 1917), pharmacist, politician
LiPR 117, ill.

MENDEZ CARDONA, José, politician
BoHP 198-99; LuO 106.

MENDEZ CARDONA, Luis (b.1879),

engineer
QEQ (1941-42) 138.

MENDEZ CARDONA, Ramón, politician
GrEPR 14:214.

MENDEZ CARDONA, Raúl G. (b. 1913), lawyer
QEQ (1941-42) 138.

MENDEZ COLON, José C. (b.1912), agronomist
QEQ (1941-42) 238, (1948-49) 110.

MENDEZ Y DE LA CRUZ, María Luisa (b.1896), banker
EGMPR 3:47-48, ill.

MENDEZ FERNANDEZ, Emiliano (b. 1892), consul
QEQ (1933-34) 105, (1936-37) 108, (1941-42) 138-39.

MENDEZ FORESTIER, Alfredo (b. 1891), engineer
QEQ (1941-42) 139.

MENDEZ JIMENEZ, Bernardo, politician
GrEPR 14:214.

MENDEZ JIMENEZ, Orlando Ramón (b.1907), engineer
QEQ (1948-49) 110.

MENDEZ LICIAGA, Andrés (b. 1943), politician
LuO 96-97; ProA 44.

MENDEZ LICIAGA, Manuel (b. 1884), pharmacist, politician
BoHP 208, ill.; CaF 99; GrEPR 14:214; QEQ (1936-37) 108.

MENDEZ MARTINEZ, Aurelio (d. 1904), politician
BoHP 98-99, ill.; GrEPR 14: 214, ill.

MENDEZ MENDEZ, Raúl G. (b.1913), lawyer
QEQ (1948-49) 110.

MENDEZ MOLL, José (b.1941), lawyer, politician
GrEPR 14:214.

MENDEZ QUIÑONES, Ramón (1847-1889), author

BrECP 294; DiLP 2, pt.2:
982-84; GrEPR 14:215; PRFAS
160.

MENDEZ RODRIGUEZ, José María,
businessman
QEQ (1948-49) 111.

MENDEZ SERRANO, Edelmiro (b.
1885), lawyer, politician
GrEPR 14:215; QEQ (1933-
34) 105, (1936-37) 108.

MENDEZ SERRANO, Lumen M. (b.
1891), pharmacist, politician
CaF 99; GrEPR 14:215; QEQ
(1941-42) 139.

MENDEZ VIGO, Santiago (b.
1790), governor, soldier
BeHNPR 2:37-45, ill.; Di-
DHM 135; DiHBC 252; EnsB
57-69; GrEPR 14:215.

MENDIA, Manuel, businessman
Tri 1:155-62.

MENDIN SABAT, José (b.1893),
doctor, politician
CaM 291; DiM 214; QEQ
(1933-34) 105-6, (1936-37)
108.

MENDIN SABAT, Luis (b.1879),
lawyer
QEQ (1936-37) 108-9.

MENDOZA, Angeles (b.1937),
professor, politician
EGMPR 2:37, ill.; GrEPR 14:
215.

MENDOZA, Cristóbal de (16th
cent.), governor
GrEPR 14:215.

MENDOZA, Inés María (b.1910),
author, wife of Gov. Muñoz
Marín
DiLP 2, pt.2:984-85; EGMPR
4:355, ill.; PQ 41; Tra
115, 168.

MENDOZA MARTINEZ, Baltasar (d.
1932), politician
Hi de Cay 248-50.

Mendoza Tió, Angeles see
Mendoza, Angeles

MENDOZA VEGA, Rosita (b. 1924),
beautician, cosmetologist
EGMPR 3:187-88.

MENDOZA VIDAL, Roger L., lawyer,
sportsman
AntHistCag 477.

MENENDEZ, Francisco J., architect
GrEPR 9:131.

MENENDEZ DE VALDES, Diego (16th
cent.), governor
GrEPR 14:216.

MENENDEZ GUILLOT, Francisco (b.
1892), veterinarian
QEQ (1933-34) 106, (1936-37)
109.

MENENDEZ Y MERCADO, José (b.
1901), doctor
QEQ (1941-42) 139-40.

MENENDEZ MONROIG, José (b.
1917), lawyer, politician
GrEPR 14:215.

MENENDEZ RAMOS, Rafael (b.
1893), agronomist
AntHistCag 430-31; GrEPR 14:
215(ill.), 216; QEQ (1933-34)
198-99, (1936-37) 109, (1941-
42) 140, (1948-49) 111-12;
Tri 1:245-49.

MERCADER, Luis (b.1889), lawyer,
politician
ProA 65, ill.; QEQ (1936-37)
109-10, (1941-42) 140-41.

MERCADO, Alonso de (16th-17th
cent.), governor
GrEPR 14:216; Hi de Pu 80-
82; HisD 55.

MERCADO, Joaquín (b.1940),
artist
GrEPR 8:410.

MERCADO, José "Momo" (1863-1911),
author, journalist
AntHistCag 256-57; AntPoeCag
27-28; BiP 276-78; BrECP
294-95; CaDeT 166-67, ill.;
CaE 802-3; DiDHM 135, ill.;
DiHBC 624-25; DiLP 2, pt.2:
985-88; ECPR 6:467; GrEPR
14:216; HoIPR 69, ill.; LPR
1040, 1041-42, 1043; PlE 1:

329-44, ill.; Por 214-16;
PRFAS 160-61, ill.

MERCADO, Manuel de (16th
cent.), bishop
Hi de la Ig 39-40.

MERCADO MONTALVO, Mario (1855-
1937), philanthropist
AlHP 278, ill.; PonY 101-2.

MERCADO ORTIZ, Wilfredo (b.
1947), politician
LiPR 126, ill.

MERGAL, Angel (1909-1971),
author, Protestant minister
BiP 278-79; BoBP 93-96; Di-
LP 2, pt.2:988-91; ECPR 6:
467-68; GrEPR 6:310; PRFAS
161.

MERGAL DE RIVERA, Isaura (b.
1942), painter
GrEPR 8:360.

MERINO, Baltasar (b.1845),
Jesuit teacher, author
Jes 150-51.

MERINO DE HAEUSSLER, Rosita,
artist
GrEPR 8:411.

MERLE, Bernardo, businessman
RepM 324, ill.

Mesenia, Dorida see Eulate
Sanjurjo, Carmen

MESSINA, Félix María de (1798-
1872), governor
BeHNPR 2:155-69, ill.; Di-
DHM 136; DiHBC 453, 625;
GrEPR 14:216, ill.

MESTRE CAPARROS, Enrique, lawyer
GenB 403-4.

MESTRE CAPARROS, Salvador (b.
1882), lawyer
GenB 403; GrEPR 14:217; QEQ
(1933-34) 199, (1936-37)
110, (1941-42) 141, (1948-
49) 112.

MESTRE Y MORA, Salvador (1852-
1894), lawyer
GenB 283-84; GenP 42; Hi de
CR 243-50; Hi de M 189-20;

Nuestr 36-38; RepM 117, ill.

MESTRE Y TOMAS, José, pharmacist
CaF 100, 206-7.

MEYER, Angela, actress
DelMu 178-83, ill.

MICARD, Augusto (19th cent.),
pharmacist
CaF 100.

MICARD, Carlos (19th cent.),
pharmacist
CaF 100.

MICHELI, Julio (b.1937), artist
GrEPR 8:362, ill.; PaG 212.

MIER, Elpidio de (1873-1939),
author, journalist
DiLP 2, pt.2:991-98.

MIGNUCCI CALDER, Armando (d.
1954), politician
GrEPR 14:217.

MILAN MARTIN, Francisco Mario
(b.1904), educator
QEQ (1941-42) 141.

MILAN PADRO, Rafael D. (b.
1919), politician
GrEPR 14:217.

MILAN SUAREZ, Fernando, politician
GrEPR 14:217.

MILES, Nelson A. (b.1839), Army
officer
DiHBC 626; GrEPR 14:217; HisP
155-60.

MILIAN, Francisco (d.1936),
musical director
PRFAS 161.

MILLAN, Félix (b.1943), baseball
player
PRUSA 19.

MILLAN, Tomás, musician
MusMP 289.

MILLAN DE PIZARRO, Candelaria
(1877-1955), spiritualist
AlHP 180.

MILLAN RIVERA, Pedro (b.1909),
author

AntHistCag 262-63; AntPoe Cag 157-59; CaDeT 185-86, ill.

MILLER, Paul Gerard (1875-1952), educator, author
    BioD 2:898; GrEPR 14:217; QEQ (1933-34) 106, (1936-37) 111, (1941-42) 141-42.

MIMOSO RASPALDO, José (b. 1907), politician
    GrEPR 14:217, ill.; QEQ (1948-49) 112.

MINTZ, Sidney (b.1922), anthropologist
    ConA nr5:374; DiHBC 627-28.

MIRABEL, Antonio (1888-1971), author
    BoBP 57-60; DiLP 2, pt.2: 998-1000; Per 101-3; PlE 2: 273.

MIRABEL, Petra (b.1870?), embroiderer
    EGMPR 4:69; MujDPR 130-31.

MIRANDA, Luis Antonio (1896-1975), author, journalist
    BiP 280-81; DiLP 2, pt.2: 1000-1003; GrEPR 14:218; Ind 123-24; Per 136-38; PlE 2:267-76, ill.; PRFAS 162.

Miranda, Luis R. see Rodríguez Miranda, Luis

MIRANDA, Neftalí (b.1898), pharmacist, composer
    CaF 102; GrEPR 14:218.

MIRANDA ARCHILLA, Graciany (b. 1910), author, journalist
    BiP 279-80; BrECP 295; CaE 808; DiLP 2, pt2:1003-5; ECPR 6:468; GrEPR 14:218; PRFAS 162.

MIRANDA CONDE, Miguel Angel (b.1932), lawyer, politician
    GrEPR 14:218; LiPR 29, ill.

MIRANDA GONZALEZ, Herminio (b. 1873), politician
    GrEPR 14:218; QEQ (1941-42) 142.

MIRANDA JIMENEZ, Maximino (b. 1931), lawyer, politician

GrEPR 14:218.

MIRANDA MONGE, Ramón (b.1873), businessman
    QEQ (1933-34) 108.

MIRANDA VILLAFAÑE, Lolita (b. 1922), lawyer
    EGMPR 3:189-90.

MIRO SOJO, Antonio (b.1900), businessman
    QEQ (1948-49) 112.

MIROS, Gilda (b.1938), journalist, actress
    Port 181, 182(ill.)

MISLA ALDARONDO, Edison (b. 1942), politician
    LiPR 35, ill.

MISLAN, Angel (1862-1911), musician, composer
    BiP 282-84; BrECP 295; Co8; DiHBC 629; ECPR 6:468; GrEPR 14:218; HoYMPR 152-61, ill.; MusMP 122-29; PRFAS 162-63.

Mita see García Peraza, Juanita

MIYARES Y GONZALEZ, Fernando (1749-1818), chronicler
    DiHBC 629; DiLP 2, pt.2: 1005-7.

MOCK, Charles T., Jr., (b.1912), manager
    QEQ (1941-42) 238.

MOCZO BANIET, Pedro (b.1864), educator
    GrEPR 14:218; QEQ (1936-37) 112, (1948-49) 142.

MOCZO GARCIA, Luis Raimundo (b.1894), doctor
    QEQ (1936-37) 112, (1941-42) 142-43.

MODESTO CINTRON, Francisco (b. 1893), teacher
    QEQ (1948-49) 112.

MOHR, Nicholasa (b.1935), author
    ConA nr1:440-41.

MOJICA MARRERO, Aguedo (b. 1910), politician, professor
    GrEPR 14:219, ill.

MOLINA, Alonso de (16th cent.), lawyer
GrEPR 14:219.

MOLINA, Antonio J. (b.1928), lawyer, art critic, artist
GrEPR 1:xiii.

MOLINA, Francisco (b.1913), author
DiLP 2, pt.2:1007-8.

MOLINA ENRIQUEZ, Enrique (19th cent.), soldier
MueYV 154-59.

MOLINA Y LOPEZ CEPERO, J. M. L. (b.1891), accountant
QEQ (1948-49) 112-13.

MOLINA LOPEZ CEPERO, Marina (1898-1979), author, journalist, teacher
DiDHM 136; DiLP 2, pt.2: 1008-9; EGMPR 3:297-98, ill.; QEQ (1941-42) 143, (1948-49) 113; Vida 35-36.

MOLINA Y VERGARA, Antonio E. (b.1823), businessman, political prisoner
Crom 88; GenP 106; Ver 165.

MOLINARY DE LA CRUZ, Aída Nilda (b.1932), policewoman, lawyer
EGMPR 3:191-92, ill.

MOLINERO CARLO, Isolina (b. 1932), policewoman
EGMPR 3:193-94, ill.

MOLL BASCANA, Arístides (1885-1964), author
CaE 809-10; DiLP 2, pt.2: 1009-10; PRFAS 163; QEQ (1933-34) 108-9, (1936-37) 112, (1941-42) 143.

MOLL BOSCANA, Josefina (1887?-1966), poet
DiLP 2, pt.2:1010-11; EGMPR 1:177-79, ill.; MujDPR 167-70, ill.; MujPu 138-45.

MONAGAS, Carlos, pharmacist
CaF 102-3.

MONAGAS, Jesús (19th-20th cent.), doctor
CaM 296.

MONAGAS, Rafael H. (1891-1921), author
DiLP 2, pt.2:1011-12.

MONAGAS Y GARCIA, Rafael, politician, pharmacist
CaF 103; GrEPR 14:219.

MONCLOVA, Juan (19th cent.), pharmacist
CaF 104.

MONCLOVA CAJIGA, José J. (19th cent.), pharmacist
HoIPR 69, ill.; RepM 196, ill.

MONCLOVA Y CAJIGAL, Santiago (19th cent.), pharmacist
CaF 105.

MONCLOVA GALLARDO, Pedro (b. 1861), pharmacist, politician
CaF 104-5; GrEPR 14:219; RepM 323, ill.

MONGE, José María (1849-1891), author, journalist
BiP 284-85; BrECP 298-99; DiHBC 637; DiLP 2, pt.2: 1012-14; ECPR 6:468; GenB 277-78; Hi de M 132, 201-2; HisD 57; LPR 998, 1000, 1001; Nuestr 55-56; PlE 1:119-36, ill.; Por 212; PRFAS 163; PuI 238-44.

MONGE, Juan A. (b.1843), author, businessman
Nuestr 43-44.

MONGE Y ARREDONDO, Alejandro, teacher
GenB 327; Hi de M 204-5, ill.

MONROIG, Antonio (b.1840), farmer
Esp 93-96.

MONROUZEAU, José Antonio, composer
ArH 575; GrEPR 7:81, ill.

MONSANTO, Juan (1887-1962), dental technician
AlHP 279, ill.

MONSERRAT, Damián (b.1887), lawyer
RepM 134, ill.

MONSERRAT, Joseph, social worker,

author
    Port 11, 12(ill.)

MONSERRAT Y SIMO, Damián (b. 1858), banker
    GrEPR 14:219(ill.), 220; QEQ (1941-42) 143-44, (1948-49) 113; RepM 110, ill.

MONSERRATE ANSELMI, Adolfo Luis (b.1909), pharmacist
    GrEPR 14:219.

MONTALBAN, Helena, actress
    DelMu 192-96, ill.

MONTALVO, Hiram, painter
    GrEPR 8:411.

MONTALVO, J. Loreto de Jesús (1834-1916), educator
    GrEPR 14:220; HoIPR 71, ill.

MONTALVO, Reinaldo (b.1944), painter
    GrEPR 8:436.

MONTALVO, William H. (b.1899), author
    DiLP 2, pt.2:1014-15.

MONTALVO GUENARD, Andrés (b. 1882), doctor
    CaM 297; GenB 414-15, ill.; QEQ (1933-34) 200, (1936-37) 113, (1941-42) 144, (1948-49) 114.

MONTALVO GUENARD, Francisco (b.1888), lawyer
    QEQ (1948-49) 114.

MONTALVO GUENARD, José Leandro (1885-1950), doctor, journalist, historian
    BiP 285-86; CaM 297-98; DiLP 2, pt.2:1015-16; DiM 214-16; ECPR 6:469; GenB 415-16, ill.; HoIPR 70-71, ill.; PRFAS 163-64; QEQ (1941-42) 144-45, (1948-49) 114-15.

MONTALVO GUENARD, Luis (1874-1920), lawyer, politician
    GrEPR 14:220, ill.; HoIPR 71, ill.; RepM 236, ill.

MONTALVO GUENARD DE GOTAY, Ana

L. (1882-1945), author
    HoIPR 69-70, ill.

MONTALVO SANCHEZ, R., lawyer
    RepM 281, ill.

MONTALVO Y TORRES, José Leandro (1853-1928), author, politician
    GenB 345, ill.; HoIPR 72, ill.

MONTANER VALLDEJULI, Ramón (b. 1892), administrator
    QEQ (1936-37) 113.

MONTANEZ, Guillermo "Willie" (b.1948), baseball player
    PRUSA 19, ill.

MONTAÑEZ, Marta (b.1937), musician
    DiDHM 136; EGMPR 4:71-72, ill.; GrEPR 14:200; PRUSA 17, ill.

MONTAÑEZ, Pedro, boxer
    EPI 1:344, ill.

MONTEAGUDO, Joaquín (1890-1966), journalist, author
    BiP 286-87; DiLP 2, pt.2: 1016-19; ECPR 6:469; Hor 315-17; Per 167-69; PlE 2: 227-34, ill.; PRFAS 164.

MONTENEGRO, José D. (b.1870), doctor
    DiM 216-17; QEQ (1933-34) 109, (1936-37) 113, (1941-42) 145-46.

MONTES, Janet, painter
    GrEPR 8:412.

MONTES, Toribio de (18th-19th cent.), governor
    DiDHM 137.

MONTESINOS, José E., lawyer, judge
    RepM 214, ill.

MONTGOMERY DE DEL VALLE, Katharene (b.1940), teacher
    QEQ (1941-42) 77, (1948-49) 189.

MONTILLA, Angeles (1869-1902), singer
    DiHBC 637; MujDPR 54-55, ill.; MusMP 181.

MONTILLA HERNANDEZ, Víctor J.
(b.1906), doctor
    QEQ (1936-37) 187.

MONTILLA JIMENEZ, Fernando
(1870-1929), engineer
    HoIPR 72, ill.; RepM 94,
    ill.

MONTILLA MONTILLA, Vinicio,
translator, teacher
    PriC 174.

MONTOJO Y PASARON, Patricio
(b.1839), naval officer
    Exp 282-83.

MONZON, Luis C. (b.1937),
painter
    GrEPR 8:436.

MOORE, Rufus H. (b.1900),
scientist
    QEQ (1941-42) 146.

MORA, María Teresa (b.1897),
doctor
    CaM 299; EGMPR 3:195-96;
    QEQ (1936-37) 113.

MORALES, Alberto (1900-1950),
poet
    AntHistCag 257-58; AntPoe-
    Cag 101-2.

MORALES, Angel Celestino
(1876-1911), musician
    HoIPR 73, ill.; LPR 1048,
    1049; MusMP 258; PRFAS 164.

MORALES, Angel Luis (b.1919),
professor, author
    BrECP 299; ConA 49-52:383-
    84; DiLP 2, pt.2:1019-21;
    GrEPR 14:220; PRFAS 164-65.

MORALES, Benjamín, actor
    DelMu 198-202.

MORALES, Gil A. (b.1928),
politician
    GrEPR 14:221.

MORALES, Hugo (b.1930), psychiatrist
    Port 7, 8(ill.)

MORALES, Jacobo, actor, author, director
    DelMu 204-8, ill.; DiDHM
    138.

MORALES, Jerry (b.1949), baseball player
    PRUSA 19, ill.

MORALES, Jorge Luis (b.1930),
author, professor
    BiP 290-91; BrECP 301; CaE
    812-13; DiDHM 137; DiHBC
    639-40; DiLP 2, pt.2:1021-
    23; DicC 69; ECPR 6:469; Gr-
    EPR 14:221; PRFAS 167.

MORALES, José, manager
    Port 89, 90(ill.)

MORALES, José C. (b.1891),
author
    Hi de CR 221, 224, ill.;
    QEQ (1941-42) 146-47.

MORALES, José Miguel, businessman, musician
    Crom 77.

MORALES, José Pablo (1828-
1882), educator, author
    Ant 113-22; BiP 291-93; Di-
    DHM 138; DiHBC 640; DiLP 2,
    pt.2:1023-25; Eco 126-35;
    ECPR 6:470; EnsB 227-34; Gr-
    EPR 14:222; HisD 57; HoIPR
    72, ill.; Ind 124-25; LPR
    978, 981; Ma 41-42; Pin 34-
    35; PlE 1:311-12; Por 221;
    PRFAS 167; PuI 144-47; Sd
    123-202.

MORALES, Luis E. (b.1896?),
auditor
    QEQ (1941-42) 238-39, (1948-
    49) 115.

MORALES, Luis M. (b.1904),
doctor
    CaM 301; DiM 217.

MORALES, Manuel (b.1870), manufacturer
    Tri 1:295-302.

MORALES, Manuel (b.1916),
politician
    LiPR 36, ill.

MORALES, Miguel, businessman
    Tri 1:201-6.

MORALES BIAGGI, Ana Cristina
(b.1935), businesswoman, manager
    EGMPR 3:49-50, ill., 4:
    337-38, ill.

MORALES BLOUIN, Egla (b.1930), poet
DiLP 2, pt.2:1025-26.

MORALES CABRERA, Pablo (1866-1933), educator, author
BiP 287-90; BrECP 299-300; DiLP 2, pt.2:1026-28; ECPR 6:469-70; GrEPR 14:221; PRFAS 165-66; QEQ (1933-34) 15-16.

MORALES CABRERA, Pedro Ramón (b.1861), teacher
QEQ (1936-37) 113-14, (1941-42) 146.

MORALES CARRION, Arturo (b. 1913), educator, author, historian
BrECP 300-301; DiDHM 137-38; DiLP 2, pt.2:1028-32; GrEPR 14:221, ill.; PolPr 1:366-67; PRFAS 166; PRUSA 20.

MORALES DE PATRICK, Nylda, stock broker
EGMPR 3:51-52, ill.

MORALES FERRER, Abelardo (1864-1894), doctor, author
AntHistCag 257; CaM 300; DiLP 2, pt.2:1032-33; DiM 217-20; GrEPR 14:222; PRFAS 166.

MORALES FORTUÑO, Awilda Milagros (b.1927), labor relations official
EGMPR 3:197-98, ill.

MORALES FORTUÑO, Nora (b. 1933), secretary
EGMPR 3:199-200, ill.

MORALES MELENDEZ, José Ramón (b.1924), politician
GrEPR 14:222.

Morales Miranda, José Pablo see Morales, José Pablo

MORALES MUNERA, Alvaro (b. 1920), singer
QEQ (1948-49) 115.

MORALES MUÑOZ, Generoso E. (1898-1956), educator, historian
DiLP 2, pt.2:1033-34; Per

79-81; QEQ (1948-49) 115-16.

MORALES-NIEVA, Ignacio (b. 1928), musician, conductor, teacher
GrEPR 14:222-23, ill.

MORALES OTERO, Pablo (1896-1971), doctor, author, politician
BiP 293-94; CaM 301; DiLP 2, pt.2:1034-36; DiM 220-21; ECPR 6:470-71; GrEPR 14:223; PRFAS 167-68; QEQ (1933-34) 109-10, (1936-37) 114, (1941-42) 147-48, (1948-49) 116.

MORALES RAMOS, Florencio, singer, composer
L 22-29, 81(ill.)

MORALES RILDON, Armando, Freemason
Nues 37-38, ill.

MORALES RODRIGUEZ, Teófilo (b. 1920), politician
GrEPR 14:223.

MORALES RUIZ, Juan Silvestre (b.1888), doctor
QEQ (1933-34) 110-11, (1936-37) 114-15, (1941-42) 147.

MORALES SENEN, Justo Ramón (b. 1904), engineer
QEQ (1933-34) 110, (1936-37) 115, (1941-42) 148, (1948-49) 116-17.

MORAN, Luis, farmer
A 30.

MORAN FERNANDEZ, José, tobacco expert
A 29-30.

MOREDA, Alice, actress
DelMu 210-13, ill.

MOREDA, José, businessman
HoIPR 73, ill.

MOREDA Y PRIETO, Francisco (19th cent.), governor
DiHBC 451.

MOREIRA VELARDO, Sixto (b.1900), author
Ind 125-26.

MOREL CAMPOS, Juan (1857-1896),

composer, musician
AlHP 53-60, ill., 404; BiP
294-96; BrECP 301-3, ill.;
CiBPI 75(ill.), 160-64; Co
9; DeADeA 227-28; DiDHM
139, ill.; DiHBC 640-42;
ECPR 6:471; EPI 1:168,
ill., 3:228, 229; GrEPR 7:
93-100, ill., 196-97; HisD
57; HoIPR 73-74, ill.; Ho-
RPR 136-40; HoYMPR 96-111,
ill.; L 36-42; LPR 1024,
1025, ill.; MueYV 128-84;
Mus en P 123-24; MusMP 130-
40; PaF 91-96; Pon 53-54;
Por 197-98; PRFAS 168,
ill.; Sil 67-77; Ver 166-
67, ill.

Morell Campos, Juan see Morel
Campos, Juan

MORELL Rivera, Pedro A. (b.
1890), dentist
QEQ (1933-34) 111, (1936-
37) 115, (1941-42) 148,
(1948-49) 117.

MORENO, Babil (1819-1899),
priest
Jes 143-44.

MORENO, Enrique, businessman,
politician
RepM 329, ill.

MORENO, Esteban, doctor, musician
DiM 221.

MORENO, Mike (b.1940), businessman
Port 147, 148(ill.)

MORENO, Pedro (16th cent.),
colonist
DiDHM 139; GrEPR 14:224.

MORENO, Rita (b.1931), actress
CuB 1985:299-302, ill.;
EGMPR 4:73-74, ill.; EPI 1:
244-45, ill., 2:231-33;
MujP 225-29, ill.; Port 3,
4(ill.); PQ 42; PRUSA 20,
ill.

MORENO CALDERON, Teresina (b.
1880), singer, teacher
EGMPR 4:75-76; MusMP 181-
83.

MORENO DE RODRIGUEZ, Barbara
(1894-1969), teacher, businesswoman
EGMPR 3:53-54, ill.

MORENO FERRAN, Patria (b.1898),
designer
EGMPR 4:77-78.

MORENO RODRIGUEZ, Narciso (b.
1889), doctor
QEQ (1933-34) 111, (1936-37)
115; Tri 1:385-88.

MORET GALLARD, Simón (1863-1923),
politician
AlHP 348, ill.; Guay 263;
Hi de Cay 242; RepM 172, ill.

MORET MUÑOZ, Simón, doctor
Ka 102-3.

MORFI, Angelina, educator,
author
GrEPR 1:xi, ill., 14:224, ill.;
PRFAS 168-69.

MORILLO DE ROMAGUERA, Providencia
(b.1898), poet
EGMPR 1:181-82.

MORSE, Samuel Finlay (1791-1872),
inventor
DiHBC 644-45.

MORRIS, Marshall (b.1942),
translator, professor
DirAS 3:365.

MOSCOSO, Guillermo Humberto (b.
1881), lawyer
QEQ (1933-34) 111, (1936-37)
115, (1941-42) 148-49, (1948-
49) 117.

MOSCOSO, Manuel Guillermo,
pharmacist
A 103.

MOSCOSO, Teodoro (1871-1948),
pharmacist
AlHP 280, ill.; GrEPR 14:225;
HoIPR 74, ill.; QEQ (1933-34)
200-201, (1936-37) 115,
(1941-42) 149.

MOSCOSO, Teodoro (b.1910), pharmacist, politician
CaF 106; CuB 1963:283-85,
ill.; DiDHM 139-40; DiHBC
645; GrEPR 14:224, ill.;
PolPr 1:372-73.

MOSQUERA, Antonio de (16th
cent.), governor
    DiDHM 140; GrEPR 14:225.

MOTA SARMIENTO, Iñigo (17th
cent.), governor
    DiDHM 140; GrEPR 14:225;
    Hi de Pu 93-95.

MOTT, Thomas D., Jr., lawyer
    RepM 40, ill.

MOTTA CEREZO, Rafael (b.1949),
artist, professor
    GrEPR 8:436.

MOURNIER ROMAN, Rafael, poet
    Hor 104-5.

MOYA, Roberto (b.1931), artist
    GrEPR 8:364, ill.; PaG 213.

MOYANO, Rafael (b.1896), author, educator
    DiLP 2, pt.2:1036-37; Ind
    127.

MUCKLEY, Robert L. (b.1928),
professor
    DirAS 3:368.

MUESAS, Miguel de (b.1715),
governor
    DiDHM 141; Hi de Cay 57-60.

MUNCH, William (b.1884), insurance agent
    QEQ (1941-42) 149.

MUNDO ARZUAGA, Francisco E.
(b.1901), politician
    GrEPR 14:225; QEQ (1941-42)
    149.

MUNIOSGUREN CASANOVA, Agustín
(19th cent.), military doctor
    CaM 304-6.

MUÑEZ ROMEU, Manuel, landowner
    Hi de Cay 245-48.

MUÑIZ, Tomás "Tommy" (b.1922),
television producer
    DiDHM 141; GrEPR 14:225.

MUÑIZ SOUFFRONT, Alfredo (b.
1899), educator
    QEQ (1936-37) 115-16,
    (1941-42) 149-50, (1948-49)
    117-18.

MUNIZ SOUFFRONT, Luis (b.1895),
teacher
    GrEPR 14:225; QEQ (1941-42)
    150, (1948-49) 118.

MUÑIZ SOUFFRONT, Tomás (b.1900),
teacher
    QEQ (1948-49) 118.

MUÑOZ, Jesús María (1867-1921),
musician, teacher
    AlDU 22, 85(ill.); GrEPR 14:
    226; Ka 153-54; MusMP 259.

MUÑOZ, José Manuel, politician
    GrEPR 14:225.

MUÑOZ, Laura P. de (b.1880),
teacher
    EGMPR 1:317-18.

MUÑOZ, Manuel (b.1920), author,
journalist
    DiLP 2, pt.2:1037-39; Ind
    127-28.

MUÑOZ, Miguel A. (b.1891),
lawyer, judge
    QEQ (1933-34) 201, (1936-37)
    116, (1941-42) 151.

MUÑOZ ARJONA, Gloriel, artist
    PaG 43.

Muñoz Colomer, Jesús M. see
Muñoz, Jesús María

MUÑOZ CUEVAS, Eugenio L. (b.1888),
engineer
    QEQ (1948-49) 118-19.

MUÑOZ DE CLAVELL, Concepción
(1890-1917), teacher
    AlHP 325, ill.

MUÑOZ DE DEL VALLE ATILES, Genara,
civic works, translator
    DiHBC 646; MujDPR 120-21,
    ill.

MUÑOZ DEL TORO, José (1863-1941),
doctor
    CaM 306-7; RepM 326, ill.

MUÑOZ DIAZ, Gustavo, doctor,
politician
    DiM 221-22.

MUÑOZ DONES, Eloisa (b.1922),
doctor
    EGMPR 3:201-2, ill.

MUÑOZ IGARTUA, Angel (b.1905),
poet, lawyer
    CaE 816; DiLP 2, pt.2:
    1039-40; QEQ (1941-42) 150.

MUÑOZ LEE, Luis, journalist,
artist
    GrEPR 8:366, ill.

MUÑOZ MARIN, Luis (1898-1980),
governor, politician, author
    A 45-46, ill.; BiP 296-98;
    BrECP 305-7, ill.; CaE 816;
    ConA 97-100:388; CuB 1942:
    615-18, ill., 1953:444-46,
    ill., 1980:460; DiDHM 142-
    43, ill.; DiHBC 646-54; Di-
    LP 2, pt.2:1040-46; ECPR 6:
    471, 473; EPI 1:205-13,
    ill.; Esb 2:36-40; GenP
    111-13; GrEPR 14:226-38,
    ill.; HePR 114-36, ill.;
    HisD 58; HoPP 325-423,
    ill.; LiPR 60-61, ill.; Oro
    118-25, ill.; PolPr 1:377-
    79, 3:445-46; PriC 63-64,
    ill., 93-94, ill.; PRFAS
    169-70, ill.; PRP 73-79,
    81-86, 91-94; QEQ (1933-34)
    111-12, (1936-37) 116,
    (1941-42) 150, (1948-49)
    119; QuR 93-114, ill.; Tra
    96-134.

MUÑOZ MORALES, Luis (1866-
1950), lawyer, politician,
author
    DiLP 2, pt.2:1046-48; GrEPR
    14:239, ill.; Hi de Cay
    243; HoIPR 74, ill.; LM
    120-21; Nues 45-48, ill.;
    Per 93-95; QEQ (1936-37)
    116-17, (1941-42) 151-52,
    (1948-49) 118-19; RepM 186,
    ill.

MUÑOZ PADIN, René (b.1925),
lawyer, politician
    GrEPR 14:238, ill.; PriC
    121-22, ill.

MUÑOZ RIVERA, José (1868*-
1937), politician, author
    BiP 298-300; DiLP 2, pt.2:
    1048-49; HoIPR 75, ill.;
    PlE 2:111-21, ill.; PriC
    46; PRFAS 170; QEQ (1933-
    34) 112, (1936-37) 117.

MUÑOZ RIVERA, Luis (1859-
1916), politician, author,
journalist, Resident Commissioner
    A1HP 116-21, ill.; BiP 300-
    302; BoHP 169-71; BrECP 307,
    ill.; CaE 816-17; CiBPI 178
    (ill.), 206-10; DeADe 209-
    13; DiDHM 143, ill.; DiHBC
    654-56; DiLP 2, pt.2:1049-
    54; DicAB 7:329-30; ECPR 6:
    472(ill.), 473-74; EPI 1:
    195-99, ill.; EntP 7-20,
    36-88, 120-34, 164-81; GenP
    30, ill.; GrEPR 14:240-42,
    ill.; HePR 84-98,ill.; HisD
    58; HisP 117-20, 138-40;
    HoDMT 20-28; HoIPR 75, ill.;
    HoRPR 121-24; HoYMPR 126-51,
    ill.; Imp 253-56, 301-3; LPR
    1029-36, 1037, ill.; Mem 129-
    32, 137-38; MueYV 191-98;
    Nues 80-85, ill.; Nuestr 94-
    98; Orad 219-22; PaE 43-48,
    ill.; PaGa 239-49, ill.; PlE
    1:365-87, ill.; Por 97-98,
    245-48; PriC 17, ill.; Proc
    108-229, ill.; PRFAS 170-71,
    ill.; QuR 35-61, ill.; RepM
    50, ill.; Se 97-125, ill.;
    SeDC 184-94; Tra 95-96; VPR
    69-85, 166-67; Ver 192.

MUÑOZ RIVERA, Luis (b.1916),
lawyer, politician
    GrEPR 14:243; PriC 123-24,
    ill.

MUÑOZ SANTAELLA, Angela Luisa
(1896-1954), teacher
    EGMPR 4:309-10, ill.

MUÑOZ SIACA, María Luisa (b.
1905), musician, teacher
    EGMPR 1:319-20.

MURGA SANZ, Vicente (b.1903),
priest, educator, historian
    DiDHM 144; DiLP 2, pt.2:
    1054-56; GrEPR 14:243; QEQ
    (1933-34) 112.

MURIEL, Diego (16th cent.),
colonist
    GrEPR 14:243.

MURILLO, Antonio Esteban
(1876*-1931), poet
    BiP 302-3; DiLP 2, pt.2:
    1056-57; PRFAS 171.

MURRAY, Carrie T. (1849-1932),
orphange director

EGMPR 4:231-32.

N

NADAL Y CUEBAS, Ramón (d. 1884), lawyer
Eco 152-57; GenB 253; Nuestr 26-27.

NADAL GRAU, José (b.1902), doctor
QEQ (1933-34) 112, (1936-37) 117.

NADAL Y GROS, Esteban (d. 1892), businessman, politician
GenB 316; Nuestr 140.

NADAL MARTINEZ, Rafael (b. 1931), Fire Department official
GrEPR 14:245.

NADAL SANTA COLOMA, Juan (1877-1943), singer
MusMP 259.

NADAL SANTA COLOMA, Matilde, musician, teacher
MusMP 259.

NADAL SANTA COLOMA, Ramón, politician
GrEPR 14:245.

NANCE, Margaret Aileen (b. 1904), educator
QEQ (1936-37) 117.

NARVAEZ SANTOS, Eliezer (b. 1927), educator, author
PRFAS 173.

NASH, Rose, professor
DirAS 3:373.

NATAL MARTINEZ, Bernabé (b. 1892), lawyer
QEQ (1933-34) 112-13, (1936-37) 117.

NATER GIRONA, Francisco, pharmacist
CaF 108.

NATER Y GONZALEZ, José Francisco (b.1848), pharmacist
CaF 108; HoIPR 75, ill.; RepM 150, ill.

NATER PABON, Justo E. (b.

1910), politician
GrEPR 14:245.

NAVARRA, Gilda, correographer, actress, teacher
EGMPR 4:79-80, ill.

NAVARRETE DE LA TEXERA, Agustín, author, historiographer, journalist
DiHBC 665; PaF 87-89.

NAVARRO, Tomás (b.1884), author, professor
BrECP 318-19.

NAVARRO ALICEA, Jorge L. (b. 1937), politician
LiPR 41, ill.

NAVARRO DE HAYDON, Rosa (b. 1905), educator
EGMPR 4:201-3, ill.

NAVARRO FUENTES, Guillermo (b. 1897), author
QEQ (1936-37) 117, (1941-42) 152.

NAVARRO ORTIZ, Antonio (b. 1895), lawyer
QEQ (1936-37) 117-18; Tri 1: 401-6.

NAVARRO ORTIZ, Francisco (b. 1879), lawyer, judge
QEQ (1941-42) 152; Tri 1: 401-6.

NAVIA, Antonio (b.1945), artist
GrEPR 8:368, ill.

NAVEIRA DE RODON, Miriam, lawyer
EGMPR 3:111-12, ill.; PQ 44.

NAZARIO Y CANCEL, José María (1838-1919), priest, author
DiHBC 689-90; DiLP 2, pt.2: 1060-61; ECPR 6:474; Ka 142-44; PuI 202-7.

NAZARIO DE FERRER, Sila (b. 1930), politician
EGMPR 2:39-40, ill.; GrEPR 14:245.

NAZARIO DE FIGUEROA, Joaquín, lawyer
RepM 280, ill.

NAZARIO DE MARTINEZ, María,

civic and social works
    EGMPR 3:339-40, ill.

NAZARIO LUGO, Amadeo (b.1879),
lawyer
    QEQ (1933-34) 113, (1936-
    37) 15-16; RepM 274, ill.

NAZARIO QUIÑONES, Emilio
Antonio (b.1914), chemist
    QEQ (1948-49) 120.

NEBOT, Celedonio Luis (b.
1778), dramatist
    DiLP 2, pt.2:1061-62.

NECHODOMA, Antonin (1877-
1928), architect
    GrEPR 9:82-85, 14:247.

NEGRON, Antonio S. (b.1940),
lawyer, judge
    GrEPR 14:247.

NEGRON, Emma Iris, professor,
musical director
    GrEPR 14:247.

NEGRON, Virgilio (b.1892),
author
    DiLP 2, pt.2:1062.

NEGRON BENITEZ, Eduardo (d.
1960), politician
    GrEPR 14:247.

NEGRON DE HUTCHINSON, Luz (b.
1920), musician
    EGMPR 4:81-82, ill.

NEGRON DE TALAVERA, Cecilia
(b.1917), musician, teacher
    EGMPR 1:321, ill.

NEGRON FERNANDEZ, Luis (1910-
1986), lawyer, judge
    GrEPR 14:246(ill.), 247;
    QEQ (1941-42) 152-53.

NEGRON FLORES, Ramón (1867-
1945), author
    BiP 303-4; CaE 820; DiLP
    2, pt.2:1063-64; GrEPR 14:
    247; PlE 1:565-92, ill.;
    PRFAS 174; QEQ (1936-37)
    118, (1941-42) 153.

NEGRON LOPEZ, Luis A. (b.
1909), politician
    GrEPR 14:247, 248(ill.);
    PriC 91-92, ill.; QEQ
    (1948-49) 120.

NEGRON MARTINEZ, Wilfredo (b.
1947), politician
    LiPR 128, ill.

NEGRON MUÑOZ, Angela (1892-
1956), author, feminist
    AlHP 278, ill.; BiP 304; Di-
    LP 2, pt.2:1064-65; EGMPR 3:
    299-300, ill.; PRFAS 174.

NEGRON MUÑOZ, María Luisa (1895-
1932), educator
    DiHBC 668; MujDPR 239-44,
    ill.

Negrón Muñoz, Mercedes see
Lair, Clara

NEGRON SANJURJO, José A. (1864-
1927), poet
    CaE 820; DiLP 2, pt.2:1067-
    68.

NEGRON SANJURJO, Quintín (1859-
1922), author
    DiLP 2, pt.2:1068-69; LM 133;
    LPR 1036, 1037, 1038; Ver
    182, ill.

NEGRONI, José C. (b.1937), author
    AlHY 177-78, 227; DiLP 2, pt.
    2:1069-70.

NEGRONI MATTEI, Francisco (1896-
1937), poet
    AlHY 163-64, 218-20; DiLP 2,
    pt.2:1070-72.

NEGRONI NIGAGLIONI, Francisco,
journalist, author
    AlHY 209-10.

NEGRONI NIGAGLIONI, Santiago,
teacher, author
    AlHY 212.

NELSON, Adrián (b.1913), author
    DiLP 2, pt.2:1072-73.

NELSON RAMIREZ, Adrián (b.1934),
artist, professor
    GrERP 8:415, 14:247.

NET, Librado, musician, artist
    AlHP 339, ill.

NEUMANN, Gustavo R. (1878-1932),
businessman
    AlHP 353.

NEUMANN GANDIA, Eduardo (1852-1913), historian, teacher, journalist
AlHP 132, ill.; BiP 305: Crom 39-40; ECPR 6:474; PRFAS 174; PuI 291-95.

NEVARES MUÑIZ, Dora (b.1948), professor, lawyer
DirAS 4:389-90.

NEVAREZ Y NEVAREZ, Francisco (b.1906), engineer
QEQ (1933-34) 113, (1936-37) 118.

NICOLAU, Nicolás, businessman
A 119.

NICOLAU BARDAGUER, Rafael (b. 1889), orator, author
Algo 107-14.

NICOLE DE MARIANI, Jane, tourism official, social activist
DiHBC 668-69; EGMPR 3:113-14, ill.; GrEPR 14:249.

NIEVES, José R., businessman, politician
RepM 226, ill.

NIEVES, Josephine, social worker
Port 91, 92(ill.)

NIEVES COLLAZO, Ida (b.1941), artist
GrEPR 8:436.

NIEVES FALCON, Luis (b.1929), author, professor
BrECP 322; DiDHM 145; GrEPR 14:249; PRFAS 174-75.

NIGAGLIONI, Antonio, teacher
AlHY 269, ill.

NIGAGLIONI FIGUEROA, Iván (b. 1929), politician
LiPR 124, ill.

NIGAGLIONI TORRUELLAS, Raquel (b.1916), lawyer
EGMPR 3:203-4.

NIN BUSTAMANTE, Manuel (b. 1874), educator
QEQ (1936-37) 118, (1941-42) 153, (1948-49) 120.

NIN RUIZ, Salvador R. (b.1898), businessman
QEQ (1936-37) 118, (1941-42) 153, (1948-49) 120-21.

NISI GOYCO, Ana (b.1950), politician
LiPR 31, ill.

NOCHERA, Domingo (b.1898), doctor
QEQ (1936-37) 118.

NOELL Y AGUAYO, Gonzálo A. (1886-1950), priest
AlHP 158, ill.

NOGUERAS, Nicolás (b.1935), lawyer, politician
GrEPR 14:249; LiPR 29, ill.

NOGUERAS MUNDIZ, Francisco (b. 1875), magistrate
QEQ (1936-37) 118-19, (1941-42) 154.

NOGUERAS RIVERA, Nicolás (b. 1902), teacher, politician
GrEPR 14:249; QEQ (1933-34) 201, (1936-37) 119, (1941-42) 154.

NOLLA, José A. B. (b.1902), politician
QEQ (1936-37) 119, (1941-42) 154-55, (1948-49) 121.

NOLLA, Miguel J. (b.1905), engineer
QEQ (1948-49) 121-22.

NONES DEL VALLE, Adolfo (b. 1879), engineer
QEQ (1933-34) 201-2, (1936-37) 119.

NONES DEL VALLE, Rafael (b. 1885), engineer, architect
QEQ (1933-34) 113-14, (1936-37) 120.

NORNIELLA HERNANDEZ, Isabel (b.1938), advertising executive
EGMPR 4:211-12, ill.

NORZAGARAY, Fernando de (b.1808), governor
BeHNPR 2:95-107, ill.; GrEPR 14:249, ill.

NOVOA, Isaac (b.1945), artist
GrEPR 8:412.

NOVOA CABALLERO, Miguel, doctor
    CaDeT 190-91, ill.

NOVOA GONZALEZ, José A. (b. 1929), lawyer, politician
    GrEPR 14:250.

NOVOA Y MOSCOSO, José de (1607-1661), soldier, governor
    Hi de P 171-75.

NOYA BENITEZ, José (b.1907), doctor
    QEQ (1941-42) 155, (1948-49) 122.

NUÑEZ, Francisco (16th cent.), apothecary
    CaF 110; GrEPR 14:250.

NUÑEZ, Gonzalo (1850-1915), composer, musician
    Co 10; GrEPR 7:199-200; Mus en P 124-25; MusMP 141-44, 272.

NUÑEZ, Guillermo (b.1927), sculptor
    GrEPR 8:413.

NUÑEZ, Guillermo (b.1936?), poet
    CaE 823.

NUÑEZ, Luis (b.1931), administrator, educator
    Port 141, 142(ill.)

NUÑEZ, M. S., businessman, politician
    RepM 256, ill.

NUÑEZ MELENDEZ, Esteban (b. 1909), pharmacist, author
    BiP 305-7; BrECP 326; CaF 109-10; GrEPR 14:250; PRFAS 175; QEQ (1948-49) 122.

NUÑEZ MELENDEZ DE BUNKER, Celia (b.1910), social worker
    EGMPR 3:205-6, ill.

NUÑEZ SALARAIN, Fernando (1839?-1910), doctor, politician
    CaM 310-11; GrEPR 14:290.

O

OCASIO BERMUDEZ, Pedro Antonio

(b.1898), politician
    GrEPR 14:251; QEQ (1941-42) 238.

OCHART, Bolívar, labor leader, politician
    GrEPR 14:251.

OCHOA DE CASTRO, Sancho (17th cent.), governor, soldier
    Hi de Pu 83-85.

OCHOTECO, Félix, politician
    GrEPR 14:251.

O'DALY, Demetrio (1780-1837), soldier, government official
    BeHNPR 1:381-404; CiBPI 68 (ill.), 84-85; DiDHM 147; EPI 1:78-79, ill.; HisD 60; PuI 55-58.

O'DALY, Jaime (18th cent.), administrator
    DiHBC 675-76; GrEPR 14:251.

O'DALY, Tomás (18th cent.), engineer
    GrEPR 14:251.

OGILVIE, John William Greene (b.1902), manager
    QEQ (1936-37) 120.

OJEDA, Félix (1903-1976), political activist
    GrEPR 14:251.

OJEDA DE BATTLE, Josefina (1910?-1972), teacher, politician
    EGMPR 2:41, ill.; GrEPR 14:251, 252(ill.); PriC 77, ill., 125-26, ill.

O'KELLY, Joseph J. (1890*-1970), architect
    GrEPR 9:87-88; QEQ (1936-37) 120.

OLDS BISSELL, Frederick (b. 1902), professor
    QEQ (1941-42) 155-56.

OLIVER, Félix, businessman
    A 124.

OLIVER, Jack John, lawyer, government official
    Port 19, 20(ill.)

OLIVER, José R. (b.1901), artist,

professor
BrECP 327; DiDHM 147; GrEPR
8:272, ill.; PaG 190-91;
PRFAS 177.

OLIVER, José Ramón (19th
cent.), pharmacist
CaF 111.

OLIVER, José Víctor, engineer
A 36-37.

OLIVER FRAU, Antonio (1902-
1945), author, lawyer
BiP 307; BrECP 327; CaE
823-24; DiLP 2, pt.2:1076-
77; ECPR 6:475; PlE 2:401-
8, ill.: PRFAS 177; QEQ
(1936-37) 120.

OLIVER GONZALEZ, José (b.
1912), doctor, researcher
DiHBC 676-77.

OLIVER ROSES, Lorenzo (b.
1875), accountant, businessman
QEQ (1936-37) 120.

OLIVERA, Ramón, artist
GrEPR 8:437.

OLIVERAS, Blas (b.1891), politician, journalist
QEQ (1936-37) 120-21,
(1941-42) 156.

OLIVERAS GUERRA, Artajerjes
(1898-1965), doctor
CaM 313.

OLIVIERI, Ulises (1862?-1939?)
poet, journalist
AlHY 211; DiLP 2, pt.2:
1077-78.

OLIVO, José A. (b.1935), artist
GrEPR 8:437.

OLOZABAL, Francisco, businessman
A 150.

OLSEN, Sally (b.1912), orphan-
age director, missionary
EGMPR 4:311-13, ill.

OLLER, Francisco (1833-1917),
artist
BgP facing p.184, ill.; BiP
308-10; BrECP 327-28; CiBPI

79(ill.), 132-35; DiDHM 148,
ill.; DiHBC 677-80; ECPR 6:
475; EPI 1:182-83, ill.;
GrEPR 8:43-117, 276, ill.;
HisD 60; HoDMT 149-52; Ho-
IPR 76; HoRPR 152-57; HoYMPR
24-37, ill.; LPR 788, 789,
791, 988, 989, ill.; MusMP
184-85; PaG 57-64, 161-63;
Por 202-3; PRFAS 177-78,
ill.; PRP 249-50.

OLLER, Jorge L. cinema owner
A 161.

OLLER Y CESTERO, Isabel (1837-
1914), singer
EGMPR 4:83-84; MusMP 185.

OLLER Y FERRER, Francisco
(1758-183?), doctor
BeHNPR 1:294-96, ill.; CaM
313; CiBPI 57-59; DiHBC
680.

OMS SULSONA, Américo, doctor
CaM 313-14.

O'NEILL, Ana María (b.1894),
educator, author
BiP 310-11; DiHBC 680-81;
DiLP 2, pt.2:1078-82; ECPR
6:475; EGMPR 1:323-26, ill.;
GrEPR 14:253; MujDPR 247-
49, ill.; Oro 26-37, ill.;
PQ 45; PRFAS 178.

O'NEILL, Gonzalo (1867-1942),
author
DiLP 2, pt.2:1082-83; ProA
46-47.

O'NEILL, Leo R. (b.1900), artist
QEQ (1948-49) 123.

O'NEILL DE MILAN, Luis (b.
1893), author
DiLP 2, pt.2:1083-84; ProA
57, ill.; QEQ (1936-37)
121, (1941-42) 156, (1948-
49) 122-23; Vida 68-70;
VisC 91-97.

O'NEILL LOPEZ, Juan, music
teacher
MusMP 260.

O'NEILL Y MARTINEZ DE ANDINO,
Luis (1861-1915?), author
AntHistCag 258; DiDHM 148;

HoIPR 76-78, ill.

ONIS, Federico de (1885-1966),
professor, author
    BiP 311-12; BrECP 328-29;
    PRFAS 178.

OPPENHEIMER, Santiago, politician
    GrEPR 14:253.

ORAMA MONROIG, Jorge (b.1938),
lawyer, politician
    GrEPR 14:252.

ORAMA PADILLA, Carlos (b.
1905), author
    AlDJ 165, ill.; BiP 312-13;
    DiLP 2, pt.2:1084-86; PRFAS
    179; QEQ (1948-49) 123.

ORDOÑEZ, Eduardo, singer
    QEQ (1948-49) 192-93.

ORDOÑEZ, Luisina (d.1975),
artist
    GrEPR 8:188-90.

ORDOÑEZ Y FERNANDEZ, Fernando
(b.1893), dentist
    QEQ (1936-37) 188.

ORDOÑEZ GOMEZ, José, doctor
    CaM 314.

O'REILLY, Alejandro (18th
cent.), soldier
    DiDHM 148-49; DiHBC 684;
    DiLP 2, pt.2:1105-8; GrEPR
    14:252, 253(ill.)

ORLANDI BAIRAN, Juan (b.1889),
Protestant minister
    QEQ (1933-34) 114, (1936-
    37) 121, (1941-42) 156-57,
    (1948-49) 123-24.

ORMAOECHEA, Fernando de, author
    DiDHM 149.

ORONOZ RODON, Joaquín, businessman
    BoHP 185, ill.

ORSINI LUIGGI, Sadí (b.
1938), author
    DiLP 2, pt.2:1109-10; Ind
    128-29.

ORSINI SANTINI, Juan André

(1837-1924), doctor
    CaM 316-17; GenB 358, ill.

ORTA, Awilda, educator
    Port 45, 46(ill.)

ORTEA, Francisco C. (1845-
1899), journalist, author
    DiLP 2, pt.2:1110-11;
    Nuestr 131-33.

ORTEGA, Cristóbal (19th cent.),
soldier
    BeHNPR 1:322.

ORTEGA, Luis (b.1910), doctor,
professor
    QEQ (1948-49) 124.

ORTEGA, Ricardo (19th-20th
cent.), governor
    DiDHM 149; DiHBC 456; GrEPR
    14:253, ill.

ORTEGA ROSADO, Enrique (b.
1893), engineer
    QEQ (1933-34) 114-15, (1936-
    37) 121, (1941-42) 157.

ORTIZ, Antonio, typographer
    A 153.

ORTIZ, Antonio Daniel (b.1891),
educator
    QEQ (1936-37) 122.

ORTIZ, Carlos (b.1936), boxer
    EPI 1:339(ill.), 340-41;
    PRUSA 21, ill.

ORTIZ, Carlos "Sueños" (b.
1952), artist
    GrEPR 8:413.

ORTIZ, Domingo Silás (b.1913),
author, journalist
    DiLP 2, pt.2:1111-12.

ORTIZ, Eduardo M., sculptor
    GrEPR 8:437; PaG 211-12.

ORTIZ, Elín, actor
    DelMu 216-21, ill.; GentI
    68-72.

ORTIZ, Emilio H., government
official
    PriC 173, ill.

ORTIZ, José Antonio (b.1915),
author, journalist

DiLP 2, pt.2:112-13.

ORTIZ, José Ramón (b.1925), musician, singer, composer
Port 179, 180(ill.)

ORTIZ, Julio B. (b.1893), educator
QEQ (1936-37) 122, (1941-42) 157-58.

ORTIZ, Liborio, educator
Tri 2:257-63.

ORTIZ, Pedro N. (1888-1949), doctor
CaM 317-18; HoIPR 81, ill.; QEQ (1933-34) 115, (1936-37) 122-23, (1941-42) 158; Tri 1:69-74.

ORTIZ ALIBRAN, Juan José (1883-1956), lawyer, author
HoIPR 80, ill.; Ind 129; QEQ (1936-37) 121-22.

ORTIZ COLLAZO, Alberto (b. 1935), artist
BrECP 330; GrEPR 8:437; PRFAS 179.

ORTIZ DE AGUDO, Raquel, lawyer pharmacist
PQ 46.

ORTIZ DE DIEZ DE ANDINO, Rita O. (b.1899), nurse
EGMPR 3:207-9, ill.

ORTIZ DE LA RENTA Y SANCHEZ, José (d.1868), politician
GrEPR 14:254; HoIPR 79, ill.

ORTIZ DE NEGRON, María (d. 1961), housewife
Desd 193-95.

ORTIZ DE ROBLES, Elsa, actress, advertising agency administrator
Port 31, 32(ill.)

ORTIZ DEL RIVERO, Ramón "Diplo" (1920-1956*), actor
DiDHM 149-50; HoIPR 80, ill.

ORTIZ GARCIA, Félix Renato (b. 1894), lawyer
QEQ (1936-37) 122.

ORTIZ GORDILLS, Humberto (b. 1930), lawyer, politician
GrEPR 14:254.

ORTIZ LEBRON, Francisco (b. 1880), businessman, politician
GrEPR 14:254; QEQ (1933-34) 115, (1936-17) 122.

ORTIZ LEON, Juan (b.1873), politician
QEQ (1936-37) 122.

ORTIZ LOPEZ, Vicente (b.1869), businessman
Tri 1:281-86.

ORTIZ ORTIZ, Benjamín (1908-1976), judge, politician
DiHBC 684-85; GrEPR 14:254, ill.

ORTIZ RIVERO, Camelia, singer, professor
GrEPR 14:254.

ORTIZ STELLA, Cruz (1900-1969), politician, author
BiP 313-14; CaE 826; Desd 68-70; DiLP 2, pt.2:1113-15; GrEPR 14:254-55; PriC 127-28, ill.; PRFAS 179; QEQ (1948-49) 124: SobM 21-24; Vida 47-48.

ORTIZ TORO, Alberto, insurance agent
A 42.

ORTIZ TORO, Arturo (b.1896), lawyer, politician
GrEPR 14:255; PriC 129-30, ill.; QEQ (1936-37) 123.

OSORIO, Carlos (b.1927), artist
BrECP 330; GrEPR 8:437; PaG 201-2; PRFAS 179-80.

OSUNA, Juan José (1884-1950?), educator
AntHistCag 258-59; BiP 314-15; BioD 2:977-78; ECPR 6:475-76; GrEPR 14:296; PRFAS 180; QEQ (1936-37) 123; Tri 1:127-32.

OSUNA, Pedro (b.1890), agronomist
QEQ (1933-34) 115-16, (1936-37) 123, (1941-42) 158.

OTERO, Ana (1861-1905), musician, teacher
    DiDHM 150; DiHBC 685; EGMPR 4:85-87, ill.; GrEPR 14:255, 256(ill.): MujDPR 58-63, ill.; MujP 122-23; MujPu 61-64; MusMP 145-52; PQ 12.

OTERO, José I. (b.1893), author
    QEQ (1936-37) 123-24, (1941-42) 158, (1948-49) 124.

OTERO, Julia, music teacher
    MusMP 289.

OTERO, Modesta (d.1912), musician, teacher
    MusMP 260.

OTERO, Olimpio (1828-1911), businessman, politician
    AlHP 347, ill.; Crom 71-72; Ka 34-37; Mem 95; Ver 173.

OTERO, Oscar (b.1904), engineer
    QEQ (1941-42) 159.

OTERO Y ARCE, Antonio (b. 1869), government official
    QEQ (1936-37) 123.

OTERO BOSCO, Rubén D. (1919-1969), politician
    GrEPR 14:255.

OTERO BOSCO DE JOVE, Elba A., politician
    EGMPR 2:43, ill.; GrEPR 14:255.

OTERO CORTES, Roque (b.1928), politician
    LiPR 119, ill.

OTERO LOPEZ, Alejandro (b. 1890), doctor
    QEQ (1933-34) 116, (1936-37) 124.

OTERO SAN ANTONIO, Alejandro, (d.1906), doctor, author
    CaM 318.

OVANDO, Francisco de (16th cent.), governor
    DiDHM 150; GrEPR 14:298.

OVANDO, Nicolás de (1451?-1511), military leader
    HisD 61.

P

PABON, Mario, actor, director
    DelMu 224-29, ill.

PABON, Regalado (d.1931), artisan
    San 50-51.

PABON RAMIREZ, Héctor Enrique (b.1902), engineer
    QEQ (1933-34) 116, (1936-37) 124.

PABON TUR, Elpidio (1902-1940), author
    DiLP 2, pt.2:1115-16.

PACHECO, Juan B., businessman
    RepM 270, ill.

PACHECO, Lorenzo, artist
    PaG 227-29.

PACHECO María del Coral, singer
    MusMP 185-86.

PACHECO DE MATOS, Domingo (18th cent.), soldier
    GrEPR 14:257.

PACHECO Y PACHECO, Sixto A. (b.1899), politician
    GrEPR 14:257, ill.; QEQ (1936-37) 124, (1941-42) 159.

PACHECO PADRO, Antonio (b. 1913), journalist, politician
    DiLP 2, pt.2:1116-18; Esb 2:128-31; GrEPR 14:257; QEQ (1948-49) 124-25.

PACHECO RUIZ, Gumersindo (b. 1901), lawyer, accountant
    QEQ (1933-34) 116, (1936-37) 124.

PADIAL, Luis (1832-1879), soldier, abolitionist
    BeHNPR 2:247-52, ill.; BgP facing p.193, ill.; BiP 315-16; BrECP 331, ill.; DiDHM 151; ECPR 6:476; EnsB 187-97; GrEPR 14:258, ill.;

HisD 62: HoIPR 81, ill.;
LPR 986, 987, 989; PRFAS
181; PuI 186-92.

PADIAL Y VIZCARRONDO, Félix
(1838-1880), newspaperman,
politician
DiDHM 151; EnsB 217-26;
GrEPR 14:257.

PADILLA, Francisco de (17th
cent.), bishop
Hi de la Ig 92-101.

PADILLA, Gustavo E. (b.1902),
engineer, lawyer
QEQ (1936-37) 124, (1941-
42) 159.

Padilla, Hernán see Padilla
Ramírez, Hernán

PADILLA, José Gualberto (1829-
1896), author, doctor
BiP 317-18; BrECP 331-32,
ill.; CaE 828-29; CaM 320-
21: DiDHM 152, ill.; DiLP
2, pt.2:1119-21; DiM 230-
40; ECPR 6:476; GenB 336-
39, ill.; GenP 28; GrEPR
14:258; HisD 44; HoIPR 56-
57, ill.; HoRPR 100-106;
LPR 980, 983, ill.; MueYV
135-39; PlE 1:405-19, ill.;
Por 216.

PADILLA CAMPIS, Mario (b.
1893), businessman
EstCR 2:52-56, ill.

PADILLA COSTA, Antonio (b.
1907), politician
GrEPR 14:258; PriC 131-32,
ill.

PADILLA DAVILA, Manuel (1847-
1898), poet
DiLP 2, pt.2:1121-22; Ho-
IPR 81, ill.; PlE 1:285;
PRFAS 181.

PADILLA DE ARMAS, Encarnación
(b.1907), political activist,
advisor on aging
Port 53, 54(ill.)

PADILLA DE SANZ, Trinidad
(1864-1958*), author, music
teacher
ArH 546-48; BiP 316-17;
CaE 829; DiHBC 689; DiLP

2, pt.2:1122-24; ECPR 6:476;
EGMPR 1:185-88, ill.; GrEPR
4:75, 14:258; MujDPR 111-15,
ill.; MujP 126-27; MujPu
110-16; MusMP 260-62; Per 21-
22; PQ 13; PRFAS 181-82, ill.;
QEQ (1936-37) 124, (1941-42)
239, (1948-49) 125; Se 33-
38, ill.; Vida 29-31.

PADILLA IGUINA, Julio (1855?-
1913), poet, translator
DiLP 2, pt.2:1124-25.

PADILLA RAMIREZ, Hernán (b.1938),
doctor, politician
DiDHM 152; GrEPR 14:259, ill.;
LiPR 126, ill.; PRUSA 20, ill.

PADILLA RECIO, Martín (b.1900),
newspaperman
QEQ (1936-37) 124, (1941-
42) 159, (1948-49) 125.

PADILLA RIVERA, Eddie A. (b.
1934), politician
LiPR 36, ill.

PADIN, José (1886-1963), author,
educator
BiP 318-20; BrECP 332; DiDHM
152-53, ill.; DiLP 2, pt.2:
1125-29; GrEPR 14:259, ill.;
PRFAS 182-83; QEQ (1933-34)
116-17, (1936-37) 124-25.

PADOWANY, Juan, Post Office
official
Ka 99.

Padre Rufo see Fernández, Rufo
Manuel

PADRO, Humberto, (1906-1958),
author, journalist
BiP 320; CaE 829; DiLP 2, pt.
2:1129-30; PRFAS 183.

PADRO PARES, Rafael (b.1891),
lawyer, politician
GrEPR 14:259; QEQ (1936-37)
125, (1948-49) 125-26.

PADRO QUILES, José, labor
leader, politician
GrEPR 14:260; LuO 1, 3-5, 9-
10, ill.

PADRON RIVERA, Lino (1897-1960),
labor leader, politician
GrEPR 14:260.

PAGAN, Avelino (1872-1927),
artisan
    San 52-53.

PAGAN, Bolívar (1879-1961),
author, lawyer, politician
Resident Commissioner
    BiP 321-22; BrECP 333,
    ill.; CiBPI 228(ill.), 293-
    95; DiDHM 153; DiLP 2,
    pt.2:1130-33; ECPR 6:477;
    Esb 2:47-50; GrEPR 14:260,
    261(ill.); HisD 62; HoPP
    157-72, ill.; PRFAS 183;
    QEQ (1933-34) 117, (1936-
    37) 125, (1941-42) 160,
    (1948-49) 126; SobM 187-90.

PAGAN, Gloria María (b.1921),
author
    DiDHM 154; DiLP 2, pt.2:
    1133-36; EGMPR 1:189-90,
    ill.; GrEPR 14:260; PRFAS
    185.

PAGAN, Juan Bautista (1907-
1964), author, journalist
    DiLP 2, pt.2:1136-38; Gr-
    EPR 14:260; Per 163-65.

PAGAN, Pedro (d.1919?), artisan
    San 51-52.

PAGAN, Vicente (1853-1920),
politician, orator
    GenB 353, ill.; Hi de M
    210, ill.; HoIPR 82, ill.

PAGAN COLON, Victoriano (b.
1890), pharmacist, chemist
    QEQ (1941-42) 160-61.

Pagán de Soto see Pagán Estela

PAGAN DONES, Carmen Junco (b.
1938), television executive
    EGMPR 3:55-56, ill.

PAGAN ESMORIS, Rafael (b.
1902), bank manager
    GenB 438-39.

PAGAN ESTELA, Gladys (b.1926),
author, educator
    DiLP 2, pt.2:1138-39; PRFAS
    183-84.

Pagán y Ferrer, Gloria María
see Pagán, Gloria María

PAGAN FORTIS, Petro América,
social worker
    EGMPR 3:115-16, ill.; PQ 47.

PAGAN MOYA, Augusto (b.1920),
politician
    LiPR 122, ill.

PAGAN ROSELL, Ernesto, politician
    GrEPR 14:260.

PAINE, Edward S., lawyer
    RepM 306, ill.

PALACIO, Romualdo (19th cent.),
governor
    DiDHM 154; GrEPR 14:262, ill.

PALACIOS, Rafael D., artist
    GrEPR 8:438.

PALACIOS RODRIGUEZ, Rafael,
lawyer
    RepM 69, ill.

PALACIOS SALAZAR, Manuel (b.
1864), politician, mace-bearer
    PriC 46.

PALERM ALFONSO, Juan A. (b.
1912), lawyer, politician
    GrEPR 14:262.

PALES ANES, Vicente (1865-1913),
poet
    DiLP 2, pt.2:1139-40; Guay
    263-68; HoIPR 82; PaGa 251-
    54, ill.; PlE 1:461-76, ill.

PALES MATOS, Gustavo (1907-1963),
author, journalist
    CaE 829; DiLP 2, pt.2:1140-
    42; Guay 273; Per 39-41.

PALES MATOS, Luis (1898-1959),
poet
    BiP 322-24; BrECP 336-37,
    ill.; CaE 829-31, ill.; Ci-
    BPI 228(ill.), 295-96; Di-
    DHM 154-55, ill.; DiLP 2,
    pt.2:1142-49; ECPR 6:477;
    EPI 1:153, ill.; GrEPR 14:
    263; Guay 268-72; HisD 62;
    HoDMT 67-71; HoIPR 83, ill.;
    Ind 129; Oro 84-91, ill.;
    Per 5-7, ill.; PlE 2:303-17;
    PRFAS 184-85, ill.; SobM
    160-63.

PALES MATOS, Vicente (1903-

1963), lawyer, author
  BiP 324-26; CaE 831: DiLP
  2, pt.2:1149-52; ECPR 6:
  477-78; Guay 272-73; PRFAS
  185; QEQ (1933-34) 117-18,
  (1936-37) 125, (1941-42)
  161.

Palma, Marigloria see Pagán,
Gloria María

PALMER, Jesús E. (b.1925),
politician
  GrEPR 14:263.

PALMER, Santiago R. (1844*-
1908), politician, journalist
  CiBPI 176(ill.), 191-93;
  DiDHM 155, ill.; GenB 28;
  GenP 66; GrEPR 14:263,
  ill.; Hi de M 194, ill.;
  HisD 62; HoIPR 83, ill.; Ka
  86; LPR 1004, 1005, 1007,
  ill.; MueYV 186-90; Nues 9-
  14, ill.; Nuestr 16-18;
  PRFAS 185-86; PuI 266-90;
  VerOr 119.

PALMER DE CLINCHARD, Marina,
artist
  GrEPR 8:414.

PALMER DIAZ, Santiago R.
(1893-1969), politician,
banker
  GrEPR 14:263; PriC 133
  (ill.), 134; QEQ (1941-42)
  239-40, (1948-49) 126-27;
  S 88.

PALMER LOPEZ, Arnaldo (b.
1917), doctor
  QEQ (1948-49) 127.

PALMER ROMAGUERA, Rafael M.
(b.1889), engineer, electrician
  QEQ (1936-37) 125-26.

PALLARES Y CUCHILLO, Juan
(19th cent.), doctor
  CaM 325.

PANDOLFI DE RINALDIS LARA,
Honorato (b.1909), lawyer
  QEQ (19341-42) 161, (1948-
  49), 127.

PANIAGUA, Alfonso, doctor
  RepM 246, ill.

PANIAGUA, Reinaldo, businessman
  RepM 166, ill.

PANIAGUA OLLER, Manuel, government official
  RepM 46, ill.

PANIAGUA PICAZO, Antonio (1904-
1966), journalist, author
  DiLP 2, pt.2:1152-53; QEQ
  (1936-37) 126, (1941-42)
  161-62, (1948-49) 128.

PANIAGUA SERRACANTE, José (b.
1905), author
  DiLP 2, pt.2:1153-54; Ind
  129-30; PRFAS 186; Vida 61-
  62.

PANTOJA, Antonia (b.1922),
educator
  Port 9, 10(ill.); PQ 49.

PANTOJA TORRES, Francisco (b.
1911), artist
  ArH 540-41.

PANZARDI, Santiago A. (d.1924),
businessman
  GenB 388-90, ill.; VerOr 149,
  194(ill.)

PAOLI, Amalia (1861-1942),
singer, music teacher
  BiP 235-37; DiHBC 691; EGMPR
  4: 89-91, ill.; GrEPR 7:215,
  ill., 14:263; MujDPR 118-19,
  ill.; MujPu 95-97; MusMP 186-
  87; Orig 301-2, 303(ill.);
  PonY 45; QEQ (1936-37) 188.

PAOLI, Antonio (1873-1946),
singer
  BiP 235-37; CiBPI 222(ill.),
  242-44; DiDHM 156; DiHBC
  691; ECPR 6:478; EPI 1:169-
  71, ill.; GrEPR 7:212-13,
  ill.; HisD 62; HoIPR 83-87,
  ill.; HoYMPR 184-93, ill.;
  Mus en P 125-26; Orig 338-
  39; Per 42-44, ill.; PRFAS
  186-87; QEQ (1933-34) 118-19,
  (1936-37) 126.

PAOLI DE BRASCHI, Olivia (b.
1854?), civic works, suffragette
  EGMPR 4:261-62, ill.; MujDPR
  102-4, ill.

PARALITICI, Alfonso (b.1907),
engineer

QEQ (1941-42) 162.

PARDO DE CASABLANCA, Coloma
(1892-1952), author, teacher
    DiLP 2, pt.2:1155-56; EGMPR
    1:327-28, ill.; MujDPR 221,
    ill.

PARDO DE MARCHENA, Miguel A.,
doctor
    A 107.

PARDO VEGA, Edith (b.1920),
lawyer
    EGMPR 3:211-12.

PAREJA, Agustín de (d.1751),
governor
    GrEPR 14:264.

PARES, Josefino (1862-1908),
musician
    GrEPR 14:264; MusMP 262-64.

PARES, Juan R. (b.1881),
accountant
    QEQ (1936-37) 127.

PARKHURST, Norman, politician
    GrEPR 14:264.

PARRA CAPO, Francisco (1872-
1952), lawyer, politician
    A 81; AlHP 284, ill.; Crom
    94; GrEPR 14:264, ill.; Ho-
    IPR 87, ill.; RepM 45, ill.

PARRA CAPO, Pedro Juan (1877-
1905), soldier
    And 181-83; SobM 201-3.

PARRA DUPERON, Francisco
(1827-1899), lawyer, banker
    AlHP 347.

PARRA TORO, Francisco, lawyer
    A 85.

PARRILLA, Arturo (b.1926),
author
    PRFAS 187.

PARRILLA, Carmen Iris, painter
    GrEPR 8:438.

PARRILLA, Joaquín R. (b.1901),
poet
    DiLP 2, pt.2:1156.

PARRILLA BONILLA, Antulio (b.

1917), Catholic priest, author
    DiDHM 156; GrEPR 6:289, 14:
    264, ill.

PARRILLA DATIS, José Joaquín
(1827-1868), revolutionary
    Añas 24-28.

PASARELL, Arturo (b.1866),
musician, composer, teacher
    GrEPR 14:265; MusMP 230-31.

PASARELL, Charles (b.1944),
tennis player
    PRUSA 21.

PASARELL, Emilio J. (b.1891),
author
    BiP 326-27; DiLP 2, pt.2:
    1156-58; ECPR 6:478; GrEPR
    14:265; Ind 130-31; PRFAS
    187; QEQ (1936-37) 127,
    (1941-42) 162, (1948-49) 128.

PASARELL, Oriol, music teacher
    AlHP 404; MusMP 289-90.

PASARELL DE COLON, Sara María
Gabriela (1895-1969), teacher
    EGMPR 1:329-30; QEQ (1941-
    42) 162.

PASARELL Y RIUS, Manuel (d.
1909?), doctor
    CaM 327-28; DiM 244-45; Med
    59-64; RepM 219, ill.

PASCUAL ARZOLA, Libertad (b.
1903), politician
    GrEPR 14:265; QEQ (1948-49)
    128.

PASSALACQUA, Luis Antonio (b.
1898), doctor
    QEQ (1936-37) 127.

PASSALACQUA-CHRISTIAN, Luis A.
(b.1926), government official
    DiHBC 700-701.

PASSARELL, Augusto (1864-1910),
lawyer
    Crom 85; HoIPR 88, ill.

PASTOR, Angeles (b.1908), author
    DiLP 2, pt.2:1158-63.

PASTOR, Jaime, businessman
    Ka 168.

PASTOR, Jorge (b.1910), poet

DiLP 2, pt.2:1163-64.

PASTOR LOPEZ, Carlos, minister, teacher
AlDJ 215, ill.

PATRON Y RAMOS, Ramón, pharmacist
CaF 113-14, 193.

PATTEN, Ryder (b.1897), lawyer
QEQ (1936-37) 127.

Pavía, Julián see Pavía y Lacy, Julián Juan

PAVIA FERNANDEZ, Antonio (b. 1895), businessman
BoHP 192, ill.; QEQ (1936-37) 127.

PAVIA FERNANDEZ, Manuel (b. 1896), doctor, politician
BoHP 190, ill.; CaM 328; DiM 246-47; GrEPR 14:265; PRFAS 187; QEQ (1933-34) 119, (1936-37) 127, (1941-42) 163, (1948-49) 128-29.

PAVIA Y LUCY, Julián Juan (1812-1870), governor
BeHNPR 2:241-45, ill.; DiDHM 156-57; DiHBC 453-54; GrEPR 14:265, ill.

PAYNE, George Calvin (b.1887), doctor
QEQ (1936-37) 127-28.

PAZ DE CABRERA, Francisca (1840-1915), civic works
DiHBC 702; EGMPR 4:161-62, ill.; GrEPR 14:265; MujDPR 82-84, ill.

PAZ FALCON, Benito (19th cent.), pharmacist
CaF 114.

PAZ GRANELA, Francisco (1894-1957). labor leader, politician
GrEPR 14:266; QEQ (1941-42) 163-64.

Peache see Hernández, José P. H.

PEDREIRA, Antonio S. (1899-1939), author, professor, bibliographer, journalist

BiP 327-30; BoBP 77-84; BrECP 340-41; CaE 833; CiBPI 223(ill.), 296-99; DiDHM 157, ill.: DiHBC 707; DiLP 2, pt. 2:1164-69; ECPR 6:478; GrEPR 14:266, ill.; HisD 67; Oro 66-72, ill.; Per 54-56, ill.; PIE 2:343-60, ill.; PRFAS 188; QEQ (1933-34) 119, (1936-37) 128; Una 185-88; VPR 111-17, 168; Vida 11-14.

PEDREIRA, José Enrique (1904-1959), composer, teacher
BiP 330-31; BrECP 341; ECPR 6:479; GrEPR 7:266-68, ill.; Mus en P 150-51; PRFAS 188-89: QEQ (1936-37) 188, (1948-49) 193.

PEDROSA, Ramón, accused assassin
AlHP 313, ill.

PEDROSA LEON, Juan (b.1887), Senate clerk
QEQ (1936-37) 128.

PELLON, Daniel, Jr. (b.1900), lawyer
QEQ (1936-37) 188, (1941-42) 164, (1948-49) 129.

PELLOT, Víctor (b.1931), baseball player
EPI 1:333, ill.

PENA, Fernando, designer
GentI 209-13.

PENNE DE CASTILLO, María Luisa, artist
GrEPR 8:438.

PENNOCK, Frederick Moisés (b. 1855), professor, gardener
QEQ (1936-37) 128.

PENNOCK, William (b.1907), agronomist
QEQ (1941-42) 164.

PEÑA, Lito, musician
GrEPR 7:141, 142(ill.)

PEÑA CLOS, Sergio (b.1927), politician
LiPR 28, ill.

PEÑA ESCABI, José Antonio (b. 1903), doctor
QEQ (1933-34) 119, (1936-37) 128.

PEÑA Y MONTILLA, Angeles
(1869-1902), singer
EGMPR 4:93-94; MujPu 65-68;
MusMP 188; Orig 304-5.

PEÑA QUIÑONES, Hernán (b.
1932), politician
LiPR 38, ill.

PEÑA Y REYES, Juan (1879-
1948), musician, composer,
director, teacher
BiP 331-32; PRFAS 189.

PEÑA SANCHEZ, Isidro R. (b.
1902), engineer
QEQ (1933-34) 119-20,
(1936-37) 128, (1948-49)
129.

PEÑARANDA, Carlos (1848-1908),
author
DiLP 2, pt.2:1169-72; Hi de
M 208-9.

PERALES, César, lawyer
Port 151, 152(ill.)

PERAZA, Gladys, artist
GrEPR 8:438.

PERCY, Fausto (1895-1963),
educator, accountant
AlHP 279, ill.; Tri 2:241-
46.

PERDOMO Y SANTIAGO, Quintín
O., priest
BoHP 148-49.

Perea, Juan Augusto see Perea
Rosello, Juan Augusto

PEREA, Juan J., lawyer
GenB 294-95; Hi de M 189;
Nuestr 74-75.

PEREA, Nelson, doctor
A 95.

PEREA FAJARDO, Pedro (1881-
1938), doctor, politician
A 109; CaM 331; DiM 247-48;
GenB 384-85, ill.; GrEPR
14:267; Hi de M 223, 224-
27, ill.; HoIPR 88, ill.;
RepM 74, ill.

PEREA ROSELLO, Juan Augusto
(1896-1959), politician, author, journalist

BiP 237-38; DiLP 2, pt.2:
1172-74; GrEPR 14:267; PRFAS
189-90; VPR 131-33, 169.

PEREA ROSELLO, Pedro Luis (b.
1906), author, translator
BiP 237-38; DiLP 2, pt.2:
1174-75.

PEREA ROSELLO, Salvador (1897-
1970), lawyer, politician, author
BiP 237-38; GrEPR 14:267;
SobM 137-39.

PEREDA, Clemente (b.1903),
author, journalist
DiLP 2, pt.2:1175-78.

PEREIRA, Luis A., businessman
A 171-72.

PEREIRA CASILLAS, Francisco
(b.1879), bus company owner
QEQ (1936-37) 188.

PERELLO CERDA, Francisco, landowner, farmer
RepM 249, ill.

PEREZ, Frank (b.1948), artist
GrEPR 8:438.

PEREZ, Guadalupe G., politician
GrEPR 14:267.

PEREZ, Josie, actress
DelMu 232-37, ill.; EGMPR
4:95-96, ill.

PEREZ, Manuel (1844-1898),
pharmacist, author
CaF 115-16; GrEPR 14:267;
PuI 301-5.

PEREZ, Vicente, businessman
Crom 89.

PEREZ, William (b.1937), poet
DiLP 2, pt.2:1178-80.

PEREZ ALMIROTY, Federico G.
(b.1880), lawyer
LM 133; QEQ (1933-34) 120,
(1936-37) 128-29.

PEREZ ALMIROTY, María M. de
(b.1881), politician, civic
works
EGMPR 2:23, ill., 4:177-78,
ill.; PQ 14; PriC 71, ill.

PEREZ AVILES, Manuel (1869-1928), politician
ArH 405, 406, 415-16; Gr-EPR 14:267; HoIP 89, ill.; RepM 157, ill.

PEREZ CRUZ, José, politician
GrEPR 14:268.

PEREZ CHANIS, Efraín E., architect
GrEPR 1:xiv, ill.

PEREZ DE GUZMAN, Juan (17th cent.), soldier, governor
DiDHM 158; GrEPR 14:264; Hi de P 175-78.

PEREZ DOMINGUEZ, Agustín (b. 1904), businessman
QEQ (1933-34) 120, (1936-37), 129.

PEREZ DURAN, Manuel, actor
DelMu 240-44, ill.

PEREZ FREYTES, Francisco Javier (1842-1890), doctor, author
CaM 333-34; DiLP 2, pt.2: 1180; DiM 248-49.

Pérez Freytes, Manuel see Pérez, Manuel

PEREZ GARCIA, Manuel (b. 1896?), author
DiLP 2, pt.2:1181-82.

PEREZ GRAU, Sergio (b.1908), accountant
QEQ (1936-37) 188-89, (1941-42) 164-65, (1948-49) 129.

PEREZ GUARDIOLA, Lydia (b. 1925), doctor
EGMPR 3:213-14, ill.

PEREZ LOSADA, José (1879-1937), journalist, author
BiP 332-33; CaE 839-40; CiBPI 222(ill.), 266-67; ComA 147-53; DiDHM 158; DiLP 2, pt.2:1182-85; GrEPR 5:127-28, 14:268, ill.; PlE 2:205; PRFAS 190; QEQ (1936-37) 129; Tri 2:247-55.

PEREZ LOZANO, Francisco (d.

1741), bishop
Hi de la Ig 118-21.

PEREZ MARCHAND, Ana Dolores (b.1886), doctor, feminist
EGMPR 3:215-17, ill.; MujDPR 202-4, ill.

PEREZ MARCHAND, Lilianne (b. 1926), poet
BrECP 342; DiLP 2, pt.2: 1185-86; EGMPR 1:191-92; PRFAS 190.

PEREZ MARCHAND, Monelisa Lina (b.1918), author
DiLP 2, pt.2:1186-89; ECPR 6:479; EGMPR 1:333-34, ill.

PEREZ MATOS, Luis, politician
GrEPR 14:268.

PEREZ MORIS, José (1840-1881), author
DiLP 2, pt.2:1189-91; GrEPR 14:268-69, ill.; HisP 96-97.

PEREZ MORIS, José Manuel (1906-1964), author, journalist
DiLP 2, pt.2:1191-93.

PEREZ MORIS, Nemesio (1875-1909), journalist
DiLP 2, pt.2:1193-94.

PEREZ NAZARIO, Iván (b.1935), artist
GrEPR 8:438.

PEREZ ORTIZ, Frances B. (b. 1940), bank official
EGMPR 3:57-58.

PEREZ PEREZ, Manuel A. (b.1890), government official
QEQ (1948-49) 129-30.

PEREZ PERRY, Ralph, radio and television station owner
A 115-16.

PEREZ PIERRET, Antonio (1885-1937), poet
BiP 333-35; BrECP 344-45; CaE 840; DiLP 2, pt.2:1194-97; GrEPR 14:269; PlE 2: 101-7, ill.; PRFAS 191.

PEREZ PIMENTEL, Pedro (b. 1904), lawyer, judge
GrEPR 14:269, ill.

PEREZ PORRATA, Rafael (b.
1897), chemist, professor
    QEQ (1933-34) 120-21,
    (1936-37) 129, (1941-42)
    165, (1948-49) 130.

PEREZ ROA, Juan, politician
    GrEPR 14:269.

PEREZ SANTALIZ, Rafael (b.
1936), politician
    LiPR 124, ill.

PEREZ TOLEDO, Adalberto F.,
doctor
    A 90.

PEREZ URRIA, Leandro, doctor
    A 93.

PERICAS DIAZ, Jaime (1870-
1939), musician, composer,
teacher
    Co 11; GrEPR 7:100-101, 14:
    269; MusMP 231-32.

PESANTE BRACETY, José R.
(1855-1905), politician
    Añas 49-53, ill.

PESQUERA, Angel M. (b.1889),
engineer
    QEQ (1933-34) 121, (1936-
    37) 129-30, (1948-49) 130-
    31.

PESQUERA, José L. (1882-1950),
politician, lawyer
    GrEPR 14:270; LM 136; QEQ
    (1936-37) 130, (1941-42)
    165, (1948-49) 131.

PESQUERA DE SURICALDAY, Carlos
M. (1902-1932), lawyer, politician
    QEQ (1933-34) 16, (1936-
    37) 16.

PESQUERA REGUERO, Rafael A.
(b.1930), lawyer, politician
    GrEPR 14:270; PriC 135-36,
    ill.

PESQUERA SOJO, Ricardo Ramón
(b.1891), businessman
    QEQ (1933-34) 121, (1936-
    37) 130.

PESQUERA UMPIERRE, Silvia L.
(b.1925), chemist
    QEQ (1948-49) 131.

PEZUELA CEBALLOS, Juan de la
(19th cent.), governor
    DiDHM 158; DiHBC 452-53;
    GrEPR 14:270, ill.; Jes 151-
    52.

PICO, Fernando (b.1941), author,
historian, professor
    DirAS 1:593.

PICO, Frank, agricultural engineer
    A 99-100.

PICO, Pedro, businessman
    A 110-11.

PICO, Rafael (b.1912), professor, geographer, politician
    BiP 335-36; ConA 45-48:440-
    41; DiHBC 710-11; ECPR 6:
    479; GrEPR 14:271, ill., 15:
    facing title page; PriC 137-
    38, ill.; PRFAS 191; QEQ
    (1948-49) 131-32.

PICO DE HERNANDEZ, Isabel, author, educator
    PQ 48.

PICO SANTIAGO, María Teresa (b.
1905), government official
    EGMPR 3:117-19, ill.

PICO VIDAL DE SILVA, Teresita
(b.1939), government official
    EGMPR 3:121-22, ill.

PICORNELL, Salvador, lawyer
    RepM 198, ill.

PIETRI, Augusto (b.1893), poet,
journalist
    DiLP 2, pt.2:1239-40.

PIETRI OMS, Rafael (b.1921),
educator
    GrEPR 14:270.

PILA IGLESIAS, Manuel de la
(1884*-1950), doctor
    AlHP 241-43, ill.; CaM 336-
    37; DiM 252-53; Pon 84-85;
    QEQ (1948-49) 57; Una 69-72.

PILAR, Basilio del (b.1896),
teacher, accountant
    QEQ (1936-37) 130.

PIMENTAL, Manuel, businessman,
politician

RepM 334, ill.

PINO, Luis V. (b.1887), industrialist
   QEQ (1948-49) 132.

PINTADO DE RAHN, María (b.
1906), social worker
   EGMPR 3:219-21, ill.

PIÑEIRO, Jesús T. (1897-1952),
governor
   BrECP 359; CiBPI 291-93;
   CuB 1946:482-84, ill.; Di-
   DHM 159, ill.; DicAB suppl.
   5:545; GrEPR 14:271, 272-
   73(ill.); HisD 68; HoPP
   175-91, ill.; PRFAS 191-92,
   ill.; QEQ (1948-49) 132.

PIÑEIRO RIVERA, Lorenzo,
politician
   GrEPR 14:271, ill.

PIÑEIRO RODRIGUEZ, Fulgencio
(b.1883), teacher, lawyer,
politician
   GrEPR 14:274; QEQ (1933-
   34) 121-22, (1936-37) 130.

PIÑEIRO, Miguel (b.1946), au-
thor, actor
   CaE 735-36; ConA 61-64:427;
   CuB 1983:301-4, ill.

PIÑERO DE LOPEZ, Dolores M.
(1892-1975), doctor
   CaM 337; EGMPR 3:223-24,
   ill.

PIÑOL, Francisco (1897-1973),
barber
   Per 183-86.

PIRELA FIGUEROA, Reinaldo (b.
1945), politician
   LiPR 117, ill.

PIZA, Pedro A. (1896), mathematician
   A 68-69; DiHBC 712-13.

PIZA GEIGEL, José (b.1897),
engineer
   QEQ (1948-49) 132.

PIZARRO, Juan "Terín" (b.
1937), baseball player
   EPI 1:334, ill.

PIZARRO, Sebastián Lorenzo
(d.1736), bishop
   Hi de la Ig 110-17.

PIZARRO RIVERA, Cereida, agronomist
   EGMPR 3:225-26, ill.

PLA, José Salvador (b.1899),
doctor
   QEQ (1941-42) 165, (1948-49)
   132-33.

PLA AYMARD DE ALFARO, Concepción M. (1891-1951), teacher
   EGMPR 1:331-32; QEQ (1933-
   34) 20, (1936-37) 20-21,
   (1941-42) 18.

PLA ESTERAS, Isidoro Luis (b.
1902), engineer
   QEQ (1941-42) 165.

PLANELLAS, Juan, politician
   GrEPR 14:274.

PLARD, Auguste Joseph (b.1876),
government official
   QEQ (1933-34) 122, (1936-37)
   130, (1941-42) 165-66.

POL MENDEZ, Emiliano (b.1900),
accountant
   QEQ (1936-37) 130, (1941-42)
   166.

POL MENDEZ, Rafael (b.1901),
chemist
   QEQ (1941-42) 166, (1948-49)
   133.

POLANCO ABREU, Santiago (b.
1920), politician, Resident
Commissioner
   GrEPR 14:274, ill.; PRUSA 22.

POLO TAFORO, María Dolores
(1887-1963), author
   DiLP 2, pt.2:1243-45; GrEPR
   14:274.

POMMAYRAC, Pedro Pablo (1819-
1880), painter
   GrEPR 8:38-39; Guay 273-74.

PONCE DE LEON, Juan (1460-1521),
soldier, governor
   BeHNPR 1:164-99, ill.; BiP
   336-37; BrECP 369; CiBPI
   22(ill.), 26-30; DiDHM 159-
   60, ill.; DiHBC 734-39; DiLP
   2, pt.2:1245-49; DicAB 8:56-

57; ECPR 6:479-80; GrEPR
14:274-75; Hi de M 41-52;
HisD 69; Por 4-7, 49-54,
57-59; PRFAS 192-93, ill.

Ponce de León II, Juan see
García Troche y Ponce de León,
Juan

PONCE DE LEON, Leonardo A.,
(1865?-1920?), author, journalist
    DiLP 2, pt.2:1249-50; GrEPR
    14:275.

PONCE DE LEON, Leonor (16th
cent.), wife of Juan Ponce de
León
    EGMPR 1:39-40.

PONCE DE LEON, Luis, priest
    GrEPR 14:275; HisD 69-70.

PONS, Miguel Antonio (b.1911),
accountant
    QEQ (1948-49) 133-34.

PONS ESCALONA, Francisco (b.
1886), engineer, architect
    QEQ (1933-34) 122, (1936-
    37) 131, (1941-42) 166-67,
    (1948-49) 133.

PONS MOLER, Gaspar (b.1906),
doctor
    QEQ (1936-37) 131.

PONS Y PICARIN, Miguel, doctor, politician
    CaM 338-39.

PONT FLORES, Rafael (1909-
1980), educator, author
    BrECP 370; DiDHM 161; DiLP
    2, pt.2:1253-54; GrEPR 14:
    276; PRFAS 193.

PONT MARCHESE, Marisara (b.
1941), librarian
    EGMPR 3:227-28.

PONTE, Rafael J., dentist
    RepM 168, ill.

PONTE JIMENEZ, Francisco,
dentist, politician
    HoIPR 90, ill.; RepM 121,
    ill.

PONTON GONZALEZ, José (1869-
1939), farmer, businessman

AlHP 343, ill.

PORTALA, César Abdallah (b.
1914), poet, translator
    DiLP 2, pt.2:1258-60.

PORTELA PEREZ, José Manuel (b.
1906), lawyer
    QEQ (1948-49) 134.

PORTELL DE TOLINCHE, Genoveva
(b.1917), businessman
    EGMPR 4:153-55.

PORTER, David (19th cent.),
naval officer
    DiHBC 739.

PORTILLA, José, politician
    GrEPR 14:276.

PORTILLA GUTIERREZ, Segundo de
la (19th cent.), governor
    DiDHM 162; GrEPR 14:276.

PORTUONDO DE CASTRO, José (b.
1909), lawyer, professor
    DirAS 4:426.

PORRAS CRUZ, Jorge Luis (1910-
1970), professor, author
    BiP 337-38; BrECP 370-71;
    DiDHM 161-62, ill.; DiLP 2,
    pt.2:1254-56; ECPR 6:480,
    GrEPR 14:276; PRFAS 193-94,
    ill.

PORRATA, Oscar E. (1908*-1981),
lawyer, educator
    QEQ (1933-34) 123-24, (1936-
    37) 131; S 88.

PORRATA DORIA, Francisco, politician
    Guay 274-75.

PORRATA DORIA, Julio L. (b.
1891), government official,
auditor
    QEQ (1933-34) 123, (1936-37)
    131.

PORRATA DORIA, Luis, politician
    PonY 109.

PORRATA DORIA, Mareb (1795-1854),
soldier
    Guay 310.

PORRATA DORIA, Osvaldo (b.1913),
engineer

QEQ (1941-42) 167, (1948-49) 134.

Porrata Doria, Providencia see Porrata Doria de Rincón, Providencia

PORRATA DORIA DE APONTE, Carmen (b.1911), author
CaE 701-2; DiLP 2, pt.2: 1256-57; EGMPR 1:193-94.

PORRATA DORIA DE RINCON, Providencia (b.1910), author
AntHistCag 259; AntPoeCag 191-92; DiLP 2, pt.2:1257-58; EGMPR 1:195-96; PRFAS 225-26.

PORRATA DORIA Y MANDES, Adolfo (b.1897), lawyer
QEQ (1933-34) 123, (1936-37) 131.

PORRATA DORIA PANDO, Franciso Luis (b.1890), architect, engineer
QEQ (1933-34) 123.

POST, Regis H. (b.1870), governor
Desf 43-49, ill.; DiDHM 162; DiHBC 438; GrEPR 14: 276; RepM 12, ill.

POU, Miguel (1880-1968), artist
A 74-75, ill.; AlHP 338-39, ill.; BiP 338-39; BrECP 371; CiBPI 268-69; DiDHM 162-63, ill.; ECPR 6:480; GrEPR 8:140-47, ill., 280 (ill.); LPR 790, 791; PaG 165-68; Pon 62-63; PRFAS 194, ill.

POVENTUD, Alberto S. (1890-1945), lawyer
AlHP 244, ill.

POVENTUD GOYCO, Irem del Carmen, singer
EGMPR 4:97-98; GrEPR 14: 276.

POVENTUD Y TORRUELLA, José A. (b.1884), lawyer
QEQ (1933-34) 124, (1936-37) 131, (1941-42) 167, (1948-49) 134; RepM 177, ill.

POWER Y GIRALT, Ramón (1775-1813), Deputy to Spanish court
BeHNPR 1:343-56, ill.; BiP 339-41; BrECP 371-72, ill.; CiBPI 46(ill.), 59-62; DiDHM 163, ill.; DiHBC 740-41; ECPR 6:480-81; EPI 1:72-74, ill.; EnsB 26-34; GenP 55; GrEPR 14:277, ill.; HePR 19-30, ill.; HisD 70; HoIPR 90, ill.; HoRPR 198-201; HoYMPR 12-22, ill.; LPR 963, 964, 965, ill.; Orad 17; Por 85-87; PRFAS 194-95, ill.; PuI 48-51.

POZO Y HONESTO, José del (18th cent.), treasurer
GrEPR 14:276.

POZUELO, Emilio, lawyer
Crom 103.

PRANN, Robert R. (b.1892), engineer
QEQ (1936-37) 131-32, (1948-49) 134.

PREY, Juan de (1904-1962), painter
GrEPR 8:438.

PRIETO AZUAR, Florentino (b. 1902), lawyer
QEQ (1941-42) 167, (1948-49) 134.

PRIM, Juan (1814-1870), governor
BeHNPR 2:55-66; DiHBC 452; GrEPR 14:277, 278(ill.); Se 137-45.

PRIMO DE RIVERA, Rafael (19th cent.), governor
DiDHM 163-64; DiHBC 454; GrEPR 14:277; Pin 48-50.

PUENTE, Tito (b.1923), musician
CuB 1977:351-53, ill.; Port 199, 200(ill.)

PUENTE ACOSTA, Lorenzo (1840-1870), author, journalist
BeHNPR 2:213; DiLP 2, pt.2: 1267-68.

PUIG DIANA, Manuel, pharmacist
Ka 186.

PUIG Y MANUEL DE VILLENA, Francisco (1854-1898), Army officer

ArH 383-91.

PUIG Y MONSERRAT, Juan Antonio (1813-1894), bishop
  BeHNPR 2:263-67, ill.; Se 83.

PUIGDOLLERS, Carmen (b.1924), author
  DiLP 2, pt.2:1268-69; PRFAS 195.

PUJADAS DIAZ, Manuel E. (1893-1962), doctor
  CaM 343-44; QEQ (1933-34) 124, (1936-37) 132, (1948-49) 134-35.

PUJALS, Eustaquio (d.1925), composer, conductor
  AlHP 404, 406, ill.

PUJALS, Rafael (1830-1889), doctor
  AlHP 326, ill.; BeHNPR 2: 215-20, ill.; CaM 344; DiM 261-63; Med 11-14; PonY 43-44; Ver 162, 163(ill.)

PUJALS SANTANA, Joaquín (b. 1877), journalist
  QEQ (1933-34) 124-25, (1936-37) 132.

PUPO, Marilyn, actress
  DelMu 246-51, ill.

PURCELL, José Norberto (1872-1953), accountant
  HoIPR 91, ill.

PURCELL RUIZ, Caridad (b. 1942), biochemist
  EGMPR 3:59-60, ill.

Q

QUERO CHIESA, Luis (b.1911), author, painter
  DiDHM 165; DiLP 2, pt.2: 1269-71; Port 83, 84(ill.); PRFAS 197.

QUEVEDO BAEZ, Manuel (1865-1955), author, doctor
  BiP 341-42; BrECP 375; CaM 345; DiDHM 165, ill.; DiLP 2, pt.2:1271-73; DiM 264-66; ECPR 6:481; GrEPR 14: 279; PaP 183-87; PRFAS 197-98, ill.; QEQ (1933-34)

125, (1936-37) 132.

QUIJANO, Domingo Miguel (1835-1885*), author, teacher
  Añas 31-35; DiLP 2, pt.2: 1273; Pin 44-45; Nuestr 45-46.

QUILES RODRIGUEZ, Waldemar (b. 1940), politician
  LiPR 127, ill.

QUILES VAZQUEZ, Carmen Iris (b. 1942), credit manager
  EGMPR 3:61-62, ill.

QUINTERO, Arturo, politician
  GrEPR 14:279.

QUINTON, José Ignacio (1881-1925), composer, teacher
  AntHistCag 345-47; BiP 342-44; BoBP 41-47; BrECP 375-76; Co 12; DiDHM 166, ill.; ECPR 6:481; EPI 3:228, 229; GrEPR 7:253-54, ill., 14: 279, ill.; Mus en P 126-27; MusMP 232-34; PRFAS 198, ill.; Sil 91-95.

QUIÑONES, Concepción, musician
  MujPu 55.

QUIÑONES, Ernesto, farmer
  A 111.

QUIÑONES, Felipe de (1758-1839), lawyer, politician
  S 82-83.

QUIÑONES, Francisco Mariano (1830-1908), politician, author
  BeHNPR 2:191-98, ill.; BgP facing p. 200, ill.; BiP 345-46; BrECP 376-77; CiBPI 173 (ill.), 185-87; DiDHM 166-67, ill.; DiHBC 770; DiLP 2, pt.2:1273-75; ECPR 6:481-82; GenP 65; GrEPR 14:280, ill.; HisD 71; HoIPR 91, ill.; Ho-RPR 57-63; Ind 134; LPR 984, 986, 987, ill.; Nuestr 154-55; PaH 1:432-36; PRFAS 199, ill.; PuI 161-65; RepM 174, ill.; S 84.

QUIÑONES, Jesús María (b.1902), doctor
  QEQ (1933-34) 125-26, (1936-37) 133.

QUIÑONES, Jesús María (b.
1890), journalist, teacher
  QEQ (1948-49) 135-36.

QUIÑONES, José (18th cent.),
soldier
  BeHNPR 1:323.

QUIÑONES, José María (1782-
183?), lawyer, Deputy to Spanish court
  BeHNPR 1:371-74; DiHBC 770;
  GrEPR 14:281; HisD 71; PuI
  54; S 83.

QUIÑONES, José Ramón (b.1895),
lawyer
  QEQ (1936-37) 133, (1941-
  42) 167-68, (1948-49) 136.

QUIÑONES, José Severo (1838*-
1909), lawyer, government
official
  CiBPI 173(ill.), 187-89;
  DiDHM 167; DiHBC 770; ECPR
  6:482; GrEPR 14:280; HisD
  79; HoIPR 91, ill.; LM 113;
  LPR 990, 991; PRFAS 199;
  PuI 208-17.

QUIÑONES, Samuel R. (1904-
1976), author, lawyer, politician
  A 51-52, ill.; BiP 346-47;
  CaE 851; DiHBC 770; DiLP 2,
  pt.2:1275-80; ECPR 6:482;
  GrEPR 14:281, 282-83(ill.);
  HoPP 105-9, ill.; Oro 40-
  49, ill.; PriC 89-90, ill.;
  PRFAS 200; QEQ (1936-37)
  133, (1941-42) 168, (1948-
  49) 136; Tri 1:379-84.

QUIÑONES, Víctor Luis (b.
1904), engineer
  QEQ (1933-34) 126, (1936-
  37) 189.

QUIÑONES CARDONA, Eleuterio
(1854-1912), doctor, composer
  CaM 346; DiM 266-68; S 86.

QUIÑONES CARRASQUILLO, Pedro
G. (b.1890), lawyer
  QEQ (1933-34) 125, (1936-
  37) 132.

QUIÑONES CHACON, Buenaventura
(b.1914), agronomist
  QEQ (1948-49) 135.

QUIÑONES CHACON, Pascasio (b.
1910), doctor
  QEQ (1941-42) 168.

QUIÑONES DE ARNALDO MEYNERS,
Delia (b.1916), journalist,
public relations officer
  EGMPR 3:301-2, ill., 4:163-
  69, ill.; QEQ (1948-49) 135,
  SobM 246-50.

QUIÑONES DE NIEVES, Delia Esther, actress
  DelMu 254-58, ill.

QUIÑONES ELIAS, Baltazar (b.
1914), lawyer, politician
  GrEPR 14:281, ill.; QEQ
  (1948-49) 135.

QUIÑONES JIMENEZ, Nicolás (b.
1892), doctor
  QEQ (1936-37) 133.

Quiñones y Nazario de Figueroa,
José María see Quiñones, José
María

QUIÑONES QUIÑONES, Edgardo (1893-
1970), doctor
  S 91.

QUIÑONES Y QUIÑONES, José Marcial (1827-1893), politician
  DiHBC 770; GrEPR 14:284.

QUIÑONES RAMIREZ, Francisco (b.
1898), teacher
  QEQ (1936-37) 133, (1941-42)
  168.

QUIÑONES Y RUIZ, José Natividad
(b.1887), lawyer, judge
  QEQ (1941-42) 168-69.

QUIÑONES VIDAL, Rafael (b.
1892), radio and television
commentator
  GrEPR 14:284, ill.

QUIÑONES Y VIZCARRONDO, Buenaventura Valentín (1804-1838),
political activist
  GrEPR 14:279; VPR 5-21, ill.

QUIROS LUGO, Miguel A. (b.
1921), author
  DiLP 2, pt.2:1280-81.

QUIROS MENDEZ, Antonio (b.
1903), lawyer, politician

GrEPR 14:284; PriC 139-40,
ill.

R

RABELO, José Juan (b.1942),
biochemist, doctor, professor
    Port 119, 120(ill.)

RABELL CABRERO, Narciso (1874-
1928), pharmacist, amateur
archeologist
    BoHP 206, 207(ill.); CaF
    122-23; DiHBC 771; GrEPR
    14:285; HoIPR 92, ill.;
    RepM 212, ill.; Tri 2:73-
    79.

RABELL Y RIVAS, Narciso, doctor
    BoHP 67, ill.

RAFFAELE, Herbert Anthony,
ornithologist
    GrEPR 1:xvi, ill.

RALDIRIS GUASP, Juan P. (1860-
1937?), author, doctor
    DiLP 2, pt.2:1282-83; DiM
    269-75.

RALDIRIS GUASP, Luis Magín
(1872-1941), journalist
    DiLP 2, pt.2:1281-82; GenB
    349-50, ill.; HoIPR 92,
    ill.

RAMERY Y ZUZUARREGUI, Dimas
de, lawyer
    Ver 188.

RAMIREZ, Adrián Nelson (b.
1934), artist
    GrEPR 8:415.

RAMIREZ, Alejandro (1777-1821)
economist, statesman
    BeHNPR 1:357-70, ill.; BiP
    347-48; BrECP 382-83, ill.;
    CiBPI 47(ill.), 62-64; Di-
    DHM 169-70, ill.; DiHBC
    772-73; ECPR 6:482-83; EPI
    1:84-86, ill.; EnsB 35-42;
    Esp 11-26; GrEPR 14:285,
    ill.; HisD 72; Por 87-89;
    PRFAS 201.

RAMIREZ, Alonso (b.1662),
sailor
    CiBPI 41-44.

RAMIREZ, Esteban (b.1897),
accountant
    QEQ (1933-34) 126-27, (1936-
    37) 134, (1948-49) 137.

RAMIREZ, Gilbert, judge
    Port 65, 66(ill.)

RAMIREZ, Luis Antonio (b.1923),
composer
    BrECP 383; ECPR 6:483; GrEPR
    14:285, 286(ill.); Mus en P
    159-60.

RAMIREZ, Mariano (d.1905), doctor
    CaM 348-49.

RAMIREZ, Pedro (b.1902), auditor
    QEQ (1933-34) 204, (1936-37)
    134, (1941-42) 171.

RAMIREZ, Rafael Roberto (b.
1900), engineer
    QEQ (1933-34) 137, (1936-37)
    134.

RAMIREZ, Ramón E. (b.1897),
doctor
    QEQ (1933-34) 127, (1936-37)
    134.

RAMIREZ, Reinaldo (b.1891), engineer
    QEQ (1933-34) 127-28, (1936-
    37) 134.

RAMIREZ, Rufino, musician,
teacher
    MusMP 264.

RAMIREZ, Tina, dancer, teacher
    Port 27, 28(ill.)

RAMIREZ BAGES, Mariano Héctor
(b.1905), lawyer
    QEQ (1933-34) 126, (1936-37)
    133, (1941-42) 169, (1948-49)
    136.

RAMIREZ BRAU, Enrique (1894-
1970), journalist, poet
    BoBP 69-73; DiLP 2, pt.2:
    1293-95: Per 140-42: QEQ
    (1948-49) 136-37.

RAMIREZ CASABLANCA, Arcadio
(1850-1890), teacher, author
    GenB 330-32, ill.; Hi de M
    207, ill.; VerOr 299-301, ill.

RAMIREZ CUERDA, Arcadio (b.

1891), apiarist
   GenB 426-27, ill.

RAMIREZ CUERDA, Temístocles
Julián (b.1889), doctor
   CaM 349; GenB 371-74, ill.;
   HoIPR 93, ill.; QEQ (1948-
   49) 137; VerOr 309-12, ill.

RAMIREZ DE ARELLANO, Alfred
(b.1940), lawyer, businessman,
banker
   GrEPR 14:288.

RAMIREZ DE ARELLANO, Clemente
(1868-1946*), pharmacist, poet
   BiP 348-49; CaF 123; DiLP
   2, pt.2:1283-85; GrEPR 14:
   288; HoIPR 93-94, ill.; PaF
   85-87; PlE 1:545-62, ill.;
   PRFAS 201-2; RepM 154,
   ill.; VPR 153-56, 169.

RAMIREZ DE ARELLANO, Diana (b.
1919), author, professor
   BiP 349-51; CaE 853; ConA
   45-48:458-59; DiDHM 170;
   DiLP 2, pt.2:1285-87; DirAS
   3:424; ECPR 6:483-84; EGMPR
   1:197-98, ill.; PQ 50;
   PRFAS 202.

RAMIREZ DE ARELLANO, Gustavo
Adolfo (1888-1972), engineer
   QEQ (1933-34) 126, (1936-
   37) 134, (1941-42) 169; S
   88.

RAMIREZ DE ARELLANO, Haydée
(b.1912), author
   DiLP 2, pt.2:1287-88; EGMPR
   1:199-201, ill.

RAMIREZ DE ARELLANO, Lorenza
(1906-1970), wife of Gov. Luis
Ferré
   EGMPR 4:359-50, ill.; SobM
   56-57.

RAMIREZ DE ARELLANO, Lorenzo,
architect
   GrEPR 9:137.

RAMIREZ DE ARELLANO, Olga (b.
1911), poet
   BiP 351-52; DiLP 2, pt.2:
   1291-93; ECPR 6:484; EGMPR
   1:203-4, ill.; PQ 50; PRFAS
   202; SobM 43-45.

RAMIREZ DE ARELLANO, Rafael W.

(1884-1974), historian, professor
   BiP 352-53; DiDHM 170, ill.;
   DiLP 2, pt.2:1288-91; GrEPR
   14:286; PRFAS 202-3, ill.

RAMIREZ DE ARELLANO, Ubaldino
(1894-1982), politician
   GrEPR 14:286; S 87.

Ramírez de Arellano de Nolla,
Olga see Ramírez de Arellano,
Olga

RAMIREZ DE ARELLANO ARRILLAGA,
Sergio (1873-1933), businessman
   Añas 84-86.

RAMIREZ DE ARELLANO Y CONTI,
Sergio (1829-1904), teacher
   Añas 29-30, ill.

RAMIREZ DE ARELLANO Y ROSELL,
Alfredo (1883-1946), politician
   GenB 365-66, ill.; HoIPR 93,
   ill.; QEQ (1936-37) 133.

RAMIREZ DE BARRETO, Eyla (b.
1918), civic works
   EGMPR 4:179-80, ill.

RAMIREZ DE CINTRON, Estrella,
bank manager
   EGMPR 3:63-64, ill.

RAMIREZ DE FUENLEAL, Sebastián
(16th cent.), bishop
   GrEPR 14:332.

RAMIREZ GARCIA, José Hipólito
(b.1890), chemist
   QEQ (1941-42) 170-71, (1948-
   49) 137-38.

RAMIREZ IRIZARRY, Marcos A.,
politician
   GrEPR 14:286, ill.

RAMIREZ MARINI, David S. (b.
1899), engineer
   QEQ (1948-49) 138-39.

RAMIREZ ORTIZ, Francisco (1844-
1900), composer
   GrEPR 7:112-14, ill., 14:
   287, ill.

RAMIREZ PABON, Rodolfo (b.
1892), politician, Freemason
   GrEPR 14:287-88, ill.; Nues
   58-62, ill.

RAMIREZ PALMER, Luis, businessman
A 126.

RAMIREZ PEREZ, Samuel (b. 1938), politician
LiPR 38, ill.

RAMIREZ RAMIREZ, Pedro (b. 1906), accountant
QEQ (1933-34) 127.

RAMIREZ RONDA, Enrique (d. 1930), politician, orator
Hi de CR 225-26.

RAMIREZ SANTIBAÑEZ, José (1895*-1950), politician, author
A 81-82; CaE 852; GrEPR 14: 288; HoIPR 94, ill.; QEQ (1933-34) 128, (1936-37) 134-35, (1941-42) 171.

RAMIREZ SANTOS, Rafael (b. 1901), doctor
QEQ (1933-34) 128, (1936-37) 135.

RAMIREZ SILVA, Amador (b. 1897), lawyer, politician
GrEPR 14:288; QEQ (1948-49) 139.

RAMIREZ SILVA, Francisco J. (b.1899), chemist
QEQ (1936-37) 135.

RAMIREZ TORRES, Osvaldo (b. 1903), chemist, professor
GrEPR 14:288; QEQ (1933-34) 128, (1936-37) 135, (1941-42) 171-72, (1948-49) 139.

RAMIREZ VELEZ, Eva (b.1912), civic works, nursing
EGMPR 4:339-41, ill.

RAMIREZ VELEZ, Gregorio (d. 1926), philanthropist
Hi de CR 233-34.

RAMIREZ VIGO, Rodolfo, notary, magistrate
RepM 283, ill.

RAMOS, Adolfo Heraclio (1837*-1891), musician, composer
ArH 527-29; BrECP 383-84; Co 13; DiHBC 773-74; GrEPR 7:191-94, ill.; HisD 46;

Mus en P 127-28; MusMP 158-61; PRFAS 203; PuI 198-201.

RAMOS, Angel (1902-1960), newspaper, radio and television executive
BiP 353-54; Desd 51-52; DiDHM 170-71, ill.; GrEPR 14: 288; PRFAS 203-4, ill.

RAMOS, Federico (b.1857), musician, composer, teacher
ArH 529, 543; Co 14; GrEPR 7: 194, 195(ill.); MusMP 234-36.

RAMOS, Francisco (d.1702), contrabandist
GrEPR 14:289.

RAMOS, Isidro, politician
GrEPR 14:289.

RAMOS, José (d.1904), artisan
San 53-54.

RAMOS, José A. (b.1946), politician
GrEPR 14:336; LiPR 126, ill.

RAMOS, José Abad (b.1906), author
DiLP 2, pt.2:1295-97; Ind 135-36.

RAMOS, José C., lawyer
RepM 131, ill.

RAMOS, Luciano (b.1888), pharmacist
QEQ (1933-34) 128-29, (1936-37) 135.

RAMOS, Modesto, businessman
Ka 84.

RAMOS, Oreste (b.1936), politician
LiPR 30, ill.

RAMOS ANAYA Y MORALES, José (1850-1921), Freemason
Nues 33-36, ill.

RAMOS ANTONINI, Ernesto (1898-1963), lawyer, politician, musician
A 52-55, ill.; AlHP 334-35, ill.; BrECP 384; CiBPI 228 (ill.), 299-302; DiDHM 171-72, ill.; GrEPR 14:289, 290-

91(ill.); HoDMT 52-66; HoPP 238-322, ill.; PRFAS 204, ill.; QEQ (1948-49) 139-40.

RAMOS BARRETO, Casimiro, politician
GrEPR 14:292.

RAMOS BARROSO, José M. (b. 1928), politician
LiPR 30, ill.

RAMOS Y BRANS, José (1866?-1900?), author, journalist
DiLP 2, pt.2:1297-98; Nuestr 135-38.

Ramos y Buensont, Adolfo Heraclio see Ramos, Adolfo Heraclio

RAMOS CASELLAS, Eduardo A. (b. 1910), advertising executive
QEQ (1941-42) 240.

RAMOS CASELLAS, Pedro (1883-1960), radiologist
CaM 350.

RAMOS CASELLAS, Ramón, engineer
ArH 548-49.

RAMOS COBIAN, Rafael (b.1904), businessman
QEQ (1936-37) 135, (1941-42) 172, (1948-49) 140.

RAMOS CONTRERAS, José (1865-1908), author, journalist
PRFAS 205.

RAMOS DE DEXTER, Raquel (b. 1902), professor, biologist
EGMPR 1:339-41.

RAMOS DE SANCHEZ VILELLA, Jeanette (b.1932), lawyer, wife of Gov. Roberto Sánchez
EGMPR 4:361-62, ill.

RAMOS ELVIRA, Enrique (b. 1914), doctor
QEQ (1948-49) 140.

Ramos Escalera, Federico see Ramos, Federico

Ramos Escalera, Heraclio Adolfo see Ramos, Adolfo Heraclio

RAMOS HERNANDEZ, Manuel (b. 1900), poet
And 237-39.

RAMOS LLOMPART, Arturo (b.1921), poet, journalist
DiLP 2, pt.2:1298-99.

RAMOS MATTEI, Carlos José (b. 1947), professor, philosopher
DirAS 4:436.

RAMOS MIMOSO, Adriana (b. 1904), author
DiLP 2, pt.2:1300-1301; EGMPR 1:335-37.

RAMOS MIMOSO, Dora, educator
EGMPR 1:345; QEQ (1933-34) 129, (1936-37) 135.

RAMOS MIMOSO, Luz María (1898-1971), home economist, teacher
EGMPR 1:343-44; QEQ (1933-34) 129, (1936-37) 135-36, (1941-42) 172, (1948-49) 140-41.

RAMOS MIMOSO, Raúl León (b. 1906), doctor
QEQ (1933-34) 204, (1936-37) 136.

RAMOS ORTIZ, José, painter
GrEPR 8:416.

RAMOS PLUNKET, Ramón (b.1907), engineer
QEQ (1933-34) 129, (1936-37) 136, (1941-42) 172-73.

RAMOS RODRIGUEZ, Luis (b.1904), politician
GrEPR 14:292.

RAMOS ROSARIO, Eli (b.1930), politician
LiPR 117, ill.

RAMOS Y SANTOS, Nicolás de (b. 1531), bishop
Hi de la Ig 42-43.

RAMOS TULIER, Arturo (1878-1968), government official
SobM 16-17.

RAMOS VAELLO, Ramón (b.1917), politician
GrEPR 14:293.

RAMOS VALLS, Ismael (b.1894),

athlete
  GenB 437-38, ill.

RAMOS VELEZ, Juan Ramón (1845-
1905), educator, politician,
lawyer
  GrEPR 14:293; LM 116-17;
  PuI 306-8.

RAMOS VILLANUEVA, Valentín (b.
1925), politician
  GrEPR 14:293.

RAMOS YORDAN, Edwin (b.1936),
politician
  LiPR 29, ill.

RAMOS YORDAN, Luis Ernesto (b.
1915), politician, doctor
  GrEPR 14:293, ill.; PRFAS
  205.

RAYMER, Paul W. (b.1897),
electrician, manager
  QEQ (1936-37) 136, (1941-
  42) 173.

RAYMOND DIAZ, Félix Antonio
(b.1900), doctor
  QEQ (1948-49) 141.

REAL, Cristóbal (1873-1966),
author, journalist
  DiLP 2, pt.2:1301-3; GrEPR
  14:294.

REAL, Matías (1874-1939), poet
  DiLP 2, pt.2:1303-5.

REAL, Romualdo (1880-1959),
journalist, author, businessman
  DiDHM 172; DiLP 2, pt.2:
  1305-7; GrEPR 14:294; HoIPR
  95-97, ill.

REBOLLO LOPEZ, Francisco (b.
1901), lawyer
  QEQ (1941-42) 173.

RECHANI AGRAIT, Carlos (d.
1971), journalist
  SobM 221-23.

RECHANI AGRAIT, Luis (b.1902),
journalist, author
  BiP 354-55; BrECP 384; CaE
  855; DiDHM 172; DiLP 2, pt.
  2:1307-9; ECPR 6:484; GrEPR
  14:294; PRFAS 205.

RECHANY, Jorge A. (b.1914),
painter
  BrECP 384-85; DiDHM 172-73;
  GrEPR 8:284, ill.; PaG 198-
  99; PRFAS 206.

RECHANY FERNANDEZ, José E. (b.
1912), doctor
  QEQ (1948-49) 141.

REED, Charles W. (b.1872),
manager
  QEQ (1936-37) 136, (1941-42)
  173.

REGUERO GONZALEZ, José (b.
1888), doctor, politician
  CaM 352.

REGUERO GONZALEZ, Julio, politician
  GrEPR 14:294.

REGULEZ Y SANZ DEL RIO, Alberto,
educator
  DiHBC 779.

REICHARD, Arturo, lawyer
  ProA 16; RepM 155, ill.

REICHARD, Augusto, teacher
  ProA 16.

REICHARD, Héctor, lawyer
  A 85-86.

REILLY, Philip Maurice (b.
1903), doctor
  QEQ (1936-37) 136.

REILY, Emmett Montgomery (d.
1954), governor
  Desf 64-84, ill.; DiDHM 173;
  DiHBC 438; GrEPR 14:994.

RENDON, José (d.1903), musician,
teacher
  MusMP 290.

RENDON, Lino, musician, teacher
  MusMP 290.

RENDON CAMACHO, Francisco (1848?-
1906*), doctor, poet
  CaM 353; Crom 102; DiLP 2,
  pt.2:1312-13; DiM 275-77;
  Ver 170.

RENOVALES, Francisco, plantation
manager
  Ka 93.

RENTAS LUCAS, Eugenio (b. 1910), poet, journalist
BiP 355-56; CaE 856; DiLP 2, pt.2:1313-15; ECPR 6: 484; PRFAS 206.

REUS GARCIA, Esteban (b.1895), Protestant minister
QEQ (1936-37) 189.

REXACH, Sylvia (1922-1961), composer
BiP 356-57; BrECP 385; Com 6; DiDHM 173; ECPR 6:484; EGMPR 4:99-100, ill.; GrEPR 7:135, 137, 139, ill.; Per 50-52, ill.; PQ 51; PRFAS 206.

REXACH BENITEZ, Roberto (b. 1929), educator, politician
DiDHM 173; GrEPR 14:295; PRFAS 206-7.

REXACH REXACH, José E. (b. 1903), engineer
QEQ (1936-37) 136, (1941-42) 173-74, (1948-49) 141.

REYES, Joaquín (b.1949), artist
GrEPR 8:416.

Reyes Correa, Antonio de los see Correa, Antonio de los Reyes

REYES DELGADO, Antonio (b. 1900), lawyer, politician
GrEPR 14:295; PriC 141-42, ill.; QEQ (1936-37) 136.

REYES GARCIA, Ismael (b.1928), author, professor
DiDHM 173-74; PRFAS 207.

REYES JIMENEZ, Ismael (b. 1898), engineer
QEQ (1933-34) 129-30, (1936-37) 136-37.

REYES PADRO, Carmen, journalist
EGMPR 3:303-4, ill.

REYES REYES, Antonio (b.1897), teacher
QEQ (1941-42) 174.

REYES RIVERA, Louis, publisher, author
Port 208.

REYES SANTIAGO, Antonio (b. 1924), politician
LiPR 122.

REYES SERRANO, Manuel, lawyer, politician
GrEPR 14:295.

REYES Y TRICOCHES, Felipe (d. 1910), militiaman
Nuestr 150.

REYES VARGAS, Pedro A., journalist
SobM 231-34.

REYMUNDI, José, actor
DelMu 260-63, ill.

RIANCHO ESCOBALES, Providencia (b.1901), poet, musician, teacher
CaE 856-57; DiLP 2, pt.2: 1315-16; EGMPR 1:205-7, ill.

Riara, Edmundo see Marín Marién, Eduardo

RIBAS SALGUERO, Julio (1868-1937), farmer
AlHP 348.

RIBERA CHEVREMONT, Evaristo (1896-1976), poet, journalist
BiP 357-59; BrECP 385-87, ill.; CaE 857-58; ComA 47-103; DiDHM 174; DiLP 2, pt.2: 1316-29; ECPR 6:485-86; GrEPR 14:295, ill.; Ind 136; Lie 216-21; Per 35-38, ill.; PlE 2:247-63, ill.; PRFAS 207-8; VPR 139-51, 169.

RIBERA CHEVREMONT, José Joaquín (b.1897), critic, poet
BiP 359-60; DiLP 2, pt.2: 1329-32; ECPR 6:485; PRFAS 208.

RIBIE DE CRISTIAN, Emilia, teacher
Ma 57-58.

RIBOT COLOMER, Antonio (b.1876), engineeer
QEQ (1936-37) 137, (1941-42) 174.

RICOI, Arturo, businessman
Ka 128.

RICHARD DE SEPTMONTS, André J. (b.1888), doctor
QEQ (1948-49) 141-42.

RICHARDSON, Carmen Belén, actress
DelMu 266-70, ill.

RICHARDSON, Donald E., customs official
RepM 41, ill.

RICHARDSON, Frank Joseph (b. 1880), government official
QEQ (1933-34) 130, (1936-37) 137, (1941-42) 174, (1948-49) 142.

RICHARDSON KUNTZ, Pedro (b. 1892), agronomist
QEQ (1948-49) 142.

RIECKEHOFF, Germán, politician
GrEPR 14:296.

RIEFKOHL, Guillermo, businessman
Ka 72-73.

RIERA LOPEZ, Mariano (1895-1944), doctor
AlHP 245, ill.; CaM 355.

RIERA PALMER, Mariano (1860-1922), author, journalist
BiP 360-61; Cre 51-55; DiLP 2, pt.2:1332-33; ECPR 6: 486; GenB 273-74, ill.; Hi de M 203, ill.; HoIPR 97, ill.; PRFAS 208; RepM 58, ill.

RIGAU, Angel (b.1916), poet, journalist
DiLP 2, pt.2:1333.

RIGAU, Marco A. (b.1919), lawyer, judge
GrEPR 14:296.

RIGGS, Francis E. (1887-1936), police official
QEQ (1936-37) 16.

RIGGS, George A. (b.1877), Protestant minister
QEQ (1936-37) 137, (1941-42) 174-75.

RIGUAL CAMACHO, Néstor (b. 1912), government official, author
PRFAS 208-9.

RILEY, Sharon (b.1946), actress, singer
DelMu 272-76, ill.

RINCON DE GAUTIER, Felisa (b. 1897), politician
A 55-56, ill.; CuB 1956:205-6, ill.; DiDHM 174-75, ill.; EGMPR 1:79-84, ill.; EPI 2: 233-37; GrEPR 14:296, ill.; HoPP 192-205; MujP 235-39, ill.; PQ 52; PRFAS 209-10, ill.; PRUSA 14.

RIO, José del, politician
GrEPR 14:297.

RIOLLANO, Arturo (b.1908), agronomist
QEQ (1936-37) 137, (1941-42) 175, (1948-49) 142-43.

RIOS, J. M., manager
QEQ (1948-49) 143.

RIOS, Juan N., artist
AlHP 338, ill.; GrEPR 8: 135, ill.

RIOS, Luis R. (b.1900), businessman
QEQ (1936-37) 137, (1941-42) 175.

RIOS, Mariano (b.1921), politician
LiPR 31, ill.

RIOS, Octavio, artist
AlHP 339.

RIOS, Rafael (b.1888), businessman
QEQ (1933-34) 130-32, (1936-37) 137-38, (1941-42) 175-76, (1948-49) 143.

RIOS, Roberto, artist
AlHP 339.

RIOS ALGARIN, Ramón A. (b. 1892), doctor
CaM 356; QEQ (1933-34) 130, (1936-37) 137, (1941-42) 175.

RIOS DUCHESNE, Isabel (b.1935), lawyer, judge

EGMPR 3:231.

RIOS LAVIENNA, Gregorio (1896-1935), educator
QEQ (1933-34) 130, (1936-37) 16.

RIOS MALDONADO, Reynaldo (b. 1946), artist
GrEPR 8:439.

RIOS OCAÑA, Manuel (b.1900), journalist, author
DiLP 2, pt.2:1339-40; Gr-EPR 14:297.

RIOS OVALLE, Juan (1863-1928), musician, composer
Co 15; MusMP 236.

RIOS REY, Rafael (1912-1980), artist
AlHP 340; GrEPR 8:417.

RIOS RIOS, Max (1897-1958), author, critic, professor
DiLP 2, pt.2:1340-41; Gr-EPR 5:129-30, 14:297; Ind 137; QEQ (1941-42) 176, (1948-49) 143-44.

RIOS ROMAN, Domingo (b.1937), lawyer, politician
GrEPR 14:297.

RIU Y BARNES, Tomás (b.1819?), doctor
CaM 357-58.

RIUS RIVERA, Juan (1846*-1924), soldier, governor of Cuba
BiP 367-68; BrECP 389-90; CiBPI 67(ill.), 143-46; Di-DHM 175; ECPR 6:486; EPI 1: 102-5; GenB 245-49, ill.; GenP 82-86, ill., 295; Gr-EPR 14:297-98, ill.; Hi de M 321-26, ill.; PRFAS 210.

RIVA AGUERO, Fernando de la (17th cent.), governor
DiDHM 175; GrEPR 14:298; Hi de Pu 97-98.

RIVAS, Benito de (d.1668), bishop
Hi de la Ig 82-84.

RIVAS, Gumersindo, businessman
Crom 66.

RIVAS, Nicolás (1883-1964), poet, journalist
DiLP 2, pt.2:1341-44; GrEPR 14:298; Per 159-61.

RIVERA, Angel (b.1930), insurance agent
Port 145, 146(ill.)

RIVERA, Carlos Raquel (b.1923), artist
BrECP 390-91; GrEPR 8:288, ill.; PaG 200; PRFAS 210.

RIVERA, "Chita" (b.1934), singer, actress
CuB 1984:351-55, ill.; GrEPR 14:298; Port 195, 196(ill.)

RIVERA, Daniel de (1824-1858?), poet
BiP 361-63; DiLP 2, pt.2: 1344-45; Pon 58-59; PRFAS 211.

RIVERA, Fernando, businessman
Crom 52.

RIVERA, Francisco, artisan
San 54-58.

RIVERA, Frank O. (1893-1941?), doctor
CaM 359.

RIVERA, Gaspar (1889-1953), poet
DiLP 2, pt.2:1345-46.

RIVERA, Geraldo (b.1943), television journalist
CuB 1975:358-61, ill.; Port 133, 134(ill.)

RIVERA, Graciela, singer, author
Port 39, 40(ill.)

RIVERA, Guillermo (b.1885), author, professor
DiLP 2, pt.2:1346-47; QEQ (1948-49) 145.

RIVERA, José R. (b.1880), salesman
QEQ (1933-34) 132, (1936-37) 139.

RIVERA, Juan de (18th cent.), governor
GrEPR 14:298.

RIVERA, Luis Antonio, actor

DelMu 42-46, ill.

RIVERA, Luis Daniel, actor
DelMu 278-82, ill.

RIVERA, María Ramona de (b.
1817), Juan Rius Rivera's
mother
GenP 87.

RIVERA, Modesto (d.1893), musician
MusMP 264-66; Orig 304.

RIVERA, Modesto (b.1897),
educator, author
DiLP 2, pt.2:1355-57;
PRFAS 213.

RIVERA, Nicomedes (d.1940),
labor leader, politician
GrEPR 14:299.

RIVERA, Pedro Amado, lawyer
RepM 250, ill.

RIVERA, Ramón Alfonso, federal
employee
RepM 268, ill.

RIVERA, Sandra, actress
DelMu 284-89, ill.

RIVERA ALVAREZ, Edmundo (b.
1917), dramatist, actor
DiLP 2, pt.2:1347-49; DelMu
292-96, ill.; PRFAS 210.

RIVERA APONTE, Pedro (b.1893),
doctor
CaM 360; QEQ (1936-37) 138,
(1941-42) 176.

RIVERA APONTE, René (b.1927),
author
DiLP 2, pt.2:1349-50.

RIVERA AULET, Rafael, doctor
CaM 361.

RIVERA AVILES, Genaro (1861-
1941), artisan
San 58-62.

RIVERA BAERGA, Manuel (b.
1902), teacher, politician
GrEPR 14:299; QEQ (1948-49)
144.

RIVERA BARRERAS, José N. (b.
1906), lawyer

QEQ (1936-37) 138, (1941-
42) 176-77.

RIVERA BENGOA, Ramón G. (b.
1902), engineer
QEQ (1948-49) 144.

RIVERA BIASCOECHEA, Rafael,
pharmacist
A 101.

RIVERA BRENES, Luis (b.1916),
agronomist, politician
GrEPR 14:299.

RIVERA CABRERA, Justo (b.1885),
journalist, government official
QEQ (1936-37) 138, (1941-42)
240, (1948-49) 144.

RIVERA CAMACHO DE LIPPITT, Margarita (b.1889), nurse
EGMPR 3:243-44, ill.

RIVERA CANDELARIA, Dolores,
politician
GrEPR 14:299.

RIVERA COLON, Angel (b.1902),
lawyer, politician
GrEPR 14:299; QEQ (1936-37)
138.

RIVERA COLON, Heraclio H. (1900-
1964), politician
GrEPR 14:299; QEQ (1948-49)
144.

RIVERA COLON, Rosendo (1868-
1899), journalist
MueYV 160-65; PuI 349; SeDC
178-80.

RIVERA CORREA, Carmen Iris (b.
1917), teacher, lawyer
EGMPR 3:233-34.

RIVERA DE ALVAREZ, Josefina (b.
1923), professor, author
And 196-98; BiP 234-35; BrECP
391; DiDHM 176; DiHBC 44;
DirAS 3:439; EGMPR 1:347,
ill.; GrEPR 1:xi, 14:299;
PRFAS 211.

RIVERA DE CASANOVA, Noelia (b.
1923), educator
EGMPR 3:235-36, ill.

RIVERA DE DIAZ, María Elisa (b.
1887), doctor

CaM 360, 481-82; DiHBC 785; EGMPR 3:237-38, ill.; GrEPR 14:300; MujDPR 215-16, ill.

RIVERA DE GARCIA, Eloísa, professor, author
EGMPR 1:349, ill.

RIVERA DE LA VEGA, Isabel (b. 1897), teacher
QEQ (1933-34) 132, (1936-37) 138.

RIVERA DIAZ, Tomás (ca.1831-1911), artisan, soldier
San 62-63.

RIVERA DIAZ, Walter (b.1910), lawyer, politician
GrEPR 14:300; QEQ (1941-42) 177-78.

RIVERA FERRER, Manuel (b. 1882), engineer
ProA 53; QEQ (1933-34) 132, (1936-37) 138-39, (1941-42) 178, (1948-49) 144.

RIVERA GARCIA, Rafael N. (b. 1929), artist, professor
BrECP 391-92; GrEPR 8:370, ill.; PRFAS 211-12; PRUSA 22, ill.

RIVERA GUTIERREZ, Justo Pastor (b.1897), manager, politician
QEQ (1948-49) 145.

RIVERA HERNANDEZ, Francisco (b.1894), gunsmith
QEQ (1941-42) 178.

RIVERA LANDRON, Francisco (b. 1907), author
DiLP 2, pt.2:1350-52; Ind 138; PRFAS 212.

RIVERA LIZARDI, Francisco M., doctor, author
PRFAS 212.

RIVERA MALDONADO, Teófilo (b. 1902), businessman
QEQ (1948-49) 145.

RIVERA MARTINEZ, Antonio (b. 1897), educator
QEQ (1936-37) 139.

RIVERA MARTINEZ, Prudencio (1887-1969), labor leader,

politician
AntHistCag 324-25; BiP 363-64; ECPR 6:486-87; GrEPR 14:300, ill.; PRFAS 212-13; QEQ (1933-34) 132-33, (1936-37) 139, (1941-42) 178-79.

RIVERA MARTINEZ DE VAZQUEZ, Genoveva (b.1908), seamstress
EGMPR 4:101-2.

RIVERA MATOS, Manuel (b.1908), author, journalist
DiLP 2, pt.2:1352-53.

RIVERA MORALES, Alejo, politician
GrEPR 14:300.

RIVERA MORALES, José C., lawyer, politician
BoHP 198.

RIVERA MORALES, Víctor M. (b. 1933), politician
LiPR 41, ill.

RIVERA MURILLO, Nora Haydee (1933-63), engineer
EGMPR 3:239-40, ill.

RIVERA NEGRON, Roberto, actor
AlDJ 123, ill., 124(ill.); Del Mu 298-302, ill.

RIVERA NEGRONI, Manuel, politician
BoHP 193; LuO 30-31.

RIVERA ORTEGA, Aurelio (b.1933), politician
LiPR 125.

RIVERA ORTIZ, Benjamín (b. 1924), lawyer, politician
GrEPR 14:300.

RIVERA ORTIZ, Gilberto (b. 1932), educator, politician
DiDHM 176; GrEPR 14:301; LiPR 32, ill.

RIVERA ORTIZ, Juan (b.1933), teacher, politician
GrEPR 14:301; LiPR 31, ill.

RIVERA OTERO, Jesús (b.1908), educator
QEQ (1941-42) 179.

RIVERA OTERO, Rafael (1903-1958), author, journalist

CaE 859; DiLP 2, pt.2:
1354-55; PRFAS 213; QEQ
(1933-34) 133, (1936-37)
139, (1941-42) 179, (1948-
49) 145-46.

RIVERA PADILLA, Graciela (b.
1921), singer
EGMPR 4:103-4, ill.

RIVERA PORRATA, Nestor (b.
1888), dentist
QEQ (1948-49) 146.

RIVERA QUIJADA, Francisco A.
(b.1897), businessman
QEQ (1948-49) 146.

RIVERA RAMOS, Rubén (b.1927),
lawyer, politician
GrEPR 14:301; PriC 143-44,
ill.

RIVERA REYES, Alvaro (b.1905),
politician, teacher
GrEPR 14:301; QEQ (1948-49)
146-47.

RIVERA RIVERA, Dominga (b.
1909), home economist, teacher, lawyer
EGMPR 3:241-42.

RIVERA RIVERA, Edil Manuel (b.
1904), engineer
QEQ (1936-37) 139.

RIVERA RIVERA, Eloisa, author,
professor
Port 29, 30(ill.)

RIVERA RIVERA, Pedro Fernando
(b.1905), engineer
QEQ (1941-42) 179-80.

RIVERA RIVERA, Ramón Luis (b.
1929), politician
GrEPR 14:301; LiPR 117,
ill.

RIVERA ROBLEDO, Manuel (b.
1947), politician
GrEPR 14:301.

RIVERA RODRIGUEZ, Juan (1906-
1963), poet
AntHistCag 264; AntPoeCag
125-26.

RIVERA ROMERO, Fidel (b.1933),
politician

LiPR 127, ill.

RIVERA ROSA, Rafael (b.1942),
artist
GrEPR 8:439.

RIVERA SALGADO, Elsa, pianist
EGMPR 4:105-7, ill.; PQ 53.

RIVERA SANTIAGO, Rafael (b.
1900), author, journalist
ComA xi-xxiv; QEQ (1936-37)
139-40, (1941-42) 180.

RIVERA SANTOS, Luis (b.1913),
economist
QEQ (1948-49) 147.

RIVERA UFRET, Carlos (b.1884),
teacher
QEQ (1933-34) 133-34, (1936-
37) 140.

RIVERA VALENTIN, Ramón (b.1923),
lawyer, politician
GrEPR 14:301.

RIVERA VASALLO, Rafael (b.
1884), poet
AntHistCag 263-64; AntPoeCag
47-48.

RIVERA VIERA, Juan (1884-1953),
author, journalist
AlHY 164-65, 215-16; BiP
365-67; DiLP 2, pt.2:1357-59;
ECPR 6:487; Per 175-77; PRFAS
214.

RIVERA VIÑAS, Ramón (b.1892),
lawyer
QEQ (1933-34) 134, (1936-37)
140, (1941-42) 180, (1948-
49) 147.

RIVERA ZAYAS, Rafael, politician
GrEPR 14:301, ill.

RIVERA ZAYAS, Rafael (1885-1958),
lawyer, judge, politician, author
GrEPR 14:302; HoIPR 94, ill.;
ProA 62; QEQ (1936-37) 189.

RIVERO, Armando (b.1920), labor
leader, politician
GrEPR 14:302; PriC 145-46,
ill.

RIVERO, Francisco H. (b.1875),
doctor
QEQ (1936-37) 189-90.

RIVERO, Horacio (b.1910), Army
officer, ambassador
   DiHBC 785; GrEPR 14:302;
   PRUSA 23, ill.

RIVERO, Juan A. (b.1923*),
scientist, professor
   BrECP 392-93; DiDHM 176;
   DiHBC 785-86; PRFAS 214.

RIVERO CHAVES, Agustín (b.
1890), government official
   QEQ (1933-34) 204-5, (1936-
   37) 140.

RIVERO MENDEZ, Angel (1856-
1930), journalist, author,
politician
   Desd 281-88; DiLP 2, pt.2:
   1359-60; GrEPR 14:302,
   ill.; RepM 202, ill.; SobM
   164-69; Tri 1:185-92.

RIVERO OTERO, Rafael (1903-
1958), professor, poet, journalist
   BiP 364-65.

ROBERT CRUZ, Rafael (b.1892),
pharmacist
   GrEPR 14:303; QEQ (1933-34)
   134, (1936-37) 140.

ROBERT DE ROMEU, Marta (b.
1890), doctor, suffragette
   CaM 361-62, 483; DiHBC
   786; EGMPR 3:245-46, ill.,
   4:265-66; GrEPR 14:303;
   MujDPR 229-30, ill.; QEQ
   (1933-34) 134, (1936-37)
   140-41.

ROBERTS DE GAETAN, Sarah Eugenia (1885-1968), teacher
   EGMPR 1:351-52, ill.; Muj-
   DPR 181-83, ill.; QEQ
   (1933-34) 134-35, (1936-37)
   141, (1941-42) 180-81.

ROBLEDILLO Y VELASCO, Diego
de, soldier, acting governor
   Hi de P 186-87.

ROBLEDO, Aura Norma, singer
   EGMPR 4:109-10, ill.; Gr-
   EPR 14:303.

ROBLEDO, Francisco, politician
   GrEPR 14:303.

ROBLES, Frank, actor, advertising agency owner
   Port 31, 32(ill.)

ROBLES, María Esther, singer
   DiHBC 786-87; EGMPR 4:111-
   12, ill.

ROBLES DE CARDONA, Mariana (b.
1904), professor, author
   BiP 369-70; DiLP 2, pt.2:
   1360-62; ECPR 6:487; EGMPR
   1:353-54; PRFAS 214-15.

ROBLES LORENZANA, Juan de (17th
cent.), governor
   GrEPR 14:303; Hi de P 189-93.

ROBLES Y SILVA, Antonio de (17th
cent.), soldier, governor
   Hi de P 206-8.

ROCA BACO, Julio C. (b.1900),
doctor
   QEQ (1933-34) 135, (1936-37)
   141, (1941-42) 181.

ROCHE, Arnaldo (b.1955), artist
   GrEPR 8:439.

ROCHER DE LA PEÑA, José (18th
cent.), sailor
   GrEPR 14:303.

ROCHET, José Luis (b.1942),
artist
   GrEPR 8:417.

RODAS, Manuel (1859-1935),
teacher
   AlHP 466, ill.

RODAS, Roberto Laureano (b.
1951), painter
   GrEPR 8:418.

RODIL Y CAMACHO, Fernando (b.
1877), educator
   GenB 418-19, ill.; HoIPR 98,
   ill.

RODON, Francisco (b.1934),
artist
   BrECP 393; GentI 198-203;
   GrEPR 8:292, ill.; PaG 207-
   8; PRFAS 215.

RODRIGUEZ, Adalberto (b.1934),
actor
   GrEPR 14:304, ill.

RODRIGUEZ, Angel Luis, painter
GrEPR 8:439.

RODRIGUEZ, Angel Manuel (b.
1945), professor, theologian
DirAS 4:452.

RODRIGUEZ, Antonio, Jr. (b.
1897), educator
QEQ (1933-34) 136-37,
(1936-37) 141-42, (1941-42)
181-82.

Rodríguez, Chi Chi see Rodríguez Vila, Juan

RODRIGUEZ, Dimas, manufacturer
A 150.

RODRIGUEZ, Emilio, manufacturer
A 152.

RODRIGUEZ, Fernando (1888-
1932), dentist
DiHBC 787; QEQ (1933-34)
16, (1936-37) 16.

RODRIGUEZ, Francisco S., industrialist
Tri 2:87-92.

RODRIGUEZ, Gladys, actress
DelMu 304-7, ill.

RODRIGUEZ, Heliodoro (b.
1894), teacher
QEQ (1933-34) 136, (1936-
37) 143, (1941-42) 184.

RODRIGUEZ, Isais, pharmacist
Ka 140-41.

RODRIGUEZ, J. A. E. (b.1883),
accountant
QEQ (1933-34) 205, (1936-
37) 143-44, (1941-42) 184,
(1948-49) 149.

RODRIGUEZ, Jaime Luis (b.
1933), author
DiLP 2, pt.2:1362-63.

RODRIGUEZ, Julio, publisher,
educator
Port 208.

RODRIGUEZ, Juan, apothecary
CaF 129.

RODRIGUEZ, Juan Zacarías

(1846-1928), author
DiLP 2, pt.2:1363-64.

RODRIGUEZ, Luisita, musician
GrEPR 14:304.

RODRIGUEZ, Margarita Sofía (b.
1944), artist, teacher
GrEPR 8:439.

RODRIGUEZ, Myrna (b.1940),
artist
GrEPR 8:419.

RODRIGUEZ, Orlando, actor
DelMu 310-13, ill.

RODRIGUEZ, Pablo Emilio (1844-
1881), journalist
PuI 300.

RODRIGUEZ, Remedios, actress
PaF 83-84.

RODRIGUEZ ACEVEDO, Gustavo
(1865-1957), lawyer
AlHP 260, ill.; QEQ (1933-34)
135, (1936-37) 141; RepM 269,
ill.

RODRIGUEZ ACOSTA, Américo, politician
Ka 109.

RODRIGUEZ AGUAYO, Arturo (b.
1886), engineer
QEQ (1936-37) 141, (1941-42)
181.

RODRIGUEZ AMADOR, Augusto A. (b.
1904), musician, composer, teacher, critic
QEQ (1936-37) 142, (1941-42)
182-83.

RODRIGUEZ AMADOR, Samuel Lucas
(b.1902), professor
QEQ (1941-42) 181.

RODRIGUEZ ARRESON, José María
(1870-1947), musician, teacher,
composer
GrEPR 7:260-62, ill.; MusMP
237-38.

Rodríguez Arreson, Manuel see
Rodríguez Arreson, José María

RODRIGUEZ BAEZ, Félix (b.1929),
artist
GrEPR 8:418.

RODRIGUEZ BARRIL, Alejandro
(b.1888), author
DiLP 2, pt.2:1365-66; QEQ
(1933-34) 136, (1936-37)
142.

RODRIGUEZ BENITEZ, Joaquín,
architect
GrEPR 9:113-14.

RODRIGUEZ BOU, Ismael (b.
1911), educator
BiP 370-71; BrECP 393; Di-
DHM 176-77; ECPR 6:487; Gr-
EPR 14:305, ill.; PRFAS
214.

RODRIGUEZ CABRERO, Luis
(1864*-1915), author, journalist
BiP 371-73; CaE 861; DiDHM
177, ill.; DiLP 2, pt.2:
1366-68; HoIPR 98, ill.;
LPR 1037, 1038, 1039; PlE
1:347-61, ill.; PRFAS 215-
16, ill.

RODRIGUEZ CABRERO, Manuel (b.
1862), businessman, politician
LuO 100-102; RepM 253, ill.

RODRIGUEZ CADIERNO, José,
businessman
A 138.

RODRIGUEZ CALDERON, Juan
(1780-1840), poet
BiP 373-75; CaE 861; DiDHM
177-78; DiLP 2, pt.2:1368-
71; HisD 74; PRFAS 216.

RODRIGUEZ COMPOAMOR, Benigno,
businessman
QEQ (1936-37) 142, (1941-
42) 183, (1948-49) 147.

RODRIGUEZ CANCIO, Francisco,
pharmacist
Ver 183, ill.

RODRIGUEZ CANCIO, Miguel
(1860-1941), doctor
BoHP 157-58; CaM 367-69;
LuO 99-100; ProA 65; RepM
255, ill.

Rodríguez Capó, Félix M. see
Capó, Bobby

RODRIGUEZ CASTRO, José (1854-
1900?), doctor

CaM 366; Crom 54; DiM 279-
80; HoIPR 99, ill.

RODRIGUEZ CASTRO, José B. (b.
1895), engineer
QEQ (1948-49) 147-48.

RODRIGUEZ CEBOLLERO, José C.,
lawyer, potlitician
RepM 297, ill.

RODRIGUEZ COLON, Charlie (b.
1954), politician
LiPR 34, ill.

RODRIGUEZ CHACON, Julio (b.
1908), engineer
QEQ (1936-37) 143.

RODRIGUEZ CHACON, Sarah (b.
1912), home economist, teacher
QEQ (1936-37) 143.

RODRIGUEZ DE ASTUDILLO, Sebastián
(d.1883), lawyer
Eco 142-45.

RODRIGUEZ DE CARRERA, María
Genoveva (b.1920), lawyer
EGMPR 3:229-30.

RODRIGUEZ DE JESUS, Juan (b.
1915), lawyer, government
official
DiHBC 787-88; GrEPR 14:306.

Rodríguez de Laguna see Rodríguez Seda de Laguna

RODRIGUEZ DE OLMEDO, Mariano (b.
1772), bishop
GrEPR 6:259-60.

RODRIGUEZ DE SAAVEDRA, Mary (b.
1914), government official
EGMPR 3:123-24.

RODRIGUEZ DE TIO, Lola (1843-
1924), author
BiP 375-77; BrECP 393-95,
ill.; CaE 864; CiBPI 74(ill.),
141-45; DiDHM 178-79, ill.;
DiHBC 789-90; DiLP 2, pt.2:
1384-88; ECPR 6:487-88; EGMPR
1:85-88, ill.; EPI 1:238-40,
ill.; GenB 280-83, ill.; GenP
56-59, ill.; GrEPR 14:308,
ill.; Hi de M 198-99, ill.;
HisD 74; HoYMPR 52-67, ill.;
MujDPR 67-82, ill.; MujP 117-
20; MujPu 71-81; PaH 1:391-93;

P1E 1:171-94, ill.; PQ 15;
PRFAS 216, ill.; S 84; SobM
181-83; VerOr 9-11.

RODRIGUEZ DIAZ, Andrés A. (b.
1867), teacher, Episcopalean
deacon
QEQ (1936-37) 143.

RODRIGUEZ EMA, Doris (b.1946),
painter
GrEPR 8:439.

RODRIGUEZ EMA, Manuel (b.
1905), doctor
QEQ (1936-37) 143.

RODRIGUEZ ESCOBAR, Angel (b.
1892), teacher, lawyer
QEQ (1936-37) 143.

RODRIGUEZ ESCUDERO, Néstor A.
(b.1914), lawyer, author
BiP 377-79; BrECP 395; DiLP
2, pt.2:1371-75; GrEPR 14:
305; PRFAS 217; QEQ (1948-
49) 148; SobM 251-54.

RODRIGUEZ FORTEZA, Félix Alberto (b.1910), doctor
QEQ (1948-49) 148.

RODRIGUEZ FRESE, Marcos (b.
1941), lawyer, poet
BrECP 395; GrEPR 14:305;
PRFAS 217-18.

RODRIGUEZ GARCIA, Carmelo,
politician
GrEPR 14:305.

RODRIGUEZ GARCIA, Tadeo (b.
1895), labor leader, politician
AntHistCag 433-35, ill.

RODRIGUEZ GEIGEL, Antonio (b.
1903), chemist
QEQ (1936-37) 143, (1941-
42) 183-84.

RODRIGUEZ GONZALEZ, Enrique
(b.1855), doctor
CaM 364-65.

RODRIGUEZ GONZALEZ, Pedro R.
(b.1920), politician
GrEPR 14:306.

RODRIGUEZ GUZMAN, Juan (b.
1899), chemist

QEQ (1948-49) 148-49.

RODRIGUEZ IRIZARRY, José Angel (b.1936), politician
LiPR 121, ill.

RODRIGUEZ LOPEZ, Francisco
(b.1881), teacher
QEQ (1933-34) 137, (1936-37)
144.

RODRIGUEZ LOPEZ, Josefina (1908-
1948), professor
EGMPR 1:355-56; QEQ (1941-42)
184.

RODRIGUEZ MCCARTY, José R. (d.
1901), teacher, poet
Pq 230-32.

RODRIGUEZ MARTINEZ, Juan, politician
GrEPR 14:306.

RODRIGUEZ MENDEZ, Antonio, businessman
A 127.

RODRIGUEZ MIRANDA, Luis (1875*-
1949), musician, composer
AlDU 23, 57-58; BiP 281-82;
CiBPI 256-58; DiHBC 788; ECPR
6:488; GrEPR 14:218, 306; Ho-
YMPR 202-10, ill.; MusMP 228-
30; PRFAS 162; QEQ (1933-34)
106-8, (1936-37) 111-12.

RODRIGUEZ MOLINA, Rafael (b.
1901), doctor
DiHBC 788-89; QEQ (1933-34)
137, (1936-37) 144, (1941-42)
184-85, (1948-49) 149-50.

RODRIGUEZ MONTAÑEZ, Agustina (b.
1867), actress
EGMPR 4:113-14; Orig 291
(ill.), 292-95.

RODRIGUEZ MORALES, Luis M. (b.
1924), historian, author
DiLP 2, pt.2:1375-77; GrEPR
14:306, ill.

RODRIGUEZ MUNDO, Juana (b.1900),
teacher, politician
EGMPR 1:357, ill., 2:45,
ill.; GrEPR 14:306, ill.;
PriC 73-74, ill.

RODRIGUEZ MUÑIZ, Tulio (b.1879),
lawyer, judge

QEQ (1933-34) 137, (1936-
37) 144, (1941-42) 185,
(1948-49) 150; Tri 2:223-
26.

RODRIGUEZ NIETZSCHE, Vicente
(b.1942), poet
    BrECP 395-96; DiLP 2, pt.
    2:1377-78; PRFAS 217.

RODRIGUEZ OLMO, Luis (b.1919),
baseball player
    EPI 1:332, ill.

RODRIGUEZ ORELLANA, Manuel,
professor
    DirAS 4:452.

RODRIGUEZ ORTIZ, Vicente,
lawyer
    RepM 195, ill.

RODRIGUEZ OTERO, Eladio (1919-
1977), lawyer
    BrECP 396; DiHBC 789; Gr-
    EPR 1:xiv-xv, ill., 14:307,
    ill.; Per 87-89; PRFAS 218-
    19.

Rodríguez Pacheco, Emilia see
Conde, Emilia

RODRIGUEZ PACHECO, Rafael,
politician
    GrEPR 14:307.

RODRIGUEZ PAGAN, Moisés (b.
1914), musician
    GrEPR 14:307.

RODRIGUEZ PASTOR, José (b.
1894*), doctor, author
    BiP 379-80; CaM 366; DiLP
    2, pt.2:1378-80; DiM 281-
    82; Ind 139-40; PRFAS 219;
    QEQ (1933-34) 137-38,
    (1936-37) 144, (1941-42)
    185-86, (1948-49) 150; Tri
    2:35-39.

RODRIGUEZ POU, Juan, businessman
    A 167, ill.

RODRIGUEZ QUIÑONES, José Monserrate (b.1902), doctor
    QEQ (1941-42) 186.

RODRIGUEZ-REMENESKI, Shirley,
legislative coordinator
    Port 139, 140(ill.)

RODRIGUEZ RIVERA, Herminio (b.
1906), chemist
    QEQ (1948-49) 150-51.

RODRIGUEZ RIVERA, Juan Francisco
(b.1897), Evangelical minister
    QEQ (1933-34) 138, (1936-37)
    144-45, (1941-42) 186, (1948-
    49) 151.

RODRIGUEZ RIVERA, Vicente
(1884*-1939), poet
    BiP 380-81; DiLP 2, pt.2:
    1380-82; Hi de Cay 238-39;
    PRFAS 219; QEQ (1933-34) 138-
    39, (1936-37) 145.

RODRIGUEZ RODRIGUEZ, Tomás, businessman
    QEQ (1936-37) 145.

RODRIGUEZ ROSARIO, Jesús María
(b.1882), decorator
    QEQ (1933-34) 139.

RODRIGUEZ RUBIO, Andrés (b.1939),
philosopher, professor
    DirAS 4:461.

RODRIGUEZ RUBIO, Luis Juan,
doctor
    CaM 367.

RODRIGUEZ SANTOS, Rodolfo, politician
    GrEPR 14:308.

RODRIGUEZ SARIEGO, Francisco
(1916-1940), poet
    AntHistCag 259-60; AntPoeCag
    217-19.

RODRIGUEZ SEDA DE LAGUNA, Asela
(b.1946), critic, professor
    Dir AS 3:443; Port 115, 116
    (ill.)

RODRIGUEZ SEÑERIZ, María, artist
    EGMPR 4:115-16; GrEPR 8:
    439; PaG 210; PQ 54.

RODRIGUEZ SERRA, Manuel (1871-
1949), lawyer
    HoIPR 99-101, ill.; LM 133-
    34: QEQ (1936-37) 145-46,
    (1941-42) 186-87, (1948-49)
    151-52.

RODRIGUEZ SUAREZ, Roberto (b.
1923), author
    DiLP 2, pt.2:1382-84.

RODRIGUEZ TORRES, Carmelo (b. 1941), poet
DiLP 2, pt.2:1388-89; GrEPR 5:130-31, 14:308; Ind 140-42; PRFAS 219-20.

RODRIGUEZ TORRES, Julio Irving (b.1930), lawyer, politician
GrEPR 14:308.

RODRIGUEZ VIDAL, José, artist
GrEPR 8:439.

RODRIGUEZ VILA, Juan (b.1935), golfer
CuB 1969:370-72, ill.

ROENA SANTIAGO, Manuel I. (b. 1911), engineer
QEQ (1941-42) 187.

ROGERS, Poligenia "Poli", dancer
Port 93, 94(ill.)

ROGLER CANINO, Lloyd (b.1930), professor, sociologist
Port 157, 158(ill.)

ROIG, Gabriel, businessman
A 128.

ROIG, Juan, author
AlHY 212-13; RepM 333, ill.

ROIG, Pablo (1866-1935), author, journalist, actor
DiLP 2, pt.2:1389-90; Hi de M 135; HoIPR 101, ill.; Orig 339-41.

ROIG CARDOSA, Francisco (b. 1870), politician
BoHP 172, 173, ill.

ROIG COLMENERO, Ramón María (b.1895), engineer
QEQ (1936-37) 146, (1941-42) 187-88, (1948-49) 152-53.

ROIG TORRELLAS, Antonio (1859-1933), businessman
DiDHM 179, ill.

ROIG VELEZ, Baldomero (b. 1909), lawyer, politician
GrEPR 14:309.

ROIG VELEZ, Eduardo (b.1903),

Protestant minister
QEQ (1936-37) 146.

ROJAS, Manuel (d.1902), revolutionary
BoHP 92-93, 95, 102, ill.; CiBPI 71(ill.), 127-30; DiDHM 179-80; HisP 84-85, 91-98, 100-101.

ROJAS, Víctor (b.1832?), sailor
ArH 271-88, 305-30; BiP 381-82; CiBPI 97-100; EnsB 289-92; GrEPR 14:309; PRFAS 220; PuI 127-30.

ROJAS NEGRON, Antonio, tobacco expert
CaDeT 194, 195(ill.)

ROJAS PARAMO, Gabriel de (d. 1620), soldier, governor
Hi de Pu 85-86.

ROJAS REYES, Julio (b.1890), pharmacist, politician
CaF 130; GrEPR 14:309.

ROJAS TOLLINCHI, Francisco (1911-1965), poet, journalist
AlHY 172-74, 222-23; DiLP 2, pt.2:1390-92; PRFAS 220.

ROLA RYAN, Emilio M. (b.1892), engineer
QEQ (1936-37) 146.

ROLAN, Manuel (b.1901), businessman
QEQ (1933-34) 139, (1936-37) 146-47, (1941-42) 188, (1948-49) 153.

ROLDAN ANCHORIZ, Amalio Faustino (b.1880), doctor
CaM 372; QEQ (1933-34) 139, (1936-37) 147.

ROLDAN BLAS, Israel (b.1929), journalist, politician
GrEPR 14:309.

ROLENSON, Julio R. (b.1889), doctor
QEQ (1933-34) 139-40, (1936-37) 147, (1941-42) 188.

ROMAGUERA, José (1873-1941), businessman
AlHP 282, ill.

ROMAGUERA, José Mariano (b. 1902), businessman
  A 66, ill.; GenB 391-92, ill.

ROMAN, Elsa, actress
  DelMu 316-21, ill.

ROMAN, Ramón Luis (b.1949), artist, teacher
  GrEPR 8:439.

ROMAN ARTIGUEZ, Diego, government official
  PriC 171, ill.

ROMAN BENITEZ, Carlos (1903-1965), politician
  GrEPR 14:309; PriC 189, ill.

ROMAN BENITEZ, Manuel (b. 1894), doctor
  CaM 373; QEQ (1941-42) 188-89, (1948-49) 153.

ROMAN CRUZ, Fortunato (b. 1896), teacher
  QEQ (1948-49) 153.

ROMAN DIAZ, Diego, doctor
  RepM 315, ill.

ROMAN GARCIA, Alfonso (b. 1914), politician
  GrEPR 14:310; QEQ (1948-49) 153-54.

ROMAN GONZALEZ, Julio César (b.1940), politician
  LiPR 116, ill.

ROMAN PRADO, María Antonia, artist
  GrEPR 8:439.

ROMANACCE, Sergio (1898-1943), journalist
  DiLP 2, pt.2:1392-93; QEQ (1936-37) 147.

ROMANI, Jorge, politician
  GrEPR 14:310.

ROMANO, Jaime (b.1942), artist
  GrEPR 8:372, ill.

ROMANY BELGODERE, Marcelino (b.1892), lawyer, judge
  QEQ (1933-34) 140, (1936-37) 147, (1941-42) 189;

VisC 63-77.

ROMERO, Alfredo, musician, composer, teacher
  GrEPR 14:310.

ROMERO, Damián, manager
  A 119.

ROMERO, José Simón (b.1815), author
  DiLP 2, pt.2:1400-1402.

ROMERO, Marta, singer, actress
  EGMPR 4:117-18, ill.

ROMERO, Pablo (b.1954), artist
  GrEPR 8:440.

ROMERO BARCELO, Carlos (b.1932), politician, governor
  CuB 1977:365-68, ill.; DiDHM 180; GrEPR 14:310, ill., 311-12(ill.); LiPR 58-59, ill.; PRFAS 221; PRUSA 23, ill.

ROMERO Y CANTERO, Calixto (1856-1911), doctor
  CaM 373; DiM 282-85; GrEPR 14:313; HoIPR 102, ill.; LPR 1020, 1021; PRFAS 221; RepM 327, ill.

ROMERO Y CANTERO, Francisco Antonio, pharmacist
  CaF 130-31.

ROMERO PEREZ DE GELPI, Carmen Alicia (b.1926), doctor
  EGMPR 3:247.

ROMERO ROSA, Ramón (19th cent.), labor leader, politician
  GrEPR 14:313.

ROMERO TOGORES, Calixto (19th cent.), doctor, political activist
  CaM 373-74; DiM 282-85; GrEPR 14:313.

ROMEU, José A. (1906), journalist
  DiLP 2, pt.2:1402-4.

RONDON TOLLENS, Salomon, politician
  LiPR 41, ill.

ROOSEVELT, Theodore, Jr. (1887-

1944), governor
CuB 1944:562-63, ill.; Desf
94-108, ill.; DiDHM 180-81;
DiHBC 438; DicAB suppl.3:
668-69; GrEPR 14:313, ill.;
PolPr 1:443-44, 2:523-25;
QEQ (1933-34) 140, (1936-
37) 147.

ROQUE DE DUPREY, Ana (1853-
1933), teacher, author, feminist
BiP 382-83; CiBPI 221(ill.)
232-34; DiDHM 181; DiHBC
790-91; DiLP 2, pt.2:1404-
6; ECPR 6:488-89; EGMPR 1:
89-90, ill.; GrEPR 14:314;
Ind 142-43; Ma 63-64; Muj-
DPR 104-11, ill.; MujP 121-
22; MujPu 82-86; PlE 1:192;
PQ 16; PRFAS 221; QEQ
(1933-34) 140-41, (1936-37)
16; VPR 95-97, 167.

ROS, Santiago (19th cent.),
artist
GenB 410-12.

ROS Y POCHET, Salvador Genaro
(19th cent.), doctor
CaM 375-76; DiM 285.

ROSA, Bibiano, lawyer
Port 99, 100(ill.)

ROSA, José A. (b.1939), painter
GrEPR 8:440.

ROSA, Martín de la (d.1938),
doctor
CaM 377.

ROSA, Pedro Juvenal (b.1897),
lawyer, author
DiLP 2, pt.2:1406-9; GrEPR
5:131-33; Ind 99-100; PRFAS
223.

ROSA, Tomás Antonio (b.1946),
artist
GrEPR 8:440.

ROSA AUDINOT, Salvador de la
(b.1898), accountant
QEQ (1948-49) 57.

ROSA DE LIMA, Santa (1586-
1617), Catholic nun, saint
DiHBC 791; EGMPR 1:9-28,
ill.

ROSA GUZMAN, Antonio (b.1931),
politician
LiPR 40, ill.

ROSA-NIEVES, Cesáreo (1901-
1974), author, critic
And 117-21; BiP 388-91; BrECP
397-98; CaE 865-66; ConA 57-
60:489-90; DiDHM 181-82; Di-
HBC 791-92; DiLP 2, pt.2:
1409-23; DicC 89-90; ECPR 6:
489; Esb 2:141-51; EsbCrit
113-24; GrEPR 5:133-37, 14:
314; Ind 143-45; PRFAS 222-
23, ill.; QEQ (1936-37) 190,
(1941-42) 189, (1948-49) 154;
Vida 18-19.

ROSADO, Hiram, political activist
GrEPR 14:314.

ROSADO, Juan A. (1891-1962),
artist
GrEPR 8:124-25.

ROSADO DEL VALLE, Julio (b.
1922), artist
BiP 383-84; BrECP 396-97,
ill.; GrEPR 8:296, ill.; PaG
203; PRFAS 223.

ROSADO PANTOJA, Rafael, politician
GrEPR 14:314.

ROSADO VELEZ, Juan (b.1942),
artist
GrEPR 8:440.

ROSALES, Ignacio (b.1860), businessman
Esp 121.

ROSALY, Johanna, actress
DelMu 324-27.

ROSALY, Pedro Juan, politician
GrEPR 14:314.

ROSALLY, Louis (b.1939), businessman
Port 135, 136(ill.)

ROSARIO, Carlos A. del, pharmacist
HoIPR 102, ill.; Ka 27-28.

ROSARIO, Charles (b.1924),
author
DiLP 2, pt.2:1423-24; PRFAS
223-24.

ROSARIO, Edwin Francisco (b. 1944), painter
  GrEPR 8:420.

ROSARIO, José Colombán (1888-1966), author
  DiLP 2, pt.2:1424-26.

ROSARIO, Leticia del (b.1914), physicist, educator
  BrECP 134-35; DiDHM 76; PRFAS 81.

ROSARIO, Miguel, banker
  Port 175, 176(ill.)

ROSARIO, Rubén del (b.1907), professor, author, philologist
  AlHY 221; BiP 385-86; BrECP 135-37, ill.; DiDHM 182, ill.; DiLP 2, pt.2:1426-29; ECPR 6:489, 491; GrEPR 14:315; PRFAS 224, ill.

ROSARIO BAEZ, Jaime (b.1908), politician
  LiPR 35, ill.

ROSARIO DE GALARZA, Gladys (b. 1943), politician
  LiPR 30, ill.

ROSARIO DE MARTINEZ, Mareb del (b. 1943), government employee, author
  BrECP 133-34.

ROSARIO GOYCO, Felipe "Don Felo" (1899-1954), composer, musician
  Com 7; GrEPR 7:125-26, ill.

ROSARIO MARRERO, Luis Antonio (b.1898), lawyer, politician
  QEQ (1936-37) 147-48.

ROSARIO NATAL, Carmelo (b. 1935), historian, professor
  GrEPR 1:xv, ill.

ROSARIO RAMOS, Ramón del (1884-1972), politician
  Añas 109-11, ill.

ROSARIO RAMOS, Tomás (1899-1950), author, evangelist
  AntHistCag 273-76, ill.

ROSARIO QUILES, Luis A. (b. 1936*), author
  BrECP 398-99; DiLP 2, pt.2:

1429-30; GrEPR 14:315; PRFAS 224-25.

ROSARIO RIVERA, Pedro (b.1897), teacher
  QEQ (1941-42) 189-90.

ROSARIO ROSADO, Angel M. (b. 1933), politician
  LiPR 125, ill.

ROSARIO SANTIAGO, José Ezequiel (b.1894), government official
  QEQ (1933-34) 141, (1936-37) 148.

ROSAS HERNANDEZ, Buenaventura (b. 1904), accountant
  A 164; QEQ (1948-49) 154.

ROSELLO, Jacqueline, artist
  GrEPR 8:440; PQ 54.

ROSELLO, José, musician
  MusMP 290-91.

ROSES ARTAU, Miguel (d. 1945), doctor
  CaM 378; Ka 77; Tri 1:133-39.

ROSES BORRAS, Lorenzo (19th-20th cent.), politician
  ArH 405, 414-15.

ROSELL Y CARBONELL, Antonio, educator
  Hi de CR 189.

ROSELLO, Juan Pablo (19th cent.), pharmacist
  CaF 132-33.

ROSSY, Cecilio S. (1892-1918), psychologist
  DiHBC 792; LPR 1050, 1051; PRFAS 225.

ROSSY, Manuel F. (1862-1932), politician, journalist, lawyer
  DiDHM 182-83; ECPR 6:491; GrEPR 14:315-16, ill.; HisD 75; HoIPR 102, ill.; LM 119-20; RepM 57, ill.; S 87.

ROSSY CALDERON, Celio, musician
  MusMP 266.

ROSSY Y CALDERON, Jesús Maria (b.1868), lawyer, judge
  LM 127

ROSSY PALMER, William (b.
1892), engineer
    QEQ (1941-42) 190, (1948-
    49) 154.

ROURA, Lorenzo, priest
    Crom 33.

ROURA DE TORRESOLA, Rosalina
(1886-1970), political activist
    EGMPR 4:253-54.

ROURE, Vicente, Jr. (b.1896),
educator, pharmacist
    QEQ (1933-34) 141-42,
    (1936-37) 148.

ROURE AMBER, Vicente, doctor
    RepM 122, ill.

ROVIRA, José (1880-1962),
businessman, politician
    GrEPR 14:316; Guay 275;
    PriC 42, ill.

ROVIRA, José María, businessman
    A 158, ill.

ROVIRA Y TOMAS, Joaquín, businessman, politician
    Guay 275.

ROYO, Manuel María (19th
cent.), Jesuit priest
    Jes 152-53.

RUANO LAIGLESIA, Argimiro (b.
1924), philosopher, professor
    DirAS 4:461.

Rubéns, Alma see Porrata Doria
de Rubéns, Providencia

RUBERT ARMSTRONG, José (b.
1906), businessman
    QEQ (1941-42) 240, (1948-
    49) 154-55.

RUBIANO, Jorge (b.1891), music
director, composer
    QEQ (1948-49) 155.

RUBIN DE CELIS, Bernardina,
artist, author
    MujPu 51-52.

RUBIO SEXTO, Pablo (b.1944),
sculptor
    GrEPR 8:420.

Rufo, Padre see Fernández, Rufo
Manuel

RUIZ, Cristóbal (d.1962), artist,
educator
    GrEPR 8:197-200, 421, ill.

RUIZ, Noemí (b.1928), artist,
educator
    BrECP 400; EGMPR 4:119-20;
    GrEPR 8:376, ill.; PRFAS
    226.

RUIZ ARNAU, Ramón (1874-1934),
doctor
    ArH 516; CaM 384; DiDHM 183,
    ill.; DiM 285-87; HoIPR 103,
    ill.; PRFAS 226-27, ill.; QEQ
    (1933-34) 142-43, (1936-37)
    16; RepM 70, ill.; Tri 1:149-
    54; Ver 185, ill.

RUIZ BELVIS, Segundo (1829-1867),
abolitionist, lawyer
    AlHP 332, ill.; BeHNPR 2:163-
    67, ill.; BiP 386-88; BrECP
    399-400, ill.; CiBPI 72(ill.),
    118-20; DiDHM 183-84, ill.;
    DiHBC 793-94; DiLP 2, pt.2:
    1430-31; ECPR 6:490(ill.),
    491-92; EnsB 129-39; GenB
    250, ill.; GenP 67-68; GrEPR
    14:317, ill.; HePR 55-62,
    ill.; Hi de M 194-95, ill.,
    294-310, ill.; HisD 75; HisP
    60, 77, 78, 80-82, 86; HoIPR
    103, ill.; HoRPR 49-53; LM
    112-13; LPR 978, 980, 981,
    ill.; Nuestr 9-12; PaI 87-99,
    ill.; Por 237-38; PRFAS 228,
    ill.; PuI 153-55; Se 73-81,
    ill.; VPR 23-36, 165.

RUIZ CESTERO, Guillermo (b.1901),
doctor
    QEQ (1936-37) 148, (1941-42)
    190, (1948-49) 155.

RUIZ CESTERO, Ramón (d.1977),
musician, conductor
    GrEPR 14:317.

RUIZ DANA, Pedro (19th cent.),
governor
    DiDHM 184; GrEPR 14:317.

RUIZ DE ARRECHE, Paquita (b.
1915), home economist, teacher
    QEQ (1941-42) 190-91.

RUIZ DE LA MATA, Ernesto J.,

artist, critic
  GrEPR 8:440.

RUIZ DE ROLDAN, Daisy, lawyer
  EGMPR 3:249-50.

RUIZ GANDIA, Manuel (1837-
1890), teacher
  AlHP 334, ill.; ArH 459;
  PRFAS 228; PuI 193-97.

RUIZ GARCIA, Zoilo (1880?-
1930?), journalist
  DiLP 2, pt.2:1431-32; Hi de
  M 134, 209.

RUIZ IRIZARRY, Eusebio, political activist
  Nuestr 62-63.

RUIZ MARI, Ricardo (1861-
1959), civic leader
  AlHP 333, ill.

RUIZ MARRERO, Eloy Guillermo
(b.1887), Protestant minister
  GrEPR 9:118-19; QEQ (1933-
  34) 100, (1936-37) 102.

RUIZ NAZARIO, Clemente (1896-
1969), lawyer, judge
  QEQ (1941-42) 191; S 90.

RUIZ PULIDO, Cristóbal (1881-
1962), professor, painter
  DiDHM 184.

RUIZ QUIÑONES, Antonio (1837-
1902), teacher, author
  DiLP 2, pt.2:1432-33; GrEPR
  14:317; Hi de M 202-3;
  Nuestr 22-23.

RUIZ RIVERA, Juan (1846*-
1924), government official,
soldier
  HisD 75; HoIPR 103-4, ill.

RUIZ ROMAN, Ruperto (b.1906),
engineer, naval architect
  QEQ (1948-49) 155.

RUIZ SOLER, Alejandro (1881-
1936), doctor
  BrECP 400-401; CaM 381-83;
  CiBPI 270-72; GrEPR 14:318,
  ill.; HoDMT 108-16; HoIPR
  104, ill.; ProA 67; PRFAS
  228-29; RepM 331, ill.

RUIZ SOLER, José (b.1879),

politician
  GrEPR 14:318; QEQ (1936-37)
  148, (1941-42) 191,
  (1948-49) 155-56.

RUIZ SOTO, Dolores (b.1941),
lawyer, judge
  EGMPR 3:251.

RULLAN, Antonio (b.1918),
doctor
  QEQ (1948-49) 156.

RULLAN MAYOL, Jaime (b.1911),
politician
  GrEPR 14:318.

RULLAN Y RIVERA, Juan (b.1884),
politician
  GenB 382-83, ill.

RUSCALLEDA, Jorge María (b.
1944), author, professor
  BrECP 401; DiLP 2, pt.2:
  1433-34; PRFAS 229.

S

SAAVEDRA, Angel Manuel (b.1900),
teacher
  QEQ (1936-37) 148-49.

SAAVEDRA BIRD, José M. (b.
1923), pharmacist
  CaF 136.

SAAVEDRA BIRD, Mercedes (b.1922),
pharmacist
  CaF 136.

SAAVEDRA GARCIA, Miguel (b.
1895), pharmacist
  CaF 136-38; GrEPR 14:371.

SABATER, Ever, artist
  GrEPR 8:441.

SABATER, Juanita, musician
  MusMP 266-67.

SABATER, Pedro (d.1963), fire-
man
  AlHP 284, ill.

SABATER Y GARCIA, José (b.
1822), lawyer, politician
  A 82; GrEPR 14:319; QEQ
  (1941-42) 192.

SACARELLO BALS, Angel (b.1901),
engineer

QEQ (1936-37) 149.

SACARELLO GOMEZ, Rafael (b.
1895), journalist
    QEQ (1936-37) 149, (1941-
    42) 192; SobM 131-33.

SAEZ, Antonia (1889-1964), author, teacher
    BiP 391-92; DiDHM 187,
    ill.; DiHBC 795-96; DiLP 2,
    pt.2:1435-38; ECPR 6:492;
    EGMPR 1:359-60, ill.; GrEPR
    14:319, ill.; MujDPR 214-
    19, ill.; Per 66-68; PQ 17;
    PRFAS 231, ill.

SAEZ, Pablo (1827-1879), lawyer, author
    DiLP 2, pt.2:1438-39; GrEPR
    14:320; HisD 75; LM 111;
    PRFAS 231; PuI 131-35.

SAEZ BURGOS, Juan (b.1943),
poet, lawyer
    BrECP 403-4; GrEPR 14:320;
    PRFAS 232.

SAEZ OLIVERAS, Florencio (b.
1895), educator, minister
    GrEPR 6:310, 14:319; QEQ
    (1933-34) 143, (1936-37)
    149, (1941-42) 192-93,
    (1948-49) 156-57.

SAGARDIA SANCHEZ, Antonio (b.
1913), journalist, politician
    GrEPR 14:320.

SAGARDIA TORRENS, Antonio,
politician
    BoHP 205-6, ill.; LuO 103-
    4.

SAINT GERMAIN, Leticia (b.
1938), artist
    GrEPR 8:441.

SAINT-JUST, José (1790-1862),
soldier
    BeHNPR 2:133-34.

SAINT-JUST, Juan (1792-1836),
soldier
    BeHNPR 2:13-19, ill.

SAINT VILLIERS URDANETA, Rafael (b.1895), politician
    GrEPR 14:320; QEQ (1933-34)
    143-44, (1936-37) 149.

SALABERRIOS DE VILLAQUIRAN,
Ivonne, painter
    PaG 237-38.

SALAMANCA, Angel (b.1938),
artist, teacher
    GrEPR 8:421.

SALAMANCA, Diego de (16th
cent.), bishop
    Hi de la Ig 40-42.

SALAS, Américo, businessman
    RepM 261, ill.

SALAS Y QUIROGA, Jacinto de
(1813-1849), author, journalist
    DiLP 2, pt.2:1439-40.

SALAVARRIA, Martín, arts patron
    Esp 77-78.

SALAZAR, Ermelindo, businessman
    Crom 27; Ka 11; RepM 335,
    ill.; Ver 174-75, ill.

SALAZAR PALAU, Andrés, doctor
    CaM 387.

SALAZAR PALAU, Guillermo (1880-
1950), doctor
    CaM 387-88; DiM 288; QEQ
    (1936-37) 149, (1941-42)
    193.

SALCEDO, Diego (16th cent.),
soldier
    DiDHM 187; GrEPR 14:320;
    HisD 76.

SALDAÑA, Eduardo J. (b.1883),
government official
    QEQ (1933-34) 144, (1936-37)
    150; Tri 1:75-79.

SALDAÑA, Jorge M., insurance
agent
    A 42-43.

SALDAÑA, José Esteban, doctor
    CaM 388.

SALDAÑA, Rafael Enrique, actor
    DelMu 330-35, ill.

SALDAÑA, Sixto M. (b.1881),
prison director
    QEQ (1936-37) 150; VisC 13-26.

SALDAÑA CROSAS, Manuel I. (b.
1891), insurance agent

QEQ (1936-37) 150.

SALDAÑA Y GUZMAN, José Manuel, doctor
CaM 388-89.

SALGADO, Ramona, mental health education
Port 117, 118(ill.)

SALGADO, Teresina (b.1901), poet, journalist
DiLP 2, pt.2:1440-42; SobM 58-61.

SALGADO SALGADO, José G. (b. 1900), accountant
QEQ (1941-42) 193-94.

SALICRUP, Alejandro (1850?-1924), journalist
DiLP 2, pt.2:1442-44.

SALICRUP, M. Alberto (b.1870), notary
RepM 234, ill.

SALICRUP, Pedro J., doctor
CaM 389-90.

SALICRUP ANEXI, Jaime, businessman
A 127.

SALICHS LOPE DE HARO, José E. (b.1919), politician
GrEPR 14:320.

SALIVA DE LERGIER, Clara Luz (b.1919), librarian, teacher, author
EGMPR 1:209-11, ill.

SALIVA SACARELLO, Georgina, poet
SobM 37-39.

SALIVA SACARELLO, Luis Alfredo (b.1890), doctor, pharmacist
CaF 138; DiM 289-91; QEQ (1933-34) 144, (1936-37) 150.

SALVA, José Alvaro, politician
GrEPR 14:321.

SAMA, Manuel María (1850-1913), author, bibliographer
CaE 869; DiLP 2, pt.2:1444-45; GenB 267-68, ill.; GenP 88-89, ill.; Hi de M 133,

201; HisD 76; HoIPR 104, ill.; LPR 1008, 1011; PlE 1:122-23; Por 210-11; PRFAS 232; VerOr 228-29, ill.

SAMALEA IGLESIAS, Luis (1890-1938), lawyer, journalist
BiP 392-94; CaE 869-70; DiLP 2, pt.2:1445-47; PRFAS 232-33; Tri 1:231-37.

SAN ANTONIO, Baldomero, author, political activist
Ver 184, ill.

SAN ANTONIO, Viriato, accountant
PriC 172, ill.

SAN ANTONIO Y DAVID, Balbino (18th-19th cent.), pharmacist
CaF 138-39.

SAN ANTONIO DE DIAZ, Laura (b. 1907), policewoman
EGMPR 3:253-54, ill.

SAN JUAN, Manuel, insurance agent
A 43, ill.

SAN MIGUEL, Juan (19th cent.), doctor
CaM 391-92.

SAN MIGUEL, Manuel (b.1930), artist
GrEPR 8:441.

SAN MIGUEL ALVAREZ, Baldomero, businessman
A 120.

SANABIA DE FIGUEROA, Carmen (1882-1954), music teacher
EGMPR 1:361, ill.; GrEPR 7: 245-47, ill.; HoIPR 105; MujDPR 184-86, ill.; QEQ (1936-37) 66.

SANABRIA, Ulises, treasurer
RepM 147, ill.

SANABRIA FERNANDEZ, Nicolás (b. 1885), doctor
QEQ (1941-42) 194.

SANCERRIT, Pascasio P. (1820?-1876), author
DiLP 2, pt.2:1447-48; EnsB 171-76; Misc 54-56.

SANCHEZ, David Samuel, artist
PaG 202.

SANCHEZ, Evelyn, painter
GrEPR 8:441.

SANCHEZ, Luis Rafael (b.1936),
author
BrECP 405, ill.; CaE 870;
DiDHM 187-88; DiLP 2, pt.2:
1448-53; DicC 94; GentI 95-
101; GrEPR 14:322; PRFAS
233.

SANCHEZ, Pablo, pharmacist
Ka 156.

SANCHEZ, Pedro Nolasco (b.
1908), lawyer
QEQ (1941-42) 194.

SANCHEZ, Rafael "Ralph" (1903-
1974), conductor
GrEPR 7:334-35, ill.

SANCHEZ, Samuel (b.1929), artist
GrEPR 8:422.

SANCHEZ, Yolanda (b.1942),
educator
Port 155, 156(ill.); PQ 55.

SANCHEZ ACEVEDO, Juan (b.
1924), politician
LiPR 125, ill.

SANCHEZ CASTAÑO, Benicio F.
(b.1899), lawyer
QEQ (1933-34) 144-45,
(1936-37) 150, (1941-42)
194.

SANCHEZ COTORRUELO, Adolf,
lawyer
Mem 174-75.

SANCHEZ DE FUENTES Y PELAEZ,
Eugenio (b.1865), author
CaE 872.

SANCHEZ DE FUENTES Y PELAEZ,
Fernando (1877-1934), lawyer,
professor
QEQ (1936-37) 16.

SANCHEZ DE SANCHEZ, Dolores,
politician
GrEPR 14:323.

SANCHEZ ESPIN, José María (d.

1860), soldier
GenB 334-36, ill.

SANCHEZ FELIPE, Alejandro (1895-
1971), artist, professor
GrEPR 8:185-86, 378, ill.;
QEQ (1936-37) 150-51.

SANCHEZ FERNANDEZ, Agustín
(1896-1966?), doctor
CaM 392.

SANCHEZ FRASQUIERI, Luis F. (b.
1884), politician
GrEPR 14:322; QEQ (1933-34)
145, (1936-37) 151, (1941-
42) 194.

SANCHEZ GARCIA, F., businessman
ProA 38, ill.

SANCHEZ HIDALGO, Efraín (1918-
1974), educator, author, psychologist
BrECP 404; ConA 57-60:506;
DiHBC 816-17; GrEPR 14:322;
Ind 146-47; PRFAS 233; QEQ
(1948-49) 157.

SANCHEZ LONGO, Manuel (b.
1918), accountant
QEQ (1948-49) 157-58.

SANCHEZ MARTINEZ, Armando (b.
1916), politician
GrEPR 14:323.

SANCHEZ MONTALVO, R., lawyer
RepM 281, ill.

SANCHEZ MORALES, Luis (1867-
1934), politician, journalist
DeADeA 11-25; DiLP 2, pt.2:
1453-55; GrEPR 14:323; HoIPR
105, ill.; PriC 59-60, ill.;
QEQ (1933-34) 145, (1936-37)
16; RepM 21, ill.; Tri 2:67-
72.

SANCHEZ MORALES, Manuel (b.
1876), politician, businessman
HoIPR 106, ill.; RepM 86,
ill.

SANCHEZ NAZARIO, Alberto, politician
GrEPR 14:323.

SANCHEZ ORTIZ, Ernesto (b.
1899), journalist
QEQ (1933-34) 145-46, (1936-

37) 151, (1941-42) 194-95,
(1948-49) 158.

SANCHEZ ORTIZ, Rafael (b.
1901), accountant
  QEQ (1936-37) 151.

SANCHEZ OSORIO, Felipe (1872-
1944), politician
  GrEPR 14:323; HoIPR 106,
  ill.

SANCHEZ PEREZ, Justo (b.1919),
politician
  GrEPR 14:323.

SANCHEZ TARNIELLA, Andrés (b.
1932), economist, professor
  GrEPR 1:xv-xvi, ill., 14:
  323-24.

SANCHEZ VILELLA, Roberto (b.
1913), politician, governor
  BrECP 405; DiDHM 188; Di-
  HBC 817; GrEPR 14:324,
  ill., 325(ill.); HoPP 367-
  70, ill.; LiPR 62-63, ill.;
  PRFAS 233-34; PRUSA 23,
  ill.

SANCHIDRIAN, Santos (1870-
1940), Freemason
  Nues 49-50, ill.

SANCHO BONET, Rafael (1893-
1945), engineer, lawyer
  HoIPR 107, ill.; QEQ (1933-
  34) 146, (1936-37) 151,
  (1941-42) 195-96.

SANCHO CARDONA, Jaime (1843-
1903), doctor, poet
  CaM 394; DiM 294-95.

SANDERS, Jorge, businessman
  ProA 8.

SANDIN, Pedro Juan (b.1917),
postmaster
  DiHBC 817.

SANDIN MARTINEZ, Andrés (b.
1884), teacher
  QEQ (1933-34) 146, (1936-
  37) 151-52.

SANDIN MARTINEZ, Angel (d.
1958), politician
  GrEPR 14:326.

SANDIN MARTINEZ, Ramón (b.

1885), teacher
  QEQ (1933-34) 146-47, (1936-
  37) 152.

SANDOVAL CRUZ, Tomás (b.1930),
lawyer, politician
  GrEPR 14:326.

SANDRA, Cecilia Elain (b.1917),
psychologist, professor
  DiHBC 818.

SANJURJO, Luis A. (b.1911),
doctor
  CaM 394; DiHBC 818.

SANLUCAR, Manuel María de (19th
cent.), missionary, poet
  DiDHM 189.

SANROMA, Jesús María (1903-
1984), musician, professor
  BiP 394-95; BrECP 411; DiDHM
  189; DiHBC 815-16; ECPR 6:
  492; GrEPR 7:278-83, ill.;
  L 76-78; Mus en P 149-50;
  PRFAS 234; PRUSA 24; QEQ
  (1936-37) 152, (1948-49)
  158.

SANTA APONTE, Jesús (b.1935),
politician
  LiPR 32, ill.

SANTA CLARA, Antonio de (16th
cent.), chronicler
  GrEPR 14:326; HisD 77.

SANTA MARIA, Juan (19th cent.),
doctor
  CaM 394.

SANTAELLA, Angela, educator
  DiHBC 818-19; EGMPR 1:363-
  64, ill.; MujDPR 157-61,
  ill.

SANTAELLA COSTAS, Alvaro (1886-
1955), doctor
  AlHP 248, ill.; CaM 394; QEQ
  (1936-37) 152, (1941-42) 196-
  97, (1948-49) 158-59.

SANTAELLA LEON, Leoncio (b.
1889), politician
  GrEPR 14:379; QEQ (1948-49)
  159.

SANTALIZ CAPESTANY, Luis (b.
1916*), politician
  GrEPR 14:327; PriC 147-48,

man
A 132, ill.

SANTO DOMINGO, Alonso (16th cent.), priest
GrEPR 14:328.

SANTOLAYA, Gregorio de (16th cent.), landowner
GrEPR 14:328.

SANTONI, Félix (1871-1959), lawyer, politician
GrEPR 14:328, ill.; HoIPR 122-23; PriC 42, ill.; RepM 76, ill.

SANTONI, Vicente (19th-20th cent.), doctor
CaM 398; Ka 12.

SANTOS, Julio A., politician
GrEPR 14:328.

SANTOS, René (b.1954), artist
GrEPR 8:423.

SANTOS FLORES, Luis Angel (b. 1925), politician
LiPR 119, ill.

SANTOS LOPEZ, Gabriel (b. 1937), politician
LiPR 123, ill.

SANTOS MORALES, José de los (1886-1939), preacher
AlDJ 20, 133, 135, ill.

SANTOS RIVERA, Julio Antonio (b.1899), doctor
DiM 295; QEQ (1933-34) 147, (1936-37) 153.

SANTOS RODRIGUEZ, José, politician
GrEPR 14:328.

SANTOS TIO, Luis Felipe (1887-1960?), doctor, politician
CaM 398-400; GenB 374-76, ill.; QEQ (1948-49) 161.

SANTOS TIO, William J. (b. 1886), lawyer
QEQ (1936-37) 153, (1941-42) 198; RepM 293, ill.

SANZ, Angel (b.1912), banker, financeer

DiHBC 820; QEQ (1936-37) 153-54, (1941-42) 198.

SANZ, José Laureano (19th cent.), governor
DiDHM 190-91; DiHBC 454; GrEPR 14:329; HisD 78.

SANZ Y AMBROS, Angel (1851-1911), soldier, customs official
HoIPR 107-8, ill.

SANZ SAN MILLAN, Carlos R., architect
GrEPR 9:120.

SARMIENTO, Antonio (b.1859), lawyer, journalist
Exp 97-98; HoIPR 108-9, ill.

Sarmiento, Camilo see Zeno Gandía, Manuel

SARVIS LOPEZ, Jeffrey (b.1949), painter
GrEPR 8:423.

SAURI, Félix, businessman, philanthropist
Ka 63; Ver 187-88.

SAVAGE, José R. F. (b.1873), lawyer
RepM 42, ill.

SBERT PRADOS, Ricardo (b.1892), pharmacist
QEQ (1933-34) 147, (1936-37) 154.

SCOVILLE, Hector Humphrey (b. 1876), lawyer
RepM 165, ill.

SCHIMMELPFINNIG, William H. (d. 1957), architect
GrEPR 9:118-19.

SCHMIDT PICKARSKI, Rebecca (b. 1922), pharmacist, nun
EGMPR 4:315.

SCHOENRICH, Otto, lawyer, judge
RepM 296, ill.

SCHOMBERG WEBER, Federico (b. 1865), businessman
QEQ (1936-37) 154.

SCHUCK, Guillermo, businessman
Ka 131-32.

SCHUCK, Oscar, philanthropist
Crom 41.

SCHWARTZ, Francis (b.1940),
musician, composer, professor
GrEPR 14:329-30, ill.

SECOLA, Francisco, businessman
Ka 100.

SEDA BONILLA, Eduardo (b.
1927*), professor, author
DiDHM 191; PRFAS 235.

SEDA RAMOS, Américo (b.1890),
lawyer
QEQ (1936-37) 154.

SEDEÑO, Antonio (16th cent.),
government official, colonist
DiHBC 820; GrEPR 14:330.

SEGARRA, Elías C. (b.1889),
doctor
QEQ (1933-34) 205, (1936-
37) 154.

SEGUER, Andrés Avelino, pharmacist
CaF 141.

SEIJO DE ZAYAS, Esther, home
economist, professor
DiDHM 191; EGMPR 1:367-68,
ill.

SEIJO TAVAREZ, Sergio, pharmacist, politician
ArH 410-11, 487-88.

SEIN, Francisco (1869-1946),
doctor, politician
Añas 75-78; CaM 401; DiM
296; GrEPR 14:330, ill.;
PriC 43, ill.; RepM 254,
ill.

SEIX, Juan, businessman
Crom 65.

SELLES SOLA, Gerardo (1887-
1946), educator
AntHistCag 260.

SEMIDEY RODRIGUEZ, José (1868-
1958), soldier
GrEPR 14:331.

SEPULVEDA, Domingo (1874-
1952), lawyer, judge
AlHP 280, ill.; QEQ (1933-

34) 147-48, (1936-37) 154,
(1941-42) 198-99; RepM 218,
ill.

SERBIA DE CARO, María Mercedes,
teacher
EGMPR 1:369-70, ill.

SERVERA SILVA, Joaquín, lawyer,
judge
Nuestr 84-85.

SERRA, Belén Milagros (b.
1923), professor, social worker
EGMPR 1:371-72.

SERRA, Guillermo (b.1913),
economist
DiHBC 823.

SERRA, José María (d.1888),
journalist
EnsB 292-94.

SERRA COLON, Américo (b.1900),
doctor
QEQ (1933-34) 148, (1936-37)
154-55, (1941-42) 199, (1948-
49) 161.

SERRA Y DE CASTRO, José María
(d.1888), teacher, journalist
GenB 287; Hi de M 126, 197;
Nuestr 47-48.

SERRA GELABERT, María, poet,
teacher
AlHP 397; MujDPR 225-28, ill.

SERRA VELEZ, Carlos (b.1944),
politician
LiPR 119, ill.

SERRALTA, Bernabé de (1530-
1598), soldier
BeHNPR 1:215-17; HisD 78; PuI
6-9.

SERRALLES, Juan E. (d.1956),
sugar industrialist
AlHP 463, ill.

SERRALLES, Juan Eugenio, sugar
industrialist
AlHP 352, ill.; Crom 26.

SERRALLES, Pedro Juan, industrialist
A 26-27; GrEPR 14:331.

SERRALLES, Sebastián (19th

cent.), sugar plantation owner
   AlHP 462, ill.

SERRANO, Guillermo (b.1950),
artist
   GrEPR 8:424.

SERRANO, Sandalio (19th
cent.), rescuer
   ArH 261-62.

SERRANO DE BRAVO, Carmen Belén (b.1925), banker
   EGMPR 3:65-66, ill.

SERRANO DE LAUGIER, Adrienne
(b.1903), teacher
   QEQ (1936-37) 190.

SERRANO MONTAÑO, Luis Antonio
(b.1895), agronomist
   QEQ (1933-34) 148, (1936-
   37) 155, (1941-42) 199.

SERRANO RAMIREZ, Francisco (b.
1893), author
   QEQ (1948-49) 161-62.

SEVERA DE ZEGRI, Polita (b.
1907), civic works
   EGMPR 4:317-18.

SEVILLA DE ARNALDO, Josefa
(1846-1890), teacher
   EGMPR 4:233-34; Hi de M
   211-12, ill.; VerOr 306-7.

SHAFROTH, John Franklin (1854-
1922), U.S. senator
   PriC 15.

SHANTON, George R., police
chief
   RepM 52-53, ill.

SHEPARD, Noah (b.1876), farmer
   QEQ (1933-34) 148-49,
   (1936-37) 155.

SHINE, James, artist, teacher
   GrEPR 8:380, ill.

SIACA PACHECO, Ramón (1861-
1936), lawyer
   QEQ (1933-34) 149, (1936-
   37) 16, 155; RepM 109, ill.

SIACA RIVERA, Manuel (b.1906),
author, critic
   CaE 877; DiLP 2, pt.2:1456-
   57; PRFAS 235-36.

SICARDO, Manuel (1803-1864),
architect, teacher
   BeHNPR 2:147-51, ill.; EnsB
   113-19; Esp 27-33, ill.

SICARDO DE CARACENA, Ramona,
musician
   MusMP 268-69.

SICARDO DE VILLAR, Alicia (1885-
1962), musician
   EGMPR 4:121-22, ill.; MujDPR
   189-92, ill.; MusMP 267-68.

SIEBERT, John Jacob, government
official
   RepM 199, ill.

SIERRA, Pedro (1889?-1937),
journalist
   BiP 116-18; BoBP 63-65; DiLP
   2, pt.2:1457-58; EsbCrit 92-
   96; GrEPR 14:331; Per 105-
   7; PRFAS 77; Una 173-75.

SIERRA BERDECIA, Fernando (1903-
1962), journalist, politician
   A 76; BrECP 413; CaE 877; DiLP
   2, pt.2:1458-62; GrEPR 14:331;
   Per 125-27; PRFAS 236.

SIFONTES, José E. (b.1925),
doctor
   DiHBC 824.

SIFRE DAVILA, Jaime (b.1887),
lawyer
   LM 132; QEQ (1933-34) 150,
   (1936-37) 155, (1941-42)
   199-200, (1948-49) 162; RepM
   106, ill.

SIFRE Y TARAFA, Jaime (1857-1941),
manager
   HoIPR 109, ill.; QEQ (1936-
   37) 190.

SIGAL, William, architect
   GrEPR 9:129.

SILEN, Iván (b.1944), poet
   DicC 96.

SILEN, Juan Angel (b.1938),
educator, author
   ConA 33-36R:714-15; PRFAS
   236.

SILVA, Ana Margarita (b.1895),
author
   DiHBC 824-25; DiLP 2, pt.2:

1462-64.

SILVA, Guillermo (b.1905),
lawyer
   QEQ (1933-34) 150, (1936-
   37) 156, (1941-42) 201.

SILVA, Jorge, teacher
   ProA 23.

SILVA, Myrta (b.1925), singer,
composer
   Com 7-8; DiDHM 191-92; ECPR
   6:492; EGMPR 4:123-26,
   ill.; GentI 180-89; GrEPR
   7:138-39, ill., 14:331,
   ill.

SILVA, Rolando A. (1945),
politician
   LiPR 30, ill.

SILVA, Rufino (b.1919), professor
   GrEPR 8:382, ill.; PaG
   199.

SILVA BAEZ, Angel (b.1905),
engineer
   QEQ (1941-42) 200.

SILVA BOUCHER, Blas C. (b.
1869), engineer
   QEQ (1936-37) 155-56,
   (1941-42) 200, (1948-49)
   162; RepM 239, ill.

SILVA COFRESI, Alfredo (b.
1897), educator
   Hi de CR 250-51; QEQ
   (1936-37) 156, (1941-42)
   200-201, (1948-49) 162-63.

SILVA COFRESI, Rosita (b.
1907), author
   DiHBC 824; DiLP 2, pt.2:
   1464-65; EGMPR 4:303-5,
   ill.; Hi de CR 250; MujDPR
   244-47, ill.

SILVA DE BESOSA, Angelina (b.
1897*), social director, civic leader
   EGMPR 3:255-57, ill.; QEQ
   (1948-49) 163.

Silva de Muñoz, Rosita see
Silva Cofresí, Rosita

Silva de Quiñones, Rosita see
Silva Cofresí, Rosita

SILVA Y FIGUEROA, Agustín de
(d.1641), soldier, governor
   Hi de Pu 95-96.

SILVA GARRASTAZU, Antonio Ramón
(b.1897), dentist
   Hi de CR 273-76; QEQ (1933-
   34) 150, (1936-37) 156,
   (1941-42) 201, (1948-49) 163.

SILVA-HUTNER, Margarda (b.1915),
doctor
   Port 125, 126(ill.)

SILVA NAVARRO, Armando (b.
1897), doctor
   QEQ (1933-34) 150, (1936-37)
   156, (1941-42) 201, (1948-49)
   163.

SILVESTRI, Reinaldo R. (b.
1935), author, journalist
   DiLP 2, pt.2:1465-67;
   PRFAS 236.

SIMON, Enrique, musician
   MusMP 269.

SIMONET GRAU, Jacobo (b.1899),
doctor, pharmacist
   QEQ (1933-34) 150-51, (1936-
   37) 156-57, (1941-42) 201-2,
   (1948-49) 163-64.

SIRAGUSA DE LA HUERTA, Sebastián
(1891-1925), journalist, businessman
   ArH 486-87; HoIPR 110, ill.

Sister Carmelita see Bonilla,
Antonia

SIVERON DE SANTIAGO, Antonia (b.
1914), designer
   EGMPR 4:127-28.

SKERRET LANDRON, Ricardo (b.
1875), engineer
   QEQ (1933-34) 151, (1936-37)
   157.

SKINNER, David A. (b.1877),
government official
   QEQ (1936-37) 157, (1941-42)
   202, (1948-49) 164; RepM 66,
   ill.

SNYDER, Cecil (b.1907), judge
   GrEPR 14:332, ill.; QEQ
   (1936-37) 157, (1941-42)
   202, (1948-49) 164.

SOBRINO, Carmelo (b.1948), artist
   GrEPR 8:424.

SOCORRO, Francisco, lawyer
   RepM 302, ill.

SOLA, Celestino, farmer
   CaDeT 55-56, ill.

SOLA, Mercedes (1879-1923*), teacher, suffragette
   DiHBC 836; EGMPR 4:247-48; GrEPR 14:333; MujDPR 173-74.

SOLA, Modesto, farmer
   CaDeT 55-56, ill.

SOLA CABALLERO, Ildefonso (d. 1944), businessman, farmer
   CaDeT 57, ill.

SOLA DE PEREIRA, Carmen (b. 1911), teacher, politician
   EGMPR 2:49, ill.; GrEPR 14:333; PriC 78.

SOLA MORALES, Ildefonso (1896-1970), politician
   AntHistCag 468-69; GrEPR 14:333; PriC 149-50, ill.

SOLA RODRIGUEZ, José D., farmer, politician
   CaDeT 59, ill.; RepM 275, ill.

SOLA RODRIGUEZ, Marcelino, tobacco grower
   GrEPR 14:333.

SOLER, Enrique, architect
   GrEPR 9:120, 125-26.

SOLER H., E., lawyer
   A 133.

SOLER LOPEZ, Emilio, businessman
   A 129.

SOLER Y MARTORELL, Carlos María (1855-1917), lawyer, judge
   GrEPR 14:333, ill.; HoIPR 110, ill.; LM 119; LPR 1018, 1019, 1021; PRFAS 237; RepM 48, ill.

SOLER Y MARTORELL, Manuel

(1853-1897), author, politician
   DiLP 2, pt.2:1470-71; GrEPR 14:333.

SOLERO FELICIANO, Narciso (b. 1896), politician
   GrEPR 14:387; QEQ (1941-42) 240-41, (1948-49) 164-65.

SOLIER Y VARGAS, Pedro (1574-1620), bishop
   Hi de la Ig 60-63.

SOLIS, Francisco de (16th cent.), governor
   DiDHM 192; GrEPR 14:334.

SOLIS COMMIS, Manuel, author
   AlHY 209.

SOLTERO, José Enrique, politician
   GrEPR 14:334.

SOLTERO HARRINGTON, Hilda, educator
   EGMPR 3:67-68, ill.

SOLTERO IRIZARRY, Nathaniel (b. 1912), journalist
   QEQ (1941-42) 241, (1948-49) 165.

SOLTERO PALERMO, Rafael (b. 1899), businessman
   A 168, ill.; QEQ (1936-37) 190, (1941-42) 202-3, (1948-49) 165-66.

SOLTERO PERALTA, Augusto Rafael (b.1893), accountant, lawyer
   QEQ (1933-34) 152, (1936-37) 157; Tri 1:429-32.

SOLTERO PERALTA, Juan Enrique (b.1895), accountant
   QEQ (1933-34) 151-52, (1936-37) 157, (1941-42) 203.

SOMOHANO, Arturo (1910-1977), conductor, composer
   BiP 396-97; BrECP 413-14, ill.; ECPR 6:492-93; GrEPR 14:334; PRFAS 237; QEQ (1948-49) 166.

SOMOZA, María E. (b.1938), artist
   GrEPR 8:384, ill.

SORIANO, Roberto E. (b.1939), politician

LiPR 37, ill.

SORRENTINI CRUZ, Benigno,
politician
    GrEPR 14:334.

SOSA, Marcos (b.1773), soldier
    BeHNPR 1:323-24.

SOSA, Michel (b.1948), artist
    GrEPR 8:425.

SOSA, Pablo L. (b.1906), lawyer, government official
    QEQ (1936-37) 158, (1941-
    42) 203-4, (1948-49) 166.

SOSA CANCEL, Carmelo (b.1892),
engineer
    QEQ (1933-34) 152, (1936-
    37) 157-58.

SOSA Y OLIVA, José (b.1873),
politician
    QEQ (1948-49) 166-67.

SOSA VILLANUEVA, Luis Angel
(b.1906), chemist
    QEQ (1948-49) 166.

SOSA VILLANUEVA, Ramón F. (b.
1903), pharmacist
    QEQ (1948-49) 166.

SOTO, Carlos H., philosopher,
professor
    DirAS 4:508.

SOTO, Juan B. (b.1882), lawyer, politician, author
    BiP 397-98; DiLP 2, pt.2:
    1471-73; ECPR 6:493; GrEPR
    14:334, 335(ill.); ProA 62;
    PRFAS 237-38; QEQ (1933-34)
    153, (1936-37) 158, (1941-
    42) 204.

SOTO, Pedro Juan (b.1928), author, professor
    BiP 398-99; BrECP 414,
    ill.; CaE 879-80; DiDHM
    192; DiLP 2, pt.2:1473-79;
    DicC 98; ECPR 6:493; GrEPR
    5:137-41, 14:334; Ind 147-
    49.

SOTO, Rafael M. de, artist,
teacher
    GrEPR 8:441.

SOTO CINTRON, José M. (b.

1926), politician
    LiPR 119, ill.

SOTO GRAS, Francisco (b.1886),
lawyer
    QEQ (1933-34) 152.

SOTO MUÑOZ, Manuel, painter
    GrEPR 8:441.

SOTO NUSSA, Isidoro, lawyer,
judge
    EntP 172-73; ProA 62-63.

SOTO RAMOS, Julio (b.1903),
author, journalist
    BiP 399-401; BoBP 7-11; CaE
    880; DiLP 2, pt.2:1479-83;
    PRFAS 238.

SOTO RAMOS, Nicolás (1897-1953),
poet, journalist
    DiLP 2, pt.2:1483-84.

SOTO ROSADO, Concepción (1873-
1936), artisan
    San 63-64.

SOTO SANCHEZ, Jorge (b.1947),
artist
    GrEPR 8:441.

SOTO VELEZ, Clemente (b.1905),
poet
    DiLP 2, pt.2:1484-86; Port
    15, 16(ill.); PRFAS 238-39.

SOTOMAYER MILETTI, Aurea María
(b.1951), professor, author
    DirAS 3:500.

SOTOMAYOR, Cristóbal de (d.1511),
colonist, soldier
    CiBPI 30-32; DiDHM 192-93; Gr-
    EPR 14:335; HisD 80-81.

SOTOMAYOR ALBERTINET, Juan (b.
1891), manager
    QEQ (1948-49) 167.

SOTOMAYOR LOPEZ, Luis (d.1950),
politician
    CaDeT 176-78, ill.

SOUFFRONT, Oscar (b.1893), lawyer
    GenB 379-80, ill.

SPENCER DE GRAHAM, Sara Isabel
(1844-1927), singer, arts patron
    AlHP 202, ill., 346, ill.;
    EGMPR 4:307-8, ill.; GrEPR

14:335; MujDPR 100-101,
ill.; MusMP 188-90.

STAHL, Agustín (1842-1917),
doctor, naturalist, author
BgP facing p.220, ill.;
BiP 401-3; BrECP 414-15,
ill.; CaM 409; CiBPI 76
(ill.), 135-38; DeADeA 237-
42; DiDHM 193, ill.; DiHBC
836-39; DiLP 2, pt.2:1486-
88; DiM 297-302; ECPR 6:
493-95, ill.; GenP 17;
GrEPR 14:335, ill., 336
(ill.); Hi de M 215; HisD
81; HoDMT 72-83; HoIPR 110,
ill.; HoRPR 115-21; HoYMPR
38-50, ill.; LPR 1002,
1003, 1004, 1005, ill.; Por
194; ProA 13; PRFAS 239,
ill.; PuI 259-65; RepM 103,
ill.

STELLA ARRILLAGA, Olga (b.
1945), lawyer
EGMPR 3:259.

STORER, Carlos F., businessman
Ka 26.

STORER DE LAGO, Genoveva de
(d.1934), educator, feminist
DiHBC 565; EGMPR 4:249-50,
ill.; GrEPR 14:336; MujDPR
150-53, ill.

STROUT, Lilia Dapaz (b.1926),
professor, author
DirAS 3:513.

STUBBE, J. D. (b.1872), farmer, businessman
QEQ (1936-37) 158, (1941-
42) 204.

STURCKE JR., Louis (b.1908),
government official
QEQ (1948-49) 167.

SUAREZ, Alfredo, engineer,
manager
A 117-18.

SUAREZ, Belarmino, tobacco
industrialist
A 30.

SUAREZ, Florencio, doctor
Ka 61.

SUAREZ, Jenaro (b.1897), doctor
QEQ (1933-34) 153, (1936-37)
158.

SUAREZ, Juan (16th cent.), soldier
GrEPR 14:336.

SUAREZ, Pedro (16th cent.),
governor, soldier
DiDHM 193; GrEPR 14:336.

SUAREZ, Ramón (b.1895), doctor
A 94, ill.; CaM 412; DiHBC
840; GrEPR 14:336.

SUAREZ CUEVAS, Ana Esther (b.
1919), advertising agency owner
EGMPR 3:69-70, ill.

SUAREZ DE LONGO, Mariana, teacher
AlHP 487, ill.

SUAREZ DE MENDOZA, Fernando (b.
1852), doctor
CaM 411.

SUAREZ DIAZ, Germán (b.1935),
politician
LiPR 125, ill.

SUAREZ MORALES, Pura Norma,
doctor, professor
EGMPR 3:261-62.

SUAREZ PEREZ, Angel (b.1864),
businessman
QEQ (1933-34) 153-54, (1936-
37) 158, (1941-42) 204-5.

SUAREZ PEREZ, Carlos M. (b.
1891), businessman
GenB 432-33, ill.

SUAREZ ROBLES, Hipólito (b.
1934), politician
LiPR 120, ill.

SUAREZ RODRIGUEZ, Rafael I.
(b.1894), engineer, accountant
QEQ (1933-34) 154, (1936-37)
158.

SUAU CARBONELL, Salvador (b.
1883), lawyer
RepM 113, ill.; Vo 194-97.

SUAU FERNANDEZ, SALVADOR, businessman
A 129-30.

SUAU MULET, Salvador (d.1902),
politician
    GenB 28, 328; Hi de M 205,
    ill.; VerOr 119.

SUCH, Miguel (1889-1952),
shipping executive, philanthropist
    A 61-63, ill.; BiP 403-4;
    DiDHM 194; DiHBC 840-41;
    PRFAS 239-40; QEQ (1933-34)
    154, (1936-37) 158-59,
    (1941-42) 205, (1948-49)
    167.

SUGRAÑES DIAZ, José G. (b.
1873), pharmacist, politician
    CaF 143; GrEPR 14:336.

SUGRAÑES LOUBRIEL, Rafael G.
(b.1898), lawyer
    QEQ (1933-34) 154-55,
    (1936-37) 159.

SULIVERAS RIVERA, Antonio,
lawyer
    RepM 201, ill.

SULSONA PELATTI DE CADILLA,
Elia (b.1922*), poet
    CaE 881-82; DiLP 2, pt.2:
    1488-89; EGMPR 1:213-14,
    ill.; PRFAS 240.

SUREDA, Guillermo (b.1912),
painter
    BiP 404; DiDHM 194; GrEPR
    8:386, ill.; PRFAS 240.

SURIA CHAVES, Fernando (b.
1862), politician
    GrEPR 14:337; QEQ (1936-37)
    159, (1941-42) 205.

SURIÑACH CARRERAS, Ricardo (b.
1928), Catholic priest
    GrEPR 6:281, 289.

SURIS Y AGRAIT, José Angel (b.
1901), lawyer
    QEQ (1936-37) 159.

SURO, Guillermo A. (b.1907),
journalist
    QEQ (1933-34) 155, (1936-
    37) 159, (1941-42) 205-6,
    (1948-49) 167-68.

SUSONI, Antonio H., doctor
    A 106.

SUSONI ABREU, Francisco M.
(1876-1954), doctor, politician
    DiM 303; GrEPR 14:337, ill.;
    PriC 43, ill.; QEQ (1948-49)
    168; Tri 2:115-19.

SUSONI LENS, Esteban, politician
    GrEPR 14:337.

SUSONI LENS, Francisco, politician
    GrEPR 14:337; HoIPR 111, ill.

SWEET, Willis (b.1856), newspaperman
    RepM 31, ill.

SWOPE, Guy J. (1892-1969),
governor
    Desf 126-28, ill.; DiDHM
    194; DiHBC 439; GrEPR 14:
    337, ill.; QEQ (1941-42) 206.

T

TADEO DE RIVERO, Francisco
(1788-1954), educator, public
servant
    HisD 81; PuI 114-20.

TALAVERA, Antonio (d.1876), author
    Esp 75-76.

TAPIA Y RIVERA, Alejandro
(1826-1882), author
    AlHY 228; Ant 101-11; BgP
    facing p.232, ill.; BiP 405-
    8; BrECP 418-22, ill.; CaE
    883-84; CiBPI 78(ill.), 108-
    10; DiDHM 195-96, ill.; Di-
    HBC 847-48; DiLP 2, pt2:
    1489-97; Eco 136-41; ECPR 6:
    495-96; EPI 1:152-53, ill.;
    EnsB 235-45; GrEPR 5:141-45,
    14:339, ill.; HisD 82; HoIPR
    111, ill.; HoRPR 78-100; Ind
    149-53; LPR 974, 975, 976,
    977, ill.; Ma 43-45; Pin 36-
    37; PlE 1:85-102, ill.; Por
    223-24; PRFAS 241, ill.; PuI
    140-43; Sd 57-95.

TARGA MAYMO, Miguel (1867-1934),
businessman
    QEQ (1933-34) 155, (1936-37)
    16.

TAVAREZ, Manuel Gregorio (1843-
1883), composer, teacher
    AlHP 61-63, ill., 404; Ant-

HistCag 349-50; BiP 408-9;
BrECP 422; CiBPI 138-40;
Co 16; DiDHM 196, ill.;
DiHBC 848; ECPR 6:496; EPI
3:228; EnsB 247-54; GrEPR
7:188-91, 14:339, ill.;
HoIPR 112, ill.; L 40; LPR
1004-5; Mus en P 128-30;
MusMP 162-69; Pin 46-47;
Pon 56-57; Por 197-98;
PRFAS 242, ill.; PuI 257;
Ver 169, 170(ill.)

TAVAREZ DE STORER, Elisa
(1879-1960), musician, teacher
AlHP 63, ill.; Desd 165-57;
DiHBC 848; EGMPR 4:129-30;
GrEPR 7:226-27, ill., 14:
340, ill.; MujDPR 164-67,
ill.; MujP 124-25; MujPu
133; MusMP 269-70; PQ 18;
QEQ (1933-34) 155, (1936-
37) 159, (1941-42) 206,
(1948-49) 168; Tri 1:413-
19.

TAYLOR, Verner Edmund (b.
1902), teacher
QEQ (1933-34) 155-56,
(1936-37) 159-60, (1941-42)
206, (1948-49) 168.

TEILLARD, Pablo Alejandro
(19th cent.), pharmacist
CaF 144-46.

TELLO DE GUZMAN, Pedro (16th-
17th cent.), sailor
GrEPR 14:340.

TERRASA, Peregrín, agronomist
A 109-10.

TERRASSA, Alberto, businessman
A 131.

TERRY, Charles H., teacher
Tri 2:29-34.

TEXIDOR, Jacinto (1870-1931),
author, lawyer
DiLP 2, pt.2:1527-28; GrEPR
14:340, ill.; Guay 276; Ho-
IPR 112, ill.; Ind 153-54;
LM 124-25; PRFAS 242; RepM
99, ill.

TEXIDOR, Jesús María (19th
cent.), industrialist, landowner
Ka 74-75.

THILLET, Félix A. (b.1831),
businessman
A 129; QEQ (1948-49) 168-69.

THOMAS, Piri (b.1928), novelist
CaE 886; ConA 73-76:604-5;
Port 37, 38(ill.)

TIMOTHEE ANDRACA, Carlos Eugenio
(b.1898), doctor
QEQ (1936-37) 160, (1941-42)
206.

TIMOTHEE ANDRACA, Rafael A. (b.
1901), doctor
QEQ (1936-37) 160, (1941-42)
206-7.

TIMOTHEE Y MORALES, Pedro Carlos
(1864-1949), author, teacher
BiP 409-11; DiLP 2, pt.2:
1528; ECPR 6:496; GrEPR 14:
341, ill.; HoIPR 113, ill.;
Ind 154; PRFAS 242-43; QEQ
(1933-34) 156, (1936-37) 160,
(1941-42) 207, (1948-49) 169;
RepM 259, ill.; Vida 56-58.

TIO, Aurelio (b.1907), historian,
author
BiP 412; DiDHM 196-97; DiHBC
861-63; DiLP 2, pt.2:1528-
30; ECPR 6:497; GrEPR 14:341,
ill.; PRFAS 243; QEQ (1936-
37) 160, (1941-42) 207-8;
S 89.

TIO, Juan Angel (1874-1965),
banker, politician
GrEPR 14:341; PriC 44, ill.;
S 89.

TIO, Salvador (b.1911), author,
journalist
A 80; BiP 411-12; DiDHM 197;
DiLP 2, pt.2:1530-32; ECPR
6:497; GrEPR 14:341; PRFAS
243.

TIO DE MALARET, Amina (b.1865),
feminist, suffragette
DiHBC 863; EGMPR 1:91-92,
ill.; GrEPR 14:341; MujDPR
121-26; PQ 19.

TIO MALARET, Félix (1855-1932),
doctor, politician, author
CaM 417; DiM 305-7.

Tió y Nazario de Figueroa, Aurelio see Tió, Aurelio

TIO RODRIGUEZ DE SANCHEZ, Patria (b.1866), author
DiHBC 863; EGMPR 1:215-17, ill.; MujDPR 138-40, ill.; MujPu 98-104; QEQ (1933-34) 156, (1936-37) 160, (1941-42) 208; VerOr 101, 103, 105.

TIO SEGARRA, Bonocio (1839-1905), journalist, politician
DiLP 2, pt.2:1532-33: GrEPR 14:342, ill.; Nuestr 39-40.

TIRADO DELGADO, Cirilo (b. 1938), politician
GrEPR 14:342; LiPR 39, ill.

TIRADO GEIGEL, Luis (b.1903), lawyer
QEQ (1933-34) 156-57, (1936-37) 160.

TIRADO VERRIER, Rafael (b. 1872), lawyer
LM 134.

TIZOL, Eusebio, musician
MusMP 270-71.

TIZOL, José de Jesús (1846-1895), doctor
CaM 417-19; DiM 307-8.

TIZOL, José de Jesús (d.1929), lawyer, politician
GrEPR 14:342; Imp 145-47; PriC 44, ill.

TIZOL, Manuel (1876-1940), musician, composer, conductor
BiP 412-14; HoIPR 112, ill.; MusMP 238-39; PRFAS 243-44; QEQ (1933-34) 157, (1936-37) 160-61; Tri 2: 181-85.

TIZOL, Mateo, musician
MusMP 271-72.

TIZOL LAGUARDIA, Lolita (1890-1933), musician, teacher
AlHP 281, ill.; PonY 45.

TODD, James F., businessman
A 136.

TODD Y BORRAS, Roberto H. (b. 1891), lawyer, judge

GrEPR 14:342; QEQ (1933-34) 157, (1936-37) 161, (1941-42) 208, (1948-49) 169-70.

TODD Y WELLS, Roberto H. (1862-1955), politician, author
And 78-83; BiP 414-15; CiBPI 221 (ill.), 234-36; DiDHM 197, ill.; DiLP 2, pt.2:1533-35; ECPR 6:497-99, ill.; GrEPR 14:342, ill.; HisD 83; PaP 9-15, ill.; Per 113-15; PRFAS 244, ill.; QEQ (1933-34) 157, (1936-37) 161, (1941-42) 208, (1948-49) 170; Vo 70-75.

TOLEDO, Tomás (1878-1943), artist
San 65-69.

TOLEDO ALAMO, Domingo (b.1904), lawyer, author, professor
ArH 542-43.

TOLEDO GONZALEZ, Rina, singer
EGMPR 4:131-32, ill.

TOLEDO MARQUES, Pedro (b.1883), prison official
QEQ (1936-37) 161.

TOLEDO RIVERA, Leonides (b.1921), politician
LiPR 118, ill.

TOLOSA Y ALVAREZ, Pedro (19th cent.), engineer
GenB 334; Hi de M 214.

TOLLINCHI CAMACHO, Esteban (b. 1932), professor, author, translator
Ind 154-55; PRFAS 244.

TORMES GARCIA, Herminia (b.1890), lawyer, judge
AlHP 445, ill.; EGMPR 3:263-64; QEQ (1941-42) 208-9.

TORMES GARCIA, Leopoldo, politician
GrEPR 14:343.

TORMES VEGA, José G. (b.1925), politician
LiPR 124, ill.

TORMOS VEGA, Nélida (b.1920), insurance agent
EGMPR 3:71-72, ill.

TORO, César A. (b.1901), poet, pharmacist

A 102; DiLP 2, pt.2:1535-
36; QEQ (1933-34) 157-59,
(1936-37) 161; S 91.

TORO, Domingo del (d.1884),
artisan, industrialist
    Eco 146-51; Hi de CR 195-
    96.

Toro, Emilio del see Toro
Cuebas, Emilio del

TORO, F. Manuel (b.1882),
lawyer
    RepM 123, ill.

TORO, Faustino del (17th-18th
cent.), soldier
    BeHNPR 1:324.

TORO, José Esteban del (b.
1902), teacher
    QEQ (1933-34) 58, (1936-37)
    59.

TORO, Josefina del (1901-
1975), librarian
    GrEPR 14:343; QEQ (1948-
    49) 171.

TORO, Luis, businessman
    Tri 1:81-87.

TORO, Manuel del (b.1911),
author
    DiLP 2, pt.2:1536; PRFAS
    245.

TORO, Osvaldo L. (b.1914),
architect
    GrEPR 9:107-10, 14:343.

TORO, Rafael Andrés (b.1897),
scientist, professor
    QEQ (1941-42) 210.

TORO, Roberto de Jesús (b.
1918), banker
    GrEPR 14:343.

TORO, Salvador, travel agent
    Ka 138.

TORO BLANCHERAUX, Juan Bautista (1851-1888), doctor,
poet
    Ver 166, ill.

TORO CABAÑAS, Luis (1899-
1933), poet
    DiLP 2, pt.2:1537.

TORO COLBERG, Miguel del (b.
1884), lawyer
    QEQ (1941-42) 209.

TORO CUEBAS, Emilio del (1876-
1955), judge, author
    BiP 415-17; DiHBC 870-71;
    DiLP 2, pt.2:1537-38; GenP
    78-81, ill.; GrEPR 14:343-
    44, ill.; Hi de CR 251-54;
    PaH 4:147-216; PlE 1:479-96,
    ill.; PRFAS 245; QEQ (1933-
    34) 57-58, (1936-37) 161,
    (1941-42) 209-10, (1948-49)
    170; RepM 27, ill.; Tri 1:
    13-23.

TORO CUEBAS, Jorge del (1884-
1950), doctor, professor
    CaM 419-21; GrEPR 14:344;
    QEQ (1933-34) 187, (1936-37)
    161-62, (1941-42) 210, (1948-
    49) 170-71; RepM 143, ill.

TORO DE LUGO, Polita (b.1906),
civic and social works
    EGMPR 3:341-42, ill.

TORO GUILLERMETY, Emilio del (b.
1913), administrator
    QEQ (1941-42) 210.

TORO NAZARIO, José M. (b.1906),
lawyer, journalist
    A 88-89, ill.; DiLP 2, pt.2:
    1538-39; GrEPR 14:343; QEQ
    (1936-37) 162, (1941-42) 211,
    (1948-49) 171.

TORO PERALTA, Manuel del (d.
1945), teacher
    Hi de CR 270.

TORO RODRIGUEZ, José (d. 1961),
politician
    AlHP 174, ill.

TORO SOLER, Ricardo del (1873-
1947), author, lawyer
    DiLP 2, pt.2:1539-40; Hi de
    CR 260-61; QEQ (1941-42)
    210; RepM 276, ill.

TORO Y URRUTIA, Teodomiro (17th-
18th cent.), soldier
    BeHNPR 1:298-99.

TORO VENDRELL, Fernando Luis (b.
1883), businessman
    A 141; QEQ (1948-49) 171.

TORRADO MARTINEZ, Manuel (b. 1883), author
QEQ (1936-37) 162, (1941-42) 211, (1948-49) 171-72.

TORRE, José Ramón de la (b. 1935), professor, author
PRFAS 80.

TORRE, Jovino de la, journalist
Nuestr 76-77.

TORRE, Miguel de la (19th cent.), governor
BeHNPR 2:21-25; DiDHM 198; DiHBC 451.

TORRE DE O'NEILL, Mercedes de la, civic works
MujDPR 163-64, ill.

TORRE MUÑIZ, José M. de la (b. 1885), government employee, journalist
QEQ (1936-37) 162-63, (1941-42) 211-12, (1948-49) 172-73.

TORRE ORMAZA, Simón de la (19th cent.), governor
GrEPR 14:344.

TORRECH GENOVES, Rafael (d. 1960), politician
GrEPR 14:344.

TORREGROSA, Angel M. (1887-1944), lawyer, author, journalist
DiLP 2, pt.2:1540-41; ProA 21-22, ill.; QEQ (1936-37) 163, (1941-42) 213.

TORREGROSA, Arturo (1882-1953), doctor, pharmacist
CaM 422; HoIPR 113, ill.; QEQ (1933-34) 159, (1936-37) 163, (1941-42) 212-13; RepM 164, ill.

TORREGROSA, Fernando (1895*-1946), author, politician
DiLP 2, pt.2:1541-42; QEQ (1933-34) 159, (1936-37) 163, (1941-42) 213.

TORREGROSA GUEVARA, Angela Luisa (b.1920), journalist
EGMPR 3:305-6, ill.

TORREGROSA LICEAGA, Luis A., pharmacist, political activist
RepM 321, ill.

TORREGROSA MORA, Luis Antonio (1854-1919), author, pharmacist
Apu 54-58; CaF 147; DiLP 2, pt.2:1542-43; GrEPR 14:344; HoIPR 113, ill.; RepM 162, ill.

TORRES, Angel R. "Pepín" (b. 1945), artist
GrEPR 8:425.

TORRES, Carlos J. (b.1894), lawyer
QEQ (1933-34) 159-60, (1936-37) 163, (1941-42) 213.

TORRES, Edwin, lawyer, judge, author
ConA 111:478-79.

TORRES, Felipe, lawyer
Port 165, 166(ill.)

TORRES, John, interior designer
Port 143, 144(ill.)

TORRES, José Arsenio (b.1926), professor, politician
GrEPR 14:345, ill.; PriC 151-52, ill.

TORRES, José "Chegui", boxer
ECPR 6:499; EPI 1:342-43; Port 23, 24(ill.); PRUSA 24.

TORRES, José G. (1863-1930), author, politician
AlHY 159-60, 208-9; DeADeA 217-19; DiLP 2, pt.2:1544-45; GrEPR 14:345, ill.; HoIPR 114, ill.; RepM 243, ill.

TORRES, Luis Angel (b.1948), politician
GrEPR 14:345.

TORRES, Magdalena, manager
Port 81, 82(ill.)

TORRES, Ramón, doctor
CaM 423.

TORRES, Ramón María (1868-1903), poet
BoHP 122, 126(ill.)

TORRES, Robustiano (b.1891),
teacher, poet
  Tri 1:433-39.

TORRES, Walter (b.1952), artist
  GrEPR 8:426.

TORRRES ALVARADO, Ramón (19th
cent.), politician
  Crom 69; Ka 38-40.

TORRES BALDORIOTY, Eustoquio
G. (b.1902), bank official
  QEQ (1948-49) 173.

TORRES CORDOVA, Rafael (b.
1905), journalist
  QEQ (1936-37) 163, (1941-
  42) 214.

TORRES CUPRILL, Onelio (b.
1896), author
  AlHY 165-66, 217-18; DiLP
  2, pt.2:1545-47.

TORRES DE LA HABA, Luis (b.
1951), artist, teacher
  GrEPR 8:426.

TORRES DE LA TORRE MUÑIZ,
Emilia F. (b. 1889), govern-
ment official
  QEQ (1936-37) 164.

TORRES DE RAMOS, Justina
(1868-1954), artisan
  San 53-54.

TORRES DELGADO, René (b.1947),
professor, author
  DiDHM 198; DirAS 3:530.

TORRES DIAZ, José (b.1891),
Catholic Church official
  QEQ (1933-34) 160-61,
  (1936-37) 164.

TORRES DIAZ, Luis (b.1897),
pharmacist, educator
  BiP 417-18; CaF 148; GrEPR
  14:346; PRFAS 246; QEQ
  (1933-34) 161, (1936-37)
  164, (1941-42) 214.

TORRES FERMOSO, José Onofre
(b.1922), baseball player,
politician
  GrEPR 14:346.

TORRES GRAU, Libertad (b.

1872), lawyer
  HoIPR 114, ill.; RepM 78,
  ill.

TORRES GRILLO, Herminio (b.1905),
teacher
  AntHistCag 294-98; QEQ (1936-
  37) 190.

TORRES LA TORRE, Luis (b.1898),
teacher
  QEQ (1936-37) 164, (1941-42)
  214.

TORRES LOPEZ, Frank (b.1900),
lawyer
  QEQ (1941-42) 214-15, (1948-
  49) 173.

TORRES MARTINEZ, Jaime (b.1903),
pharmacist
  QEQ (1933-34) 161, (1936-37)
  164.

TORRES MARTINO, José A. (b.
1916), artist
  BiP 418-19; GrEPR 8:427;
  PRFAS 246.

TORRES MAZZORANNA, Rafael
(20th cent.), journalist
  A 76-77, ill.

TORRES MIRO, Carlos A. (b.
1936), politician
  LiPR 116, ill.

TORRES MONGE, Sandalio (b.
1868), lawyer
  QEQ (1936-37) 165.

TORRES MORALES, José Antonio
(b.1922), author, anthropologist
  DiLP 2, pt.2:1547-48.

TORRES OLIVER, Fremiot (b.
1925), lawyer, Catholic bishop
  S 87.

TORRES QUILES, Herbert (b.
1930), politician
  LiPR 36, ill.

TORRES RIGUAL, Hiram (b.1922),
lawyer, judge
  GrEPR 14:346.

TORRES ROSADO, Félix Juan (b.
1913), author
  DiLP 2, pt2:1548-50; Ind
  156-58; PRFAS 245-46.

TORRES SANTIAGO, Carlos Luis
(b.1938), politician
    GrEPR 14:346; LiPR 39, ill.

TORRES SANTIAGO, José M. (b.
1940), poet
    BrECP 431; DiLP 2, pt.2:
    1550-52; GrEPR 14:346;
    PRFAS 246.

TORRES SANTOS, Lucas, politician
    GrEPR 14:346.

TORRES SEGARRA DE BERMUDEZ,
Lucía (b.1902), nurse, author
    EGMPR 3:265-66.

TORRES TORRES, Adrián (b.
1921), teacher, politician
    AlDJ 233, ill.; GrEPR 14:
    347.

TORRES Y TORRES, Antonio Juan
(b.1907), chemist
    QEQ (1936-37) 165, (1941-
    42) 215.

TORRES TORRES, César (b.
1944), politician
    LiPR 122, ill.

TORRES TORRES, Mercedes, politician
    LiPR 32, ill.

TORRES VARGAS, Diego de
(1590-1649), chronicler,
priest
    BiP 419-20; CiBPI 24(ill.),
    37-38; DiDHM 199; DiHBC
    871-72; DiLP 2, pt.2:1553-
    55; ECPR 6:499; GrEPR 14:
    347, ill.; HisD 83; PRFAS
    247; PuI 10-12.

TORRETTI, Roberto (b.1930),
philosopher
    DirAS 4:540-41.

TORRUELLA CORTADA, Juan (1880-
1948), industrialist
    AlHP 350, ill.

TORRUELLA CORTADA, Sergio
(1884-1944), businessman
    AlHP 350, ill.

TORRUELLA DE ARTEAGA, Nicola-
sa, musician, teacher
    MusMP 190-91.

TORRUELLAS CORREA, Alicea (b.
1919), educator
    EGMPR 1:373-75.

TOTTI TORRES, Etienne (b.1887),
engineer, politician
    A 96-97; GrEPR 14:347; QEQ
    (1933-34) 161-62, (1936-37)
    165, (1941-42) 215, (1948-
    49) 174.

TOTTI TORRES, Noel (b.1885),
engineer
    QEQ (1941-42) 216.

TOUS SOTO, José (1874-1933*),
lawyer, politician
    AlHP 258, ill.; DiDHM 199;
    GrEPR 14:347-48, ill.; HoIPR
    114, ill.; LM 128; PriC 45,
    ill.; QEQ (1933-34) 16,
    (1936-37) 16; RepM 167, ill.

TOUS SOTO, Manuel, (b.1880),
lawyer
    RepM 222, ill.

TOVAR DE BURGOS, Gladys, advertising executive, journalist
    EGMPR 4:199-100, ill.

TOWNER, Horace M. (1855-1937),
governor
    Desf 85-93, ill.; DiDHM 199-
    200; DiHBC 438; GrEPR 14:348,
    ill.; QEQ (1933-34) 162,
    (1936-37) 166.

TRAVIESO FERNANDEZ, Luis F.
(b.1907), accountant
    QEQ (1948-49) 174.

TRAVIESO Y NIEVA, Martín
(1882-1971), lawyer, politician
    GenB 405-8, ill.; GrEPR 14:
    348; HisD 83; LM 132-33; PriC
    45, ill.; QEQ (1933-34) 205-6,
    (1936-37) 166, (1941-42) 216,
    (1948-49) 174-75; RepM 24,
    ill.; VerOr 232-33, 236-37,
    ill.

TRAVIESO Y QUIJANO, Martín
(1851-1920), doctor, author
    CaM 424-25; DiLP 2, pt.2:
    1567-68; GenB 278-79, ill.;
    Hi de M 190; HoIPR 115, ill.

TRELLES, Francisco (1855-1899),
doctor, author
    DiLP 2, pt.2:1568-70; DiM

309-13; Hi de Cay 241-42.

TRELLES DE VAZQUEZ, Blanca (b.
1908), doctor
EGMPR 3:267-68; QEQ (1941-
42) 216.

TRELLES Y OLIVA, Vicente,
politician
RepM 158, ill.

TRESPALACIOS Y VERDEJA, Felipe
José de (d.1799), bishop
Hi de la Ig 148-51.

TRIAS, Antonio (19th cent.),
banker
Crom 25.

TRIAS MONGE, José (b.1920),
judge
GrEPR 14:349, ill.

TRICOCHE, Rafael, cartoonist
PaG 235.

TRICOCHE, Valentín (19th
cent.), businessman
BeHNPR 2:143-45; CaM 426;
PonY 44.

TRIGO, Luis Camilo (b.1896),
lawyer
QEQ (1933-34) 162-63,
(1936-37) 166, (1941-42)
216, (1948-49) 175.

TRIGO GONZALEZ, Dionisio (b.
1932), businessman
GrEPR 14:349; Tri 1:177-83.

TRISTANI, Enrique, Jr. (b.
1895), lawyer
QEQ (1936-37) 166, (1941-
42) 217.

TROYO, Rafael Angel, poet
Cre 65-66.

TRUJILLO, Dionisio (b.1912),
poet
DiLP 2, pt.2:1570.

TUFIÑO, Rafael (b.1918*), art-
ist
BiP 420-21; BrECP 432; Di-
HBC 875; GrEPR 8:300, ill.;
PaG 193-95; PRFAS 247; PRP
251.

TUFIÑO, Rafael (b.1951), art-

ist
GrEPR 8:442.

TUGWELL, Rexford Guy (1891-
1979), governor
ConA 85-88:596-97, 89-92:526;
CuB 1941:874-76, ill.,
1979:474; Desf 129-33, ill.;
DiDHM 200; DiHBC 439; GrEPR
14:349, 350(ill.); HisD 83-
84; PolPr 4:568-70; QEQ
(1936-37) 166, (1941-42)
217, (1948-49) 175; Tra 193-
209.

TUR VICTORIA, Jacobo (b.1864),
engineer
Ka 20-21; RepM 185, ill.

TUYA, Carmen, artist
GrEPR 8:442.

TYSON, Lawrence Davis (1861-
1929), soldier, governor
DicAB 10:104-5.

U

UBARRI CAPETILLO, Pablo (d.
1894), businessman, politician
GrEPR 14:351; HisD 84.

ULANGA, Francisco (d.1860),
businessman, civic works
Esp 59.

ULLOA Y VARELA, Darío (19th
cent.), lawyer
Crom 75.

UMPIERRE, Luz María (b.1947),
professor, literary critic
DirAS 3:537.

UMPIERRE CARMONA, Ramón (b.
1892), doctor
CaM 429; QEQ (1933-34) 163,
(1936-37) 166.

UMPIERRE ORTIZ, Artemio (19th
cent.), doctor
CaM 428-29.

UMPIERRE SIERRA, Francisco (b.
1896), dentist
QEQ (1933-34) 163, (1936-37)
190, (1941-42) 217.

URAYOAN, Taíno Indian chief
DiHBC 189; GrEPR 14:351.

URBINA URBINA, David (b. 1937), lawyer, politician
GrEPR 14:351.

URGELL, Francisco C. (b.1893), architect, educator
QEQ (1936-37) 166-67, (1941-42) 217-18, (1948-49) 175-76.

URIAGA, Pedro de la Concepción (d.1713), missionary, bishop
Hi de la Ig 104-7.

URRUTIA, Dennis (b.1941), artist
PaG 234-35.

URRUTIA, Enrique (b.1887), Army officer
QEQ (1941-42) 218, (1948-49) 176.

USERA, José (19th-20th cent.), politician
GrEPR 14:351; RepM 228, ill.

USERA, Vicente (1861-1943), politician
AlHP 349, ill.; Crom 93; GrEPR 14:351; QEQ (1936-37) 167, (1941-42) 218; RepM 182, ill.

UZEDA, Raimundo (19th-20th cent.), doctor
CaM 430.

V

VADI, Alberto, artist
GrEPR 8:442.

VADI BENELLI, Luis (1846*-1936), doctor
CaM 431-33; GenB 356, ill.

Valbuena, Bernardo de see Balbuena, Bernardo de

VALDECILLA, Raimundo, businessman
Crom 96.

VALDES, Antonio G. A., dentist
Crom 83.

VALDES, Grace, tennis player
MujP 241.

VALDES, Ramón (1854-1913), businessman
HoIPR 115, ill.; RepM 68, ill.

VALDES COBIAN, Alfonso, politician
GrEPR 14:353.

VALDES COBIAN, Ramón (1886-1962), politician, engineer
GrEPR 14:353, ill.; PriC 46, ill.; QEQ (1936-37) 167, (1941-42) 218; RepM 175, ill.

VALDES COBIAN, Sabino (b.1896), manager
QEQ (1936-37) 167, (1941-42) 218, (1948-49) 176.

VALDES LINARES, Manuel (1838-1875), statesman
BeHNPR 2:275-79, ill.; DiHBC 529-30; GrEPR 14:354; LM 111.

VALDES QUESADA, Leopoldo (b. 1879), author, publicity agent
QEQ (1936-37) 167.

VALDIVIA, Fernando de (d.1725), bishop
Hi de la Ig 108-10.

VALDIVIESO, Jorge Lucas (b. 1899), politician
GrEPR 14:354; QEQ (1936-37) 167, (1941-42) 218-19.

VALDIVIESO, Lucas, businessman
Crom 80.

VALDIVIESO, Lucas, politician
GrEPR 14:354.

VALDIVIESO LLOMPART, Dolores, politician
GrEPR 14:354.

VALENTIN ACEVEDO, Freddy (b. 1952*), politician
GrEPR 14:354; LiPR 34, ill.

VALENTIN VEGA, Antonio (b. 1928), politician
LiPR 116, ill.

VALENTIN VIZCARRONDO, Augusto, politician
GrEPR 14:354.

VALENTINE Y MARTINEZ, Miguel Angel (b.1894), Protestant minister
QEQ (1933-34) 164, (1936-37) 167, (1941-42) 219, (1948-49) 176.

VALERO, Antonio (1790*-1863), soldier
BeHNPR 2:135-42, ill.; BiP 421-22; BrECP 439; CiBPI 66 (ill.), 85-86; DiDHM 201; DiHBC 915-18; ECPR 6:499-500; EPI 1:76-77, ill.; GrEPR 14:354; HisD 85; HisP 19-25, 32; HoIPR 51, ill.; HoRPR 183-92; MueYV 117-27; PaI 29-52, ill.; PRFAS 249; PuI 67-80.

VALERO, Eduardo (b.1889), federal employee
QEQ (1933-34) 164, (1936-37) 168.

VALL SPINOSA, Federico (b. 1879), businessman
QEQ (1933-34) 164-65, (1936-37) 168, (1941-42) 219, (1948-49) 176.

VALLDEJULI, Sandalio, customs official
Ka 162.

VALLDEJULI RODRIGUEZ, Juan (b. 1896), lawyer, author
DiLP 2, pt.2:1571-72; QEQ (1933-34) 163-64, (1936-37) 168, (1941-42) 219.

VALLDEJULY, Arturo, businessman
A 126.

VALLE, Adrián del (d.1906), politician
ProA 57, ill.

VALLE, Edwin del (b.1951), painter
GrEPR 8:399.

VALLE, Manuel Maximino del (19th cent.), pharmacist
CaF 151-52.

VALLE, Marta, social worker
EPI 2:237-41.

VALLE, Marta (1934-1975), educator, consultant
PQ 57.

VALLE, Pedro G. del (b.1897), dentist
QEQ (1933-34) 58, (1936-37) 59.

Valle, Rafael del see Valle Rodríguez, Rafael del

VALLE, Rodulfo del (1871-1948), government official
AlHP 330, ill.; ProA 51, ill.

VALLE, Rodulfo del (b.1900), engineer
QEQ (1948-49) 57-58.

VALLE, William A. del (b.1898), engineer
QEQ (1941-42) 78.

VALLE ATILES, Francisco del (1852-1928), doctor, author
CaM 435-38; DiM 314-15; DiLP 2, pt.2:1572-74; Exp 289, ill.; GrEPR 5:146-47, 14:354; HoIPR 116, ill.; Ind 158-59; PRFAS 249; RepM 56, ill.

VALLE ATILES, Francisco del, Jr., lawyer, judge
RepM 272, ill.

VALLE ATILES, Manuel V. del (b.1871), dentist
QEQ (1933-34) 187-88, (1936-37) 59, (1941-42) 77.

VALLE ATILES, Pedro del (b.1860), doctor, pharmacist
CaM 438; QEQ (1936-37) 182.

VALLE ESCOBAR, Miguel A. del (b.1923), politician
GrEPR 14:355.

VALLE RODRIGUEZ, Rafael del (1846*-1917), doctor, author, politician
BiP 423-24; CaM 438-39; DiLP 2, pt.2:1575-77; DiM 319-25; ECPR 6:500; GrEPR 14:355, ill.; HoIPR 116, ill.; Ind 159-60; LPR 1004, 1006, 1007, 1009, ill.; PIE 1:291-306, ill.; ProA 13; PRFAS 249-50; RepM 22, ill.

VALLE SARRAGA, Rafael (b. 1881), chemist, pharmacist
CaF 153; QEQ (1933-34) 58-59, (1936-37) 59, (1941-42) 77-78, (1948-49) 58.

VALLE TALAVERA, Belisario del (19th cent.), humorist, orator
GenB 303-5; Nuestr 106-10.

VALLE ZENO, Carlos del (b. 1881), engineer
QEQ (1933-34) 59, (1936-37) 59-60, (1948-49) 58.

VALLE ZENO, Rafael del (b. 1878), engineer
QEQ (1933-34) 188-89, (1936-37) 60, (1948-49) 58-59.

VALLECILLO, Gerónimo, businessman
Tri 1:215-21.

VALLECILLO, Irma Luz (b.1946), musician
EGMPR 4:133-34, ill.

VALLECILLO MANDRY, Arsenio, doctor
CaM 440; RepM 264, ill.

VALLEJO, Luis (16th cent.), governor
GrEPR 14:355.

VAN DEUSEN, Elizabeth K. (b. 1902), author, teacher
QEQ (1933-34) 165, (1936-37) 168.

VAN DEUSEN, Richard James (b. 1879), lawyer, author
QEQ (1933-34) 165-66, (1936-37) 168-69; Tri 2: 103-4.

VAN VOLKENBURG, Horatio Luther (b.1893), parasitologist
QEQ (1936-37) 169.

VARAS, Jaime (b.1915), economist, professor, author
BrECP 439-40; GrEPR 1:xvi, ill., 14:355; PRFAS 250.

VARELA, Justo Enrique (b. 1911), engineer
QEQ (1936-37) 169.

VARELA Y FIGUEROA, Manuel F. (b. 1893), government official
ProA 50-51, ill.; QEQ (1933-34) 166, (1936-37) 169, (1941-42) 220.

VARELA TORRES, Víctor M. (b. 1903), bank official
QEQ (1948-49) 176-77.

VARGAS, Juan de (d.1631), governor
GrEPR 14:356; Hi de Pu 88-89; Misc 34-38.

VARGAS, Pedro Pablo (1848-1914?), poet
DiLP 2, pt.2:1577.

VARGAS, Urbino, businessman
BoHP 193.

VARGAS BADILLO, Pablo (1906-1971), journalist
BiP 424-25; DiLP 2, pt.2: 1577-78; GrEPR 14:356; Per 151-53; PRFAS 250; QEQ (1948-49) 177.

VARGAS FOURNIER, María Soledad (b.1944), doctor
EGMPR 4:345-46, ill.

VARGAS RODRIGUEZ, Alfredo (b. 1897), politician
QEQ (1933-34) 166-67, (1936-37) 169.

VARONA SUAREZ, Narciso (b.1858), teacher
ArH 460-61.

VASALLO, Vanessa, musician
EGMPR 4:135-36, ill.

VASCO Y PASCUAL, Juan (18th-19th cent.), governor
DiDHM 201.

VASQUEZ Y COLON, F., doctor, politician
RepM 266, ill.

VASSALLO Y CABRERA, Francisco (1823-1867), doctor, author
BeHNPR 2:161-62, ill.; BiP 425-26; CaM 441; DiDHM 201; DiLP 2, pt.2:1578-80; DiM 325-31; ECPR 6:500; HisD 85; Ind 160; PlE 1:43-53, ill.; PRFAS 250-51; PuI 102.

VASSALLO Y FORES, Francisco (1789-1849), author
   BeHNPR 2:67-68, ill.; BiP 426-27; DiLP 2, pt.2:1580-81; Esp 35-37, ill.; PlE 1: 46; PRFAS 251.

VASSALLO Y JULIA, Mariano Bartolomé, priest, church official
   QEQ (1941-42) 220, (1948-49) 177.

VAZQUEZ, Alejandro (b.1943), singer
   GrEPR 14:356.

VAZQUEZ, Diego (1890?-1922), author
   AntHistCag 260-61; AntPoe-Cag 59-60.

VAZQUEZ, Gladys, painter
   GrEPR 8:442.

VAZQUEZ, Héctor, economist
   Port 33, 34(ill.)

VAZQUEZ, Isabel, painter
   GrEPR 8:427.

VAZQUEZ, José Antonio, author
   Guay 277-78.

VAZQUEZ AGUILAR, Eduardo, politician
   Guay 276-77.

VAZQUEZ ALAMO, Francisco (b. 1913), accountant
   QEQ (1948-49) 177.

VAZQUEZ ALAYON, Manuel (1861-1943), journalist
   DiLP 2, pt.2:1581-82; GrEPR 14:356; QEQ (1933-34) 167-68, (1936-37) 169-70, (1941-42) 220-21.

VAZQUEZ DE ARCE, Martín (d. 1609), bishop
   Hi de la Ig 47-59.

VAZQUEZ DE COLON, Myrna (1935-1975), actress
   EGMPR 4:137-38, ill.

VAZQUEZ DE RIVERA, Margarita (b.1925), professor
   GrEPR 1:x, ill., 14:357; PRFAS 251-52.

VAZQUEZ DE SANTOS, Africa (b. 1913), labor leader
   EGMPR 4:251-52.

VAZQUEZ DE UMPIERRE, María (1901-1975), politician
   EGMPR 4:171-72, ill.

VAZQUEZ DIAZ, Francisco (b. 1898), sculptor
   GrEPR 8:397.

VAZQUEZ DIAZ, Manuel (1886?-1969?), painter, musician, poet
   And 132-34; SobM 46-48.

VAZQUEZ FEBUS, Julián (b.1903), teacher
   QEQ (1933-34) 168, (1936-37) 170.

VAZQUEZ GOTTLEIB, Aida, music producer
   Port 103, 104(ill.)

VAZQUEZ MILAN, Hiram (b.1903), pharmacist
   CaF 153; QEQ (1933-34) 168, (1936-37) 190-91, (1941-42) 221, (1948-49) 178.

VAZQUEZ RIVERA, Luzgarda (b. 1940), lawyer
   EGMPR 3:269.

VAZQUEZ Y RIVERA, Tomás (1852-1918), doctor
   CaM 443-44; DiM 331-32; GenP 107, ill.; Ka 135.

VAZQUEZ TORRES, Ernesto (b. 1908), agronomist, professor
   QEQ (1941-42) 221.

VAZQUEZ URBINA, Antonio (b. 1900), government official
   QEQ (1941-42) 221-22, (1948-49) 178.

VAZQUEZ VELE, Carlos A., politician
   GrEPR 14:357.

VEGA, Carola, artist, teacher
   GrEPR 8:428.

VEGA, Eladio José de la (1837-1931), teacher
   Apu 63-64; ProA 38, ill.

VEGA BERRIOS, Baudilio, politician
A 170, ill.; GrEPR 14:357.

VEGA BERRIOS, Pedro (b.1902), labor leader, politician
GrEPR 14:357; QEQ (1948-49) 178.

VEGA CAPRILES, José Angel (b. 1903), pharmacist
QEQ (1948-49) 178-79.

VEGA Y LOUBRIEL, Laureano (d. 1888), government official
EnsB 286-87; HoIPR 117.

VEGA MORALES, Arturo (b.1865), teacher
Apu 65-66.

VEGA MORALES, Ignacio (b. 1875), teacher
Apu 65.

VEGA NEVARES, Félix (b.1863), calligrapher
QEQ (1933-34) 168, (1936-37) 170.

VEGA PESQUERA, Luis B. de la (b.1888), doctor
QEQ (1936-37) 58, (1941-42) 77.

VELA DE FELIU, Esther Ileana (b.1925), teacher
EGMPR 3:343.

VELA RODRIGUEZ, Ricardo (d. 1966), businessman
And 124-27.

VELASCO, Jerónimo de, soldier, governor
Hi de P 178-81.

VELASCO ALONSO, Domingo, businessman
A 135, ill.

VELAZQUEZ, Federico (1904-1955), doctor
CaM 444-45.

VELAZQUEZ, Juan Ramón (b. 1951), artist
GrEPR 8:388, 14:357, ill.

VELAZQUEZ, Luis Magín (b. 1920), politician

GrEPR 14:358.

VELAZQUEZ, Sancho (d.1521), governor
GrEPR 14:358.

VELAZQUEZ FELICIANO, Gil (b. 1886), engineer
QEQ (1933-34) 168, (1936-37) 170, (1941-42) 222.

VELAZQUEZ FLORES, Modesto (b. 1912), lawyer, politician
GrEPR 14:358; QEQ (1941-42) 222, (1948-49) 179.

VELAZQUEZ IGLESIAS, Orlando (b. 1938), lawyer, politician
GrEPR 14:358.

VELEZ, Agustín A., politician
GrEPR 14:358.

VELEZ, Ismael (1908-1970), scientist, professor
BrECP 441-42; DiDHM 922-23; GrEPR 14:358; PRFAS 252.

VELEZ, Lucas Luis (1870-1940), pharmacist
CaF 153-54; GrEPR 14:358; HoIPR 117-18, ill.; QEQ (1936-37) 170.

VELEZ, Otto (b.1950), baseball player
PRUSA 24, ill.

VELEZ, Ramón S. (b.1933), politician, government employee
EPI 2:167-68; Port 75, 76 (ill.)

VELEZ, Secundino, police official
A 67, ill.

VELEZ ALVARADO, Antonio (1864-1948), journalist
CiBPI 221(ill.), 236-38.

VELEZ DE ACEVEDO, Mabel (b. 1944), politician
LiPR 37, ill.

VELEZ DEJARDIN, José E. (b. 1937), teacher, author
S 103.

VELEZ DIAZ, Angel (b.1924), politician

LiPR 121, ill.

VELEZ GONZALEZ, Sigfredo (b. 1915), politician
  GrEPR 14:358.

VELEZ ITHIER, Manuel (b.1914), politician
  GrEPR 14:358.

VELEZ LOPEZ, Evaristo, singer
  MusMP 191; Orig 341.

VELEZ LOPEZ, Rafael (1872?-1934), doctor
  CaM 445-46; DiM 332-33.

VELEZ MERCADO, Francisco M. (b.1912), lawyer, politician
  GrEPR 14:358; QEQ (1941-42) 222, (1948-49) 179.

VELEZ RAMIREZ, Walter (b. 1939), politician
  LiPR 122, ill.

VELEZ RODRIGUEZ, Antonio (b. 1888), customs official
  QEQ (1936-37) 170, (1941-42) 222-23.

VELEZ RODRIGUEZ, Enrique (b. 1950), lawyer, professor
  DirAS 4:552.

VELEZ VIALIZ, Julio Enrique, journalist
  GenB 291-92; Nuestr 66-70.

VELILLA, Manuel, politician
  GrEPR 14:359.

VENDRELL, Fernando A., businessman
  Ver 191-92.

VENDRELL Y RUIZ, Ramón, lawyer
  Ver 172.

VENDRELL Y TORO, Adolfo, agronomist
  Ver 188.

VENEGAS, Carlos V. (b.1900), accountant
  QEQ (1933-34) 169, (1936-37) 170-71, (1941-42) 223, (1948-49) 179.

VENEGAS, Luis (1846-1905), political activist

Guay 286; Ka 98.

VENEGAS CORTES, Luis (d.1964), lawyer, poet
  Hor 265-67.

VENEGAS LLOVERAS, Guillermo (b. 1915), musician, author
  BiP 427-28; Com 8; GrEPR 7:144(ill.), 145-47; SobM 140-42.

VENEGAS Y ORTIZ DE ZARATE, Leopoldo (b.1890), dentist
  QEQ (1933-34) 169, (1936-37) 171, (1941-42) 223.

VENTURA, Juan Bautista (1840-1923), doctor
  CaM 446; DiM 334.

VERA, Arturo, Jr. (b.1918), engineer
  QEQ (1948-49) 179.

VERA, Estrellita, actress
  GenB 430, ill.

VERA BADRENA, Luis, actor
  DelMu 338-41, ill.

VERA CORTES, Eduardo (b.1926), artist
  GrEPR 8:429.

VERA ITHIER, Rafael (1861-1926), doctor
  CaM 446-48; GenB 272, ill.; HoIPR 118, ill.; RepM 231, ill.

VERA ITHIER, Tomás C. (1860-1919), teacher
  GenB 269-71; HoIPR 118-19, ill.

VERAR, Francisco (b.1850), musician
  GrEPR 14:359; MusMP 291-92.

VERAR DE REAL, Cruz, conductor
  MusMP 191-92.

VERAY MARIN, Francisco, dentist, singer
  AlHY 228-29.

VERAY HERNANDEZ, José (b.1903), lawyer
  QEQ (1936-37) 170, (1941-42) 223, (1948-49) 179.

VERAY TORREGROSA, Amaury (b. 1923), musician, composer
AlHY 176, 224-25; BiP 428-29; BrECP 442; DiLP 2, pt. 2: 1582-83; ECPR 6:500-501; GrEPR 7:311-14, ill., 14:359-60, ill.; L 101-3; Mus en P 153-54; PRFAS 252-53.

VERGARA, Gregorio (19th cent.), pharmacist
CaF 154.

VERGNE Y CASTELO, Jesús J. (b. 1882), lawyer
QEQ (1941-42) 223-24.

VERGNE CASTELO, Ramón (b. 1890), doctor
CaDeT 180-81; QEQ (1936-37) 171, (1941-42) 224, (1948-49) 179-80.

VETANCOURT, Manuel Norberto (b.1892), diplomat
QEQ (1933-34) 169-70, (1936-37) 171.

VEVE, Juan, doctor
RepM 309.

VEVE Y CALZADA, José Antonio, politician
GrEPR 14:360.

VEVE Y CALZADA, Santiago Manuel (1858*-1931), doctor, politician, orator
CaM 449-50; DeADeA 233-36; DiM 334-37; GenP 51-54, ill.; GrEPR 14:360, ill.; HoIPR 119, ill.; PaP 173-80; ProA 55-56, ill.; RepM 116, ill.

VEVE CALZADA, Santiago Miguel, doctor
DiM 335-37.

VIAS OCHOTECO, Juan F., politician
GrEPR 14:360, ill.; RepM 23, ill.

VICE, Celia, civic leader
EPI 2:241-44.

VICENS, Enrique (b.1926), doctor, politician
GrEPR 14:360.

VICENS, Nimia (b.1914), poet
AntHistCag 261; AntPoeCag 208-10; BrECP 442; CaE 897-98; DiLP 2, pt.2:1601-2; EGMPR 1:219-20, ill.; PRFAS 253.

VICENS RIOS, Antonio (b.1896), businessman
QEQ (1936-37) 171, (1941-42) 224, (1948-49) 180.

VICENS RIOS, Cristóbal, doctor
AlDJ 125, 127, ill.

VICENTE GONZALEZ, Avelino (1859-1928), hospital administrator
HoIPR 120, ill.

VICENTE MARTINEZ, Elvira, teacher
EGMPR 1:377-78, ill.

VIDAL ALVAREZ, Felipe Félix (b. 1893), engineer
QEQ (1936-37) 171, (1941-42) 224.

VIDAL ARMSTRONG, Mariano (b. 1931), author, historian
DiLP 2, pt.2:1602-4; Pon 95.

VIDAL LOPEZ, Lilliam (b.1942), artist
GrEPR 8:442.

VIDAL Y RIOS, Esteban (19th cent.), doctor, poet
CaM 450-51; Crom 79; DiM 337-39; Ka 183.

VIDAL RODRIGUEZ, Rafael S. (b. 1890), lawyer
QEQ (1941-42) 224.

VIDAL SANCHEZ, Manuel (19th cent.), notary
PonY 68-69.

VIDAL SANTAELLA, Irma, lawyer
PQ 58.

VIDARTE, Juan Bautista (b.1826), doctor, author
CaM 452; DiLP 2, pt.2:1604-5; DiM 339-40.

VIDARTE, Santiago (1828-1848), poet
BeHNPR 2:51-54, ill.; BiP 429-31; BrECP 442-43; CaE 898; DiDHM 202, ill.; DiHBC

925; DiLP 2, pt.2:1605-7;
ECPR 6:501; EnsB 79-86;
GrEPR 14:361; HisD 86; PlE
1:29-40, ill.; Por 209-10;
PRFAS 253; PuI 110-13.

VIENTOS GASTON, Nilita (b.
1908), lawyer, author, critic,
professor
    A 64-65; BiP 431-32; BrECP
    443; DiDHM 202-3; DiHBC
    925; DiLP 2, pt.2:1607-10;
    ECPR 6:501; EGMPR 1:379-80,
    ill.; GrEPR 14:361, ill.;
    PQ 59; PRFAS 254; QEQ
    (1936-37) 171-72, (1941-42)
    224-25.

VIERA DE TORRES, Tania (b.
1924), educator
    EGMPR 3:127-28, ill.

VIERA MARTINEZ, Angel (b.
1915), lawyer, politician
    DiDHM 203; GrEPR 14:361;
    LiPR 33, ill.; PRFAS 254.

VIERA MORALES, Julio (b.1916),
lawyer, politician
    GrEPR 14:361.

VIERA SOSA, Deogracías, race
track owner
    A 142, ill.

VIGOREAUX RIVERA, Luis (1928-
1983), television host
    GrEPR 14:361, ill.

VIGUIE, Juan E. (b.1891),
cinematographer
    QEQ (1936-37) 191, (1941-
    42) 225.

VILA MAYO, Rafael (b.1891),
chemist
    QEQ (1936-37) 172, (1941-
    42) 225.

VILA MAYO, Ramón, pharmacist,
politician
    CaF 155; GrEPR 14:362.

VILANOVA Y CANCEL, Joaquín (b.
1890), teacher
    QEQ (1936-37) 172, (1941-
    42) 225-26.

VILAR DALMAU, Ramón (d.1923),
businessman
    CaDeT 54, ill.

VILELLA, Salvador, businessman
    RepM 146, ill.

VILELLA Y POL, Pablo, businessman, politician
    RepM 170, ill.

VILELLA VELEZ, Félix M. (b.1883),
doctor
    QEQ (1933-34) 170, (1936-37)
    172, (1941-42) 226.

VILLAFAÑE CINTRON, Josefina,
doctor
    CaM 453-54, 482-83; DiHBC
    925-26; EGMPR 3:271-72, ill.;
    MujDPR 223-25, ill.

VILLAHERMOSA RODRIGUEZ, Gloria
(b.1929),accountant, union
official
    EGMPR 4:263-64, ill.

VILLALOBOS, Miguel de (16th
cent.), doctor
    CaM 454-55, 472-75; DiDHM
    203; GrEPR 14:362.

VILLAMIL, Angel M. (b.1831*),
lawyer, author
    BiP 432; DiLP 2, pt.2:1610-
    11; PRFAS 254.

VILLAMIL, Félix (b.1876), doctor
    RepM 191, ill.

VILLAMIL, Fernando A. (b.1902),
engineer
    A 100; QEQ (1948-49) 180.

VILLAMIL, Joaquín, businessman
    DeTUP 13-16.

VILLAMIL DE MARTINEZ, Carmen
(b.1934), accountant
    EGMPR 3:75, ill.

VILLAMIL ORTIZ, Angel (b.1873),
Protestant minister
    QEQ (1933-34) 170-71, (1936-
    37) 172.

VILLANUEVA, Asencio de (16th
cent.), horse breeder
    GrEPR 14:362.

VILLANUEVA, Bernardino, politician
    GrEPR 14:362.

VILLAR ROCES, Mario (b.1912),

lawyer
    GrEPR 1:xviii.

VILLARES RODRIGUEZ, José,
lawyer, judge
    CaDeT 189-90, ill., 229-30.

VILLARINI, Pedro (b.1933),
artist
    GrEPR 8:442; PaG 225-26.

VILLARINI DE VELEZ, Juanita
(b.1897), pharmacist
    QEQ (1933-34) 171, (1936-
    37) 172.

VILLARONGA, Eduardo (d.1897),
intellectual
    MueYV 149-53.

VILLARONGA, Gabriel (19th
cent.), doctor
    CaM 456; Crom 34-35; DiM
    340-41; Med 17-19; RepM
    124, ill.

VILLARONGA, Luis (1891-1964),
author, journalist
    BiP 433-34; CaE 899-900;
    DiLP 2, pt.2:1611-14; Gr-
    EPR 5:147-49, 14:362; Ind
    161-63; P1E 2:343; PRFAS
    254-55; QEQ (1948-49) 180-
    81.

VILLARONGA CHARRIEZ, José (b.
1901), author
    DiLP 2, pt.2:1615.

VILLARONGA DE ARMSTRONG,
Emilia (b.1875), author
    DiHBC 926; DiLP 2, pt.2:
    1614-15; EGMPR 1:221-22;
    MujDPR 161-62, ill.; MujPu
    125-32.

VILLARONGA DE MOSCOSO, Emilia
(b.1916), businesswoman
    EGMPR 3:77-78, ill.

VILLARONGA TORO, Mariano (b.
1906), educator
    GrEPR 14:362; QEQ (1948-
    49) 181.

VILLASANTE, Blas de (d.1536),
Royal Treasurer
    GrEPR 14:362.

VILLENUEVE BONELLI, Antonio
(b.1885), doctor

QEQ (1936-37) 191, (1941-42)
226.

VINCENTY, Francisco, industrialist
    A 143-44, ill.

VINCENTY, Francisco, teacher,
lawyer
    ProA 39.

VINCENTY RAMIREZ, Néstor, author,
educator
    Tri 2:265-72.

VIÑAS CAAMAÑO, Manuel, politician
    ArH 407.

VIÑAS MARTINEZ, Vicente, politician
    GrEPR 14:365, ill.; RepM 292,
    ill.

VIÑAS SORBA, Luis A. (b.1926),
doctor
    GrEPR 14:365.

VIÑAS RODRIGUEZ, Ramón (b.1878),
politician
    RepM 303, ill.

VIRELLA, Federico E., politician
    GrEPR 14:365, ill.

VIRELLA RIVERA, María S. (b.
1934), bank manager
    EGMPR 3:73-74, ill.

VIRELLA URIBE, Valeriano, businessman, politician
    RepM 318, ill.

VISO LORENZO, Bautista, landowner
    RepM 152, ill.

VIVAS CAPO, Francisco (1888-
1953), politician
    AlHP 245, ill.

VIVAS MALDONADO, José Luis (b.
1926), author, professor
    CaE 903; DiLP 2, pt.2:1616-
    18; GrEPR 14:365; PRFAS 255.

VIVAS ROSALY, José Guillermo (b.
1914), lawyer
    QEQ (1941-42) 226-27.

VIVAS VALDIVIESO, Guillermo (b.

1881), businessman, politician
  Ka 13; QEQ (1936-37) 172-73 (1941-42) 226, (1948-49) 181; RepM 240, ill.

VIVES, Guillermo, doctor, inventor
  Ka 133-34.

VIVO, Paquita, author, civic leader
  PQ 60.

VIVONI, Pedro S., politician
  GrEPR 14:365.

Vizcarrondo, Andrés Cayetano see Vizcarrondo Martínez, Andrés Cayetano

VIZCARRONDO, Carmelina (b. 1906), author
  BrECP 445; CaE 903; DiLP 2, pt.2:1618-20; EGMPR 1:223-24, ill.; GrEPR 14:364; PRFAS 255.

VIZCARRONDO, Fortunato (b. 1896*), poet
  CaE 903; DiLP 2, pt.2: 1620-22; PRFAS 255.

VIZCARRONDO, José (d.1809), soldier
  BeHNPR 1:299, 317.

VIZCARRONDO, Sicinio (b.1850), doctor
  RepM 316, ill.

VIZCARRONDO Y CANALES, Lorenzo Francisco de (1887-1934), government official
  QEQ (1933-34) 171-72, (1936-37) 16.

VIZCARRONDO Y CORONADO, Felipe, doctor
  DiM 341-42.

VIZCARRONDO Y CORONADO, Julio (1830-1889), abolitionist, author, journalist
  BgP facing p.248, ill.; BiP 435-36; BrECP 445-46; CiBPI 71(ill.), 120-22; DiDHM 203-4; DiHBC 927-28; DiLP 2, pt.2:1622-23; ECPR 6: 501-2; GrEPR 14:364, ill.; HisD 86; HoIPR 119, ill.;

HoRPR 57-63: Hor 201-5; LPR 982, 983, 985, ill.; Mem 59-61; Nuestr 141-43; Por 237-40; PRFAS 255-56; PuI 175-80; Ver 221-22, ill.

VIZCARRONDO MARTINEZ, Andrés Cayetano (1774-1838), soldier
  BeHNPR 1:299; GrEPR 14:364.

VIZCARRONDO MORELL, Francisco (b.1883), teacher, lawyer
  DiHBC 926; QEQ (1933-34) 171, (1936-37) 173, (1941-42) 227; Tri 2:23-28.

VOGEL, Carlos (19th cent.), doctor
  CaM 459; RepM 114, ill.

VONDERLEHR, Raymond Aloysius (b.1897), doctor
  QEQ (1948-49) 181-82.

W

WAGENHEIM, Kal (b.1935), author
  ConA 29-32R:61-70.

WAINMAN RYAN, Mary Margaret (b. 1923), nun
  EGMPR 4:319.

WALLACE, Henry A. (b.1888), federal official
  QEQ (1936-37) 173, (1941-42) 227.

WARD, George Cabot (b.1876), auditor, lawyer
  RepM 13-14, ill.

WARREK, George, artist
  GrEPR 8:428.

WATSON, James (b.1884), doctor
  QEQ (1933-34) 172, (1936-37) 173.

WATSON, James (b.1884), doctor
  QEQ (1933-34) 172, (1936-37) 173.

WAYMOUTH, Thomas George (b. 1856), businessman
  RepM 93, ill.

WELTY, Frank M., bank official
  RepM 43, ill.

WELLS, Ira Kent (1871-1933),

lawyer, judge
 QEQ (1933-34) 172, (1936-
 37) 16.

WESTERBAND, Carlos, politician
 GrEPR 14:365.

WHITE, John (16th cent.),
artist
 GrEPR 14:365.

WILCOX, Elías Bunn (b.1869),
lawyer
 QEQ (1936-37) 191; RepM
 32-33, ill.

WILLEMSEN, Madelline (d.
1982), actress
 DelMu 344-48, ill.; EGMPR
 4:139.

WILLIAMS, Clarence Russell
(1870-1949), historian
 QEQ (1933-34) 172, (1936-
 37) 173, (1941-42) 227.

WILLINGER, Aloysius J. (1886-
1973), Catholic bishop
 GrEPR 6:285; QEQ (1936-37)
 173, (1941-42) 227.

WINSHIP, Blanton (1869-1947),
governor
 DicAB suppl.4:902-3; Desf
 117-21, ill.; DiDHM 205;
 DiHBC 438, 940; GrEPR 14:
 365, ill.; QEQ (1936-37)
 173-74, (1941-42) 227-28.

WINTER, Charles Edwin (1870-
1948), Attorney General
 QEQ (1933-34) 172-73,
 (1936-37) 174.

WINTHROP, Beekman (1874-
1940), governor
 CuB 1940:877; Desf 26-42,
 ill.; DiDHM 205; DiHBC 437-
 38; GrEPR 14:366, ill.;
 QEQ (1933-34) 173, (1936-
 37) 174; RepM 10, ill.

WIRSHING, Herman (d.1932),
engineer
 AlHP 462-63, ill.

WOLF, Adolph Grant (b.1869),
judge
 QEQ (1933-34) 173, (1941-
 42) 228.

WRIGHT, John W. (1876-1952),
Army officer
 DiHBC 940-42; QEQ (1936-37)
 191-92, (1941-42) 228-29.

X

XINORIO, José (19th cent.),
apothecary
 CaF 158.

XIORRO Y VELASCO, Miguel (1743-
1801), philanthropist, monk
 EPI 1:68-69; HisD 87; PuI
 22-24.

Y

YAGER, Arthur (b.1858), governor
 Desf 57-63, ill.; DiDHM 207;
 DiHBC 438; GrEPR 14:367,
 ill.; QEQ (1933-34) 173,
 (1936-37) 174.

YAHUREIBO (d.1514), Taíno Indian chief
 CiBPI 18-21.

YAÑEZ PINZON, Vicente (14th-
15th cent.), sailor, colonist
 DiDHM 158-59, 207; GrEPR
 14:367; HisD 87; Por 309-10.

YDRACH YORDAN, Rafael L., politician
 GrEPR 14:367.

Ygaravídez see Igaravídez

Yo Yo Boing see Rivera, Luis
Antonio

YORDAN DAVILA, Luis (1869-1932),
politician
 AlHP 245, ill.; GrEPR 14:
 368.

YORDAN PASARELL, Luis Angel (b.
1893), radiologist
 CaM 463; QEQ (1933-34) 173-
 74, (1936-37) 174, (1941-42)
 229.

YORDAN RODRIGUEZ, Joaquín, politician
 GrEPR 14:368.

Ysern see Isern

Yuisa see Luisa, "La Cacica"

YUMET, Antonio, pharmacist
    Ka 138; Ver 192.

YUMET, Fernando, politician,
businessman
    ProA 14-15.

YUMET MENDEZ, José (1887-
1955), journalist, poet, orator
    BiP 437; DiLP 2, pt.2:
    1624-25; PRFAS 257.

YUSTI, José (19th cent.),
apothecary
    CaF 159-60.

Z

ZABALA DE LOCKHEIMER, Carmen
(b.1931), civic leader
    EGMPR 4:347-48, ill.

ZABALA VAZQUEZ, Marianita (b.
1935), nun, teacher
    EGMPR 3:345-46, ill.

ZALDUENDO, Johnny, businessman
    A 116-17, ill.

ZAMBRANA, José, politician
    GrEPR 14:369.

ZAMORA, Pedro, doctor
    ProA 36.

ZAPATA ACOSTA, Ramón (b.
1917), author, professor
    CaE 907; DiLP 2, pt.2:1625-
    27; GrEPR 14:369; PRFAS
    259.

ZAPATA MUÑOZ, José A., businessman
    GenB 420-21, ill.

ZAPATER MARTINEZ, Fernando
(1891), educator
    Hi de CR 254-55.

ZAPATER MARTINEZ, Fernando
(1891-1951), lawyer
    AlHP 331, ill.; QEQ (1933-
    34) 174, (1936-37) 175,
    (1941-42) 229, (1948-49)
    182.

ZARATT, Jacinto (b.1875),
doctor
    QEQ (1936-37) 175, (1941-

42) 229-30, (1948-49) 182;
    RepM 244, ill.

ZAVALA, Iris M. (b.1936), author, critic
    ConA nr1:731-32; DiDHM 209;
    DiLP 2, pt.2:1627-29; DirAS
    3:581.

ZAVALA RODRIGUEZ, Manuel Antonio (1857*-1925), doctor,
politician
    CaM 465-66; DiM 343-45; GenP
    96; Med 51-55; RepM 311, ill.

ZAVALA RODRIGUEZ, Romualdo,
pharmacist, politician
    CaF 161; GrEPR 14:369, ill.

ZAYAS, Alberto "Beco", actor
    DelMu 350-55, ill.

ZAYAS, Dean, director, actor,
professor
    GentI 72-76.

ZAYAS APONTE, Juan, pharmacist,
politician
    GrEPR 14:369.

ZAYAS BONILLA, José Uriel (b.
1940), politician
    LiPR 39, ill.

ZAYAS COLON, Carmen Sonia (b.
1936), judge
    EGMPR 3:275-76, ill.

ZAYAS LOPEZ, Raúl (b.1946),
artist
    GrEPR 8:442.

ZAYAS MICHELI, Luis O., professor, critic
    PRFAS 259.

ZAYAS Y ZAYAS, Florencio (19th
cent.), pharmacist
    CaF 161-62.

ZEGRI VIVAS, Day, businesswoman
    EGMPR 3:79-80.

ZENGOTITA Y BENGOA, Juan Bautista (1731-1802), bishop
    BeHNPR 2:1-5, ill.; Hi de la
    Ig 170-96.

ZENO, Francisco M. (1886-1971),
politician, journalist

Bibliography of Sources Indexed

Abril, Mariano. Sensaciones de un cronista: literatura, viajes, semblanzas, cuentos. San Juan, P. R.: Tipografía de "La Democracia", 1903.

Album de Jayuya, 1962-1963. San Juan, P. R.: Círculo Social Jayuyano, 1964.

Album de Utuado. Utuado, P. R.: Imprenta Modelo, 1967.

Amy, Francisco J. Predicar en desierto... San Juan, P. R.: Tip. "El Alba", 1907.

Angelis, María Luisa de. Mujeres puertorriqueñas que se han distinguido en el cultivo de las ciencias, las letras y las artes desde el Siglo XVII hasta nuestros días. [San Juan, P. R.]: Tip. del Boletín Mercantil, 1908.

Angelis, Pedro de. Españoles en Puerto Rico: bocetos biográficos de españoles que han cooperado al desenvolvimiento moral e intelectual de esta isla... San Juan, P. R.: Imprenta de M. Burillo & Co., 1911.

Añeses Morell, Ramón. Apuntes para la historia de Aguadilla. Río Piedras, P. R.: Imprenta Falcón, 1949.

Arana Soto, Salvador. Catálogo de farmacéuticos de Puerto Rico (desde 1512 a 1925). San Juan, P. R.: 1966.

_____. Catálogo de médicos de P. R. [sic] de siglos pasados (con muchos de éste). Burgos, Spain: Imprenta de Aldecoa, 1966.

_____. Diccionario de médicos puertorriqueños: que se han distinguido fuera de la medicina. San Juan, P. R., 1963.

Arillaga Roqué, Juan. Memorias de antaño: historia de un viaje a España. Ponce, P. R.: Tipografía Baldorioty, 1910.

Asenjo, Conrado, ed. Quien es quien en Puerto Rico: diccio-
    nario biográfico de record personal. 4 vols. San Juan,
    P. R.: Real Hermanos, Inc., etc., 1933-1947.

Atiles García, Guillermo. Kaleidoscopio. Ponce, P. R.:
    Est. Tip. de Manuel López, 1905.

Balasquide, Lorenzo A. Médicos notables del antaño ponceño.
    San Juan, P. R.: Instituto de Cultura Puertorriqueña,
    1984.

Bloch, Peter. La-Le-Lo-Lai: Puerto Rican Music and Its
    Performers. New York: Plus Ultra Educational Pub-
    lishers, Inc., 1973.

_____. Painting and Sculpture of the Puerto Ricans.
    New York: Plus Ultra Educational Publishers, Inc., 1978.

Braschi, Wilfredo. Perfiles puertorriqueños. San Juan, P. R.:
    Biblioteca de Autores Puertorriqueños, 1978.

Brau, Salvador. Ecos de la Batalla. San Juan, P. R.: Imp.
    de J. González Font, 1886.

Callejo Ferrer, Fernando. Música y músicos puertorriqueños.
    [San Juan, P. R.]: Tip. Cantero Fernández & Co., 1915.

Campo Lacasa, Cristina. Historia de la Iglesia en Puerto Rico
    (1511-1802). San Juan, P. R.: Instituto de Cultura
    Puertorriqueña, 1977.

Carreras, Carlos N. Hombres y mujeres de Puerto Rico. México:
    Editorial Orión, 1966.

_____. Oradores puertorriqueños. San Juan, P. R.:
    Editorial Cordillera, 1973.

Carrero Concepción, Jaime A. Añasco y sus hombres, 1475-1893.
    Mayagüez, P. R.: Imprenta y Litografía Torres, 1975.

La ciudad de los poetas: antología en homenaje a siete poetas
    representativos de Lares... Santurce, P. R.: Publica-
    ciones Orsini-Bristto, 1965?

Coll, Edna. Indice informativo de la novela hispanoamericana.
    Vol. 1. Las Antillas. Río Piedras, P. R.: Editorial
    Universitaria, Universidad de Puerto Rico, 1974.

Coll y Toste, Cayetano. Puertorriqueños ilustres; segunda
    selección. Compiled by Isabel Cuchí Coll. Bilbao,
    Spain: Editorial Vasco-Americana, n. d.

Comité Constituído para la Celebración del Bicentenario de la
    Fundación de Mayagüez. Historia de Mayagüez, 1760-1960.
    Mayagüez, P. R.: Talleres Gráficos Interamericanos, Inc.,
    1960.

Compositores de música popular. San Juan, P. R.: Centro de
    Investigaciones y Ediciones Musicales de Puerto Rico,
    1981.

Contemporary Authors; A Bio-Bibliographical Guide to Current
    Authors and Their Works. Detroit: Gale Research, 1962-

Cuchí Coll, Isabel. Del mundo de la farándula. Cataño, P. R.:
    Litografía Metropolitana, Inc., 1980.

_____. Oro nativo; colección de semblanzas puerto-
    rriqueñas contemporáneas. San Juan, P. R.: 1936.

Current Biography. New York: H. W. Wilson, 1940-1985.

Chavier, Arístides. Siluetas musicales. Ponce, P. R.: Tip.
    El Día, 1926.

Dalmau y Canet, Sebastián. Crepúsculos literarios. San Juan,
    P. R.: Boletín Mercantil, 1903.

_____. Próceres. San Juan, P. R.: Imp. Correo
    Dominical, 1929.

Delgado Cintrón, Carmelo. Libro de matrículas del ilustre
    Colegio de Abogados de Puerto Rico, 1840-1910. San Juan,
    P. R.: Instituto de Historia del Derecho Puertorriqueño,
    Colegio de Abogados de Puerto Rico, 1970.

Delgado Votaw, Carmen. Puerto Rican Women: Some Biographi-
    cal Profiles. Washington, D. C.: National Conference
    of Puerto Rican Women, Inc., 1978.

Dictionary of American Biography. 20 vols. New York:
    Scribner, 1928-37; Supplements 1-7. New York: Scribner,
    1944-1981.

Diez de Andino, Juan. Andanzas y perfiles. San Juan, P. R.:
    1969.

_____. Desde mi rascacielo. San Juan, P. R.:
    1963.

_____. Horizontes y verdades. San Juan, P. R.:
    1967.

_____. Sobre la marcha... San Juan, P. R.: 1972.

_____. Voces de la farándula: crítica contempo-
    ránea. Barcelona, Spain: Ediciones Rumbos, 1959.

Directory of American Scholars. 8th ed. 4 vols. New York:
    R. R. Bowker, 1982.

Enciclopedia clásicos de Puerto Rico. Selection, edition,
    and notes by Lucas Morán Arce. 6 vols. Barcelona,
    Spain: Ediciones Latinoamericanas, 1971.

Enciclopedia grandes mujeres de Puerto Rico. Selection and
    notes by Lola Krüger Torres. Hato Rey, P. R.: Ramallo
    Bros. Printing, 1975.

Farr, Kenneth R. Historical Dictionary of Puerto Rico and the
    U. S. Virgin Islands. Metuchen, N. J.: Scarecrow Press,
    1973.

Fernández García, E., ed. El libro de Puerto Rico. The Book
    of Porto Rico. San Juan, P. R.: El Libro Azul Pub-
    lishing Co., 1923.

Fernández Juncos, Manuel. Antología de sus obras. Selection,
    prologue and notes by José Antonio Torres Morales. México:
    Editorial Orión, 1965.

_____. Semblanzas puertorriqueñas. San Juan, P. R.:
    Tip. de José González Font, 1888.

Ferrer, Rafael. Lienzos. San Juan, P. R.: 1965.

Figueroa, Sotero. Ensayo biográfico de los que más han con-
    tribuído al progreso de Puerto Rico. San Juan, P. R.:
    Editorial Coquí, 1973 (1888).

Fonfrías, Ernesto Juan. Sementera; ensayos breves y biogra-
    fías mínimas. San Juan, P. R.: Editorial Club de la
    Prensa, 1962.

Fortuño Janeiro, Luis, comp. Album histórico de Ponce, 1692-
    1963; contentivo de los más importantes datos históricos
    y de una exposición gráfica de su cultura y progreso.
    Ponce, P. R.: Imprenta Fortuño, 1963?

Foster, David William, comp. A Dictionary of Contemporary
    Latin American Authors. Tempe, Arizona: Center for
    Latin American Studies, Arizona State University, 1975.

Gaudier, Martín. Genealogías, biografías e historia del
    Mayagüez de ayer y hoy y antología de Puerto Rico.
    San Germán, P. R.: Imprenta "El Aguila", 1959.

_____. Genealogías puertorriqueñas: partidas de
    bautismos y biografías. Burgos, Spain: Imprenta de
    Aldecoa, 1963-64.

_____. El verdadero orígen de "La Borinqueña".
    Santurce, P. R.: Imprenta Soltero, 1957.

Geigel Polanco, Vicente. Valores de Puerto Rico. San Juan,
    P. R.: Editorial Eugenio María de Hostos, 1943.

Geigel y Zenón, José and Abelardo Morales Ferrer. Biblio-
    grafía puertorriqueña. Barcelona, Spain: Editorial
    Araluce, 1934.

Góngora Echenique, Manuel and Amelia Góngora de Parker.
    Actualidades y semblanzas puertorriqueñas. Caracas,
    Venezuela: Tipografía Vargas, 1949.

Gotay, Modesto. Hombres ilustres de Puerto Rico. Barcelona,
    Spain: Ediciones Rumbos, 1966.

La gran enciclopedia de Puerto Rico. 15 vols. San Juan,
P. R.: Puerto Rico en la Mano y la Gran Enciclopedia
de Puerto Rico, 1976-1980.

Grismer, Raymond L. and César Arroyo. Vida y obra de autores
puertorriqueños. Habana, Cuba: Editorial "Alfa", 1941.

Guerra, Ramón H. De todo un poco: riqueza sacarina, comer-
cio e industria, biografías de hombres del día; cróni-
cas, cuentos cortos y artículos varios. Ponce, P. R.:
Tipografía Matías & Sobrino, 1911.

_____. Del rincón boricua. San Juan, P. R.:
Tipografía Venezuela, 1925.

Hanson, Earl Parker. Transformation: The Story of Modern
Puerto Rico. New York: Simon and Schuster, 1955.

Herdeck, Donald E., ed. Caribbean Writers: A Bio-Biblio-
graphical-Critical Encyclopedia. Washington, D. C.:
Three Continents Press, Inc., 1979.

Hostos, Adolfo de. Diccionario histórico bibliográfico
comentado de Puerto Rico. San Juan, P. R.: Academia
Puertorriqueña de la Historia, 1976.

_____. Hombres representativos de Puerto Rico.
San Juan, P. R.: Imprenta Venezuela, 1961.

Huyke, Juan B. Páginas escogidas. Boston: D. C. Heath y
Compañía, 1925.

_____. Triunfadores. 2 vols. San Juan, P. R.:
Negociado de Materiales, Imprenta y Transporte, 1926.

Ibern Fleytas, Ramón. Historia de Cabo Rojo. Trujillo,
P. R.: Editorial Montalvo, 1960.

Infiesta, Alejandro, ed. La exposición de Puerto Rico:
memoria. San Juan, P. R.: Imprenta del "Boletín
Mercantil, 1895.

Jesús Castro, Tomás de. Esbozos. Barcelona, Spain: Rumbos,
1957-

_____. Esbozos críticos. San Juan, P. R.: Talle-
res Tipográficos Baldrich, 1945.

_____. Vistos de cerca (reportajes). San Juan,
P. R.: Editorial Club de la Prensa, 1962.

LeCompte, Eugenio. Impresiones del momento (no-partidaris-
tas): colección de editoriales y artículos periodísti-
cos. Ponce, P. R.: Tipografía "El Aguila", 1930?

Lefebre, Enrique. Paisajes mentales: estudios críticos,
bocetos y perfiles, impresiones de arte, personalidades
políticas, necrologías. San Juan, P. R.: Tip. Cantero,
Fernández & Co., 1918.

Lidin, Harold.   History of the Puerto Rican Independence
    Movement.   Vol. 1:   19th Century.   Hato Rey, P. R.:   1981.

Limón de Arce, José.   Arecibo histórico.   Arecibo, P. R.:
    1938.

_____.   Poetas arecibeños, 1832-1904.   Arecibo,
    P. R.:   Editorial Harry C. del Pozo, 1926.

López Cantos, Angel.   Historia de Puerto Rico (1650-1700).
    Seville, Spain: Escuela de Estudios Hispano-Americanos,
    1975.

López de Santa Anna, Antonio.   Los Jesuítas en Puerto Rico de
    1858 a 1886.   Santander, P. R.:   Taller de Artes Gráfi-
    cas de los Hermanos Bedia, 1958.

López Martínez, Pío.   Historia de Cayey.   San Juan, P. R.:
    Cooperativa de Artes Gráficas Romualdo Real, 1972.

Lugo Silva, Enrique.   Antología histórica de Caguas.   Caguas,
    P. R.:   Edición Club de Leones de Caguas, 1975.

Lugo Toro, Sifredo.   Estampas de Cabo Rojo.   2 vols.   Mayagüez,
    P. R.:   Imprenta y Litografía Torres, 1973-1974.

Lluch Negroni, Francisco R., ed.   Album histórico de Yauco
    (Puerto Rico).   Valencia, Spain: Editorial Guerri, 1960.

Malaret, Augusto.   Medallas de oro.   5th ed.   México: Edito-
    rial Orión, 1966.

Maldonado, Adál Alberto.   Portraits of the Puerto Rican Expe-
    rience.   Edited by Louis Reyes Rivera and Julio Rodríguez.
    New York: IPRUS Institute, 1984.

Maldonado, Teófilo.   Hombres de primera plana.   [San Juan,
    P. R.]:   Editorial Campos, 1958.

Martínez Acosta, C.   Algo.   San Juan, P. R.:   Editorial
    Imprenta Puerto Rico, 1937.

_____.   Entre próceres.   San Juan, P. R.:   Edito-
    rial Imprenta Puerto Rico, 1938.

Matos Bernier, Félix.   Cromos ponceños.   By Fray Justo.   Ponce,
    P. R.:   Imprenta "La Libertad", 1896.

_____.   Muertos y vivos.   San Juan, P. R.:   Tip.
    "El País", 1905.

_____.   Páginas sueltas.   Ponce, P. R.:   Tipografía
    de "La Libertad", 1897.

Mayoral Barnés, Manuel.   Ponce y su historial geopolítico-
    económico y cultural; con el árbol genealógico de sus
    pobladores.   Ponce, P. R.:   Editorial "Promisión del
    Porvenir", 1946.

Medina y González, Zenón. Pinceladas: colección de artículos. Puerto Rico: Tipografía Viuda de González, 1895.

Medina Ramírez, Ramón. Patriotas ilustres puertorriqueños. 2nd ed. San Juan, P. R.: Editora Nacional, 1975.

Melón de Díaz, Esther M. Puerto Rico: figuras, apuntes históricos, símbolos nacionales. Río Piedras, P. R.: Editorial Edil, 1975.

Méndez Liciaga, Andrés. Boceto histórico del Pepino. Mayagüez, P. R.: Tipografía "La Voz de la Patria", 1925.

Millán Rivera, Pedro. Antología poética de Caguas. San Juan, P. R.: Editorial Club de la Prensa, 1964.

Morales Miranda, José Pablo. Misceláneas históricas. San Juan, P. R.: Tip. "La Correspondencia de Puerto Rico", 1924.

Morales Otero, Pablo. Hombres de mi tierra. San Juan, P. R.: Biblioteca de Autores Puertorriqueños, 1965.

Moretti, Darcia. Gente importante. New York: Plus Ultra Educational Publishers Inc., 1973.

Muñoz, María Luisa. La música en Puerto Rico: panorama histórico-cultural. Sharon, Conn: Troutman Press, 1966.

Negrón Muñoz, Angela. Mujeres de Puerto Rico, desde el período de colonización hasta el primer tercio del Siglo XX. San Juan, P. R.: Imprenta Venezuela, 1935.

Neumann Gandía, Eduardo. Benefactores y hombres de Puerto Rico: bocetos biográfico-críticos. 2 vols. Ponce, P. R.: Imprenta del "Listín Comercial", 1896-1899.

_____. Verdadera y auténtica historia de la ciudad de Ponce, desde sus primitivos tiempos hasta la época contemporánea... San Juan, P. R.: 1913.

Notable American Women. Vol. 4: The Modern Period. Cambridge, Miss.: Belknap Press of Harvard University Press, 1980.

Ohles, John F., ed. Biographical Dictionary of American Education. 3 vols. Westport, Conn.: Greenwood Press, 1978.

Padró Quiles, José. Luchas obreras y datos históricos del Pepino 60 años atrás. San Sebastián, P. R.: 1950.

Palacín Mejías, Juan. Nuestros grandes maestros. Santurce, P. R.: Imprenta Soltero, 1961.

Pasarell, Emilio J. Orígenes y desarrollo de la afición teatral en Puerto Rico. San Juan, P. R.: Editorial Universitaria, Universidad de Puerto Rico, 1951.

Political Profiles. 5 vols. New York: Facts on File, Inc., 1976-1979.

Porrata-Doria, Adolfo. Guayama: sus hombres y sus institu-ciones. Barcelona, Spain: Jorge Casas, 1972.

Primer cincuentenario Senado de Puerto Rico, 1917-1967. San Juan, P. R.?: Talleres de Artes Gráficas, Departamento de Instrucción Pública, 1968.

Puerto Rico. Instituto de Cultura Puertorriqueña. Composi-tores puertorriqueños del Siglo XIX. San Juan, P. R.: Centro de Investigaciones y Ediciones Musicales de Puerto Rico, 1981.

Puerto Rico USA: Biographies. Washington, D. C.: Federal Affairs Administration, 1980.

Quintana, Pepe. Pro-Aguadilla. Aguadilla, P. R.: Tip. Libertad, 1923.

Quiñones Calderón, Antonio, ed. El libro de Puerto Rico 1983. San Juan, P. R.: Ediciones Nuevas de Puerto Rico, 1983.

The Representative Men of Porto Rico. Compiled and edited by F. E. Jackson & Son. C. Frederiksen, artist and photo-grapher. N. p.: F. E. Jackson & Son, 1910.

Reynal, Vicente. Diccionario de hombres y mujeres ilustres de Puerto Rico y de hechos históricos. Río Piedras, P. R.: Editorial Edil, 1983.

Ribes Tovar, Federico. 100 [cien] biografías de puertorri-queños ilustres. New York: Plus Ultra Educational Publishers, Inc., 1973.

_____. Enciclopedia puertorriqueña ilustrada. The Puerto Rican Heritage Encyclopedia. 3 vols. San Juan, P. R.; New York: Plus Ultra Educational Pub-lishers, Inc., 1970.

_____. La mujer puertorriqueña: su vida y evolu-ción a través de la historia. New York: Plus Ultra Educational Publishers, Inc., 1972.

Rivera de Alvarez, Josefina. Diccionario de literatura puertorriqueña. 2nd rev. ed. San Juan, P. R.: Insti-tuto de Cultura Puertorriqueña, 1970-1974.

Rivera Santiago, Rafael. Comprensión y análisis: entrevis-tas biográficas, conferencias, artículos. San Juan, P. R.: Imprenta Venezuela, 1938.

Rodríguez Troche, Concha. Maestro. Ponce, P. R.: n. p., n. d.

Rosa-Nieves, Cesáreo and Esther M. Melón. Biografías puerto-rriqueñas: perfil histórico de un pueblo. Sharon, Conn.: Troutman Press, 1970.

Rosa-Nieves, Cesáreo. Plumas estelares en las letras de Puerto Rico. 2 vols. San Juan, P. R.: Ediciones de la Torre, Universidad de Puerto Rico, 1967-1971.

Rosario, Rubén del, Esther Melón de Díaz, and Edgar Martínez Masdeu. Breve enciclopedia de la cultura puertorriqueña. San Juan, P. R.: Editorial Cordillera, 1976.

Ruiz García, Zoilo. Nuestros hombres de antaño. Mayagüez, P. R.: Mayagüez Publishing Co., 1920.

Sánchez Morales, Luis. De antes y de ahora: colección de artículos y discursos. Madrid, Spain: Centro Editorial Rubén Darío, 1936.

Soto Ramos, Julio. Bocetos biográficos puertorriqueños. Barcelona, Spain: Talleres Gráficos de Manuel Pareja, 1973.

_____. Una pica en Flandes (ensayo y otros artículos). San Juan, P. R.: Editorial Club de la Prensa, 1959.

Sterling, Philip and María Brau. The Quiet Rebels: Four Puerto Rican Leaders. Garden City, N. Y.: Doubleday & Co., 1968.

Todd, Roberto H. Desfile de gobernadores de Puerto Rico 1898 a 1943. San Juan, P. R.: Impreso en Casa Baldrich, 1943.

_____. Patriotas puertorriqueños: siluetas biográficas. Madrid, Spain: Ediciones Iberoamericanas, 1965.

Toro y Cuebas, Emilio del. Patria: artículos, discursos, informes y entrevistas. 4 vols. San Juan, P. R.: Biblioteca de Autores Puertorriqueños, 1950-1960.

Tuck, Jay Nelson and Norma Coolen Vergara. Heroes of Puerto Rico. New York: Fleet Press Corporation, 1969.

Van Deusen, Richard James and Elizabeth Kneipple Van Deusen. Porto Rico, a Caribbean Isle. New York: Henry Holt and Co., 1931.

Vélez Dejardín, José E. San Germán: notas para su historia (un pueblo con profunda historia). San Juan, P. R.: 1983.

Vidal, Teodoro. Santeros puertorriqueños. San Juan, P. R.: Ediciones Alba, 1979.

Vidal Armstrong, Mariano. Ponce: notas para su historia. San Juan, P. R.: Model Offset Printing, 1983.

Vila Vilar, Enriqueta, Historia de Puerto Rico (1600-1650). Seville, Spain: Escuela de Estudios Hispano-Americanos, 1974.

Vilar Jiménez, Adolfo. _El Caguas de todos los tiempos_. San Juan, P. R.: Editorial Florete, 1950.

Wagenheim, Kal. _Puerto Rico: A Profile_. New York: Praeger, 1970.

Selective Bibliography
of Related Materials

Alonso Fernández, Jorge. Colección de semblanzas. Guayama,
    P.R.: Imp. Alvarez, 1905.

Arana Soto, Salvador. Catálogo de poetas puertorriqueños. San
    Juan, P.R.: Sociedad de Autores Puertorriqueños, 1968.

Arce de Vázquez, Margot, Laura Gallego, and Luis de Arrigoíta.
    Lecturas puertorriqueñas; poesía. Sharon, Conn.; Trout-
    man Press, 1968.

_____ and Mariana Robles de Cardona. Lecturas puertorriqueñas:
    prosa. Sharon, Conn.: Troutman Press, 1966.

Biography Index. New York: H. W. Wilson, 1946-

Cabassa Túa, Regino. Antología de oradores puertorriqueños del
    pasado. San Juan, P.R.: Instituto de Cultura Puertorri-
    queña, 1978.

Carrión Maduro, Tomás. Oradores parlamentarios y hombres nota-
    bles de la Asamblea Legislativa de P.R. San Juan, P.R.:
    Boletín Mercantil, 1904.

Cifre de Loubriel, Estela. Catálogo de extranjeros residentes
    en Puerto Rico en el siglo XIX. Río Piedras, P.R.: Edi-
    ciones de la Universidad de Puerto Rico, 1962.

_____. La inmigración a Puerto Rico durante el siglo XIX.
    San Juan, P.R.: Instituto de Cultura Puertorriqueña, 1964.

Fernández Juncos, Manuel. Varias cosas. San Juan, P.R.: Imp.
    Bellas Artes, 1884.

Foster, David William, comp. Puerto Rican Literature: A Bibli-
    ography of Secondary Sources. Westport, Conn.: Greenwood
    Press, 1982.

Guerrero, César H. Sanjuaninos del ochenta. San Juan, P.R.:
    Sanjuanina, 1965.

Hill, Marnesba D. and Harold B. Schleifer. Puerto Rican Authors: A Bio-Bibliographic Handbook. Metuchen, N.J.: Scarecrow Press, 1974.

Hostos, Adolfo de. Tesauro de datos históricos. San Juan, P.R.: Departamento de Hacienda, 1948-1951.

Huyke, Juan B. Esfuerzo propio: entrevistas con portorriqueños que se han formado por su propio esfuerzo. San Juan, P.R.: Negociado de Materiales, Imprenta y Transportación, 1922.

Indice biográfico; breves apuntes para un diccionario de puerto-riqueños distinguidos. San Juan, P.R.: Colección HIPATIA, 1985.

McNeil, Barbara, ed. Biography & Genealogy Master Index, 1981-85. 5 vols. Detroit: Gale Research, 1985.

Maestros de la educación en Cabo Rojo: historia y homenaje. San Juan, P.R.: Club Caborrojeño del Area Metropolitana, 1979.

Marqués, René, comp. Cuentos puertorriqueños de hoy. Río Piedras, P.R.: Editorial Cultural, 1971.

Matos Bernier, Félix. Isla de arte. San Juan, P.R.: Imprenta La Primavera, 1907.

Mundo Lo, Sara de. Index to Spanish American Collective Biogra-phy. Vol.3: The Central American and Caribbean Countries. Boston: G. K. Hall, 1984.

Picó, Fernando. Registro general de jornaleros: Utuado, Puerto Rico (1849-50). Río Piedras, P.R.: Ediciones Huracán, 1976.

Rosa-Nieves, Cesáreo, comp. Aguinaldo lírico de la poesía puertorriqueña. 3 vols. Río Piedras, P.R.: Editorial Edil, 1971.

_____ and Félix Franco Oppenheimer, comps. Antología general del cuento puertorriqueño. 2nd ed. 2 vols. San Juan, P.R.: Editorial Edil, 1970.

Tió, Aurelio. Fundación de San Germán y su significado en el desarrollo político, económico, social y cultural de Puerto Rico. San Juan, P.R.: Biblioteca de Autores Puertorri-queños, 1956.

Webster's American Biographies. Springfield, Mass.: G. & C. Merriam, 1974.

Bibliographies Consulted

Pedreira, Antonio A. Bibliografía puertorriqueña (1493-1930).
New York: Burt Franklin Reprints, 1974.

Rivera, Guillermo. A Tentative Bibliography of the Belles-Lettres
of Porto Rico. Cambridge, Mass.: Harvard University
Press, 1931.

Toro, Josefina del. "A Bibliography of the Collective Biography
of Spanish America." The University of Puerto Rico Bulle-
tin. Series IX. 1(Sept. 1938):61-72.

United States. Library of Congress. Library of Congress Catalog. Books: Subjects. Washington, D.C.: 1950-

Velázquez, Gonzálo, comp. Anuario bibliográfico puertorriqueño:
índice alfabético de libros, folletos, revistas y periódicos
publicados en Puerto Rico... Río Piedras, P.R.: Biblioteca
de la Universidad, 1950-

Vivó, Paquita, ed. The Puerto Ricans: An Annotated Bibliography.
New York: R. R. Bowker, 1973.

About the Compiler

FAY FOWLIE-FLORES is Coordinator of Public Services for the Ponce Technical University College Library of the University of Puerto Rico. She is the coauthor of *Manual de Adiestramiento de Referencia* and author of articles published in *Ceiba* and *Redes de Comunicacion*.